Praise for Jumpstart: A Sentence-to-Paragraph Worktext with Readings, *2e, by Barbara Fine Clouse*

"Barbara Fine Clouse is to be commended for writing a text that is so useful to teachers and students!"

> —*Kathryn Sheffield*, Mesa Community College

"I have not come across a better textbook."

> —*Sheri Van Court*, Brookhaven College

"This is a clear text, easily accessible, that offers the proper blend of challenge and support. I find the text to be very approachable for both students and college instructors."

> —*Maria Tabor*, Hartnell College

"The format is great. The activities are varied and focus on multiple skills to meet the needs of all students."

> —*Karen Moenkhaus*, Casper College

"I especially like the cross-disciplinary approach put forth in this new edition. It is a pragmatic way to show students how what they are learning applies to 'real world' situations. I am impressed with the diversity in your choice of readings."

> —*Dustin Greene*, Caldwell Community College and Technical Institute

"The style and organization of this text are reader-friendly and easily navigated."

> —*Jason Murray*, Bacone College

JUMPSTART:

A SENTENCE-TO-PARAGRAPH WORKTEXT WITH READINGS

TO ACCESS PREMIUM CONTENT IN

WWW.MHHE.COM/JUMPSTART

PLEASE USE THE FOLLOWING CODE:

G8JR-Y9P7-TTEH-9487-THW4

SECOND EDITION

JUMPSTART:
A SENTENCE-TO-PARAGRAPH
WORKTEXT WITH READINGS

Barbara Fine Clouse

Boston   Burr Ridge, IL   Dubuque, IA   Madison, WI   New York   San Francisco   St. Louis
Bangkok   Bogotá   Caracas   Kuala Lumpur   Lisbon   London   Madrid   Mexico City
Milan   Montreal   New Delhi   Santiago   Seoul   Singapore   Sydney   Taipei   Toronto

Higher Education

JUMPSTART: A SENTENCE-TO-PARAGRAPH WORKTEXT WITH READINGS
Published by McGraw-Hill, a business unit of The McGraw-Hill Companies, Inc., 1221 Avenue of
the Americas, New York, NY, 10020. Copyright © 2007, 2002 by The McGraw-Hill Companies,
Inc. All rights reserved. No part of this publication may be reproduced or distributed in any form
or by any means, or stored in a database or retrieval system, without the prior written consent of
The McGraw-Hill Companies, Inc., including, but not limited to, in any network or other electronic
storage or transmission, or broadcast for distance learning.
Some ancillaries, including electronic and print components, may not be available to customers
outside the United States.

This book is printed on acid-free paper.

1 2 3 4 5 6 7 8 9 0 VNH/VNH 0 9 8 7 6

ISBN-13: 978-0-07-298203-9
ISBN-10: 0-07-298203-9
AIE ISBN-13: 978-0-07-298204-6
AIE ISBN-10: 0-07-298204-7

Vice President and Editor-in-Chief: *Emily Barrosse*
Senior Sponsoring Editor: *John Kindler*
Freelance Development Editor: *Ann Grogg*
Editorial Assistant: *Jesse Hassenger*
Permissions Coordinator: *Marty Granahan*
Marketing Manager: *Lori DeShazo*
Managing Editor: *Jean Dal Porto*
Project Manager: *Ruth Smith*
Art Editor: *Katherine McNab*
Cover Designer: *Srdjan Savanovic*

Cover image: © Digital Vision Punchstock
Photo Research Coordinator: *Natalia
  C. Peschiera*
Production Supervisor: *Janean A. Utley*
Media Project Manager: *Stacy Dorgan Bentz*
Media Producer: *Alexander Rohrs*
Composition: *10/12 Sabon, by Techbooks*
Printing: *45# New Era Matte,
  Von-Hoffmann*

Credits: The credits section for this book begins on page C-1 and is considered an extension of the
copyright page.

Library of Congress Cataloging-in-Publication Data

Clouse, Barbara Fine.
    Jumpstart!: a sentence-to-paragraph worktext with readings / Barbara Clouse.— 2nd ed.
        p. cm.
    Includes index.
    ISBN-13: 978-0-07-298203-9 (softcover : alk. paper)
    ISBN-10: 0-07-298203-9 (softcover : alk. paper)
    1. English language—Rhetoric—Problems, exercises, etc. 2. English language—Grammar—
Problems, exercises, etc. 3. Report writing—Problems, exercises, etc. 4. College readers. I. Title.

    PE1413.C47 2007
    808'.042—dc22   2006041853

    AIE ISBN-13: 978-0-07-298204-6
    AIE ISBN-10: 0-07-298204-7

The Internet addresses listed in the text were accurate at the time of publication. The inclusion of a
Web site does not indicate an endorsement by the authors or McGraw-Hill, and McGraw-Hill does
not guarantee the accuracy of the information presented at these sites.

www.mhhe.com

About the Author

Barbara Clouse is a seasoned writing instructor who has taught all levels of college composition, first at Youngstown State University in northeastern Ohio and then at Slippery Rock University in western Pennsylvania. She has written several composition textbooks for McGraw-Hill, including *The Student Writer: Editor and Critic, Patterns for a Purpose: A Rhetorical Reader,* and *A Troubleshooting Guide for Writers.* In addition, she has developed *Cornerstones: Readings for Writers,* which is a short prose reader for Primis Online, McGraw-Hill's electronic database that allows instructors to build their own textbooks. Barbara's publications also include *Progresseions* for Longman Publishing. Barbara often presents at national and regional conferences, and she frequently conducts workshops for writing teachers.

Also by Barbara Fine Clouse

PATTERNS FOR A PURPOSE: A Rhetorical Reader
ISBN: 0-07-298257-8 (Copyright © 2005)

THE STUDENT WRITER: Editor and Critic
ISBN: 0-07-301880-5 (Copyright © 2004)

A TROUBLESHOOTING GUIDE FOR WRITERS:
Strategies and Process
ISBN: 0-07-287689-1 (Copyright © 2005)

In loving memory of
Faye Elizabeth Clouse

Contents in Brief

Table of Contents

PART FOUR   UNDERSTANDING PRONOUNS
CHAPTER 15 USING PRONOUNS   252

Recognizing Nouns and Pronouns   252

Using Pronouns as Subjects   253

Using Pronouns as Objects   253

Object Pronouns   253
Objects of Verbs   253
Objects of Prepositions   254

Using Pronouns as Possessives   254

Possessive Pronouns   255

Comparing Subject, Object, and Possessive Pronouns   255

Choosing Subject and Object Pronouns in Special Situations   256

In Compounds   257
In Comparisons   258
When the Antecedent Follows Immediately   260

Using Reflexive and Intensive Pronouns   262

If English Is Not Your First Language   263

Getting in Gear: Ideas for Writing   265
Recharge: Lesson Summary   266

CHAPTER 16 ACHIEVING PRONOUN-ANTECEDENT AGREEMENT   267

Recognizing Singular and Plural Pronouns   267

Making Pronouns Agree with Their Antecedents   268

Achieving Agreement in Special Situations   268

Phrases after the Antecedent   268
Compound Antecedents   269
Collective Noun Antecedents   271
Indefinite Pronoun Antecedents   272
Composing at the Computer   273
Avoiding Sexist Pronoun Usage   273
References to People in General   274

If English Is Not Your First Language   276

Getting in Gear: Ideas for Writing   278
Recharge: Lesson Summary   279

CHAPTER 17 ELIMINATING COMMON PRONOUN ERRORS   280

Avoiding Inappropriate Person Shifts   280

Avoiding Problems with Demonstrative Pronouns   281

Eliminating Unnecessary Pronouns   282

Avoiding Unclear Antecedents   283

Avoiding Unstated Antecedents   284

Composing at the Computer   285

If English Is Not Your First Language   286

Getting in Gear: Ideas for Writing   287
Recharge: Lesson Summary   288

PART FOUR REVIEW   288

Index of "Connect for Success" Boxes

Preface

In this major revision of a successful text, *Jumpstart: A Sentence-to-Paragraph Worktext with Readings* expands its mission. In addition to helping students write correct sentences and proficient paragraphs, this new edition lays a solid foundation for academic success by infusing instruction with academic content. New reading and study skills features, a cross-curricular emphasis, exercises derived from textbook excerpts, and writing applications across the disciplines prepare students for the kinds of reading and writing they will do in college. In addition, this edition engages a tech-savvy (or –hungry) generation by offering guidance in the use of computers, expanded opportunities to learn from the Web, and writing assignments that integrate visual and verbal rhetoric. In short, because *Jumpstart: A Sentence-to-Paragraph Worktext with Readings* is aligned with the interests of college students and all aspects of college-level work, those who use this book will be poised for a successful transition to college writing and to writing competence in all of their courses.

THE CHIEF FEATURES OF THE NEW EDITION

To carry out its expanded mission, *Jumpstart* includes the following features.

An emphasis on academic content

- "Connect for Success" features show students how to use what they are learning in *Jumpstart* to achieve success in other classes and in the workplace.
- Exercises adapted from biology, art, education, speech, psychology, sociology, business, music, childcare, medical assisting, communications, history, and political science textbooks expose students to important academic content across the disciplines and help them become more comfortable with college-level language, information, and ideas.
- "Getting in Gear" writing assignments at the end of every chapter are based in academic content and cultural literacy materials. Students have a chance, for example, to learn about and draw inspiration from Auguste Rodin's *The Thinker*, Jesse Owens's success at the 1936 Olympics, marriage ceremonies in different cultures, advertising, and Robert Frost's famous poem "Mending Wall."
- Weblinks in the "Getting in Gear" assignments send students to sites where they can learn more about academic subjects.
- End-of-unit cumulative exercises ask students to analyze the structure and grammar of textbook passages, as well as the content, and to write a response to what they have read.

A stronger foundation in the fundamentals of writing

- A new opening chapter introduces the importance of writing in college and in the workplace.
- A new chapter on revising and editing emphasizes the importance of these stages in the writing process.
- An expanded chapter on writing essays supports students who are ready for more complex writing forms.
- A solid chapter on paragraph writing continues as the centerpiece of this sentence-to-paragraph worktext.

Varied exercises with high-interest academic and cultural literacy content

- A wide variety of exercise formats (one-third of all the exercises are new to this edition) give students a range of practice and keep them interested. Exercise formats include whole discourse, continuous discourse, sentence combining, collaborative activities, and mix-of-error activities.
- Exercises drawn from academic and cultural literacy material expose students to college-level content and ideas. Academic topics include the Underground Railroad, the concept of status, the freedom of the press, cell structure, and music theory. Cultural literacy topics include the history of shoes, Oreo cookies, reality TV, and the origin of Crayola crayons.
- A new appendix includes eight multi-paragraph exercises with a mix of errors, so students can practice editing the way they should edit their own writing—for more than one kind of mistake.

Extra support for basic writers

- Troubleshooting tips in the margins point out common pitfalls and offer specific strategies for avoiding them.
- "Composing at the Computer" features outline strategies for students who use the computer for all or part of the writing process.
- "If English Is Not Your First Language" features in every grammar chapter provide targeted help for non-native users of English.
- A reconfigured unit on the writing process explains specific strategies for every stage of writing.
- "Getting in Gear" writing assignments are accompanied by suggestions for generating ideas, drafting, revising, and editing.
- "Grammar, Spelling, and Punctuation Alerts" highlight important grammar and usage points.

A variety of writing opportunities

- Writing assignments at the end of each chapter are designed to build success by guiding students with suggestions for prewriting, drafting, revising, and editing.
- Brief, informal writing prompts based on quotations appear at the beginning of each unit.
- More formal and complex writing prompts based on textbook excerpts appear at the end of each unit.
- Every reading includes related writing assignments and strategies for completing those assignments.

An emphasis on reading

- An expanded introduction to reading explains the importance of reading, the connection between reading and writing, and the reading process.
- Instruction in the use of context clues helps students figure out the meaning of unfamiliar vocabulary.
- New readings (almost half the readings are new) engage students' interest in topics such as judging people by what they wear, e-mail and privacy, and attention deficit disorder.
- New post-reading questions focus on critical thinking and students' reading processes, as well as on reading comprehension.
- Responses to each reading are framed in a writing assignment that includes a weblink and an image, as well as strategies for completing the assignment.

An emphasis on technology

- "Composing at the Computer" features describe efficient strategies for all stages of the writing process.
- Weblinks accompanying "Getting in Gear" writing assignments send students to additional information on their writing topics.

An updated design that includes more images

- A refreshed design increases *Jumpstart*'s appeal and highlights its most important features.
- A generous number of images complements the instruction.
- Images frame the "Getting in Gear" writing assignments.

ACKNOWLEDGMENTS

I am deeply appreciative of the extraordinary McGraw-Hill editorial team. Alexis Walker was the original sponsor of this edition. Her vision is responsible for the *Jumpstart*'s substantive academic and cultural literacy content. John Kindler stepped in to guide this edition across the finish line and deal with all the tricky final details. He did so most ably and with gentle good humor, which I very much appreciate. Joshua Feldman and Jesse Hassenger provided invaluable research assistance with the "Getting in Gear" images and websites. They are talented, energetic, and very smart.

Guiding *Jumpstart* through production was Ruth Smith. Very simply, I cannot overstate my gratitude for her grace under pressure, hand holding, and problem solving. Ruth makes everything possible, no matter what the constraints. She is unflappable; she is the best. Art Director Katherine McNab and Photo Editor Natalia Perschiera are responsible for the wonderful images, and talented designer Srdjan Savanorvic gave the book its terrific look. Marty Granahan did her ususal amazing job securing permissions.

Once again, I had the privilege of working with Development Editor Ann Grogg. Ann's elegance makes every project better. She is wise and knowing.

I also owe an inestimable debt to the following reviewers, who so graciously gave of their time and expertise. I thank them profoundly.

Andrea Alonzo, Borough of Manhattan Community College; Jana Carter, Montana State University—Great Falls College of Technology; Kathleen Dorantes, Imperial Valley College; Dustin Greene, Caldwell Community College and Technical Institute; David Merves, Miami-Dade College – North Campus; Karen Moenkhaus, Casper

College; Jason Murray, Bacone College; Nancy Sanders, Marymount College; Kathryn Sheffield, Mesa Community College; Rebecca Stapay Potter, Colorado Mountain College; Steve Stewart, West Central Technical College; Ann Stotts, Gateway Technical College; Maria Tabor, Hartnell College; Sheri Van Court, Brookhaven College; Emilie Vardaman, Cochise Community College; Ralph Velazquez, Rio Hondo College; Maria Villar-Smith, Miami-Dade College

Finally, as always, I thank my amazing husband, Denny. He makes it all possible and worthwhile.

Barbara Fine Clouse

EVERYTHING IN *JUMPSTART* IS DESIGNED WITH YOU IN MIND!

Like all learners, you need plenty of opportunity to practice new skills, and you need a variety of practice activities so you don't get bored. That's why *Jumpstart* offers you so many different kinds of practice activities—so many, in fact, that you probably won't get to them all.

In addition to an abundant number and variety of practice activities, *Jumpstart* has many compelling features to help you learn. Take a few moments to review the following pages. They introduce you to some of the unique features of *Jumpstart*, features designed specifically with you mind.

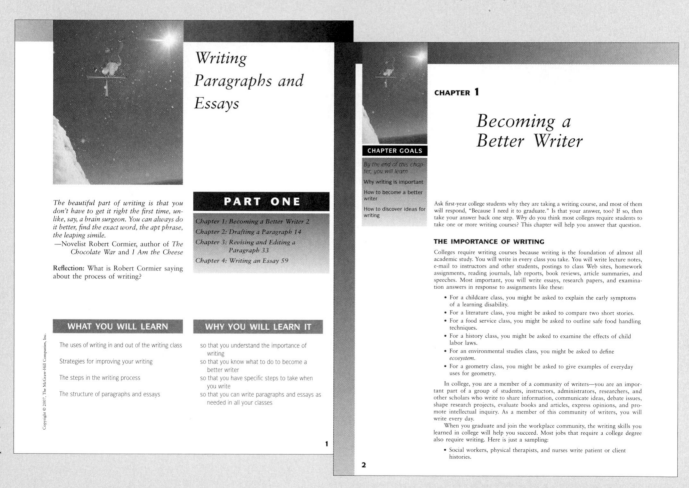

YOU ALWAYS KNOW WHAT YOU WILL LEARN AND WHY

You deserve to be in the know, so at the beginning of every unit and every chapter, *Jumpstart* specifies what you are studying and why the material is important.

CONNECT FOR SUCCESS: Outline Examination Answers

Before writing an essay examination answer, write an informal outline that states the main points your answer will include. The outline will keep your answer organized and serve as a reminder, in case you forget something in the heat of the moment.

YOU SEE HOW TO APPLY YOUR LEARNING BEYOND YOUR WRITING CLASS

Of course, the material in *Jumpstart* is important in your writing class, but much of it has important applications in your other classes as well. *Jumpstart* shows you those connections, so you will be even more motivated to learn.

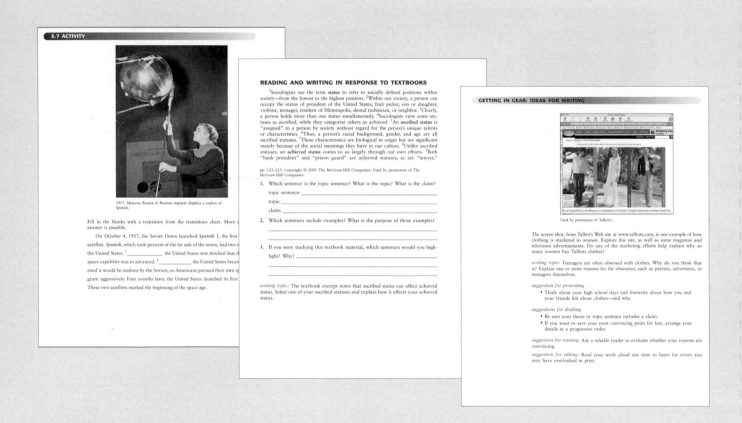

YOU LEARN ACADEMIC CONTENT

Who says you can't learn about Benjamin Franklin while you study sentence structure, or the psychology of self-esteem while you learn punctuation? You are in college because you want to learn, so *Jumpstart* includes academic content in its exercises and images to capture your interest, excite your curiosity, and extend your knowledge.

The elderly are the fastest-growing age group in the United States. As the photographs depict, some older Americans will be blessed with good health and other circumstances, so they will be able to maintain an active, independent lifestyle, but others will need more care. To learn about issues important to both active seniors and those needing more care, visit the American Association of Retired Persons Web site at www.aarp.org and www.aging-parents-and-elder-care.com/index.html.

writing topic: What do you think of the way we treat the elderly in this country? You can consider such issues as whether we respect the elderly appropriately, help them maintain a satisfactory quality of life, and provide adequate healthcare, housing, and assisted living facilities and nursing homes. Are there any changes that should be made? If so, what are they?

suggestions for discovering ideas
- If you have any elderly friends, relatives, or neighbors, think about how these people are treated and about the quality of their lives.
- Freewrite about how we treat the elderly and about how they should be treated.

suggestions for drafting
- Include examples to show how the elderly are treated, or cite reasons you think they are or are not treated well.
- If you recommend a change, explain why that change is a good idea, or explain how the change can be made.

suggestion for revising: Use the checklist for revising a paragraph on pages 33–34 or the checklist for revising an essay on page 65.

suggestion for editing: Edit twice. The first time, look for the kinds of errors you have made in the past; the second time, look for all other errors.

YOU ARE WELL SUPPORTED AS YOU WRITE PARAGRAPHS AND ESSAYS

With some textbooks, you feel like you are on a high wire without a net beneath you, but not with *Jumpstart* because your writing assignments are accompanied by step-by-step procedures that build in confidence and success.

YOU LEARN HELPUL HINTS

Do you ever feel that you aren't in on all the cool writing tips? You won't feel that way after using *Jumpstart* because Troubleshooting notes and Alerts offer abundant strategies for avoiding writing problems and working efficiently.

Troubleshooting

To check whether a clause is necessary or not, try dropping it out of the sentence. Whatís lost? Is the person or thing referred to still clearly identified?

GRAMMAR ALERT

Who and *whose* refer to people. *Which* refers to things and animals. *That* refers to people and things.

No: *He is the person <u>which</u> gave me the letter.*
Yes: *He is the person <u>who</u> gave me the letter.*

PUNCTUATION ALERT

How you punctuate a relative clause depends on whether or not the clause is necessary for identifying who or what is referred to. If the clause is *not* necessary for identification, set it off with commas. If it *is* necessary for identification, do not use commas.

Necessary for
identification: *The person who studies hard will get good grades.*

Unnecessary for
identification: *My roommate, who studies hard, will get good grades.*

YOU RECEIVE ADDITIONAL SUPPORT IF ENGLISH IF NOT YOUR FIRST LANGUAGE

Is English your second or third language? If so, you will find extensive help in the "If English Is Not Your First Language" sections that appear in almost every chapter. Even if English is your <u>first</u> language, these sections are helpful.

 IF ENGLISH IS NOT YOUR FIRST LANGUAGE

1. If your native language does not use English script, punctuation may be new to you. Ask a writing center tutor or someone else you trust to help you edit for punctuation.
2. Do not use a comma whenever you would pause in speaking. This method, used in some languages, is unreliable in English.

YOU CAN TAKE ADVANTAGE OF TECHNOLOGY

Do you like to use a computer? *Jumpstart* suggests helpful strategies for writing at the computer, and it gives you access to helpful online materials.

Composing at the computer

If you like to compose at the computer, you may find the following revision strategies helpful.

- **Use your computer's thesaurus (dictionary of synonyms) when you cannot think of the right word.** However, be sure you understand the word's shades of meaning before using it.
- **Revise at least once on paper copy.** When you revise on screen, you may see only part of your draft at one time, which can make it hard for you to get a good overview. It is best to print out your writing, double-spaced, so there is plenty of room to make corrections and to revise in pencil or pen at least once.
- **If you use Microsoft Word, keep track of your revisions with the "Track Changes" function.** Go to "Tools," then "Track Changes." All your revisions will become visible.
- **Use your computer to secure reader response.** E-mail your draft to a reader who can insert comments and e-mail back the draft. If you use Microsoft Word, go to "Insert," then "Comment."

GETTING IN GEAR: IDEAS FOR WRITING

What Happens to Wildlife

The poster, from the New York Public Library's web site, depicts animals in danger of extinction because they are losing their habitats to human development and other encroachments. When we lose species, we lose some of the diversity, some of the variety that enriches life. If you want to read more about the dangers to species and the threatened loss of diversity, visit the New York Public Library site at www.nypl.org/admin/exhibitions/endangered/whatz.html.

writing topic: In this chapter, you learned that varying sentence openers is important for creating interest in your writing and enriching your writing style. Variety is important in other areas as well. For example, the variety of animal species and habitats enriches our lives; variety in workout routines helps people maintain interest in exercise. Discuss other ways that variety is important for maintaining interest or for enriching lives.

suggestions for discovering ideas
- Freewrite about variety for about ten minutes.
- If you need additional ideas, do a second, focused freewriting or try mapping.

suggestion for drafting: Before beginning your draft, develop an informal outline or outline map.

suggestion for revising: Read your draft aloud. If you hear passages that sound either sing-songy or choppy, revise to vary the sentence openers.

suggestions for editing
- Edit a separate time, looking for each of the kinds of errors you make habitually.
- Edit again to find any other kinds of errors.

Writing Paragraphs and Essays

The beautiful part of writing is that you don't have to get it right the first time, unlike, say, a brain surgeon. You can always do it better, find the exact word, the apt phrase, the leaping simile.

—Novelist Robert Cormier, author of *The Chocolate War* and *I Am the Cheese*

Reflection: What is Robert Cormier saying about the process of writing?

PART ONE

WHAT YOU WILL LEARN

The uses of writing in and out of the writing class

Strategies for improving your writing

The steps in the writing process

The structure of paragraphs and essays

WHY YOU WILL LEARN IT

so that you understand the importance of writing

so that you know what to do to become a better writer

so that you have specific steps to take when you write

so that you can write paragraphs and essays as needed in all your classes

1

CHAPTER 1

Becoming a Better Writer

CHAPTER GOALS

By the end of this chapter, you will learn

Why writing is important

How to become a better writer

How to discover ideas for writing

Ask first-year college students why they are taking a writing course, and most of them will respond, "Because I need it to graduate." Is that your answer, too? If so, then take your answer back one step. *Why* do you think most colleges require students to take one or more writing courses? This chapter will help you answer that question.

THE IMPORTANCE OF WRITING

Colleges require writing courses because writing is the foundation of almost all academic study. You will write in every class you take. You will write lecture notes, e-mail to instructors and other students, postings to class Web sites, homework assignments, reading journals, lab reports, book reviews, article summaries, and speeches. Most important, you will write essays, research papers, and examination answers in response to assignments like these:

- For a childcare class, you might be asked to explain the early symptoms of a learning disability.
- For a literature class, you might be asked to compare two short stories.
- For a food service class, you might be asked to outline safe food handling techniques.
- For a history class, you might be asked to examine the effects of child labor laws.
- For an environmental studies class, you might be asked to define *ecosystem*.
- For a geometry class, you might be asked to give examples of everyday uses for geometry.

In college, you are a member of a community of writers—you are an important part of a group of students, instructors, administrators, researchers, and other scholars who write to share information, communicate ideas, debate issues, shape research projects, evaluate books and articles, express opinions, and promote intellectual inquiry. As a member of this community of writers, you will write every day.

When you graduate and join the workplace community, the writing skills you learned in college will help you succeed. Most jobs that require a college degree also require writing. Here is just a sampling:

- Social workers, physical therapists, and nurses write patient or client histories.

2

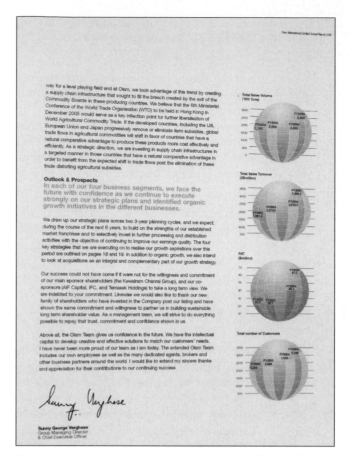

This page from a business report is one example of work place writing

- Police officers write crime reports.
- Teachers write lesson plans, study sheets, and letters to parents.
- Plant and office safety officers write out steps to take in the event of an emergency.
- Nutritionists write diets and explanations of dietary concerns, such as cholesterol and carbohydrates.
- Human resources managers write employee handbooks.
- Real estate agents write copy for advertisements and brochures.

Like reading, writing is something you will do for the rest of your life. This course and this book aim to give you a "jumpstart" on the way to writing well.

TEN WAYS TO BECOME A BETTER WRITER

Perhaps writing has not been easy for you in the past. This book rests on the assumption that, like so many things, writing will get easier with practice, so this book and this class will give you many chances for practice—beginning with this chapter. But you must also give your writing its best chance to improve. Here are ten ways to do that:

1. TAKE A WRITING CLASS. Because you are already doing this, you have made an excellent decision and have taken that important first step.

2. GET COMFORTABLE AND CONCENTRATE. Find a quiet place to write that is free of distractions. If you have one eye on *The Simpsons* and one eye on your writing, you will make mistakes. Get comfortable and use the tools that put you at ease, such as a favorite pen, a particular kind of paper, or a computer. Be

sure to choose the best time of day to write, because you cannot do good work when you are tired.

3. PACE YOURSELF.   Avoid putting yourself in the situation of writing up to the deadline. You may *think* you perform better under pressure and, therefore, put off your writing until the last minute. However, most writing done at the last minute is rough and unsatisfactory. To give your writing its best chance, set intermediate goals. Break down your writing project into smaller steps, and focus on one step at a time. For example, the first time you sit down, work to think of several ideas; the next time, work to think of a few more. Make one day's goal to write a usable first draft and another day's to improve that draft.

4. EXPECT PROBLEMS, BUT DO NOT EXPECT INSPIRATION.   Remember that mistakes are a natural part of learning, so expect to make them and embrace them as learning opportunities. *All* writers delete and revise, change their minds, and get frustrated, but they push on anyway, even in the absence of inspiration. If the lightning bolt of inspiration does not strike you, do not wait around for it. Just write. Because writing is a *discovery process*, the ideas are not just in your head, waiting to get written. The act of writing often *creates* the ideas.

5. WORK WITH YOUR INSTRUCTOR.   As part of your community of writers, your instructor is dedicated to helping you improve, so ask questions and ask for help. Your instructor cannot anticipate everything that is on every student's mind, so if you have a question, ask it—and ask it when it occurs to you, or you may never get around to it. When your instructor responds to your writing by noting strengths and weaknesses, be sure you understand every point. Can you repeat the strengths in future writings? Do you understand why certain aspects of your writing need improvement and how to make the changes? If not, speak to your instructor.

6. COLLABORATE WITH YOUR CLASSMATES.   Your classmates are part of your community of writers, so discuss your ideas with them on the phone, over e-mail, and face-to-face. Later in this book, you will learn strategies for sharing drafts to give and receive feedback. You might also form a writers' group with some of your classmates, so you can share your ideas and writing regularly and give and receive both encouragement and constructive criticism.

7. VISIT YOUR CAMPUS WRITING CENTER.   There you will be in the company of other writers who can keep you motivated and sensitive readers who will help you think about your writing and consider possibilities. You can also meet with tutors who can give you specific guidance. Many writing centers also sponsor workshops on common writing problems, such as writer's block. Remember that writing centers are not just for students in writing classes. You can use the center anytime you have a writing task in any of your courses.

8. KEEP A JOURNAL.   Write every day, because the more you write the more comfortable you will become with writing. Journaling gives you an opportunity to record your thoughts, practice your writing, and become more fluent as a result. A journal can also serve as an "idea bank" for writing projects in many of your classes. (Journal writing is discussed in more detail in this chapter on page 10.)

9. READ EVERY DAY AND NOTICE HOW OTHERS WRITE.   Every day, read something you like in addition to your textbooks, whether it is a book, magazine, newspaper, or Web page. Even if it is only for fifteen minutes a day, regular reading exposes you to the ways others use words, compose sentences, and write paragraphs and essays—and that is information you can bring to your own

writing. If you read enough, your language instincts will improve and you will grow as a writer.

10. USE THIS BOOK TO ITS BEST ADVANTAGE.   Many features in this book are designed to help you jumpstart your writing. If you have not already done so, study the book's "Visual Preview," beginning on page xxxi, to learn about these and other features of *Jumpstart!* designed to help you learn efficiently. Finally, apply what you are learning about writing in your other classes. As you read your textbooks, notice how the principles you have learned in this book are applied in your other textbooks. When you write in other classes, follow the grammar and writing principles you have studied in *Jumpstart!* To help you make the connections, "Connect for Success" boxes, like the following one, will show you specific ways to apply what you learn in other classes.

CONNECT FOR SUCCESS: Use Writing in All Your Classes

Writing helps you learn. To master the content in your other courses, try writing it. Keep a notebook for each course, and take class and lecture notes in it, as in the photo. Keep a list of your assignments with dates due. Write summaries of textbook chapters and other assigned reading. List main points you want to study for exams, write out study questions, and outline answers. If you like, you can reflect in your notebook on reading assignments and class lectures, indicating ideas you agree and disagree with, how you can use the information you have learned, and how that information relates to your own experiences and other learning. Using writing this way "sets" information to help you learn it and understand it better.

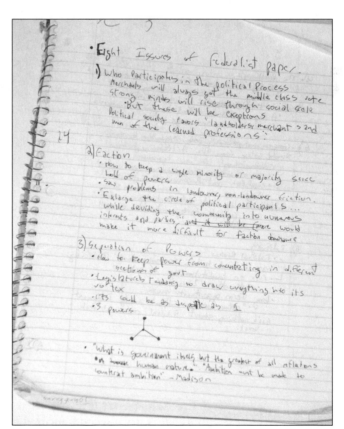

WRITING AS A PROCESS

Writing is a *process*—a process of discovery played out over time. As writers sit down to begin a writing task, try out ideas, scratch out what they have written, and try again, they discover what they want to say and how they want to say it. Almost always, as they work through the writing process, they change their minds and move in new directions, or they come to new understandings. As a result, a piece of writing can start out one way and end up to be something very different. And that's fine.

Because writing is a process of discovery played out over time, you cannot expect to do it all at once—especially not all at once right before the deadline. Instead, respect the process. You will give your writing its best chance to succeed by staging it across several days. Like experienced writers, take time to work through these steps of the process:

1. **prewriting** to discover ideas
2. **drafting** to create an early version of the writing
3. **revising** to improve the draft
4. **editing** to find and correct errors

In this chapter, you will try out prewriting strategies—ways to discover ideas for writing. The next chapters will help you through the remaining steps of writing.

PREWRITING

Inspiration is nice, but you do not need inspiration to write. If you have a writing task, but inspiration fails you, use one or more of the **prewriting** strategies explained next. These include *freewriting, listing, mapping,* and *journaling.* These strategies can jumpstart your writing and help you discover ideas to write about.

Freewriting

To **freewrite,** write without stopping for five to ten minutes. Do not worry about spelling, grammar, or neatness. Just write whatever occurs to you (even silly ideas) without censoring yourself. If you run out of ideas to write, then write the alphabet or write about how you feel. Even as you do this, new ideas will occur to you, and you can continue your freewriting.

Here is a freewriting to discover ideas for a writing about stress and college students:

> *Stress and college students. I'm not sure I can even take it anymore and the semester just began I just don't know how I can do 3 classes and work to but I can't give anything up. What am I going to do? I can't let anyone down. Now what? What to do, what to write. what to write. This is hard, I'm stuck. A B C D E F Does everyone feel as stressed out as I do? My classes are so hard, I don't get algebra at all. I'm supposed to go to the math lab but how am I supposed to find time for that? I'm so tired all the time I'd like to quit work but what will I do for money? Tuition will be due again soon. And the cost of books is insane. Maybe I should drop a course. Would that be cheaper? But then I'll never get out of here. I don't know what to do but I better do something or I'll explode. Actualy this freewriting is making me stressed out. Very funny.*

A single freewriting may give you all you need to get started. However, if you need a few more ideas, try a second, **focused freewriting,** which concentrates, or "focuses," on one or more of the ideas in the first freewriting. For example, the following is a focused freewriting that concentrates on this idea in the first freewriting: why the writer feels stress. Notice that the writer reread the focused freewriting and underlined ideas that could be used in a paper.

Why do I feel stress? <u>My parents are on me all the time about grades, they call all the time and ask tons of questions. What if I let them down? Work is killing me,</u> but I can't quit because I need the money. It takes up too much time though and my grades are hurting. Hmmm. I'm really stuck good. <u>Maybe I could find a job on campus that was easier on me.</u> What should I write now? <u>Even little stuff stresses me out like I might sleep in and miss my early class and what if I get the flu?</u> And I'm getting fat. I need exercise.

CONNECT FOR SUCCESS: Freewrite to Solve Academic Problems

Freewriting is an excellent problem-solving technique. What academic problems do you have? Are you trying to stop procrastinating? Are you trying to find a major, choose an advisor, or improve your math grade? Freewrite for ten minutes, focusing on possible solutions to your problem, and a good one may surface.

1.1 ACTIVITY

On a separate sheet, freewrite for about ten minutes on the advantages or disadvantages of cell phones. Do not worry about correctness or how good your ideas are. If you run out of ideas to write, write the alphabet, names of family members, or "I don't know what to write" until new ideas strike you. When you are finished, underline ideas you could focus on and possibly expand. Then respond to the following questions.

1. How many ideas did you underline? List them here.

   _____

   _____

   _____

2. Which idea do you like the best? Why?

   _____

   _____

1.2 ACTIVITY

On a separate sheet, do a focused freewriting for ten minutes on one of the ideas you listed in Activity 1.1. Underline the ideas that you could write in a paper and then answer the following questions.

Note: Save your freewriting to use in an activity in Chapter 2.

1. How many ideas did you underline? List them here.

   _____

   _____

   _____

2. Which idea do you like the best? Why?

   _____

   _____

Listing

To **list,** write every idea that occurs to you in a column down the page, without stopping to decide how good the ideas are. When you run out of ideas to list, you can study what you have and cross out any ideas you do not like. One list may give you all the ideas you need to get started. If it does not, try a second, **focused list,** which concentrates on one or more of the ideas in the first list. Or if you prefer, do a focused freewriting on one or more of the ideas you listed. You can also use listing after freewriting for additional ideas. Just write a focused list on one or more of the ideas in your freewriting.

Here is a list of ideas about what can be done to reduce student stress:

make counseling available to students

provide massage therapy for stressed students

make employers give time off to students at exam time

have stress management workshops

test students to learn who is stressed out

have "catch-up" days when classes are canceled, so students can catch up on their work

let students drop courses without penalty

make extensions easier to get

provide more parking spaces

train teachers to recognize signs of stress

give out more scholarships, so students do not have to work

colleges will have fewer dropouts and make more money

tell profs to lighten up on the work and tough grading

show students how to study and take tests

1.3 ACTIVITY

On a separate sheet, write a list to discover ideas for one of the following subjects. When you cannot think of any more ideas, review your list and write a focused list if necessary. Then answer the questions that follow.

Note: Save your list to use in an activity in Chapter 2.

computer voting	blogging	a campus problem	bias in news reporting
reality television	Instant Messaging	a popular musician	the American family

1. How many ideas did you discover that you could write in a paper? Write them here.

_____

_____

_____

2. Which idea do you like best? Why?

_____

_____

_____

CONNECT FOR SUCCESS: List to Stay Organized in Your Classes

You can use listing to stay organized in all your classes and remember important details. Keep a master list of your assignments in your course notebook, and review that list each evening. Then make a second list of things to do the next day. Consider breaking down assignments into intermediate steps and placing those steps on your lists.

Mapping

Many writers like **mapping** because it allows them to discover ideas *and* to see how those ideas relate to each other. To map, place an idea or a subject for writing in a circle in the center of a page, like this:

(effects of stress on college students)

Then as each idea occurs to you, connect it to the circle it most closely relates to. A map of ideas for developing a paper about the effects of stress on college students might look like this:

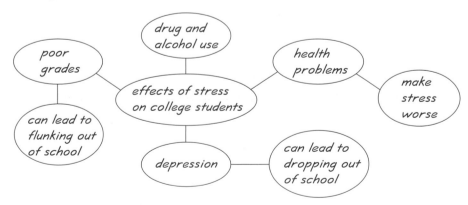

One mapping may give you the ideas you need. If it does not, you can write a second, **focused map,** which concentrates on one of your circles, or you can do a focused freewriting or listing on one of your circles.

> **CONNECT FOR SUCCESS:** Write Maps to Remember
> Course Content
>
> If you have trouble remembering how the ideas in a textbook or lecture relate to each other, try mapping them for an easier to remember visualization.

1.4 ACTIVITY

Select one of the following subjects and write a map on a separate sheet. Then answer the questions that follow.

friendship	Internet dating	EBay	immigration
television news	college life	body piercing	final exams

Note: Save your map to use in an activity in Chapter 2.

1. How many ideas did you discover that you could write in a paper? Write them here.

   _____

   _____

   _____

2. If you were to write a focused map, focused freewriting, or focused list for more ideas, which circle would you write it on? Why?

   _____

   _____

Journaling

A journal is a place to write for yourself. Your instructor may collect your journal and respond to some of what you have written, but he or she will not evaluate your writing, so you can write what you want in the way you want.

A journal is *not* a diary, because in it you do much more than record the events of your day. Instead, you can think things through in these ways:

1. You can explore ideas just to see where they take you.
2. You can react to the events of your day and write about how they affect you and others.
3. You can write to discover what you think about an issue or event.
4. You can write about your feelings and unleash emotions.
5. You can experiment with writing styles and drafts.

When you need ideas for writing, check your journal entries.

To give you an idea of what a journal entry is like, here is a sample:

November 29, 2006

Today I saw a student in a wheelchair. Whenever I see someone in a wheelchair, I try not to make eye contact because I don't want the person to think I'm staring or feeling pity. It's my way of being courteous. Then I realized that lots of times I was making eye contact with people not in wheelchairs, and I

Troubleshooting

If you are unsatisfied with the ideas you discover during prewriting, you are probably expecting too much too soon. Remind yourself that you are not looking for polished ideas. You need only raw material, which you can polish later as you move through the writing process.

was smiling at them. Now I wonder if people in wheelchairs feel like they're being ignored when people try to avoid looking at them. I think that by trying to be polite, I was being rude. From now on, when I see people in wheelchairs, I'm going to smile at them.

To keep a journal, do the following:

1. Buy a sturdy notebook about 8½ × 11 inches. The best notebooks are sewn at the binding, but a spiral notebook will do. If you prefer, set up a computer file.
2. Write in your journal each day for at least ten or fifteen minutes. Many writers like the discipline of writing at the same time each day.
3. Date each entry and begin each one on a new page. This makes rereading your journal easier.
4. Do not worry about grammar, spelling, or how good your writing is. Just write the best you can in a way that satisfies *you*.

If you are ever stuck for a topic for a journal entry, review this list for ideas:

1. Record your feelings about something that happened to you or to someone else.
2. Explore the meaning of something that happened to you or to someone else.
3. Write about one of your hopes, fears, or anxieties.
4. Explain what you worry about and why.
5. Tell what you like best (or least) about yourself and why.
6. Explain what you think is right (or wrong) with the world.
7. Record a vivid childhood memory.
8. React to something you have read in a newspaper.
9. Write about a person you admire, respect, like, or dislike. Try to determine why you feel as you do about the person.
10. Write about your goals for the next year.

CONNECT FOR SUCCESS: Keep Journals in Other Classes

Many successful students keep reading journals, where they record their reactions to their reading, how ideas they read connect to what they have learned in other classes, and how they can use the ideas they have read about. Consider keeping a separate journal for each of your courses to help you learn material and understand its significance, or set aside a section of your course notebook for journaling.

Composing at the computer

Most of the prewriting strategies explained in this chapter can be done at the computer. In addition, you may find the following prewriting strategies helpful if you like to compose at the computer.

- **Try "blindfolded" writing.** Freewrite with the light turned down on your monitor, so your screen is dark. You will likely have many typos, but not seeing your work on the screen can help your thoughts flow more freely.

- **"Talk" to others.** Discuss your writing subject in e-mail correspondence, in real-time messaging, and on class message boards to get input and ideas to consider for your writing.

1.5 CHAPTER REVIEW ACTIVITY

1. What kinds of writing do you expect to do in your other courses this term or in courses you expect to take soon? (If you do not know the answer to this question, speak to instructors, writing center tutors, and other students to find out.)

    _____

    _____

    _____

    _____

2. Will you try any of the "Connect for Success" strategies in this chapter? If so, which ones? What other ways do you think you can apply what you learn in this writing class to your other classes?

    _____

    _____

    _____

    _____

3. When you write, how do you usually come up with the ideas? Do you normally feel inspired? Do you have any trouble coming up with ideas to write?

    _____

    _____

    _____

    _____

4. The next time you write, will you use any of the prewriting strategies described in this chapter? If so, which ones? Why? How do you think they will help you?

    _____

    _____

    _____

    _____

5. Did you learn anything in this chapter about writing that you did not know before? If so, what?

    _____

    _____

    _____

    _____

The photograph is of a bronze sculpture called *The Thinker,* sculpted by Auguste Rodin (1840–1917). Rodin thought of the man he sculpted as a dreamer whose dreams evolved into ideas that inspired him to create. To learn more about this sculpture and Rodin, visit www.artcyclopedia.com.

writing topic: The Thinker is engaged in a discovery process different from the process for discovering ideas explained in this chapter. Use the prewriting strategies in this chapter to consider how *The Thinker*'s process differs from the way this chapter recommends you discover ideas. If you prefer, you can use the following prewriting suggestions.

suggestions for prewriting

- Make a list of all the ideas that occur to you on the writing topic.
- Select one of the ideas from your list and do a focused mapping.
- Select one or more of the ideas from your mapping and do a focused freewriting.
- Study all your prewriting material and make a master list of potentially usable ideas.

RECHARGE: Lesson Summary

1. Writing is important to success in your college courses and in most jobs that require a college degree.
2. You can take specific steps to become a better writer.
3. Writing is a process that starts with discovering ideas to write about.
4. In the absence of inspiration, using these prewriting strategies (individually or in combination)—freewriting, listing, mapping, and journaling—can help you discover ideas.

CHAPTER 2

Drafting a Paragraph

CHAPTER GOALS

By the end of this chapter, you will learn to

Identify the parts of a paragraph

Explain the characteristics and function of each part

Draft a paragraph

In Chapter 1, you learned prewriting strategies to discover ideas for your writing. In this chapter, you will use that prewriting as the foundation for drafting a paragraph.

THE DEFINITION OF A PARAGRAPH

A **paragraph** is a group of sentences that develop one main idea. Sometimes a paragraph stands alone as a brief composition, and sometimes it is combined with other paragraphs to form longer writings. Stand-alone paragraphs are used for brief essay examination answers and homework responses, short business memos and letters, and brief thank you and sympathy notes. Writing composed of several paragraphs includes essays, lab reports, book reviews, business reports, and long letters and long e-mail.

THE PARTS OF A PARAGRAPH

A paragraph has three parts:

- The **topic sentence** expresses the main idea of the paragraph.
- The **supporting details** explain or prove the topic sentence.
- The **closing** ends the paragraph by referring to the topic sentence idea, by drawing a conclusion from the supporting details, or by providing closure some other way.

To help you recognize the parts of a paragraph, here is a sample with the topic sentence, supporting details, and closing labeled. Notice that the first word of a paragraph is indented.

The topic sentence expresses the main idea of the paragraph. The first line is indented five spaces to show where a paragraph begins.

The supporting details prove and explain the main idea with examples of different family arrangements.

Family arrangements vary from culture to culture. Among Tibetans, a woman may be married to more than one man at the same time, usually brothers. This system makes it easier for brothers to share the limited amount of land. In Sumatra, Indonesia, a bride and her husband live with the bride's family, and all property passes from mother to daughter. A Trobriand Island couple signals marriage by sitting in public on a porch, eating yams provided by the bride's mother. She continues to cook yams for a year while the groom's family provides

14

The **closing** provides closure by referring to the topic sentence idea.

valuables, such as stone axes and clay pots. In the United States, divorce is a complicated legal process, but a Hopi woman may divorce her husband by placing her belongings outside the door. Clearly, across the world family arrangements take many forms.

Source: Adapted from Richard T. Schaefer, *Sociology,* 7th ed. (New York: McGraw-Hill, 2001), p. 343. Copyright © 2001 The McGraw-Hill Companies. Used by permission of The McGraw-Hill Companies.

2.1 ACTIVITY

Read the following paragraph and then answer the questions that follow it.

The oyster toadfish is a very strange animal. With flaps of slimy skin hanging from its face like melted candle wax, it looks like a creature from a monster movie. Unlike most fish, the toadfish is not afraid of people and will dart straight toward divers if they come too close. Most other fish would just swim away. Oyster toadfish are not only unusually aggressive; they are also surprisingly loud. Both males and females make loud grunting sounds, and during mating season the male makes a sound like the blast of a foghorn. In fact, mating toadfish are so loud that people living near coasts have been kept awake all night by their loud noises. Certainly, the oyster toadfish is one of the most unusual fish in the sea.

1. What is the main idea of the paragraph? Which sentence best expresses the main idea?

2. What name is given to the sentence that expresses the main idea?

3. To prove the main idea, the supporting details give three reasons the oyster toadfish is strange. What are they?

4. What detail proves the idea that the fish looks like a creature from a monster movie?

5. What detail proves the idea that the fish does not fear people and is aggressive?

6. What details prove the idea that the fish is loud?

7. What purpose does the last sentence serve?

_____

THE TOPIC SENTENCE

A paragraph explains or proves one main point, and the sentence that expresses that main point is the **topic sentence.** The purpose of the topic sentence is to let the reader know what the paragraph is about.

The topic sentence can appear anywhere in a paragraph—at the beginning, in the middle, or at the end. For now, you may be more comfortable placing your topic sentence first. That way, you can refer to it easily as you write and stay on course. Later, after you have had more practice, you can try different placements for your topic sentence.

To express a paragraph's main point, an effective topic sentence usually has two parts. One part states the topic, and the other part expresses your claim (opinion) about that topic. Here is an example:

> Topic: *my brother*
>
> Claim: *He expects too much of people.*
>
> Topic sentence: *My brother expects too much of people.*

This topic sentence lets the reader know that the paragraph will show that the writer's brother expects too much of people. Now look at this example:

> Topic: *cultural anthropology courses*
>
> Claim: *They teach that different cultures solve the same problems in different ways.*
>
> Topic sentence: *Cultural anthropology courses teach that different cultures solve the same problems in different ways.*

This topic sentence lets the reader know that the paragraph will be about how cultural anthropology courses teach that different cultures solve the same problems in different ways. Here is one last example:

> Topic: *side air bags*
>
> Claim: *They should be required in all new cars.*
>
> Topic sentence: *Side air bags should be required in all new cars.*

This topic sentence lets the reader know that the paragraph will be about why side air bags should be required in all new cars. As a reader, you will expect to learn why, and you might anticipate that the paragraph will be about their safety benefits for all passengers.

CONNECT FOR SUCCESS: Use Topic Sentences as a Study Aid

If you highlight material when you study your textbooks, look for the topic sentence of every paragraph. Be sure to mark these sentences, because they include main points you will want to remember. To take this study technique a step further, highlight the most important supporting details in a contrasting color. For a quick review, look only at the topic sentences; for a more thorough review, read the main supporting details as well.

2.2 ACTIVITY

For the following topic sentences, draw one line under the words that give the topic and two lines under the words that give the writer's claim about the topic.

EXAMPLES More schools should adopt a twelve-month calendar.

Computers simplify our lives.

1. Traveling by train offers many advantages over air travel.
2. Billboards should be banned along scenic highways.
3. Of all my friends, Dana has the most ambition.
4. Nurses are not appreciated as much as they should be.
5. Pornography on the Internet should be regulated.
6. Being an only child is a lonely existence.
7. Many parents believe that rock videos encourage sexual experimentation.
8. Freedom of speech does not mean what many people think it does.
9. Mozart was one of the world's most versatile composers.
10. Several theories explain why people forget.

2.3 ACTIVITY

Underline the topic sentence in each of the following paragraphs, keeping in mind that the topic sentence may not be the first sentence.

1.   In 1932, when Cleveland, Ohio, teenagers Jerry Siegel and Joe Shuster created the comic book character Superman, comic books were only a few years old. Legend has it that, in 1934, Jerry Siegel had a dream about what the Superman character should be like, and by morning he had created the Man of Steel. In all, the duo labored six years to get their superhero into the newspaper comic strip page. Finally, in 1938 the publisher of DC Comics decided to introduce Superman in Action Comics #1. Superman was an instant hit and remains one of our most enduring comic book characters. Nonetheless, Siegel and Shuster made little money from Superman, for it was not until 1975 that DC Comics finally paid the men a small annuity for their creation. Certainly, the history of the Superman character is a story of perseverance and injustice.

2.   Spider-man is very different from Superman. For one thing, Spidey is more human and less "super" than Superman. Spider-man catches colds, misses appointments, falls behind in paying his bills, and forgets where he has put his keys. Thus, whereas Superman is the "Man of Steel," Spider-man is your "friendly, neighborhood Spider-man." Their motivation is also different. Spider-man is motivated by guilt. He could have prevented the murder of his beloved Uncle Ben if he had not been distracted by a desire for revenge against a man who had cheated him out of some money. In his 1962 debut, Spider-man became a crime fighter to compensate. Superman, on the other hand, is motivated by a pure desire to right wrongs in the name of "truth, justice, and the American way." At first, Marvel Comics hesitated to publish Spider-man, because his alter-ego, Peter Parker, is an alienated, troubled teenager, and the company feared negative response to such a dark character. They need not have worried, for response to Spider-man was enthusiastic and continues so to this day.

3.   The popular and enduring Batman character was introduced in 1939. Batman is very different from both Superman and Spider-man. A superhero without any

super powers, Batman fights crime by relying on equipment, including the Bat-mobile, the Bat signal, smoke bombs, grappling hooks, and the Bat plane. Because his morals are often questionable and he has a violent streak, Batman is not a role model the way Superman and Spider-man are. For example, in the first installment of the comic, Batman causes the villain to fall into a vat of acid. He responds to this hideous event with the cold comment "A fitting end for his kind." Finally, whereas Superman's alter-ego, Clark Kent, is a bumbler, and Spider-man's alter-ego, Peter Parker, is a troubled teenager struggling with his relationships, Batman's alter-ego, Bruce Wayne, is a polished millionaire who moves effortlessly among Gotham's social elite. The world of comic book heroes calls for all types of crime fighters. Whereas people like Superman for his pure goodness and Spider-man for his teenage angst, they like Batman because a side of him is as dark as the black bat suit he wears.

DRAFTING YOUR TOPIC SENTENCE

Sometimes when you start out, you already have a good idea of what your topic sentence will say. For example, if you want to write a one-paragraph letter to the editor of your campus newspaper to remind students to recycle their soda cans, you know you will begin with a sentence that says something like this:

> *Students should remember to recycle their soda cans.*

Other times you cannot write your topic sentence until you have studied your prewriting material—your freewriting, listing, mapping, or journaling—to determine what you want your main idea to be. For example, consider again this freewriting on stress and college students that first appeared on page 6:

> *Stress and college students. I'm not sure I can even take it anymore and the semester just began I just don't know how I can do 3 classes and work to but I can't give anything up. What am I going to do? I can't let anyone down. Now what? What to do, what to write. what to write. This is hard. I'm stuck. A B C D E F Does everyone feel as stressed out as I do? My classes are so hard, I don't get algebra at all. I'm supposed to go to the math lab but how am I supposed to find time for that? I'm so tired all the time I'd like to quit work but what will I do for money? Tuition will be due again soon. And the cost of books is insane. Maybe I should drop a course. Would that be cheaper? But then I'll never get out of here. I don't know what to do but I better do something or I'll explode. Actualy this freewriting is making me stressed out. Very funny.*

This freewriting suggests topic sentences about the stress of working and going to school, about the stress of taking difficult classes, and about the stress of financial pressures. In other words, topic sentences like these emerge from the freewriting:

- Working and going to school at the same time is very stressful.
- Difficult classes cause stress in college students.
- Financial pressures are a source of stress for college students.

If you have trouble discovering a topic sentence idea in your prewriting material, try asking the following questions about the material. The answers to one or more of them can suggest a topic sentence.

- What ideas do I mention?
- What conclusion can I draw?

Troubleshooting

If you have trouble drafting your topic sentence, you may be blocked by the thought that you will be stuck with whatever you write. Remember that you are *drafting* now; you can change your topic sentence later if necessary.

- What opinions are expressed?
- What ideas interest me?

If asking these questions does not help you find a topic sentence, do additional prewriting—perhaps a second, focused freewriting or list. Or try switching to a different prewriting strategy.

You have already learned that your topic sentence should state your topic and express your claim. In addition, make sure that your topic sentence is neither too broad nor too narrow.

Limiting your topic sentence

When you draft your topic sentence, keep your topic and claim at manageable proportions for a single paragraph. Topic sentences that take in too much territory give you too much to say in one paragraph. These sentences, for example, make poor topic sentences because they take in too much territory:

> *College athletics should be reformed.* [All of college athletics will be discussed in one paragraph?]
>
> *My childhood was a happy time.* [All of the writer's childhood will be discussed in one paragraph?]
>
> *Social class affects a person's family life, health, and education.* [Every aspect of family life, health, and education will be discussed in one paragraph?]

If you find that you have drafted a topic sentence that takes in too much, limit by focusing on a single aspect you can write about, as in these examples:

Too broad:	*College athletics should be reformed.*
Limited:	*Instead of awarding football scholarships, colleges should pay their football players to play.*
Too broad:	*My childhood was a happy time.*
Limited:	*Camping in the backyard with my twin brother is my happiest childhood memory.*
Too broad:	*Social class affects a person's family life, health, and education.*
Limited:	*Social class affects a person's choice of spouse.*

Broadening your topic sentence

When you draft your topic sentence, keep your topic and claim from being a simple statement of fact about which there is nothing more to say. The following statements of fact, for example, make poor topic sentences, because there is nothing to add—nothing needs to be proven or explained.

> *Students take many tests during their college years.*
> *I own a late-model Honda Accord.*
> *In 1979, the Soviet Union invaded Afghanistan.*

To broaden statements of fact so you have something to say, rewrite them into topic sentences that require proof or explanation, like these:

Too narrow:	*Students take many tests during their college years.*
Broader:	*The test-taking technique I use can help students manage their time.*
Too narrow:	*I own a late-model Honda Accord.*

Troubleshooting

You may find a broad topic sentence comforting because you fear not having enough to say. However, broad topic sentences lead to superficial supporting details, so use prewriting strategies, not a broad topic sentence, to ensure enough detail.

Broader:	*The Honda Accord is the best car on the road today.*
Too narrow:	*In 1979, the Soviet Union invaded Afghanistan.*
Broader:	*The Soviet Union's 1979 invasion of Afghanistan was a costly economic mistake.*

CONNECT FOR SUCCESS: Use Topic Sentences in Examination Answers

When you write one-paragraph exam answers, use a topic sentence and place it first to focus your response.

2.4 ACTIVITY

Five of the following topic sentences are acceptable. Three are unacceptable because they are narrow statements of fact, and two are unacceptable because they are too broad to be developed in a single paragraph. Label each topic sentence "narrow," "broad," or "acceptable," whichever is appropriate.

EXAMPLE _narrow_ I am a first-year college student.

1. _____ Women hold different positions than men do on many issues.

2. _____ I attended the Browns-Dolphins football game.

3. _____ Taking a year off between high school and college is a good idea.

4. _____ Carla's practical jokes are more cruel than funny.

5. _____ The neighborhood watch program reduced crime in the city by 15 percent.

6. _____ In my family, Sunday evening is the best part of the week.

7. _____ Public education should be reformed in every way.

8. _____ Students can overcome exam anxiety if they follow these steps.

9. _____ Children need to be loved.

10. _____ Dr. Garcia is the best teacher I ever had.

2.5 ACTIVITY

For each subject area below, write an acceptable topic sentence. Be sure to include the topic and claim.

EXAMPLE   friends:

Nothing comes between friends as fast as jealousy.

1. a favorite movie or television show

_____

_____

2. a difficult decision

_____

_____

3. college life

_____

_____

4. family life

_____

_____

5. the difference between two cities

_____

_____

6. sports

_____

_____

7. adolescence

_____

_____

8. a funny experience

_____

_____

9. shopping

_____

_____

10. one of your goals

_____

_____

2.6 ACTIVITY

Read the following paragraphs, which lack topic sentences. Compose suitable topic sentences, and write them in the blanks. Be sure to include the topic and claim.

1. _____ Originally, the pitcher's mound in baseball was 50 feet from home plate. Fifty feet is not very far, so pitchers found it easy to throw perfect pitches. Baseball became boring, so in 1893 officials decided to move the mound to 60 feet from home plate. A diagram was drawn up for the surveyor to map out new fields. However, the surveyor misread the diagram, thinking 60' 0" was 60' 6" and that is how he designed the new fields. The blueprints were drawn up and several new mounds were built before anyone noticed the mistake, so the incorrect measurement became the standard.

2. _____ During our country's first century, many wealthy people feared that an educated public would challenge their power, so they opposed free public education. However, those who favored a more equal society wanted to use education as a way to help ordinary people get ahead. Fortunately, this latter view won out, and free public schools sprang up in nearly every community.

Source: Adapted from Thomas E. Patterson, *We the People,* 5th ed. (New York: McGraw-Hill, 2004), p. 526. Copyright © 2004 The McGraw-Hill Companies. Used by permission of The McGraw-Hill Companies.

3. _____ In a study of 3,781 high school students, how much parents monitored their teenagers' behavior and schoolwork, encouraged achievement, and allowed joint decision making influenced school performance. It also affected whether or not adolescents used drugs and how independent they were. Parents' behavior also influenced what groups their teenagers joined. That is, parental behavior determined whether teenagers joined peer groups that were the "populars, jocks, brains, normals, druggies, and outcasts."

Source: Adapted from Diane E. Papalia and Sally Olds, *Human Development,* 6th ed. (New York: McGraw-Hill, 1999). Copyright © 1999 The McGraw-Hill Companies. Used by permission of The McGraw-Hill Companies.

2.7 COLLABORATIVE ACTIVITY

Select an article from a newsmagazine and follow the directions below. If you want to find an article online, you can find *Time* magazine at www.time.com/time/ and *Newsweek* at www.msnbc.msn.com/id/3032542/site/newsweek/.

Note: Keep your article and responses to use for a later activity.

A. Place brackets around the topic sentences in three paragraphs. (Remember, the topic sentence is not always the first sentence.) If you cannot find the topic sentence in a paragraph, move on to another paragraph.

B. Underline once the words that state the topic, and underline twice the words that express the claim.

C. Form a group with two or three classmates and trade articles. First, determine whether the topic sentences, topics, and claims in the article you receive have been correctly identified. Discuss any disagreement.

D. Discuss how the topic sentences in the articles make the reader's job easier.

SELECTING YOUR SUPPORTING DETAILS

The **supporting details** are the sentences in a paragraph that explain or prove the topic sentence. For example, reread the paragraph in Activity 2.1. The topic sentence is

The oyster toadfish is a very strange animal.

To explain or prove that topic sentence, these supporting details are included:

It looks like a monster.
It is not afraid of people.
It is aggressive.
It is very loud.
It makes a grunting sound.
The male sounds like a foghorn.
Mating toadfish are so loud that they keep people awake.

2.8 ACTIVITY

Reread the paragraph about families and culture on page 14, and answer these questions:

1. What is the topic sentence?

   _____

   _____

2. List the five examples that make up the supporting details.

   A. _____

   B. _____

   C. _____

   D. _____

   E. _____

2.9 COLLABORATIVE ACTIVITY

Reread the magazine article you used to complete Collaborative Activity 2.7 and answer the following questions with a classmate with whom you completed that activity.

1. How many supporting details are provided in each of the three paragraphs you examined earlier?

   Paragraph 1 _____

   Paragraph 2 _____

   Paragraph 3 _____

2. Do the supporting details explain the topic sentence or do they prove the topic sentence?

   Paragraph 1 _____

   Paragraph 2 _____

   Paragraph 3 _____

3. Trade articles with one other classmate and decide whether you agree with each other's conclusions. Discuss any areas of disagreement.

Considering your claim

After drafting your topic sentence and before drafting the rest of your paragraph, return once again to your prewriting. This time, you are looking for supporting details—for ideas to help you prove or explain the claim in your topic sentence. Some of your prewriting ideas will be usable, and some will not.

List all your prewriting ideas and cross out the ones that do not help you explain or prove the claim in your topic sentence. For example, the following is a list of prewriting ideas for the topic sentence "The Dean of Students office can do more to help students who are stressed." The ideas that do not help explain or prove the claim in the topic sentence have been struck out. Ask yourself why as you read the list.

> make counseling available to students
> ~~provide massage therapy for stressed students~~
> ~~make employers give time off to students at exam time~~
> have stress management workshops
> ~~test students to learn who is stressed out~~
> have "catch-up" days when classes are canceled, so students can catch up on their work
> let students drop courses without penalty
> ~~make extensions easier to get~~
> ~~provide more parking spaces~~
> train teachers to recognize signs of stress
> ~~give out more scholarships, so students do not have to work~~

2.10 ACTIVITY

The following is a list of prewriting ideas for the topic sentence "The shopping mall is more than a place to buy goods." Cross out the ideas that do not help prove or explain that topic sentence. Next to each idea you omit, explain why you deleted it.

> a place for teens to socialize
> a place for seniors to socialize
> mall walking for exercise
> health fairs there
> can be dangerous places
> can see a movie
> many specialty stores
> celebrity appearances
> restaurants
> entertainment opportunities
> getting too big

Considering your purpose

Your **purpose**, which is your reason for writing, can also help you select appropriate supporting details. To determine your writing purpose, ask yourself these questions:

- Do I want to entertain my reader?
- Do I want to express my feelings?
- Do I want to relate my experience?
- Do I want to inform my reader about something?
- Do I want to convince my reader to think or act a particular way?

To understand how considering your purpose will help you determine your supporting details, follow this example. Say you are writing about your school's general education requirements. To *inform* your reader of the importance of the requirements, you could explain what the requirements are and why they exist. However, to *persuade* the reader that the requirements should change, you would explain why the changes would improve the curriculum.

Considering your audience

Like purpose, your audience affects your supporting details. Your **audience** is your reader. Are you writing for your classroom teacher, for your classmates, for your boss, for coworkers, for the readers of a city newspaper, or for another audience? If you are arguing for a change in your school's general education requirements and your audience is the dean of your college, you need not define *general education requirements*. However, if you are writing a letter to the editor of your local newspaper, the definition may be necessary.

Audience affects more than *what* you say; it also affects *how* you say it. For example, the following are two definitions of *velocity*. The first is for readers of a college-level physics textbook, and the second is for users of a standard dictionary. Notice how the different audiences affect how the definition is expressed.

> *From a college textbook:* The velocity of an object is the rate of change of its position vector. Velocity tells how fast the object is traveling and the direction it is heading at the same instant of time. Velocity is the vector quantity because it is defined as a displacement divided by a time interval.

> *From a standard dictionary:* Velocity is the rate of change of position along a straight line with respect to time.

2.11 ACTIVITY

For each topic sentence, indicate an appropriate audience and purpose. (More than one answer is possible for each.)

EXAMPLE Daylight savings time creates more problems than it solves.

Possible purpose: *to persuade reader that daylight savings time is a bad idea*

Possible audience: *state legislators*

1. My happiest birthday was my sixteenth.

   Possible purpose: _____

   Possible audience: _____

2. Performing CPR is not as difficult as you might think.

   Possible purpose: _____

   Possible audience: _____

3. Everyone should learn how to perform CPR.

    Possible purpose: _____

    Possible audience: _____

4. The ringtone on an individual's cell phone says something about the person's personality.

    Possible purpose: _____

    Possible audience: _____

5. The differences between Internet phone service and traditional telephone service are significant.

    Possible purpose: _____

    Possible audience: _____

2.12 COLLABORATIVE ACTIVITY

Form a group with two of your classmates, and assume you are writing an article for your campus newspaper with this topic sentence: "Off-campus employers who hire college students should allow these students extra time off to study for exams." Now assume you want to rewrite the article to submit to your city's local newspaper. With the members of your group, respond to the following questions on a separate sheet.

1. How would you change the details for your new audience?
2. Why is the change necessary?

2.13 ACTIVITY

The following is the list of ideas generated for a paragraph about stress and college students. Assume you are planning to write a paragraph for other students about the causes and effects of stress on college students. Also assume you plan to make the paragraph humorous, so that you can entertain your audience. Circle the details you are likely to use for this audience and purpose, and be prepared to explain the reasons for your choices.

> make counseling available to students
>
> provide massage therapy for stressed students
>
> make employers give time off to students at exam time
>
> have stress management workshops
>
> test students to learn who is stressed out
>
> have "catch-up" days when classes are canceled, so students can catch up on their work
>
> let students drop courses without penalty
>
> make extensions easier to get
>
> provide more parking spaces
>
> train teachers to recognize signs of stress
>
> give out more scholarships, so students do not have to work
>
> colleges will have fewer dropouts and make more money

tell profs to lighten up on the work and tough grading
show students how to study and take tests

Asking questions

You have selected supporting details that explain or prove the claim in your topic sentence, that carry out your purpose, and that suit your audience. Do you have enough ideas to write a draft? Perhaps you do. If not, you can ask these questions about your topic sentence to discover additional ideas:

What can I describe?	Can I compare or contrast something?
What examples can I give?	Can I tell how something is made or done?
Can I explain any causes?	Can I define something?
Can I explain any effects?	Can I argue something?

Here is an example of asking questions to discover supporting details for the topic sentence "Colleges should offer a stress management workshop":

1. Question: What can I describe?

   Answer: the anxiety that many students feel

2. Question: What examples can I give?

   Answer: examples of other colleges that offer stress management workshops

3. Question: Can I explain any causes?

   Answer: the most common causes of stress in college students

4. Question: Can I explain any effects?

   Answer: the positive effects the workshop would have

5. Question: Can I compare or contrast something?

   Answer: contrast students who do and do not know techniques for managing stress

6. Question: Can I tell how something is made or done?

   Answer: explain how the workshop would work

7. Question: Can I define something?

   Answer: define *stress*.

8. Question: Can I argue something?

   Answer: that colleges will benefit if their students are less stressed

You may not be able to answer all the questions for your topic sentence, and you do not need to include all the ideas your answers generate. However, some of the answers may give you the additional ideas you need for your supporting details.

2.14 ACTIVITY

On a separate sheet, answer the eight questions for one of the topic sentences you wrote for Activity 2.5. Write three ideas you came up with on the following spaces.

1. _____

2. _____

3. _____

DRAFTING AN EFFECTIVE CLOSING

A stand-alone paragraph has a **closing sentence** to bring it to a satisfying finish. Many times, an appropriate closing sentence suggests itself to you. When it does not, try one of these approaches:

- Refer to the topic sentence idea. (The paragraph on families and culture on page 14 is an example of this approach.)
- Draw a conclusion from the supporting details. (Paragraph 3 of Activity 2.3 is an example of this approach.)

2.15 ACTIVITY

One of the following paragraphs needs a closing sentence to be added, and one does not. If the paragraph needs a closing sentence, add one. If the paragraph does not need a closing sentence to be added, explain why.

1.   Many people start their own businesses because they see the risks as similar to those of working for someone else—but the rewards are much greater. The workplace as a whole is becoming more risky. Many jobs are more uncertain than they were ten years ago because downsizing and restructuring are undermining job security. Pay increases are no longer automatic and fringe benefit packages are shrinking. Because working for someone else is more uncertain than it was, the incentive for some risk-taking with a payoff of independence, high job satisfaction, and possible high profits just might entice you to start your own business.

_____

Source: Adapted from William G. Nickels, James M. McHugh, and Susan M. McHugh, *Understanding Business,* 5th ed. (New York: McGraw-Hill, 1999), p. 193. Copyright © 1999 The McGraw-Hill Companies. Used by permission of The McGraw-Hill Companies.

2.   To succeed in business, you need certain qualities. First, you must be willing to take risks. Taking risks does not mean being reckless. It means being comfortable with trying things that could possibly fail. You must also be able to see the possibilities in new ways of doing things. You must be able to "see the big picture" with both creativity and practicality. You cannot be too set in the old ways of doing things or of perceiving reality. To succeed, you also need to be a self-starter—someone who doesn't need to have others tell you what to do and when. You need to be internally motivated. Getting up in the morning should be exciting and challenging rather than threatening or depressing. Finally, you need to be ambitious and competitive enough that you are willing to work hard and long hours. You must see yourself as a winner and *expect* to win. _____

_____

Source: Adapted from William G. Nickels, James M. McHugh, and Susan M. McHugh, *Understanding Business,* 5th ed. (New York: McGraw-Hill, 1999), p. 193. Copyright © 1999 The McGraw-Hill Companies. Used by permission of The McGraw-Hill Companies.

OUTLINING YOUR FIRST DRAFT

After selecting your prewriting ideas, develop an **informal outline** by placing the draft of your topic sentence at the top of a page and numbering your ideas in the order you will write them in your draft. (If you do not have enough ideas for an informal outline, do additional prewriting—including asking questions, as explained on page 27—until you do have enough ideas.) At the end of your list, sketch an idea for your closing. Here is an informal outline for a paragraph on what the Dean of Students office could do to help students who are stressed:

Draft of topic sentence: The Dean of Students office can do more to help students who are stressed.

⑤ *.make counseling available to students*

③ *.have stress management workshops*

① *.have "catch-up" days when classes are canceled, so students can catch up on their work*

④ *train teachers to recognize signs of stress*

② *show students how to study and take tests*

Idea for closing: Dealing with their stress would help students improve the quality of their lives.

CONNECT FOR SUCCESS: Outline Examination Answers

Before writing an essay examination answer, write an informal outline that states the main points your answer will include. The outline will keep your answer organized and serve as a reminder, in case you forget something in the heat of the moment.

2.16 ACTIVITY

Review the prewriting ideas you discovered when you completed Activity 1.2, Activity 1.3, and Activity 1.4 in Chapter 1. (If you did not complete those activities, complete one of them now.) Then do the following on a separate sheet.

A. Using the set of ideas you like best, draft a topic sentence that could guide a first draft.

B. Evaluate your supporting details and cross out ones that do not help prove the claim in your topic sentence.

C. Decide on the purpose and audience. Write them down, and use them to help you select supporting details.

D. Do you need more ideas? If so, try asking questions and add ideas to your list.

E. Using your list, write an informal outline. Be sure to sketch an idea for a closing.

WRITING YOUR FIRST DRAFT

With your informal outline as a guide, you are ready to write your first draft. Begin with your topic sentence. Then write the number 1 point in your informal outline. When you are finished writing that point, write the number 2 point, and so on. Although the informal outline is guiding you, you can respond to good thoughts as they occur to you by adding ideas, deleting ideas, or changing the order of ideas. Remember, writing is a process of discovery, so take advantage of any new ideas or even inspiration that comes to you as you write.

Remember, too, that a first draft is merely a first attempt to express yourself, so it will have problems, which is why a first draft is often called a **rough draft**. Do not be concerned about the rough spots, and do not get bogged down trying to fix things. Keep pushing forward; you will have ample opportunity to improve the draft later, during revising and editing (which you will learn about in Chapter 3). If you cannot think of a word, leave a blank and press on. If you are unsure how to express an

Troubleshooting

If you have trouble drafting, return to mapping, freewriting, or listing. You may need more ideas. Or try writing your draft as a letter to a friend.

idea, jot down anything you can and deal with the problem later. The key to drafting is focusing on what you *can* do without worrying about what you cannot do.

The following is an example of a first draft written from the informal outline in the section "Outlining Your First Draft." When you read it, you may notice several problems. These problems can be addressed later. As it is, the draft offers valuable material to shape into a finished product.

The Dean of Students office can do more to help students who are stressed. One good idea being "catch-up" days. Catch-up days are when classes are canceled, so students can catch up on their work and assignments. One day each semester should do it. Another idea is showing students how to take tests, because tests are a big reason for stress for students who do not know how to take tests and have trouble as a result of not knowing this. Stress management workshops would help because they would teach student how to deal with any stress that comes up before the student explodes from the stress. Teachers should be trained to recognize the signs of stress, so they can interveen as necessary. Counseling should be available to students who need it because of stress. If the Dean of Students office could do these simple things and they would help students cope with their stress and improve the quality of their lives.

Composing at the computer

If you like to compose at the computer, you may find these suggestions helpful:

- **Use your copy and move functions.** You can use these functions to arrange items in your prewriting list into an informal outline.
- **Paste your outline in your draft.** If you have trouble writing one part of your draft, paste in the relevant portion of your outline as a placeholder and reminder of what goes in that spot. Then push on.

CONNECT FOR SUCCESS: Rewrite Lecture Notes

As a study aid, rewrite your lecture notes into paragraphs. Put each main idea in a topic sentence. Make the relevant examples, definitions, and clarifying points the supporting details. For a closing, draw a conclusion or state the importance of the information in the paragraph.

2.17 ACTIVITY

1. Using the informal outline you wrote for Activity 2.16 as a guide, write a first draft of your paragraph on a separate sheet of paper.

Note: Save your draft; you will need it for an activity in Chapter 3.

2.18 CHAPTER REVIEW ACTIVITY

1. What did you learn about writing in this chapter that you did not know before?

_____

_____

2. Will your writing process change as a result of what you have learned? Explain.

   _____

   _____

3. What did you learn in this chapter that you can use in other courses?

   _____

   _____

4. How can an informal outline make drafting easier?

   _____

5. Why are first drafts often called rough drafts?

   _____

GETTING IN GEAR: IDEAS FOR WRITING

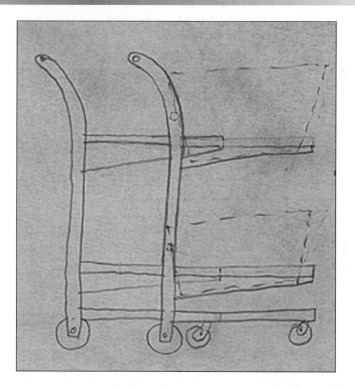

The photograph is of a drawing by Orla E. Watson (1896–1983), who invented a telescoping shopping cart that could be fitted into another cart for easy storage in minimal space. To see more drawings that preceded inventions, vist the Smithsonian Institution's industrial drawings site at www.sil.si.edu/exhibitions/doodles/cf/doodles_alt.cfm.

writing topic: Like writing, inventing useful items is a process that involves idea generation, planning, and trial and error—and some of that may be done on paper, as the drawing of the telescoping shopping cart illustrates. Explain how a process you perform is either similar to or different from the process of writing. You might consider processes such as studying for an exam, giving a party, working out in the gym, taking a road trip, decorating a Christmas tree, scheduling your classes, or buying a present.

suggestions for prewriting

- List five to ten processes you perform regularly. Review the list and pick one to write about.
- The writing process involves generating ideas, planning, outlining, making a first effort (drafting), and making changes (revising). List the ways your process is either similar to or different from the process of writing

suggestions for drafting

- Plan your draft by writing a topic sentence that states your topic (the process you are writing about) and expresses your claim (whether the process is or is not similar to the writing process).
- List your ideas for supporting details; if you think you need more, return to prewriting, perhaps by asking questions.
- Identify your purpose and audience, and use them to help you select your supporting details.
- Write your draft in one sitting, allowing it to be rough. If you get stuck on a word or phrase, leave room and push on. Try to write at least ten sentences.

RECHARGE: Lesson Summary

1. A paragraph is a group of sentences that develop one main idea. The parts of a paragraph are the topic sentence, the supporting details, and the closing.
2. The topic sentence
   - expresses the paragraph's main idea.
   - includes the topic and the writer's claim about the topic.
   - should be limited, but not a narrow statement of fact.
3. The supporting details
   - prove or explain the topic sentence.
   - should suit your purpose and audience.
4. The closing
   - brings the paragraph to a satisfying close.
   - can refer to the topic sentence idea or draw a conclusion.
5. Freewriting, listing, mapping, journaling, and asking questions can help you decide on your topic sentence and discover supporting details.
6. An informal outline can guide a draft.
7. A first draft is a rough draft that will be improved later.

CHAPTER 3

Revising and Editing a Paragraph

No matter how rough your first draft is, it provides raw material you can improve with *revising* and *editing*. **Revising** is the process of improving the content, organization, and wording of your draft. **Editing** is the process of correcting mistakes in grammar, spelling, punctuation, and capitalization. You will learn about these important processes in this chapter.

DECIDING WHAT TO REVISE

The first step in revising is deciding what changes to make in your draft. The strategies explained in this section can help you. However, before you start revising, take a break for a day. The time away will help you view your draft more objectively. Then, when you start to revise, do it in stages over a period of days. The first time, make the easiest changes. Then go down each point in the revising checklist that follows, taking a break whenever you need to. Because revising is time-consuming, spread the work out over several days. Each time away will also give you an opportunity to rethink your draft and changes. As you revise, you may notice some errors in grammar, spelling, punctuation, and capitalization. You may correct mistakes now if you want, but do not make editing a priority, because it diverts your attention from revising concerns.

Troubleshooting

If you have trouble deciding what to revise, listen to your draft. Have someone read it to you, or read it aloud yourself. You may *hear* problems you do not *see*.

Using a revising checklist

Answering the questions in this checklist can help you decide what to revise. Later sections of this chapter will offer additional guidelines on these topics.

REVISING CHECKLIST FOR A PARAGRAPH

- What is my topic sentence? Where does it appear? Does it state the topic and express a claim? Does it avoid making an overly broad statement or an overly narrow statement of fact?
- Do the supporting details fulfill my writing purpose and meet my audience's needs?
- Is the content adequate and convincing?

> **REVISING CHECKLIST FOR A PARAGRAPH CONTINUED**
>
> - Do the supporting details show and not just tell?
> - Are the ideas in a logical order and connected by transitions, so the paragraph has coherence?
> - Does every sentence relate to the topic sentence, so the paragraph has unity?
> - Are the words concise and specific?
> - Does the closing provide a satisfying finish?

Revising with reader response

You can get additional revision suggestions if you ask people to react to your *revised* draft. It is best to do your own revising first, so you can show readers a draft you think is satisfactory. Then their comments can help you make that draft even better. Use people with good judgment about writing. Good choices include writing center tutors, students who have successfully taken writing courses, and classmates who are doing well in your course. Poor choices include a friend who is uncomfortable giving criticism and a roommate who is failing three classes. Try to use two or three readers, so you can look for consensus. If your readers disagree and you cannot decide who is right, speak to your instructor.

You can secure helpful reader response in several ways:

- Make a list of questions you would like your readers to answer, questions such as "What do you think of the example in the fourth sentence?" and "Does my closing provide a satisfying finish?"
- Ask your readers to write responses directly on the draft. (See page 52 for an example.)
- Give your readers an unmarked copy of your draft with a photocopy of the form on page 35 to complete.

3.1 ACTIVITY

The following is the first draft of a paragraph meant to persuade an audience of state legislators. Assume the writer gave the draft to you for reader response. Photocopy and complete the reader response form on page 35.

It's wrong to require students to pass a state test in order to get their teacher certification. Some people who would make excellent teachers are not any good at taking tests. Should these people be punished just because they aren't any good at taking standardized tests? If a person passes the necessary college courses, then how can the state come along, give a test, and say those courses don't mean anything if you fail the state test? College teachers are the best judge of preparedness to teach, not tests devised by the state. We should abolish the state teacher's exam and let college teachers decide who is and is not ready to get teacher certification.

READER RESPONSE FORM FOR A PARAGRAPH

1. What is the topic sentence of this paragraph? What is the topic? What is the claim about the topic? _____

   _____

   _____

   _____

   _____

2. What do you like best about this paragraph? _____

   _____

   _____

   _____

   _____

3. Do the supporting details prove or explain the topic sentence? If not, what ideas could be added? _____

   _____

   _____

   _____

   _____

4. Does the paragraph end in a satisfying way? Why or why not?

   _____

   _____

   _____

   _____

5. On the draft, do the following:

   A. Place a ! next to any wording you particularly like.

   B. Place a ? next to anything you do not understand.

   C. Circle any words or phrases that are not concise or specific enough.

6. What is the most important revision the writer should make?

   _____

   _____

   _____

   _____

REVISING FOR PARAGRAPH CONTENT

As you begin to revise, look first at your paragraph's content. Do your supporting details prove or explain your topic sentence? To improve your paragraph's content, improve your supporting details. You can do that through examples, stories, descriptions, and reasons. These kinds of supporting details help you do more than *tell* your reader that something is true. They allow you to *show* your reader that something is true.

Giving examples

Examples (instances, models, or cases that are representative of something) are an excellent way to prove or explain a topic sentence; they are an excellent way to *show* rather than merely *tell*. Notice how two examples explain the topic sentence in the following paragraph from a psychology textbook. The topic sentence is underlined as a study aid.

> *Concepts are categories of objects, events, or people that share common properties and, therefore, help us understand the world more readily on the basis of past experience. For example, we can surmise that a small, rectangular box with buttons that is on a chair near a television is probably a remote control—even if we have never encountered that specific brand before. That is, we understand the concept of a remote control because we have had prior experience with other remote controls and know what their characteristics are. Ultimately, concepts influence behavior. We assume, for instance, that it might be appropriate to pet an animal after determining that it is a dog, because our concept of dog tells us that petting one is generally safe. However, we would behave differently after classifying the animal as a wolf because our concept of wolf tells us that the animal is not safe.*

Source: Adapted from Robert S. Feldman, *Essentials of Understanding Psychology,* 4th ed. (New York: McGraw-Hill, 2000), p. 243. Copyright © 2000 The McGraw-Hill Companies. Used by permission of The McGraw-Hill Companies.

If your first draft needs more supporting details to prove or explain the topic sentence, consider including one or more examples. Study the improvements that the addition of examples can make by comparing the first version of the following paragraph with the second, revised version. The supporting details in the first draft do not prove or explain the topic sentence idea because they *tell* the reader that much of what circulates on the Internet is untrue, but they do not *show* that it is untrue.

> *Much of what circulates on the Internet is untrue. People assume that the stories they read on the Internet are true, so they pass them along in e-mails. However, often the stories are hoaxes. Some stories have been circulating for years, but people still believe them. It doesn't even matter how preposterous the stories are. Particularly persistent are false stories about making money or receiving gifts by sending e-mail. If the Internet proves anything, it's that people will fall for any ridiculous story.*

Notice in the following revised paragraph that adding examples solves the problem of telling, not showing.

> *Much of what circulates on the Internet is untrue. People assume that the stories they read on the Internet are true, so they pass them along in e-mails. However, often the stories are hoaxes. One false story making the rounds these days says that we can end the funding of terrorists if we all stop buying gasoline*

on the same day. Some stories, like the one that says students get 220 points on the SAT if they spell their names correctly, have been circulating for years, but people still believe them. It doesn't even matter how preposterous the stories are. A ridiculous story stating that a girl's jaw swelled because she ate cockroach eggs when she was licking envelopes is currently on the Internet and believed by many people. Particularly persistent are false stories about making money or receiving gifts by forwarding e-mail. Different versions of these hoaxes say you can get cash from Microsoft, shoes from Nike, clothes from the Gap, and computers from IBM. One even states that you can receive a trip to Disney World, just by forwarding e-mail. If the Internet proves anything, it's that people will fall for any ridiculous story.

Telling a story

Narration (storytelling) is another way to explain or prove your topic sentence, as the following paragraph from a psychology textbook illustrates. The topic sentence is underlined as a study aid.

<u>Bodily kinesthetic intelligence, which is skill in using the body, is one kind of intelligence.</u> Fifteen-year-old Babe Ruth played third base. During one game, his team's pitcher was doing very poorly and Babe loudly criticized him from third base. The coach called out, "Ruth, if you know so much about it, you pitch!" Babe was surprised and embarrassed because he had never pitched before, but the coach insisted. Ruth said later that, at the very moment he took the pitcher's mound, he knew he was supposed to be a pitcher. In other words, he knew he could use his body that way. That's bodily kinesthetic intelligence.

Source: Adapted from Robert S. Feldman, *Essentials of Understanding Psychology,* 4th ed. (New York: McGraw-Hill, 2000), p. 284. Copyright © 2000 The McGraw-Hill Companies. Used by permission of The McGraw-Hill Companies.

Stories are powerful ways to show, not tell. In the following pair of paragraphs, the second one is revised to tell the full story of how Coach McGregor reached out and boosted the writer's self-confidence. When you read it, you will see the drama that narrative details add.

When I was an awkward boy in eighth grade, Coach Dennis McGregor reached out to me and boosted my confidence. In eighth grade, I was an awkward boy who was the last one picked for teams in gym class. I was also the first one to make a stupid mistake. I felt worthless and unpopular. Then one day Coach McGregor taught me to kick a football, and I made second string on the team. I will always be grateful to Coach McGregor.

The following revised paragraph *shows* with narration how the coach boosted the writer's confidence.

When I was an awkward boy in eighth grade, Coach Dennis McGregor reached out to me and boosted my confidence. In eighth grade, I was an awkward boy who was the last one picked for teams in gym class. I was also the first one to make a stupid mistake. I felt worthless and unpopular. Then one day Coach McGregor asked me to stay after school. He asked me if I wanted to learn to kick a football. I told him I probably couldn't do it, but he insisted on teaching me, anyway. He worked with me after school three days a week, and over the summer he coached me twice a week. Then came the shocker. In July before high school, he told me he expected me to try out for the high school football team as a field goal kicker. I was terrified, but Coach made me try because he said he knew I could do it. On the day of tryouts, he was there. When it was my turn to try out, I glanced at Coach and he gave me his famous thumbs-up sign. Suddenly, his confidence became my own, and I had a successful tryout. I became a second stringer, but just making the team did more for my confidence than anything since. I will always be grateful to Coach McGregor.

Describing something

Sometimes **description** (telling how something looks, sounds, tastes, feels, or smells) can help you prove or explain your topic sentence, as the following paragraph from an American history textbook demonstrates. The topic sentence is underlined as a study aid.

November 1914, Scotland Neck, Halifax County, North Carolina—Eleven-year-old Nannie Coleson sewing stockings at Crescent Hosiery for which she makes three dollars a week.

<u>Work was difficult for women in the garment factories in early twentieth-century New York.</u> At seven in the morning, Sadie Frowne sat at her sewing machine in a Brooklyn garment factory. The factory was crowded and dark, filled with immigrant women like Sadie sitting straight-backed and ready. It was nothing at all like the small, open village in Russia where her people had started. The boss, a man she barely knew, dropped a pile of unfinished skirts next to her. She pushed one under the needle and began to rock her foot quickly on the pedal that powered her machine. Sometimes Sadie pushed the skirts too hastily, and the needle pierced her finger. There was pain and usually a moment's confusion; perhaps those at nearby machines stopped to help, but then it was

back to stitching. To stop, even to slow down, was ordinarily unthinkable. "The machines go like mad all day because the faster you work the more money you get," Sadie explained of the world of industrial work in 1902.

Source: Adapted from James West Davidson et al., *Nation of Nations*, 3rd ed., (New York: McGraw-Hill, 1998), PP. 621–22. Copyright © 1998 The McGraw-Hill Companies. Used by permission of The McGraw-Hill Companies.

Description can help your reader see what you see or feel what you feel. Notice the difference that descriptive details make between the following original and revised paragraphs. In the revised paragraph, you can *see* how unappealing the Thanksgiving buffet was.

Instead of going home for Thanksgiving, my roommate and I ate Thanksgiving dinner at the Sunshine Buffet and Grill. This was a mistake, because the buffet was very unappealing. The food was typical, but the turkey was an alarming color. The side dishes were greasy and limp. Worst of all, the pumpkin pie was not fresh. Believe me, next year I will do whatever it takes to get to my mother's table at Thanksgiving.

The revised paragraph convinces the reader with descriptive details that show that the buffet was unappealing.

Instead of going home for Thanksgiving, my roommate and I ate Thanksgiving dinner at the Sunshine Buffet and Grill. This was a mistake, because the buffet was very unappealing. The entrees at the front of the buffet table included some of the traditional Thanksgiving dishes, but they also included some very strange choices, like pork chops drowning in brown glop and liver smothered in greasy onions. There was turkey, but it was laced with streaks of pink, so I wasn't sure it was safe to eat. Actually, the pork chops in glop looked better. The side dishes behind the entrees were unappealing, too. Apparently, the cook thought that butter would improve all the side dishes, because they were swimming in pools of it. The cook must also have been afraid of undercooking the vegetables, because they had been steamed so long that the carrots were soggy, the green beans were limp, and the asparagus was mushy. It was like eating baby food in butter broth. Worst of all, even dessert was a disappointment, as the pumpkin pie had been frozen and had the "freezer flavor" that frozen food gets when it has been not been properly wrapped. Believe me, next year I will do whatever it takes to get to my mother's table at Thanksgiving.

Giving reasons

You can prove your topic sentence with **reasons** (statements that justify or explain why something is true), as the following excerpt from an education textbook illustrates. The topic sentence is underlined as a study aid.

In the 1950s, economist Milton Friedman suggested schools would improve if parents could choose the public schools their children attended. Friedman believed that public schools were not working well because there was no competition, no incentive for them to do their best. Parents were forced to send their children to the neighborhood school, and the neighborhood school had no incentive to compete with other schools to improve. It had a "trapped" clientele. But not everyone was trapped. Because they could afford private school tuition, wealthy parents were able to bail out if the public school was performing *poorly. Friedman believed that everyone needed the same freedom to choose what the wealthy enjoyed.*

Source: Adapted from Myra Pollack Sadker and David Miller Sadker, *Teacher, Schools, and Society*, 5th ed. (New York: McGraw-Hill, 2000), p. 152. Copyright © 2000 The McGraw-Hill Companies. Used by permission of The McGraw-Hill Companies.

Reasons may, at times, seem obvious to you, but they will not be obvious to your readers. If your first draft seems weak, elaborate your reasons, one by one. The supporting details in the following first draft only repeat the claim in the topic sentence; they do not prove that it is a good idea for all first-year students to take a study skills course. Compare this draft with the revised draft that specifies reasons.

All first-year students should be required to take a one-week study skills course prior to the start of classes. A study skills class is a good idea because many first-year students would benefit from the class, and so would the university. There is really no reason not to offer the course, because it would be such a service to students. Often, many students try hard, but no matter how hard they try, they still do not do as well as they should or could. These students would certainly benefit from a study skills course. In fact, students who would flunk out without the course are more likely to stay in school. Thus, a mandatory study skills course would be a great benefit.

In the following revision, the reasons are explained to show the reader that that a mandatory study skills course is a good idea. Look for the distinct reasons the writer puts forward.

All first-year students should be required to take a one-week study skills course prior to the start of classes. First of all, many first-year students are returning to school after a long absence. These people probably need to brush up on their study skills. A greater concern is the fact that many 18-year-old students have never had a study skills course and need to learn how to study. Also, techniques that were used to study in high school may not be effective in college, particularly since students often take courses unlike anything they encountered in high school. Perhaps most important is the fact that colleges need to decrease the number of students who flunk out, so they can stay in business. A mandatory study skills course prior to the start of classes can help colleges achieve this goal.

Combining strategies

You can prove or explain your topic sentence by combining strategies. Reread, for example, the revised paragraph about the Thanksgiving buffet on page 39. Notice that it uses both examples and descriptions. Notice, too, the textbook excerpt about factory work on page 38. That paragraph combines descriptions, narration, and reasons.

Troubleshooting

If you have trouble thinking of examples, stories, descriptions, or reasons for supporting details, take some time to think about your past experiences, what you have observed recently, and what you have read on your own and for your classes.

CONNECT FOR SUCCESS: Prove or Explain Topic Sentences in Examination Answers

When you write one-paragraph essay exam answers, you should use examples, stories, descriptions, and reasons from your textbooks and lecture notes to prove or explain your topic sentence.

3.2 ACTIVITY

Pick five of the topic sentences you wrote in response to Activity 2.5. Indicate whether the supporting details are likely to be descriptions, examples, a story, reasons, or a combination. If the details are likely to be a combination, state what the combination will be.

EXAMPLE Topic sentence: *To get the best bargains, shop outlet stores with caution.*

Supporting details: *reasons to be cautious and examples of what happens when not cautious*

1. Topic sentence: _____

   _____

   Supporting details: _____

   _____

2. Topic sentence: _____

   _____

   Supporting details: _____

   _____

3. Topic sentence: _____

   _____

   Supporting details: _____

   _____

4. Topic sentence: _____

   _____

   Supporting details: _____

   _____

5. Topic sentence: _____

   _____

   Supporting details: _____

   _____

3.3 ACTIVITY

Each of the sentences below *tells*. After each one, add a sentence that *shows*.

EXAMPLE Americans are becoming more health-conscious. *For example, they are eating fewer fatty foods.*

1. The history exam was very difficult. _____

   _____

2. The storm caused much hardship. _____

   _____

3. Gloria's apartment is filthy. _____

   _____

4. Students who work while they attend school often have a difficult time.

   _____

5. College offers students many rewarding experiences. _____

   _____

3.4 ACTIVITY

After each topic sentence, list three supporting details that could be written to prove or explain the topic sentence.

EXAMPLE   My sixteenth birthday was the best ever.

   I was given a surprise party.

   My sister bought me a leather coat.

   My parents took me out to dinner.

1. The scene at Boltin Department Store's going-out-of-business sale was one of complete chaos.

   _____

   _____

   _____

2. Advertising makes people want things they do not really need.

   _____

   _____

   _____

3. We would be better off if we threw out our television sets.

   _____

   _____

   _____

4. I will never forget the time I got a traffic ticket.

   _____

   _____

   _____

5. Laricia's is an excellent restaurant.

_____

_____

_____

The following paragraph could be improved with more details, so it would show and not just tell. On a separate sheet, rewrite the paragraph by adding the following:

A. a sentence or two after sentence 2 to show that the father drives too fast

B. a sentence or two after sentence 3 to show that he does not watch the road

C. a sentence or two after sentence 4 to show that he tries to get the best of other drivers

[1]If you drive with my father, you take your life in your hands. [2]For one thing, he drives too fast. [3]He also does not watch the road the way he should. [4]Worst of all, he is very aggressive when he gets behind the wheel, so he is always trying to get the best of other drivers. [5]He is so bad, in fact, that my mother and I now refuse to get in the car with him unless one of us drives.

REVISING YOUR DRAFT FOR COHERENCE

Writing has **coherence** when readers can tell how all the ideas relate to each other. One way you can achieve coherence is to arrange your ideas in a logical order. Another way to achieve coherence is to use **transitions,** which are words and phrases that _show_ the reader how ideas relate to each other. These methods will be explained next.

Arranging ideas in a logical order

When you revise, be sure your supporting details are arranged logically, so your reader can follow your progression of thought. In your draft, you may have followed an informal outline that put your list of supporting details in sequence. Now examine that sequence to see if it is still the best way to present your ideas. The following are common ways to arrange your supporting details.

- _Chronological order (time order)._ With **chronological order,** you arrange your supporting details in time order—in the order events occur or occurred. Write the event that happens or happened first, then the event that happens or happened next, and so on to the last event. You will use chronological order when you tell a story or explain how to do something (such as perform CPR). For an example of chronological order, reread the paragraph about Coach McGregor on page 37.
- _Spatial order (space order)._ With **spatial order,** you arrange your supporting details in a pattern across space, such as near to far, top to bottom, left to right, or front to back. You will often use spatial order when you describe a scene or place. For example, a real estate brochure might start at the front door and describe a house by moving clockwise through the rooms. For an example of spatial order, reread the revised paragraph about the Thanksgiving buffet on page 39 and notice that

the description of entrees and side dishes is arranged in spatial order from front to back.

- *Progressive order (order of importance).* With **progressive order,** you arrange your supporting details from the least to the most important, or from the most to the least important. When you give examples or reasons, you will use progressive order when you want to save the best for last or when you want to open with your strongest point. For an example of progressive order that saves the best for last, reread the paragraph urging a mandatory study skills course on page 40.

3.6 ACTIVITY

For each paragraph, indicate the logical order or combination of orders for supporting details (chronological, spatial, or progressive). Be prepared to explain your choice.

EXAMPLE   a paragraph about the best new programs on television in a media
critic's column *progressive order*

1. a paragraph explaining how to program an IPod in an e-mail to a friend

   _____

2. a paragraph about your favorite childhood Halloween celebration in your journal

   _____

3. a paragraph explaining why public employees unionize in an essay examination answer for a labor studies class _____

4. a paragraph describing a cell viewed under a microscope in a biology lab report

   _____

5. a paragraph explaining how your car accident happened in a report to your insurance company

   _____

6. a paragraph giving the reasons pay raises will not be given this year in a letter to company employees

   _____

7. a paragraph for a fire science class explaining the chief benefits of a particular fire prevention program

   _____

8. a paragraph describing the public baths in ancient Rome for a world history homework assignment

   _____

9. a paragraph for an office management class explaining how to organize work space for maximum efficiency

   _____

10. a paragraph explaining the advantages of new health care benefits for a company newsletter

Using transitions

Transitions are words and phrases that show your reader how ideas relate to each other. The following chart gives some common transitions, the relationships they signal, and example sentences. When you revise, add transitions from the chart as needed to show your reader the connections among your ideas.

TRANSITIONS CHART

TRANSITIONS THAT SIGNAL CHRONOLOGICAL (TIME) ORDER					
first	next	now	then	meanwhile	later
at that time	finally	afterward	earlier	eventually	soon after
Example: Interest rates should rise next month. <u>Soon after</u>, mortgage rates will rise.					

TRANSITIONS THAT SIGNAL SPATIAL (SPACE) ORDER					
near	nearby	across from	beyond	beside	to the right
next to	alongside	above		below	in front of	underneath
Example: The new school is well located. <u>Nearby</u> is a library and a bookstore.					

TRANSITIONS THAT SIGNAL PROGRESSIVE ORDER					
first	more/most important	least of all	above all	first of all
finally	more significant	worst of all	moreover	less important
Example: <u>First of all</u>, a tax increase is necessary to pay down the deficit. <u>More important</u>, a tax increase will slow the inflation rate.				

TRANSITIONS THAT SIGNAL EXAMPLES			
for example	for instance	to illustrate	specifically
Example: Catherine is very superstitious. <u>For example</u>, she will not leave the house on Friday the 13th.			

TRANSITIONS THAT SIGNAL ADDITION						
in addition	further	furthermore	also	second	third	finally
Example: City council approved tax incentives for new industry. <u>In addition</u>, council members voted to fund a new convention bureau.						

TRANSITIONS THAT SIGNAL CAUSE AND EFFECT					
therefore	so	thus	as a result	because	consequently
Example: The drought has damaged the citrus crop. <u>As a result</u>, the cost of orange juice has gone up dramatically.					

> **GRAMMAR ALERT!**
>
> *Plus* is not a transition that can be substituted for *and* or *in addition*.
>
> No: *Palo won first prize in the art show. Plus, he sold one of his paintings.*
>
> Yes: *Palo won first prize in the art show. In addition, he sold one of his paintings.*

3.7 ACTIVITY

1957, Moscow, Russia–A Russian engineer displays a replica of Sputnik.

Fill in the blanks with a transition from the transitions chart. More than one answer is possible.

On October 4, 1957, the Soviet Union launched *Sputnik I*, the first artificial satellite. *Sputnik*, which took pictures of the far side of the moon, had two effects on the United States. [1]_____ the United States was shocked that the Soviet space capability was so advanced. [2]_____ the United States became frightened it would be outdone by the Soviets, so Americans pursued their own space program aggressively. Four months later, the United States launched its first satellite. These two satellites marked the beginning of the space age.

³ _____ the Soviets and Americans realized they needed to prove that living creatures could survive in space, so they could eventually launch a vehicle with humans in it. ⁴ _____ the Soviets sent a dog into space. Unfortunately, the dog died a few days into orbit. The Americans had better luck, ⁵ _____ The monkeys they launched into space survived the experience. For the next three decades, the Soviet and American rivalry fueled the space race, leading to one advancement after another. Each country had its shining moments. ⁶ _____ a Soviet cosmonaut, Yuri Gagarin, was the first person in space in 1961, and American astronaut Neil Armstrong was the first person to walk on the moon, in 1969. ⁷ _____ we are thinking of sending people to Mars. Unfortunately, funding for space exploration is currently a low priority for the United States. ⁸ _____ our space program is not what it once was.

CONNECT FOR SUCCESS: Listen for Transitions in Lectures

Listen for transitions, such as *for example, first,* and *therefore,* in your class lectures. They will help you organize your notes and understand how important ideas relate to each other. For example, when your instructor says, "First," you have a clue that the ideas coming up can be organized into a list. When your instructor says, "Therefore," you know that the idea spoken is the *result* of a previously spoken point.

REVISING FOR UNITY

A paragraph has **unity** when all the supporting details relate to the topic and claim in the topic sentence. Consider, for example, a paragraph with this topic sentence:

> *Before beginning their job interviews, students should learn how to dress for success.*

This topic sentence allows you to discuss clothing style, but it does not allow you to discuss how to behave. Now read the following paragraph and determine which sentence creates a problem with unity.

> *¹If you decide to try online dating, remember these safety guidelines. ²As you correspond with an individual, look for red flags, such as inappropriate displays of anger or aggression, undue interest in your financial situation, requests for money, or inappropriate questions. ³Also be on guard if the person has no solid contact number, such as a reliable land line or cell phone number. ⁴Be sure to talk on the phone several times before meeting anyone in person, again staying on the lookout for red flags. ⁵If you are not comfortable with the phone conversation for any reason—even if you cannot name the problem—do not agree to meet the person. ⁶If you do decide to meet for a date, do so in a public place, and let at least one person know where you will be. ⁷Stay in public places for several dates. ⁸Try to do something you both enjoy, so you are both more likely to have fun. ⁹If you become uncomfortable for any reason, end the relationship. ¹⁰If you follow these guidelines, you can enjoy online dating safely.*

You probably noticed that sentence 8 does not belong in the paragraph, because it does not relate to safe online dating. When you revise your paragraphs, be sure that none of your details creates a problem with unity because of straying from the topic and claim in your topic sentence.

CONNECT FOR SUCCESS: Maintain Unity in Examination Answers

Students who are not sure of the correct response sometimes pad their answers to examination questions with details not strictly related to the question. Avoid this impulse, because instructors will recognize the lack of unity and possibly penalize you for the padding.

3.8 ACTIVITY

Cross out the sentences that create a problem with unity because they do not stick to the point.

1.   Although it may have seemed so at the time, the 2000 election between Al Gore and George Bush was not the closest, most controversial U.S. presidential election. That distinction belongs to the election between Republican Rutherford B. Hayes and Democrat Samuel J. Tilden in 1876. Tilden won the popular vote by a very small margin—4,284,020 to 4,036,572. But Florida, South Carolina, and Louisiana sent in disputed returns, and one electoral vote in Oregon was disputed. Both Republicans and Democrats charged election fraud. Congress established a fifteen-member electoral commission to decide the matter. Because the Republicans had a majority in Congress, they had a majority on the commission, and every disputed vote was awarded to Hayes, who then won the presidency by a single electoral vote. Although they were not controversial decisions, both of Bill Clinton's elections were achieved without a majority vote. He had 43 percent in 1992 and 49 percent in 1996. Clearly, the U.S. system of government is resilient enough to survive election disputes.

2.   In the United States, government has little power to block the press from reporting information that could damage national security. The principle of "no prior restraint" holds that government cannot stop a publication or broadcast program unless it can convince a court that grave harm to the nation would result from that release of information. Britain's government, however, can easily prevent news organizations from reporting on national security issues. The U.S. press is also protected by an imposing legal standard for libel. It is nearly impossible for a U.S. official to win a libel suit against a newspaper, magazine, or broadcast organization, even in situations where his or her reputation has been destroyed by false allegations.

Source: Adapted from Thomas E. Patterson, *We the People*, 5th ed. (New York: McGraw-Hill, 2004), p. 310. Copyright © 2004 The McGraw-Hill Companies. Used by permission of The McGraw-Hill Companies.

REVISING FOR WORD CHOICE

During revising, you have the opportunity to improve the way you express your ideas by considering how concise and how specific your words are. These matters are explained next.

Concise word choice

To be concise, avoid using many words when you can express yourself equally well in a few words.

Wordy: *My physician, who happens to be an allergy specialist, tells me on a frequent basis that I should always be sure to avoid processed sugar.*

Concise: *My physician, an allergy specialist, frequently tells me to avoid processed sugar.*

One way to be concise is to reduce wordy phrases to a single word.

Wordy	Concise
at this point in time	now
on a frequent basis	frequently
in the event that	if
in society today	today
in today's modern world	today
has the ability to	can

Another way to be concise is to revise to eliminate repetitious phrases.

Repetitious	Concise
the color green/green in color	green
mix together	mix
the final conclusion	the conclusion
a true fact	a fact
the reason why	the reason
very necessary	necessary
very unique	unique

Troubleshooting

If you use a dictionary or thesaurus (dictionary of synonyms) to find specific words, be sure you understand the shades of meaning of the words you take from these sources. You can't always substitute one word for a similar one. For example, calling someone "smart" is very different from calling that person "cunning."

Specific word choice

Words can be general or specific. **General words** are vague and do not give the reader a very detailed idea. **Specific words** are more exact and give the reader a more detailed, precise idea. To appreciate how specific words convey a more detailed idea, consider these examples:

General: *The child ate a snack.*

Specific: *The two-year-old boy gleefully sucked on a cherry Popsicle.*

When you revise, substitute specific words for some of your general ones.

General	Specific
walk	stroll/wander/strut
feel good	elated/excited/optimistic
feel bad	depressed/apprehensive/nervous
nice	colorful/playful/spirited/
hat	red stocking cap
drink	slurp
meat	rare roast beef
book	*The Color Purple*

3.9 ACTIVITY

Revise each sentence to make it more concise.

EXAMPLE   At a point in time about 5,000 years ago, the Chinese discovered how to make the fabric silk. *About 5,000 years ago, the Chinese discovered how to make silk.*

1. The Chinese learned how to make silk from silkworm cocoons, but for about 3,000 years of time they kept this discovery a secret to themselves.

2. Because of the fact that the poor people could not afford real silk cloth, they tried to make other cloth look silky.

3. Women would beat on cotton with sticks for the purpose of softening the fibers of cloth, and then they would rub the cloth against a big rock stone to make it shiny bright.

4. The shiny cotton was called by the name of "chintz."

5. Because chintz was a cheaper reproduction copy of silk, calling something "chintzy" means it is cheap in price and not a good quality.

3.10 ACTIVITY

Revise the following sentences to make the words more specific.

EXAMPLE   The food was terrible. *The baked chicken tasted greasy and too salty.*

1. The noise bothered me.

2. The view was beautiful.

3. Later on, the girl began to feel bad.

   _____

   _____

4. The room was a terrible mess.

   _____

   _____

5. The kitchen smelled funny.

   _____

   _____

3.11 COLLABORATIVE ACTIVITY

Bring to class a magazine or newspaper article you find interesting. (You can select one online, if you wish.) Pair up with a classmate and do the following.

- Identify the specific words in two paragraphs of each article.
- Discuss how the specific words help make the articles interesting.
- Is there any wordiness you can trim?

Composing at the computer

If you like to compose at the computer, you may find the following revision strategies helpful.

- **Use your computer's thesaurus (dictionary of synonyms) when you cannot think of the right word.** However, be sure you understand the word's shades of meaning before using it.
- **Revise at least once on paper copy.** When you revise on screen, you may see only part of your draft at one time, which can make it hard for you to get a good overview. It is best to print out your writing, double-spaced, so there is plenty of room to make corrections and to revise in pencil or pen at least once.
- **If you use Microsoft Word, keep track of your revisions with the "Track Changes" function.** Go to "Tools," then "Track Changes." All your revisions will become visible.
- **Use your computer to secure reader response.** E-mail your draft to a reader who can insert comments and e-mail back the draft. If you use Microsoft Word, go to "Insert," then "Comment."

A FIRST DRAFT PARAGRAPH WITH REVISIONS

In this section are three paragraphs. The first paragraph is the first draft from Chapter 2, page 30. The second paragraph is the revision of the draft that was made using the revising checklist on page 33. The third paragraph is the same revision, but with the remarks made by a trustworthy reader.

The first draft

If you want to review the idea generation material that prompted this draft, return to page 8.

> **Troubleshooting**
>
> Because a copy printed from your computer looks so much better than a handwritten one, you can be fooled into thinking your computer draft does not need much editing. Computer-generated writing needs the same careful editing as handwritten material.

The Dean of Students office can do more to help students who are stressed. One good idea being "catch-up" days. Catch-up days are when classes are canceled, so students can catch up on their work and assignments. One day each semester should do it. Another idea is showing students how to take tests, because tests, are a big reason for stress for students who do not know how to take tests and have trouble as a result of not knowing this. Stress management workshops would help because they would teach student how to deal with any stress that comes up before the student explodes from the stress. Teachers should be trained to recognize the signs of stress, so they can interveen as necessary. Counseling should be available to students who need it because of stress. If the Dean of Students office could do these simple things and they would help students cope with their stress and improve the quality of their lives.

The second draft

The author used the revising checklist on page 33 and produced the following second draft. The changes appear in bold type as a study aid.

The Dean of Students office can do more to help students who are stressed. One good idea being "catch-up" days. Catch-up days are when classes are canceled so students can catch up on their work and assignments. **Many students fall behind because of the circumstances of their lives.** *One day each semester should* ~~do~~ **help students catch up, so difficult circumstances don't create more problems at school.** ~~it.~~ **Also, during catch-up days, teachers could be in their offices during regular class time to meet with students who need extra help. This individual attention could eliminate the stress felt by students who do not completely understand material. Also, some students cannot make an instructor's regular office hours, so office hours during class would help them.** *Another idea is showing students how to take tests, because tests are a big reason for stress for students who do not know how to take tests and have trouble as a result of not knowing this. Stress management workshops would help because they would teach student how to deal with any stress that comes up before the student explodes from the stress. Teachers should be trained to recognize the signs of stress, so they can interveen as necessary. Counseling should be available to students who need it because of stress. If the Dean of Students office could* ~~do these simple things and~~ **make these changes,** *they would help students cope with their stress and improve the quality of their lives.*

Reader responses to the second draft

The following is the second draft with remarks made by a trustworthy reader. See if you agree with the reader's responses.

What circumstances? Can you give an example?

The Dean of Students office can do more to help students who are stressed. One good idea being "catch-up" days. Catch-up days are when classes are canceled, so students can catch up on their work and assignments. Many students fall behind because of the circumstances of their lives. One day each semester should help students catch up, so difficult circumstances don't create more problems at school. Also, during catch-up days, teachers could be in their offices during regular class time to meet with students who need extra help. This individual attention could eliminate the stress felt by students who do not completely understand material. Also, some students cannot make an instructor's regular office *Why not?* hours, so office hours during class would help them. Another idea is showing students how to take tests, because tests are a big reason for stress for students who do not know how to take tests and have trouble as a result of not knowing this. Stress management workshops would help because they would teach student how to deal with any stress that comes up before the student explodes from the stress. Teachers should be trained to recognize the signs of stress, so they can interveen as necessary. *Another good idea* Counseling should be available to students who need it because of stress. If the Dean of Students office could make these changes, they would help students cope with their stress and improve the quality of their lives.

This is a great idea.

What do you mean by "explode"?

We already have counseling on campus.

The third draft

The revision here includes changes made in response to the reader's reactions to the previous draft. What do you think of the changes?

The Dean of Students office can do more to help students who are stressed. One good idea being "catch-up"days. Catch-up days are when classes are canceled, so students can catch up on their work and assignments. Many students fall behind because ^ *of their work schedules, illness, or child care problems.* ~~of the circumstances of their lives.~~ One day each semester should help students catch up, so difficult circumstances don't create more problems at school. Also, during catch-up days, teachers could be in their offices during regular class time to meet with students who need extra help. This individual attention could eliminate the stress felt by students who do not completely understand material. Also, some students cannot make an instructor's regular office hours ^ *because of schedule conflicts*, so office hours during class would help them. Another idea is showing students how to take tests, because tests are a big reason for stress for students who do not know how to take tests and have trouble as a result of not knowing this. Stress management workshops would help because they would teach student how to deal with any stress that comes up before the student ^ *drops out of school because the stress is too much.* ~~explodes from the stress.~~ Teachers should be trained to recognize the signs of stress, so they can interveen as necessary. ~~Counceling should be available to students who need it because of stress.~~ If the Dean of Students office could make these changes, they would help students cope with their stress and improve the quality of their lives.

Reread the revising strategies on page 33–36. On a separate sheet, revise the draft you wrote for Activity 2.17. Then answer these questions:

1. Which of the revising strategies did you find the most helpful?

   _____

   _____

   _____

2. Did you notice problems in your draft that you did not see at the time you wrote it? _____

   _____

   _____

3. Do you like your revision better than your first draft? If so, in what way(s)?

   _____

   _____

   _____

Save your revised draft; you will need it for a later activity.

EDITING YOUR DRAFT

Editing is the process of finding and correcting errors in grammar, spelling, punctuation, and capitalization. Because errors distract and sometimes annoy a reader, eliminating them is important. The best time to edit is *after* revising; the procedures described next can help.

    1. TAKE A BREAK FOR A DAY.   The time away will help you view your revision more objectively, so you have a better chance of noticing mistakes.

    2. EDIT SLOWLY.   If you move quickly, you will overlook mistakes, so linger over each word and punctuation mark for a few seconds. Try placing a ruler under each line and pointing to each item with a pencil or pen. (Be sure your eyes do not look beyond the word or mark you are pointing to.)

    3. LOOK FOR MISTAKES YOU OFTEN MAKE.   If you frequently misspell words, make a special effort to check spellings. If you write sentence fragments, edit carefully for this error.

    4. EDIT MORE THAN ONCE.   The first time through, look for mistakes you often make. The second time, look for and correct other errors. If you tend to make many errors, edit a third time.

    5. TRUST YOUR INSTINCTS.   If you have a feeling that something is wrong, it probably is. Even if you do not know the name of the problem or how to solve it, assume that something is wrong and talk to your instructor or a writing center tutor.

    6. READ YOUR REVISED DRAFT ALOUD. If something sounds "off," assume you have a problem.

7. LEARN THE RULES. You cannot edit confidently if you do not know the grammar, spelling, punctuation, and capitalization rules. The chapters in this book starting with Part Two will help you learn them.

Composing at the computer

If you like to compose at the computer, these editing strategies may be helpful:

- **Use your computer's search function to locate trouble spots.** For example, if you often misuse *there* and *their,* have your computer find every use of these words, so you can check each one.
- **Use your computer's grammar check cautiously.** This program is often unreliable, so do not automatically accept its flagged errors and corrections. Check everything yourself.
- **Use your computer's spell check.** This program is very helpful, but it is not foolproof. For example, it does not distinguish between soundalikes (such as *know/no,* and it does not recognize an incorrect word that is spelled correctly (*fled* instead of *sled*).
- **Edit a print copy at least once.** Sometimes you notice errors on paper that you overlooked on the screen.

CONNECT FOR SUCCESS: Edit in All Your Classes and in the Workplace

Teachers in your other classes and employers care about correctness. If your writing has many mistakes, these people will react negatively. They may even question your ability. Thus, you should edit everything you write for your instructors and employers—even seemingly casual e-mail—carefully.

An Edited Paragraph

The revised paragraph on page 53 was revised again. (Writers usually revise many times until they are satisfied.) The following is the more polished version of the paragraph, with the editing shown as a study aid.

The Dean of Students office can do more to help students who are stressed. One good idea ~~being~~ is "catch-up" days, ~~Catch-up days are~~ when classes are canceled, so students can catch up on their work and assignments. Many students fall behind because they work while going to school, or they are single parents who miss class, when ~~When~~ their children get sick or the baby-sitter ~~cancells.~~ cancels. One free day each semester should ~~releieve~~ relieve stress by giving these students time to catch up. During catch-up days, teachers could be in their offices during regular class time to meet with students who need extra help but cannot make an instructor's regular office hours because of schedule conflicts. In addition, colleges should show students how to take tests, because tests are a big cause of stress. College tests are not like high schools tests, so many students do not know good strategies. Stress management workshops would also help because they would teach students how to deal with any stress that comes up before ~~the student~~ *they* drops out of school because the stress is too much. Teachers should be trained to recognize the signs of stress, so they can ~~interveen~~ *intervene* as necessary. Counseling should be available to students who need it because of stress. The Dean of Students office should make these changes to help students cope with stress and improve the quality of their lives.

3.13 ACTIVITY

Reread the editing strategies on page 54–55. Then, on a separate sheet, edit the draft you revised for Activity 3.12. When you are finished, answer these questions. (Save the edited draft, because your instructor may ask you to submit it.)

1. Which editing strategies did you use? Have you used these strategies before?

   _____

   _____

   _____

2. Did you like these strategies enough to use them again? Why or why not?

   _____

   _____

   _____

3. How many editing errors did you find and correct?

   _____

PROOFREADING YOUR FINAL COPY

After editing your draft, type or copy it into its final form, the one you will submit to your reader. Because it is easy to make copying or typing mistakes, you should check for errors one last time. This last check for errors in the final copy is **proofreading**. When you proofread, you should go very slowly, checking each correction from the edited draft to the final copy. Check every word and punctuation mark.

3.14 CHAPTER REVIEW ACTIVITY

1. Why is it important to *show* rather than *tell*? What strategies will help you show your reader that something is true?

   _____

   _____

2. When does writing have coherence?

   _____

   _____

3. What are transitions?

   _____

   _____

4. When does a paragraph have unity?

    _____

    _____

5. How do concise, specific words improve writing?

    _____

    _____

6. Will using the revising checklist and the reader response form help you revise your drafts? Why?

    _____

    _____

7. Which strategies do you think will best help you edit your drafts? Why?

    _____

    _____

    _____

GETTING IN GEAR: IDEAS FOR WRITING

This photograph of an early draft of the Declaration of Independence illustrates that all writers revise—even writers as accomplished as Thomas Jefferson, the primary architect of the Declaration of Independence. When writers revise, their work often looks the way this draft does, filled with cross outs and writing above the lines.

To learn more about the drafting of the Declaration of Independence visit this site: www.loc.gov/exhibits/declara/declara1.html

writing topic: For the "Getting in Gear" assignment in Chapter 2, you were asked to write a first draft that explains how a process you perform is either similar to or different from the process of writing. Now you will improve that draft to make it ready for your reader.

suggestions for revising

- Attend to each concern in the revising checklist on page 33. Take a break whenever you feel tired or blocked.
- Ask a reliable reader to read your draft and complete the reader response form on page 35. Consider your reader's comments and make the changes you think are appropriate. Then take a break.
- Go over your draft one more time, looking for improvements to make.

suggestions for editing

- Edit once for the mistakes you habitually make and a second time for any other errors. Be sure to move very slowly. If you are composing at the computer, edit a print copy of your draft.
- Read your work aloud to listen for errors.
- If you have trouble finding and correcting your errors, set up regular appointments at your campus writing center to learn ways to improve your editing skills.

RECHARGE: Lesson Summary

1. Revision strategies include setting aside your draft for a short time, so you can read it with fresh eyes; revising in stages; using a revising checklist; and getting reader response.

2. Revision concerns include improving the content, organization, and wording of your draft.

   - Add examples, a story, descriptions, and/or reasons if needed to prove or explain your topic sentence.
   - Rearrange your ideas, so they are in chronological, spatial, progressive, or another logical order to improve coherence.
   - Add transitions to improve coherence.
   - Delete details that do not relate to the topic sentence to improve unity.
   - Make words more concise and specific to improve word choice.

3. Editing strategies include setting your draft aside for a short time, so you can read it with fresh eyes; going slowly; editing more than once; trusting your instincts; reading aloud; and learning the rules.

4. Editing involves finding and correcting mistakes in grammar, spelling, punctuation, and capitalization.

5. Proofreading involves checking your final copy for copying or typographical errors.

CHAPTER **4**

Writing an Essay

An **essay** is a composition of several paragraphs that work together to develop one central idea. You will write essays in and out of college when your topic requires fuller treatment than you can give in a single-paragraph writing. This chapter will show you how to write an essay, so you can write one when necessary.

THE PARTS OF AN ESSAY

Like a one-paragraph composition, an essay has a beginning, a middle, and an end. The beginning is the *introduction,* the middle is the *body,* and the end is the *conclusion.*

The introduction

The first paragraph of an essay is the introduction. The introduction has two functions: It creates interest in the essay so your readers will want to read on, and it states your topic and your claim about your topic in a sentence called the **thesis.** Thus, the thesis of an essay is like the topic sentence of a one-paragraph composition.

The body

Two or more paragraphs follow the introduction. These paragraphs, called the **body,** explain or prove the thesis. Each body paragraph develops a single point related to the thesis. Thus, if you want to present two points to explain or prove the thesis, you will have two body paragraphs. Three points will mean three body paragraphs, and so on. A body paragraph is structured the same way as a one-paragraph composition: with a topic sentence and supporting details.

The conclusion

The **conclusion** is the final paragraph. Like the closing of a one-paragraph composition, the conclusion provides a satisfying finish by creating closure.

The following chart shows how the parts of an essay correspond to the parts of a one-paragraph composition.

	PARAGRAPH	ESSAY
BEGINNING	Topic sentence	Introduction
MIDDLE	Supporting details	Body paragraphs
END	Closing	Conclusion

A SAMPLE ESSAY

In the following student essay, the parts are labeled as a study aid.

WHAT'S REALLY IMPORTANT
DREW STAHL

Introduction
Opening creates interest

[1]I come from a large family. I am the third youngest of seven children. Being a member of a large family has its economic disadvantages. For one thing, every item our family owned was secondhand. When I was nine and wanted a bike, shiny and new like my friends had, I was told that I could have my brother's old ten-speed, since he was driving. At nine, I didn't understand what it cost to keep a family of our size up and running. The bike, along with all the other hand-me-downs, gave me the impression that my father was cheap. As a result, I felt

Thesis Notice the topic and claim.

deprived and cheated. Then, my senior year of high school I realized just how well I was provided for.

Body paragraph
Topic sentence

[2]I believed Dad was cheap because I was always comparing our family belongings to those of my friends. It never occurred to me that income or family size had much to do with what a person had. I just expected to get what the other kids got. My friends wore clothes from the Gap; I wore clothes from Hal, who got them from Dave, who got them from who knows which brother. My friends

Supporting details
Notice the examples.

had CD players and CDs of all the latest teen sensations; I had the radio. My friends wore the cool Nikes to cruise the mall on Saturdays; I wore K-Mart specials, which don't "cruise" very well.

Body paragraph
Topic sentence

[3]My parents' belongings also convinced me that Dad was cheap. Dad drove a blue Buick Century with dented front fenders and no hub caps. Mom owned a faded blue minivan with more rust than paint on it. Neither one of these was

Supporting details
Notice the examples and description.

bought new, nor could either one compare with the shiny Cadillacs and Acuras my friends were being dropped off at school in. Our washer, dryer, dishwasher, color television set, and furniture—all bought used—were scratched and dented. They were so old that they constantly broke down, supporting my theory that Dad was too cheap to buy decent stuff.

Body paragraph
Topic sentence

[4]Then a tragedy changed my mind. My senior year, a classmate was killed in an auto accident. A few days later, a group of friends and I paid a visit to his mother. I was shocked to see the house in which my classmate had lived. The walls

Supporting details
Notice the description.

were yellowed and stained, the ceiling was cracking, a pool table served as the dining room table, and the refrigerator looked like a warehouse for frozen dinners. This classmate had worn expensive Gap clothes and the cool Nikes. He had had the CD player and latest CDs. But his house didn't compare to mine. Suddenly, I realized that Dad wasn't cheap. He just knew what was important—the basics, like clean, well-maintained surroundings, decent food, and comfortable furniture. Everyday things that I failed to appreciate, like having a well-kept home to live in, a good dinner every night, a real dining room table to eat off of, and home-cooked meals to eat with my family suddenly became very meaningful.

Conclusion
Brings the essay to a satisfying finish by drawing a conclusion and looking to the future.

[5]I am ashamed to say it took me seventeen years and the death of a friend to realize how well off I was. Now that I know, I do not think Dad is cheap. I think he is incredible, because he knows what is important and he sees that we get it. Maybe after I get my degree, I'll buy some new things—but they won't be for me. I'd like to give them to my parents, especially to my dad.

DRAFTING YOUR INTRODUCTION

To discover ideas for the introduction and the thesis for your writing, you can use the prewriting techniques you learned in Chapter 1: freewriting, listing, mapping, and journaling.

Interesting your audience

One important function of the introduction is to interest your reader in your essay. You can create interest many ways, but two useful strategies are

- providing background information
- explaining why your writing topic is important

Reread the introduction of "What's Really Important" on page 60, and notice that the writer peaks your interest with background information. That background information includes details about the large size of the writer's family, the economic disadvantages of the large size, and how the writer reacted to the disadvantages.

To see how it is possible to create interest by explaining why the writing topic is important, read this version of the introduction:

We always want what we don't have, so we fail to appreciate what we do have. That's too bad, because we waste a lot of time feeling dissatisfied for no reason. We would be much happier if we focused on the positive aspects of our circumstances. I learned this lesson my senior year of high school, when I realized just how well I was provided for.

This version indicates that the writing topic is important because it teaches a valuable life lesson.

Developing an effective thesis

By expressing the central point, the **thesis** lets your reader know what your essay is about. Like the topic sentence of a one-paragraph composition, your thesis should state your topic and express your claim. Here is an example:

Topic:	*identity theft*
Claim:	*A person must follow specific procedures to guard against it.*
Thesis	*To guard against identity theft, a person must follow specific procedures.*

The topic and claim expressed in your thesis should be limited enough that you can manage it in a single essay.

Too broad: *Public education should be reformed.*

Better: *Public education should not be funded by property taxes.*

Finally, your topic sentence should not be a narrow statement of fact, because such statements give you nothing to write about.

Too narrow: *Many people use their cell phones while they drive.*

Better: *It should be illegal to use a cell phone while driving.*

If you like, your thesis can also state the points you will discuss in each of your body paragraphs, in the order in which you will discuss them. Here is an example:

Reality television shows depict people as greedy, foolish, and cruel.

This thesis provides an outline. It indicates that the first body paragraph will show that reality television programs portray people as greedy; the next body paragraph will show that they portray people as foolish, and the last body paragraph will show that they depict people as cruel.

CONNECT FOR SUCCESS: Identify Important Ideas in Your Textbooks

When you read your textbooks and other classroom materials, the first paragraph of a chapter will often tell you what is to follow, because it gives the thesis. Look for the most important ideas, the ones to highlight for study, in the opening sentences of the following paragraphs.

4.1 ACTIVITY

Select two of the following subjects and write an acceptable thesis and ideas for interesting your audience. If necessary, prewrite for ideas.

drug testing   sports fans   freedom of speech   a high school experience
your favorite or least favorite teacher   something you do well
television commercials

Thesis 1 _____

_____

Ideas for interesting your audience _____

_____

Thesis 2 _____

_____

Ideas for interesting your audience _____

_____

DISCOVERING IDEAS TO DEVELOP YOUR THESIS

The ideas to prove or explain your thesis will appear in your body paragraphs. To come up with those ideas, you can use the prewriting strategies you learned in Chapters 1 and 2: freewriting, listing, mapping, journaling, and questioning. An essay should have at least two body paragraphs, so you will need to discover at least two main ideas to develop in separate paragraphs.

When you consider ideas for your essay, be sure to think about your purpose and audience, because they will influence your selection of main ideas and details. Consider whether your purpose is to entertain, express feelings, relate experience, inform, or convince your reader of something. Also assess how much your audience knows about your topic and how much you will have to explain. If you need to review how to consider your purpose and audience, refer to pages 24–25 in Chapter 2.

4.2 ACTIVITY

Select one of the thesis sentences you wrote for Activity 4.1. Using one or more of your favorite prewriting strategies, generate as many ideas as you can for proving or explaining that thesis. Save your prewriting to use in Activity 4.3.

PLANNING YOUR DRAFT WITH AN OUTLINE MAP

On the next page is a model outline map written to plan the first draft of "What's Really Important" on page 60. Study the map to see that it guides the draft by plotting the details to appear in each paragraph. To plan your own draft, write up a map similar to this one, but fill it in with your own notes about what you will write. Or if you prefer, you can make the outline map a computer file and use it as needed.

4.3 ACTIVITY

Using the ideas you discovered for Activity 4.2, write an outline map on a separate sheet.

Troubleshooting

If you have trouble thinking of a way to generate interest in your introduction, draft you thesis and move on the first body paragraph. You can come back later and work on a way to create interest in your essay.

WRITING A FIRST DRAFT

Using your outline map as a guide, you can write your first draft, being sure you have at least two body paragraphs. Remember that your first draft is supposed to be rough, so do not polish as you go; just express yourself the best way you can and push on. Also remember that you can alter your outline by adding and deleting ideas—always respond to good ideas as they occur to you.

REVISING

When you revise, use the strategies explained in Chapter 3 to improve the content, organization, and wording of your draft. You can also answer the questions in the revising checklist on page 65 to decide what improvements to make.

OUTLINE MAP

Introduction

Idea for generating interest *Give family background. Tell about bike and hand-me-downs.*

Thesis *In my senior year, I learned how well I was provided for.*

Body Paragraph

Topic sentence *I was always comparing our family belongings to those of my friends.*

Supporting details *Clothes, CDs and CD players, Nikes*

Body Paragraph

Topic sentence *My parents' belongings made me think my dad was cheap.*

Supporting details *Minivan, washer and dryer, television, furniture-all old*

Body Paragraph

Topic sentence *The death of a friend changed my mind.*

Supporting details *His house had stained ceilings and walls, a pool table for a dining table, and only frozen food.*

Conclusion

Now that I know Dad is not cheap, I want to use my degree to buy them things.

REVISING CHECKLIST FOR AN ESSAY

- Are your opening sentences likely to engage your reader's interest?
- Does your introduction include a thesis that states your topic and expresses your claim about that topic?
- Does each body paragraph have a topic sentence and supporting details, just like a one-paragraph composition?
- Do your supporting details show rather than merely tell?
- Does your essay have coherence because you have arranged details in a logical order and used transitions?
- Does your essay have unity because each topic sentence relates to your thesis and all supporting details relate to their topic sentence?
- Are your ideas expressed in concise, specific words?
- Does your conclusion create a sense of closure?

EDITING AND PROOFREADING

Because mistakes in grammar, spelling, punctuation, and capitalization can distract readers from your ideas, edit carefully using the strategies explained in Chapter 3—*after* you revise. Then copy or type your essay into its final form and check for copying or typographical errors.

4.4 CHAPTER REVIEW ACTIVITY

Answer the following questions about "What's Really Important" on page 60.

1. What topic and claim does the thesis express?

    _____

    _____

2. Does the introduction stimulate your interest in the essay? Why or why not?

    _____

    _____

3. Which body paragraph do you like the best? Why? Does this paragraph show as well as tell? Explain.

    _____

    _____

4. What transition appears in the topic sentence for paragraph 3? In the topic sentence for paragraph 4? How do those transitions contribute to the essay's coherence?

    _____

    _____

5. Does the essay have unity? Why or why not?

_____

_____

6. How does the conclusion bring the essay to a satisfying finish?

_____

GETTING IN GEAR: IDEAS FOR WRITING

© Reprinted with permission of King Features Syndicate.

The boy in the cartoon is having a difficult time writing because he is experiencing writer's block. (Someone needs to show him the prewriting strategies explained in Chapters 1 and 2.) He is expressing admiration for the prolific author of the Harry Potter series, J. K. Rowling. What he doesn't know, however, is that all writers—including professional writers—experience writer's block. For an interesting take on writer's block, visit www.writersblock.com/, a site dedicated to "helping musicians and writers help themselves."

writing topic: Write about your most vivid writing memory—your best remembered positive or negative experience with writing in school, at home, or on the job. For example, you might write about the time you wrote a love poem to your first-grade teacher, the time your essay was read in history class, a time you got a strong reaction to a letter you wrote, or—like the boy in the cartoon—a time you experienced a difficult bout of writer's block. Explain what happened and how you were affected by the experience.

suggestions for prewriting

- Think about the different writing situations you have been in, because your essay can be about writing at any time or any place for any reason. Then list as many writing memories as you can.
- Pick one of those memories and freewrite about it for ten minutes.

suggestions for drafting

- Draft a thesis that mentions the writing occasion (that's your topic) and how you were affected by the experience (that's your claim about the topic).
- Write an outline map to guide your drafting. One or two body paragraphs can explain what happened, and one or two body paragraphs can explain how you were affected.

suggestions for revising

- Use the revising checklist on page 65 to identify changes to make.
- Ask a reliable reader to note whether there is anything he or she does not understand and whether there are any points that need more explanation.

suggestions for editing

- Edit once for the mistakes you habitually make and a second time for any other errors.
- Read your essay aloud once to listen for errors you may not have seen.

RECHARGE: Lesson Summary

1. The parts of an essay are the introduction, body, and conclusion.
2. The introduction creates interest and states the thesis.
3. The thesis

    - states the topic.
    - expresses your claim about the topic.
    - should not be too broad.
    - should not be a narrow statement of fact.
    - may state the points you will discuss in each of your body paragraphs in the order in which you will discuss them.

4. The body paragraphs

    - explain or prove the thesis by showing and not just telling.
    - each have a topic sentence and supporting details.
    - have coherence and unity.

5. The conclusion provides a sense of closure.
6. Freewriting, listing, mapping, journaling, and questioning can help you discover ideas for your essay.
7. An outline map can help you plan your essay.

PART ONE REVIEW

Reviewing paragraph and essay writing

1. If the sentence would make a satisfactory topic sentence or thesis, write "yes" in the blank. If it would not, write "too broad" or "too narrow" on the blank.

   A. _____ Levi Strauss began selling blue jeans in 1874.

   B. _____ The kind of blue jeans a person wears is an indication of that person's personality.

   C. _____ For good reasons, baseball is considered our national pastime.

   D. _____ Over the years, many extraordinary athletes have played professional baseball.

   E. _____ In 1896, the U.S. Supreme Court ruled in *Plessy v. Ferguson* that separate but equal facilities for black and white people were constitutional.

   F. _____ The Supreme Court's decision in *Plessy v. Ferguson* was its darkest hour.

2. The following prewriting list of ideas is for a paragraph with this topic sentence: "Left-handed people in this country are not treated fairly." Read the prewriting list and respond as indicated.

   in school, left-handed children are often forced to switch hands

   left-handed people have to learn to used right-handed scissors
      left handed people can have an advantage in some sports

   irons have cords hanging out on the left, which is awkward for lefties

   the word *right* is positive and the word *left* is negative (unfocused people are out in "left field" but focused people are "right on target")
      lefties annoy hostesses at dinner parties because they have to be seated away from right handed people or they bump elbows

   side-arm desks in classrooms are for right-handed people

   spiral notebooks and pencil sharpeners are hard for lefties to use
      people should not be discriminated against for qualities they are born with

   A. Cross out any ideas that create a problem with unity.

   B. Number the ideas to create an informal outline. Be prepared to explain why you numbered as you did.

READING AND WRITING IN RESPONSE TO TEXTBOOKS

[1]Sociologists use the term **status** to refer to socially defined positions within society—from the lowest to the highest position. [2]Within our society, a person can occupy the status of president of the United States, fruit picker, son or daughter, violinist, teenager, resident of Minneapolis, dental technician, or neighbor. [3]Clearly, a person holds more than one status simultaneously. [4]Sociologists view some statuses as *ascribed,* while they categorize others as *achieved.* [5]An **ascribed status** is "assigned" to a person by society without regard for the person's unique talents or characteristics. [6]Thus, a person's racial background, gender, and age are all ascribed statuses. [7]These characteristics are biological in origin but are significant mainly because of the social meanings they have in our culture. [8]Unlike ascribed statuses, an **achieved status** comes to us largely through our own efforts. [9]Both "bank president" and "prison guard" are achieved statuses, as are "lawyer,"

"pianist," "advertising executive," and "social worker." [10]A person must do something to acquire an achieved status—go to school, learn a skill, establish a friendship, or invent a new product. [11]Ascribed status influences achieved status. [12]Being male, for example, will decrease the likelihood that a person would become a child care worker.

Source: Adapted from Richard T. Schaefer, *Sociology,* 7th ed. (New York: McGraw-Hill 2001), pp. 122–123. Copyright © 2001 The McGraw-Hill Companies. Used by permission of The McGraw-Hill Companies.

1. Which sentence is the topic sentence? What is the topic? What is the claim?

    topic sentence: _____

    topic: _____

    claim: _____

2. Which sentences include examples? What is the purpose of those examples?

    _____

    _____

3. If you were studying this textbook material, which sentences would you highlight? Why? _____

    _____

    _____

writing topic: The textbook excerpt notes that ascribed status can affect achieved status. Select one of your ascribed statuses and explain how it affects your achieved status.

Understanding the Sentence

I type in one place, but I write all over the house.

—Novelist Toni Morrison, author of *The Bluest Eye, Tar Baby,* and *Beloved*

Reflection: What is Toni Morrison saying about the process of writing?

WHAT YOU WILL LEARN

How to identify subjects and verbs
How to find and eliminate sentence fragments
How to use coordination

How to use subordination

How to find and eliminate run-on sentences and comma splices

WHY YOU WILL LEARN IT

so that you can write correct sentences
so that you can write correct sentences
so that you can join clauses of equal importance and avoid choppiness
so that you can join clauses of unequal importance and avoid choppiness
so that you can write correct sentences

CHAPTER 5

Identifying Subjects and Verbs

To write correct English sentences, you must be able to identify their two most basic components—the subject and the verb. Because the ability to find the subject and verb of a sentence is so basic, this chapter deals exclusively with helping you master that skill.

IDENTIFYING SUBJECTS

Every sentence must have a subject. The **subject** indicates whom or what the sentence is about. You can find the subject by answering these questions:

Who or what does or did something?
About whom or what is something being said?

Here are two examples:

Heavyweight wrestler Tom Schotsky won the state championship.

Ask: *Who or what does or did something?*

Answer: *heavyweight wrestler Tom Schotsky*

Subject (who or what the sentence is about): *heavyweight wrestler Tom Schotsky*

My coat is too small.

Ask: *About whom or what is something being said?*

Answer: *my coat*

Subject (whom or what the sentence is about): *my coat*

Simple and complete subjects

The most important word in the subject is called the **simple subject.** The simple subject is a *noun* or *pronoun.* A **noun** is a word that names a person, a place, an object, an idea, or an emotion (such as *father, Nashville, table, freedom,* or *fear*); a **pronoun** is a word that substitutes for a noun (such as *I, you, he, she, it, we, they*). The **complete subject** consists of the simple subject and all the other words in the subject.

Sentence:	*Pitcher Hillary Simmons was hit in the head by a fly ball.*
Simple subject:	*Hillary Simmons*
Complete subject:	*pitcher Hillary Simmons*

Sentence:	*The horror movie had a surprise ending.*
Simple subject:	*movie*
Complete subject:	*the horror movie*

Sentence:	*My oldest and dearest friend is coming to town.*
Simple subject:	*friend*
Complete subject:	*my oldest and dearest friend*

5.1 ACTIVITY

Underline the complete subjects and circle the simple subjects.

EXAMPLE   A Bavarian |immigrant| invented blue jeans.

1. The California Gold Rush was going strong in 1850.
2. Bavarian immigrant Levi Strauss arrived in San Francisco with dry goods for sale.
3. A gold prospector asked what Strauss was selling.
4. The salesman sold him rough canvas for tents and wagon covers.
5. The frustrated prospector was disappointed.
6. Strong pants were needed much more than tent canvas.
7. The enterprising businessman had the canvas made into strong pants.
8. Most miners liked the pants but complained about their roughness.
9. The clever Strauss substituted a twilled cotton from France.
10. This twilled cotton was called "serge de Nimes," now know as denim.

5.2 ACTIVITY

Fill in the blanks with any appropriate complete subject.

EXAMPLE   *The lost wallet*_____ is behind the sofa.

1. _____ explained how to use the computerized card catalog in the library reference room.

2. _____and _____ are my favorite breakfast foods.

3. _____ was the best act in the talent show.

4. _____ needed expensive repairs.

5. _____ should be thrown away.

5.3 ACTIVITY

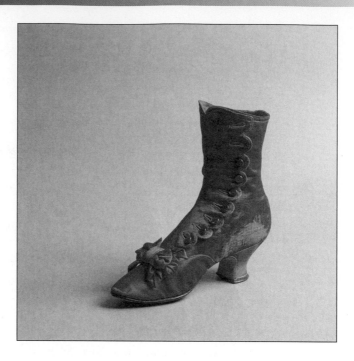

For each of the following sentences, write the complete subject in the first blank and the simple subject in the second blank.

EXAMPLE   The first shoes were made of a single piece of rawhide.

Complete subject: *the first shoes* _____

Simple subject: *shoes* _____

1. Pointed toes were fashionable on shoes from the eleventh to the fifteenth century.

    Complete subject: _____

    Simple subject: _____

2. Six-inch-high heels were worn by the upper classes in the seventeenth century.

    Complete subject: _____

    Simple subject: _____

3. Right and left shoes were identical until the nineteenth century.

    Complete subject: _____

    Simple subject: _____

4. Women's shoes became different from men's in the eighteenth century.

    Complete subject: _____

    Simple subject: _____

5. The first lady's boot was designed for Queen Victoria in 1840.

Complete subject: _____

Simple subject: _____

The location of the subject

You have probably noticed that the subject usually comes at or near the beginning of a sentence. Sometimes one or more words come before the subject, as in these examples:

Sentence:	*In the afternoon, Milana volunteers at the Senior Citizens Center.*
Ask:	Who or what does or did something?
Answer:	*Milana*
Subject:	*Milana*
Words before the subject:	*in the afternoon*
Sentence:	*For the time being, the labor union is experiencing a membership decline.*
Ask:	About whom or what is something being said?
Answer:	*the labor union*
Subject:	*the labor union*
Words before the subject:	*for the time being*

5.4 ACTIVITY

Underline the complete subjects and circle the simple subjects. The first one is done as an example.

[1]Once in a while, a person will bite into an apple and find a worm. [2]These worms get into apples in a surprising way. [3]The little critters are born there. [4]In the middle of summer, small apples are growing on apple trees. [5]At that time, female flies lay their eggs inside some of the apples. [6]The eggs hatch into tiny worms called larvae. [7]These worms begin eating the apples. [8]If unpicked, the apples fall from the tree in autumn. [9]The larvae crawl out and bury themselves in the ground. [10]Then, a hard skin forms around each one. [11]The next summer, a fly emerges from the skin. [12]A person biting into an apple at the wrong time can find a worm.

Action-word subjects

The simple subject of a sentence can be a form of an action word (which functions as a noun). This form can end in *-ing* (a **gerund**) or begin with *to* (an **infinitive**), as in the following examples.

Running is an excellent activity for reducing stress.
Seeing you again is a pleasure. [The simple subject is *seeing*.]
To win is my only goal.
To win the game will take a miracle. [The simple subject is *to win*.]

The simple subjects in the following sentences are forms of action words. Underline the complete subjects and circle the simple subjects.

EXAMPLE   Teenage dating varies around the world.

1. To go on a date in Afghanistan is rare.

2. Teenage pairing is not allowed until the age of fifteen in many parts of South America.

3. Studying in groups is the preferred way for Korean and Japanese teens to spend time together.

4. To meet in pairs is against the law for Iranian teenagers.

5. Gathering for parties at a home is popular among Italian and Swiss teens.

Subjects with prepositional phrases

Prepositions show the relationship of one thing to another.

The kitten sat <u>in</u> the corner.

In is a preposition that shows the relationship of the kitten to the corner: it was *in* the corner.

The following is a list of words often used as prepositions. Study it to familiarize yourself with these words.

Troubleshooting

If you have trouble identifying prepositions, think of a ball and a box. Many words that can describe the relationship of the ball to the box are prepositions. For example, a ball can be in the box, near the box, or above the box, so *in, near,* and *above* are prepositions.

about	before	in	toward
above	behind	into	under
across	beside	like	until
after	between	of	up
against	by	off	with
along	during	on	without
among	except	over	
around	for	through	
at	from	to	

A **prepositional phrase** is a preposition and the words that go with it. The following are prepositional phrases. The prepositions are underlined as a study aid.

<u>among</u> the ruins	<u>by</u> day	<u>of</u> the people
<u>around</u> the corner	<u>for</u> me	<u>over</u> the hill
<u>between</u> us	<u>in</u> the night	<u>without</u> a doubt

A complete subject often includes a prepositional phrase, but the simple subject will *never* be a word in that prepositional phrase.

Sentence:	*Six of the scouts earned merit badges.*
Complete subject:	*Six of the scouts*
Prepositional phrase:	*of the scouts*
Simple subject:	*six*

Sentence:	*Three members of the band are absent.*
Complete subject:	*Three members of the band*
Prepositional phrase:	*of the band*
Simple subject:	*members*

The complete subject can include more than one prepositional phrase, like this:

The car at the side of the road has stalled.

Complete subject:	*the car at the side of the road*
Prepositional phrases:	*at the side/of the road*
Simple subject:	*car*

5.6 ACTIVITY

In the following sentences, underline the prepositional phrases.

EXAMPLE   <u>Throughout history</u>, pepper has been considered the universal spice.

1. True pepper is made from a pepper plant with the scientific name of *Piper nigrum.* [*Hint:* This sentence contains three prepositional phrases.]

2. Other kinds of pepper are obtained from plants of entirely different families. [*Hint:* This sentence contains three prepositional phrases.]

3. Pepper is considered the most important spice in the world.

4. In ancient times and during the Middle Ages, only the rich could afford pepper.

5. It was carried by caravan from the Far East, which made it an item fit for a king. [*Hint:* This sentence contains three prepositional phrases.]

5.7 ACTIVITY

Rewrite the following sentences, adding one or more prepositional phrases of your choice before or after the subject of each sentence.

EXAMPLE   The baby began crying for a bottle.

In the middle of the night, the baby began crying for a bottle.

_____

1. The score was 12–14.

_____

_____

2. Grandpa caught three large-mouth bass and some bluegills.

_____

_____

3. The audience began to leave in disgust.

_____

_____

4. Delores accepted a basketball scholarship.

_____

_____

5. All the children dressed in scary costumes.

_____

_____

5.8 ACTIVITY

Underline the complete subject. Draw a line through any prepositional phrases that appear in the complete subject, and circle the simple subject.

EXAMPLE   The [invention] ~~of the pop-top can~~ illustrates that necessity is the mother of invention.

1. An engineer from Dayton, Ohio, was on a picnic with his family in 1959.

2. The engineer by the name of Fraze became thirsty for a beer.

3. None of the utensils in the picnic basket included a can opener, however.

4. The bumper on his car provided Fraze with the idea to open the can on that bumper, thereby leading him to invent the easy-open can.

5. The device in its earliest form pulled off the entire top of a can.

6. In this form, the device was patented in 1963.

7. An improvement on this invention came in 1965.

8. On the top of the can, a ring of metal pulled a prepunctured tab, to form the pop-top can.

9. The patent by Fraze of the "push in, fold-back" top occurred in 1965, and the rights to his invention were sold to Aluminum Company of America (Alcoa).

10. Each of the 150 billion cans of beer, soda, and juice sold every year in the United States earned Fraze a royalty payment.

Compound subjects

A simple subject can be made up of two or more nouns and pronouns. In this case, the sentence has a **compound subject**.

Sentence:	_Louise and I save $500 a year with grocery coupons._
Ask:	Who or what does or did something?
Answer:	_Louise and I_
Compound simple subject:	_Louise and I_

Sentence:	_Exercise and proper diet are important._
Ask:	About whom or what is something being said?
Answer:	_exercise and proper diet_
Complete subject:	_exercise and proper diet_
Compound simple subject:	_exercise and diet_

Sentence:	*The right attitude and a winning personality will get you the job.*
Ask:	Who or what does or did something?
Answer:	the right attitude and a winning personality
Complete subject:	*the right attitude and a winning personality*
Compound simple subject:	*attitude and personality*

Sentence:	*Rundown motels, boarded-up restaurants, and an aging amusement park are reminders of the town's more prosperous days.*
Ask:	About whom or what is something being said?
Answer:	rundown motels, boarded-up restaurants, and an aging amusement park
Complete subject:	*rundown motels, boarded-up restaurants, and an aging amusement park*
Compound simple subject:	*motels, restaurants, and amusement park*

5.9 ACTIVITY

Underline the complete subject and write the compound simple subject in the blank.

EXAMPLE   The roots and development of American music lie in other cultures.

roots and development

1. West Africa, Asia, and Europe are the principal influences on American music.

   _____

2. The many similarities and differences among various musical styles flavor American music.

   _____

3. Both classical music and popular musical styles have influenced the evolution of American music.

   _____

4. Pop music, rock and roll, folk songs, and country melodies are derived from African and West European musical traditions.

   _____

5. Both jazz and blues are the result of blending a variety of musical cultures and traditions.

   _____

5.10 ACTIVITY

Fill in the blanks in the following sentences with compound subjects.

EXAMPLE   _Businesspeople_ and _senior citizens_ were unhappy with the new tax law.

1. Both _____ and _____ decided to change their majors to criminal justice.

2. _____ and _____ are necessary for a successful party.

3. _____ , _____ , and _____
are the car's best features.

4. _____ and _____ gathered outside the auditorium to await the arrival of the rock stars.

5. _____ , _____ , and _____
are on sale this week at the mall.

5.11 ACTIVITY

Combine each pair of sentences into one sentence with a compound subject.

EXAMPLE   Two cups of sugar are needed for this recipe.
Three eggs are also needed.

Two cups of sugar and three eggs are needed for
_____

this recipe.
_____

1. Antonio drove to Pittsburgh for the Steelers game.
Karl drove with him.

_____

_____

2. This fall, three classroom buildings were closed for repairs.
Two dormitories were also closed for repairs.

_____

_____

3. Apartment buildings will be constructed on that land.
A small park will be constructed there, too.

_____

_____

4. Damaging winds will accompany the storm.
Hail will also accompany it.

_____

_____

5. The movie's plot annoyed me.
The background music also annoyed me.

_____

_____

6. Your test scores are very good.
   Your recommendations are very good as well.

   _____

   _____

7. In this store, the prices are excellent.
   The selection of merchandise is excellent, too. [*Hint:* Your verb will be *are.*]

   _____

   _____

8. The president visited the flood-ravaged town along the Mississippi River.
   The vice president went with him.

   _____

   _____

9. For many parents, teenage hairstyles are a mystery.
   Teenage fashions are also a mystery to them.

   _____

   _____

10. Many movies are unsuitable for children.
    Some television programs are also unsuitable.

    _____

    _____

Troubleshooting

When you are unsure whether a sentence is a command or request with the unstated *you* as the subject, try this test: If you can rephrase the sentence as a question beginning with *Would you,* you have a command or request. For example, "Leave me alone" becomes "Would you leave me alone?"

Unstated subjects

When a sentence gives a command or makes a request, the subject is not always written out. Then the subject is the unstated word *you.*

Command with unstated subject:	*Leave me alone!*
Unstated subject:	*you*
Command with stated subject:	*You leave me alone!*
Request with unstated subject:	*Close the curtains, please.*
Unstated subject:	*you*
Request with stated subject:	*You close the curtains, please.*

5.12 ACTIVITY

Rewrite the following commands and requests so that the subject is stated.

EXAMPLE   Go to the store for me, please.

   You go to the store for me, please.

1. Leave to pick up Julio at eight o'clock.

   _____

2. Answer me right now.

_____

3. Try to understand what I am telling you.

_____

4. Call the police immediately!

_____

5. Turn off the television and study.

_____

IDENTIFYING VERBS

Every sentence must have a verb. The **verb** is the word that expresses an action (such as _jump, sneeze, carry, fall_) or a state of being (such as _is, were, be, seem_). Because verbs show present, past, and future time, you can locate them by finding the word or words that work in these sentences:

1. Today I (we or it) _____ .

2. Yesterday I (we or it) _____ .

3. Tomorrow I (we or it) _____ .

Consider this sentence:

Heavyweight wrestler Tom Schotsky won the state championship.

The verb is _won_, because you can say, "Today I win," "Yesterday I won," "Tomorrow I will win."

Remember that a verb can be more than one word, as in these examples:

Heavyweight wrestler Tom Schotsky <u>might win</u> the state championship.

Heavyweight wrestler Tom Schotsky <u>will win</u> the state championship.

Heavyweight wrestler Tom Schotsky <u>could have won</u> the state championship.

Action verbs

Most verbs are action verbs.

As their name suggests, **action verbs** show activity or movement. They can also show some kind of process or thought.

Action verbs that show activity or movement:	_eat, run, go, hit, fall, sing, throw, jump, drive_
Action verbs that show thought:	_think, consider, reflect, desire_
Action verbs that show process:	_rest, review, try, enjoy, answer_

Some action verbs are made up of two words. Examples are

burn up	look over	pick up	send out
drop in	look up	put on	take off
fill up	make up	quiet down	think over

CONNECT FOR SUCCESS: Identify Action Verbs in Examination Questions

Pay attention to the action verbs in essay examination questions. Verbs such as *analyze, discuss, compare, define, explain,* and *demonstrate* direct the nature of your response.

5.13 ACTIVITY

Underline the action verbs in the following paragraph. A sentence may have more than one action verb. The first sentence is done as an example.

[1]Scientists <u>realized</u> long ago that we need a classification system for the animals and plants on earth. [2]In fact, ancient Greek philosopher Aristotle developed a primitive classification system over two thousand years ago. [3]However, it was not until the 1700s that a Swedish biologist, Carolus Linneaus, developed the classification system that is used today. [4]In that system, a name consists of two Latin words, as in *Homo sapiens* for humans. [5]No two species are given the same name. [6]An organism is classified according to its relationship to other organisms. [7]Thus, if a new toad were found in the rainforest, its structure and behavior would be compared to that of other toads. [8]This comparison would determine the name and classification of the new species. [9]So far, the system that Linneaus developed has served us well.

Source: Adapted from Sylvia S. Mader, *Biology,* 7th ed. (New York: McGraw-Hill, 2001), p. 489. Copyright © 2001 The McGraw-Hill Companies. Used by permission of The McGraw-Hill Companies.

5.14 ACTIVITY

Fill in the blanks with action verbs.

EXAMPLE   The hail *pounded* _____ the cars in the parking lot.

1. The children _____ when the circus clown _____ .

2. At the checkout counter, the cashier _____ when the customer _____ her money on the floor.

3. Deanne _____ carefully before buying the used Toyota.

4. This is a difficult decision, so I must _____ carefully.

5. The hotel manager _____ the staff because they were not polite to guests.

6. Jeff and Ann _____ in Yellowstone National Park before they _____ to Alabama for a week.

7. Wanda _____ chocolate chip cookies, but they give her migraine headaches.

8. The photographer _____ a park scene for the bride's wedding picture, but the unexpected rain shower _____ his plan.

9. Many people _____ computers by mail rather than _____ them in retail stores.

10. The architect _____ a modern office tower, but the mayor _____ a more traditional structure.

5.15 COLLABORATIVE ACTIVITY

Pair up with a classmate. Separately, see how many action verbs you can list in sixty seconds. Then trade lists and sort the verbs into three categories: verbs that show activity or movement, verbs that show thought, and verbs that show process. Trade lists again and check each other's work.

Linking verbs

Although most verbs show action, some do not. Instead, these verbs link the subject to something that renames or describes the subject. For this reason, these verbs are called **linking verbs.** Here are four examples:

Chris <u>is</u> my oldest and closest friend.

Complete subject:	*Chris*
Linking verb:	*is*
Renames the subject:	*my oldest and closest friend*

Black olives <u>are</u> an essential ingredient in the salad.

Complete subject:	*black olives*
Linking verb:	*are*
Renames the subject:	*essential ingredient*

The soup <u>seems</u> too hot to eat.

Complete subject:	*the soup*
Linking verb:	*seems*
Describes the subject:	*too hot*

The man <u>appears</u> confused.

Complete subject:	*the man*
Linking verb:	*appears*
Describes the subject:	*confused*

Troubleshooting

If you are unsure whether a verb is a linking verb, remember that most linking verbs are forms of *be* or sensory verbs (related to sight, sound, smell, taste, and touch).

Study the following list of linking verbs, so you will recognize them easily in sentences.

am	was	appear/appeared	taste/tasted
be	were	feel/felt	smell/smelled
is	been	seem/seemed	look/looked
are	being	sound/sounded	become/became

5.16 ACTIVITY

Circle each linking verb. Underline the complete subject and the words after the linking verb that rename or describe the subject.

EXAMPLE   Cells are the basic unit of life.

1. I am interested in cellular biology.

2. The basic unit of both structure and function is the cell.

3. Cells of similar structure become muscle tissue, nervous tissue, connective tissue, or epithelial tissue.

4. All organs are combinations of different tissue types.

5. Muscle tissue often looks striated.

6. The walls of the stomach appear smooth because of the smooth muscle tissue.

7. A gland is epithelial tissue specialized for secretion.

8. Under the microscope, connective tissue seems elastic.

9. The majority of cells are less than 1 cubic millimeter.

10. Cell division is one of the most amazing of life's processes.

5.17 ACTIVITY

If the underlined verb is an action verb, write AV above it. If it is a linking verb, write LV above it.

EXAMPLE   The Underground Railroad helped many fugitive slaves to freedom.

[1]The Underground Railroad was not really a railroad. [2]It was a network of people who helped Southern slaves over paths, across rivers, through forests, and over fields to freedom in the North and Canada. [3]No one knows when it started. [4]It seems, however, that slave runaways used the railroad as early as the 1700s. [5]At first, the Underground Railroad lacked any formal organization. [6]By the 1800s, the flights had become more organized. [7]Quakers and other abolitionists (those who opposed slavery and worked for its abolition) helped the runaways. [8]Although no one knows for sure how many slaves were helped to freedom, it appears that between 1810 and 1850 approximately 100,000 slaves escaped on the railroad.

5.18 ACTIVITY

On a separate sheet, write ten sentences, five with action verbs and five with linking verbs. Underline the action verbs and circle the linking verbs.

Helping verbs

The **complete verb** can be made up of more than one word. The action verb or the linking verb is the **main verb.** The other verb is the **helping verb.** The helping verb often "helps" the main verb express time or ask a question.

You *did ask* Dr. Brezinski that question.

Action verb:	*ask*
Helping verb:	*did*
Complete verb:	*did ask*

You *will be* the winner of the contest.

Linking verb:	*be*
Helping verb:	*will*
Complete verb:	*will be*

The complete verb can also include more than one helping verb.

Karen and Tony *have been studying* for hours.

Action verb:	*studying*
Helping verbs:	*have been*

So that you will recognize them easily, study this list of helping verbs.

am	were	might	will	has
be	been	can	do	had
is	being	could	did	shall
are	may	should	does	
was	must	would	have	

GRAMMAR ALERT

Some of the helping verbs on this list (*am, is, are, was,* and *were,* for example) are also on the list of linking verbs on page 84. When these verbs appear alone, they are linking verbs. When they appear with action or other linking verbs, they are helping verbs.

GRAMMAR ALERT

The descriptive words *not, just, never, only, already,* and *always* often appear with helping verbs, but they are not verbs themselves. Rather, they are adverbs as they answer the question "when" on "how often."

I will never agree to that plan.

Descriptive word:	*never*
Complete verb:	*will agree*

5.19 ACTIVITY

Underline the complete verbs and circle the helping verbs. Remember, the complete verb can include more than one helping verb, and descriptive words are not verbs.

EXAMPLE   Solid waste is harming our environment.

1. In the United States, solid waste is generated at the rate of 4.5 tons annually.

2. Typically, paper has accounted for most of the solid waste.

3. Most of this paper is sent to landfills.

4. We should not rely on landfills indefinitely, however.

5. The capacity of landfills has steadily declined since 1995.

6. Recycling can be an important part of the solution.

7. For example, recycling a ton of paper will save more than 3 cubic yards of landfill space.

8. Recycling can also preserve trees.

9. A 4-foot stack of newspaper can be considered the equivalent of a 40-foot tree.

10. Then we will be saving forests.

5.20 ACTIVITY

Underline each verb and label it AV if it is an action verb, LV if it is a linking verb, and HV if it is a helping verb.

EXAMPLE   Many people <u>have</u> <u>learned</u> little about the Pledge of Allegiance because its history <u>is</u> rarely <u>taught</u> in schools.
                                  HV AV
                                HV AV

[1]The Pledge of Allegiance was written in 1892 by Francis Bellamy in honor of Columbus Day. [2]Originally, the words were "I pledge allegiance to my Flag and the Republic for which it stands—one nation indivisible—with liberty and justice for all." [3]The pledge was popular in schools and was recited daily. [4]In 1923, the U.S. Flag Association made some changes. [5]It replaced "my Flag" with "the flag of the United States of America." [6]In 1954, Congress made another change, when it added "under God."

A sentence can have two or more verbs for the same subject. In this case, the sentence has a **compound verb.** Compound verbs are connected by the conjunctions *and* and *or.* Here is an example:

Sentence:	*The untrained puppy <u>chewed</u> the rug and <u>ruined</u> the sofa.*
Compound verb:	*chewed, ruined*
Conjunction:	*and*
Sentence:	*The developer will <u>renovate</u> the hotel or <u>demolish</u> it.*
Compound verb:	*renovate, demolish*
Conjunction:	*or*

A compound verb can include action verbs, linking verbs, and helping verbs:

　　　LV　　　　AV
I <u>was</u> ill and <u>stayed</u> home.
　　　　　LV　　　　　　　　LV
Cobina <u>appears</u> happy and <u>looks</u> fit.
　　　　　HV　AV　　　　　　　　AV
Airlines <u>are cutting</u> costs and <u>increasing</u> fares.
　　　HV　AV　　　　　AV
I <u>will rest</u> and then <u>go</u> with you.

GRAMMAR ALERT

A verb that follows *to* is not part of the complete verb. It is a special form known as an **infinitive.**

> *The child wants to go with his mother.* [The complete verb is *wants*, not *go*, which follows *to.*]

5.21 ACTIVITY

The following sentences have compound verbs. Underline those verbs. Remember, a verb that follows *to* (an infinitive) is not part of the complete verb.

EXAMPLE   George Washington <u>oversaw</u> construction of the White House but never <u>lived</u> there.

1. The White House has been known as the "President's Place" and has been called the "President's House" and the "Executive Mansion."

2. Most people do not know the number of rooms in the White House or appreciate its great size.

3. The White House has 132 rooms and 35 bathrooms, and it extends over six floors.

4. A tennis court, jogging track, billiard room, bowling lane, movie theater, and swimming pool provide residents opportunities to exercise and give them recreational opportunities.

5. With five full-time chefs, the White House kitchen is able to serve dinner to as many as 140 guests and can prepare hors d'oeuvres for more than 1,000 people.

5.22 ACTIVITY

Combine each pair of sentences into one sentence with a compound verb. To do so, eliminate the subject of the second sentence. (Item 4 requires you to combine three sentences into one.)

EXAMPLE   A low-fat diet prevents heart disease.
　　　　　　　It also causes weight loss.

A low-fat diet prevents heart disease and causes weight

loss.

1. The newspaper advertisement misrepresented the product.
The advertisement created confusion.

_____

_____

2. The judge heard the attorney's closing arguments.
He made his decision.

_____

_____

3. My morning run begins promptly at seven o'clock.
It ends at eight-fifteen.

_____

_____

4. Before our guests arrive, we must shop.
We must cook the meal.

We must clean the house.

_____

5. The supermarket melons smell sweet.
They look ripe.

_____

_____

6. The salesperson explained the car's features.
She offered us a test drive.

_____

_____

7. Janet studied her biology text.
She read over her class notes.

_____

_____

8. I studied the map for ten minutes.
I found the fastest route to Omaha.

_____

_____

9. Mario went to summer school for six weeks.
Then he worked as a lifeguard at the city pool.

_____

_____

10. Carefully, I selected the most beautiful plant.
I presented it to Grandmother for her eightieth birthday.

_____

_____

5.23 ACTIVITY

Circle the verbs in the following paragraph. Remember, descriptive words are not verbs, and verbs that follow _to_ (infinitives) are not part of the complete verb. The first one is done as an example.

[1]Nevada resident Gary Murray's dog ⟨was hurt⟩ in a car accident. [2]As a result, Murray invented the Love Belt, a seat belt for dogs. [3]The Love Belt comes in three sizes—small, medium, and large. [4]In case of an accident, it restrains the dog to minimize injury. [5]A dog owner can even use the Love Belt as a leash outside the car. [6]Thousands of dogs are hurt or killed every year in car accidents. [7]However, the Love Belt reduces the risk of serious injury and provides valuable protection for beloved pets.

5.24 COLLABORATIVE ACTIVITY

Select a newspaper article and circle the first ten verbs. Trade articles with a classmate and label each circled verb an action verb, a linking verb, or a helping verb. Check each other's work and get help from your instructor to resolve areas of disagreement.

CONNECT FOR SUCCESS: Identify Subjects and Verbs in Difficult Material

If you are having trouble understanding difficult reading material, look first for the subjects and verbs in each sentence for the most important information about meaning.

IF ENGLISH IS NOT YOUR FIRST LANGUAGE

1. Remember that helping verbs come _before_ action verbs.

       _HV AV_
  Marco will go with us.

A word can come between the helping verb and the action verb.

       _HV_   _AV_
  Marco will ⟨not⟩ go with us.

       _HV_   _AV_
  Marco will ⟨always⟩ go with us.

2. These verbs are helping verbs; they appear with action verbs or linking verbs:

can	might	should
could	must	will
may	shall	would

With action verb: *Joe <u>can play</u> the piano.*
With linking verb: *Jackie <u>can be</u> annoying.*

Note: Can can be an action verb, as in this example:

I <u>can</u> tomatoes every summer.

3. The forms of *do (do, does,* and *did)* and the forms of *have (have, has,* and *had)* can be either action verbs or helping verbs.

Action verb:	*The dog <u>had</u> puppies.* [*Had* means "gave birth to."]
Helping verb:	*Connie <u>had spoken</u> first.*
Action verb:	*Alejandro <u>did</u> all the work.*
Helping verb:	*You <u>did help</u> me.*

4. As helping verbs, *do, does,* and *did* can be used three ways: (A) with *not* or *never* to express a negative, (B) to ask a question, (C) to emphasize the action verb.

A. *I <u>do</u> not know the answer. I never <u>did</u> see that.*
B. *Where <u>do</u> you live?*
C. *They <u>do drive</u> very fast.*

5. The forms of *be (am, is, are, was,* and *were)* can be either helping verbs or linking verbs.

Helping verb:	HV AV *Traffic <u>is moving</u> slowly.*
Linking verb:	LV *This shirt <u>is</u> too tight.*

6. A number of English verbs are made up of two words. Some of these two-word verbs can be separated, but some cannot be separated. For example, *give in* cannot be separated, but *put off* can be separated. However, verbs that *can* be separated do not always *have* to be separated.

Separable:	*I must <u>put</u> that appointment <u>off</u> until next week.*
	I must <u>put off</u> that appointment until next week.
Inseparable:	*The police will not <u>give in</u> to the protestors' demands.*

If you are unsure which verbs are separable and which are not, consult the list that follows. Example sentences appear with some of the verbs in each list.

Separable Two-Word Verbs

ask out:	*I will ask her out.*
burn down:	*We must burn the tree down.*
	We must burn down the tree.

Troubleshooting

Listen and learn! You can gain practice recognizing the rhythms and conventions of English by listening to how people speak. For example, listen to talk radio while you are washing the dishes or driving the car; watch and listen to television while you are folding your laundry.

burn up: *The fire burned the papers up.*
The fire burned up the papers.

bring up: *Bring the issue up at the next meeting.*
Bring up the issue at the next meeting.

call off: *The umpire called the game off when the rain began.*
The umpire called off the game when the rain began.

call up: *Call the porter up to get our bags.*
Call up the porter to get our bags.

clean up: *You should clean this mess up yourself.*
You should clean up this mess yourself.

cut up: *The butcher cut the meat up into chops.*
The butcher cut up the meat into chops.

drop off: *I dropped Marcel off at school this morning.*
I dropped off Marcel at school this morning.

fill out	help out	point out	take off [clothes]
fill up	leave out	put away	take out
give away	look over	put off	think over
give back	look up	put on	throw away
hand in	make up	put together	try on
hand out	pick out	quiet down	wake up
hang up	pick up	shut off	wrap up

Inseparable Two-Word Verbs

come across: *I came across old letters in the attic.*

drop in
  [on someone]: *My neighbor drops in every day to visit.*

get along
  [with someone]: *My sister and I never got along.*

get away
  [with something]: *Students rarely get away with cheating.*

give in: *The parents gave in to the crying child.*

give up: *The robber gave up and put down his gun.*

go out
  [with someone]: *Jean and I go out every Saturday.*

go over
  [something]: *Let's go over the notes together.*

grow up	run into [someone	stay away from
play around	or something]	take care of
run across [someone	run out [of	take off [airplane]
or something]	something]	wake up
	speak up	

5.25 CHAPTER REVIEW ACTIVITY

Draw one line under each simple subject and two lines under each complete verb.

EXAMPLE   <u>Areas</u> of space <u>are accumulating</u> more and more pieces of junk.

[1]Pieces of junk are traveling in space around our planet. [2]This space junk will travel in orbit around earth for many years. [3]Five thousand pieces of the space junk are the size of baseballs. [4]Almost 40,000 pieces are the size of golf balls or smaller. [5]Each piece of junk orbits earth once every hour. [6]At that speed, peanut-sized metal and plastic could wreck a spaceship. [7]The junk will also pose a threat to future space stations.

[8]The junk got into space in different ways. [9]Some pieces slipped through the fingers of astronauts or broke off old satellites. [10]For safety's sake, astronauts may have to collect the space junk. [11]The cost of such an operation could be enormous. [12]In addition, spaceships may need covers to protect them from the pieces. [13]Engineers will have to design these covers. [14]Of course, their efforts will create another expense. [15]The problem is a serious one and must be solved.

5.26 CHAPTER REVIEW ACTIVITY

In the following paragraph,

- draw one line under the complete subject and two lines under the complete verb.
- circle the simple subject.
- label each verb AV if it is an action verb, LV if it is a linking verb, and HV if it is a helping verb.

EXAMPLE   The [history] of many streets <u>can be</u> interesting to learn.

[1]New York City's financial district is called Wall Street. [2]You have probably heard of this street but do not know its history. [3]The street itself is a narrow thoroughfare in lower Manhattan and runs from Broadway to the East River. [4]It became the first permanent home of the New York Stock Exchange. [5]Wall Street got its name in an interesting way. [6]In the seventeenth century, the Dutch on the Manhattan island controlled New Amsterdam, New York's name at the time. [7]British forces and some Indian tribes were planning an invasion. [8]For defense, the Dutch built a 9-foot wall around their troop headquarters. [9]After that, the area within the wall became known forever as Wall Street. [10]Perhaps you have heard of *The Wall Street Journal*. [11]This prestigious publication was named in reference to Wall Street.

GETTING IN GEAR: IDEAS FOR WRITING

The track star in the photo is Jesse Owens, who won four gold medals at the 1936 Olympics, held in Berlin, Germany. His wins are particularly memorable because Adolf Hitler, the dictator of Germany at the time, wanted to make the Olympics a showcase for German racial superiority. The fact that an African American had beaten German athletes publicly discredited his racism. Jesse Owens was remarkable as both a man and an athlete. To learn more about him, visit www.jesseowens.org/about1.html.

writing topic: Tell about a positive or negative experience you had with sports and what you learned as a result. You can tell about an experience you had as a player, spectator, fan, or coach. You can even discuss what it is like to be a member of a sports-crazed family, or a family that is not interested in sports. The experience can have occurred in or out of school, as a child or an adult.

suggestions for prewriting
- List three happy experiences you have had with sports.
- List three unhappy experiences you have had with sports.
- From which experience did you learn the most valuable lesson? Answer the following questions about that experience:

Who was involved?	When did it happen?
What happened?	Why did it happen?
Where did it happen?	How did it happen?

suggestion for drafting: Your thesis or topic sentence (depending on whether you are writing an essay or a paragraph) can mention the experience and what you learned from the experience.

suggestion for revising: Because action verbs are more lively and vivid than linking verbs, look for opportunities to replace linking verbs with specific action verbs, like this:

Draft: I <u>was</u> angry when I left the room.

Revision: I <u>stormed</u> out of the room angrily.

suggestion for editing: Check each of your sentences separately to be sure each has a subject, a verb, and a complete thought. If any word group seems as if it should not be a sentence, add the missing component.

RECHARGE: Lesson Summary

1. To identify the **subject**, ask, "Who or what does or did something?" or "About whom or what is something being said?"
2. The **simple subject** is the most important word in the subject, and the **complete subject** is the simple subject and all the other words in the subject.

The sudden (storm) surprised the picnickers.

- The simple subject is a **noun** or **pronoun.**
- The simple subject can be a form of an action word (a **gerund** or an **infinitive**).
- The simple subject will not be a word in a **prepositional phrase.**
- A simple subject is **compound** when it is made up of two or more nouns or pronouns.

3. The subject is usually at or near the beginning of the sentence.
4. The subject can be the unstated word *you* in a command or request.
5. To identify the **complete verb**, find the word or words that show time.

- The complete verb can be an **action verb** that shows activity, thought, or a process.

The teacher <u>took</u> the class on a trip to the museum.

- The complete verb can be a linking verb that connects the subject to something that renames or describes that subject.

The child <u>is</u> a good swimmer.

- The complete verb can include a **helping verb** with the action or linking verb. The helping verb can help express time or ask a question.

A winter storm (is) <u>approaching</u> the East Coast.

- The verb is **compound** when two or more verbs connected by *and* or *or* appear with the same subject.

CHAPTER 6

Eliminating Sentence Fragments

A sentence is *not* just any word group that begins with a capital letter and ends with a period. For example, here is a word group with a capital letter and a period, but it is not a sentence:

Understanding the new tax law.

If you speak those words out loud, you can probably sense that the words do not form a sentence. The following is another word group with a capital letter and a period. Speak these words aloud, and you can probably sense that this word group *is* a sentence:

I need help understanding the new tax law.

This chapter will help you find sentence fragments in your writing and eliminate them.

RECOGNIZING SENTENCE FRAGMENTS

To be a sentence, a word group must meet these requirements:

- It must have a subject.
- It must have a verb.
- It must stand independently, because it expresses a complete thought.

A word group missing one or more of these requirements is a **sentence fragment**.

Fragment:	*Eats pizza every day for lunch.* [Who eats pizza? The subject is missing.]
Sentence:	*Hans eats pizza every day for lunch.*
Fragment:	*Students registering for summer school on Monday.* [Part of the verb is missing.]
Sentence:	*Students are registering for summer school on Monday.*
Fragment:	*When the interstate is complete.* [What will happen when the interstate is complete? Information necessary for completeness is missing.]
Sentence:	*When the interstate is complete, business will expand in our area.*

Each word group below looks like a sentence because it has a period and a capital letter. However, five of the word groups are really sentence fragments because one of the sentence elements is missing (the subject, all or part of the verb, or information necessary for completeness). Read each word group aloud and listen to determine whether something is missing. If the word group is a sentence, write S on the blank; if it is a fragment, write an F.

EXAMPLES _F_ Joseph Mallord William Turner often known as M.W. Turner.

_S_ He painted around 300 landscapes.

1. _____ The British painter Joseph Turner lived from 1775 to 1851.

2. _____ Renowned for his landscape paintings.

3. _____ His paintings have spectacular color effects.

4. _____ That capture the play of light on a scene.

5. _____ For example, a sunset or a storm of dramatic intensity.

6. _____ Turner wanting to see what a storm at sea looked like.

7. _____ He had himself tied to the mast of a ship.

8. _____ The ship was sailing through a storm.

9. _____ People often do unusual things.

10. _____ When they are passionate about their art.

Troubleshooting

If you are unsure how to locate subjects and verbs, review Chapter 5.

MISSING SUBJECT AND VERB FRAGMENTS

Some sentence fragments occur because the subject has been left out. In the following example, the fragment is underlined.

Sentence and fragment: *I needed to be awake by six o'clock. But forgot to set the alarm.*

Who forgot to set the alarm? The word group does not say, so the subject is missing. Perhaps you are thinking that the subject is *I*. But that word appears in the previous sentence and is the subject of that sentence. It is not the subject of the underlined word group because it does not appear in that word group.

To eliminate a fragment that results from a missing subject, you have two choices:

- Add the missing subject.
- Join the fragment to a sentence.

Sentence and fragment: *I needed to be awake by six o'clock. But forgot to set the alarm.*

Add the missing subject: *I needed to be awake by six o'clock. But I forgot to set the alarm.*

Join the fragment
to a sentence: *I needed to be awake by six o'clock but forgot to set the alarm.*

Some sentence fragments occur because both the subject and the verb have been left out.

Sentence and fragment: *Marcus bought a new suit. <u>With wide lapels and baggy pants.</u>*

To eliminate a fragment that results from a missing subject and verb, you have two choices:

- Add the missing subject and verb.
- Join the fragment to a sentence.

Sentence and fragment: *Marcus bought a new suit. <u>With wide lapels and baggy pants.</u>*

Add the missing subject and verb: *Marcus bought a new suit. <u>It had</u> wide lapels and baggy pants.*

Join the fragment to a sentence: *Marcus bought a new suit with wide lapels and baggy pants.*

6.2 ACTIVITY

All but one of the following pairs of word groups consist of one fragment and one sentence. The fragments have missing subjects or missing subjects and verbs. First underline the fragment. Then eliminate it, using the correction method of your choice. Remember, one pair of word groups is already correct.

Troubleshooting

Here's a test to try when you are unsure whether a word group is a command or a request, (and, therefore, a complete sentence and not a fragment): If you can rephrase the words as a question beginning with *Would you,* you have a command or request. "Close the door" becomes "Would you close the door?" to become a sentence.

EXAMPLE   Clarence Birdseye made cooking easier. <u>And freed cooks from a great deal of drudgery.</u>

Clarence Birdseye made cooking easier and freed cooks from a great deal of drudgery.

or

Clarence Birdseye made cooking easier. He freed cooks from a great deal of drudgery.

1. Clarence Birdseye was a naturalist and fur trader. Traveling in Labrador in 1916.

_____

_____

2. With his keen scientific mind. He understood Inuit fish-freezing techniques.

_____

_____

3. He recognized that speed was the key. And could revolutionize the food industry.

_____

_____

4. Slow freezing is a problem. Large ice crystals will form within and outside the cells.

_____

_____

5. During the thawing period, the large crystals cause damage. In the cell walls of plants and the membranes in animals.

_____

_____

6. Damaged to a significant extent. Vegetables become mushy and meat becomes tough.

_____

_____

7. However, the Inuits laid freshly caught fish on the ice. To freeze quickly.

_____

_____

8. Their fish had the flavor and texture of the fresh catch. And did not suffer from the freezing process.

_____

_____

9. Birdseye returned home. Then established Birdseye Seafoods.

_____

10. Later he expanded his business to include meats, fruits, and vegetables. Making frozen foods the forerunner of convenience foods.

_____

_____

6.3 ACTIVITY

Find and eliminate the fragments that occur because a subject or both a subject and a verb are missing. Use the correction method of your choice. (*Hint:* Do not simply read over the paragraph. Instead, examine each word group separately to be sure each has both a subject and a complete verb.)

EXAMPLE   It is traditional for students to wear a cap and ~~gown. For~~ *gown for* graduation.

[1]You are probably aware that high school and college students wear academic dress for graduation. [2]But may not know the reason. [3]Academic dress started in the twelfth and thirteenth centuries, when universities were first formed. [4]Whether a student or a teacher. [5]Everyone wore clerical garb. [6]Most medieval scholars had made religious vows. [7]And belonged to a religious order. [8]Therefore, clerical robes were their customary dress. [9]Even outside the university. [10]The cap and gown

customarily worn for graduation today harkens back to the clerical robes worn by early university students and teachers. [11]In the United States in the late 1700s. [12]Colors were assigned to designate different areas of study. [13]For example, green was the color of medieval herbs. [14]And was, therefore, assigned to medical studies.

INCOMPLETE VERB FRAGMENTS

Troubleshooting

If you need to review helping verbs, see page 85.

Some verbs cannot appear alone. They must appear with one of the following **helping verbs:**

am	was	may	could	do	has
be	were	must	would	did	had
is	been	might	should	does	shall
are	being	can	will	have	

Here are two examples:

> *helping verb*
> The party ⏐is⏐ ending now.

> *helping verb*
> The runner ⏐has⏐ broken the school record.

If a necessary helping verb is left out, a sentence fragment results.

> Fragment: *The party ending now.*

> Fragment: *The runner broken the school record.*

To eliminate a fragment that results from an incomplete verb, you have two possibilities:

- Add the missing helping verb.
- Change the verb form.

Add the Missing Helping Verb

Sentence and fragment: *We raced down the pier. However, the ferry gone by the time we arrived.*

Correction: *We raced down the pier. However, the ferry was gone by the time we arrived.*

Change the Verb Form

Sentence and fragment: *Arina enjoys early morning exercise. At six a.m. she jogging down neighborhood streets.*

Correction: *Arina enjoys early morning exercise. At six a.m. she jogs down neighborhood streets.*

 GRAMMAR ALERT

Words ending in *-ing* cannot be complete verbs by themselves; they must appear with helping verbs.

> Fragment: *The storm slowing rush hour traffic.*

> Sentence: *The storm is slowing rush hour traffic.*

> Fragment: *Judd considering three job offers.*

> Sentence: *Judd was considering three job offers.*

6.4 ACTIVITY

1911, New York City: Ruins after fire swept the Triangle Shirtwaist Company.

Underline the fragments that result from incomplete verbs and rewrite to eliminate those fragments. One is already correct.

EXAMPLE   The fiery deaths of 146 people at the Triangle Shirtwaist Company shocking the nation. Following the fire, New York enacted the most ambitious labor code in the country.

The fiery deaths of 146 people at the Triangle Shirtwaist Company shocked the nation. Following the fire, New York enacted the most ambitious labor code in the country.

1. On March 25, 1911, people pouring into the streets of lower Manhattan on their way home from work. They saw "a great swirling, billowing cloud of smoke."

    _____

    _____

    _____

2. The Asch Building, home of the Triangle Shirtwaist Company, was on fire. Inside, 500 workers been cutting and sewing since dawn.

    _____

    _____

3. The workers making tailored blouses called "shirtwaists," popular among young office women. Most of the factory workers were young women, too, Italian and Jewish immigrants or their daughters.

_____

_____

_____

4. Many workers were under twenty-five. Some were children.

_____

_____

_____

5. The fire broken out in the lofts. In minutes, the top stories were ablaze.

_____

_____

_____

6. Terrified seamstresses groping through the black smoke. However, they found exits locked or clogged with bodies.

_____

_____

7. All but one of the working fire escapes collapsed. Ladders on the fire trucks not reaching the top stories.

_____

_____

8. Children, with their hair on fire, jumping to their deaths. Girls hugged each other as they leaped.

_____

_____

9. By the time the fire was extinguished, 146 people been killed. A few days later, 80,000 New Yorkers joined the silent funeral procession on Fifth Avenue.

_____

_____

_____

10. Partly as a result of that tragedy, a progressive movement of reform emerged. Clearly, the Triangle fire shaken the nation.

_____

_____

6.5 ACTIVITY

Find and eliminate the fragments that occur because of incomplete verbs. Use the correction method of your choice.

EXAMPLE Most people know that Henry Ford invented the Model T. How-

                                  do   *realize*
ever, many people ˄not ~~realizing~~ that he created the assembly line
                                        ˄

[1]Henry Ford (1863–1947) was the founder of the Ford Motor Company. [2]He credited with creating the assembly line. [3]An assembly line being an arrangement of machines and workers. [4]Each worker performs a single, repetitive operation on an incomplete unit as it passes by. [5]The assembly line was an important innovation that changed manufacturing forever. [6]It allowing factory managers to control the pace of production. [7]As a result of the assembly line, goods produced cheaper. [8]Soon after Ford introduced the assembly line, other manufacturers began using it. [9]With the spread of assembly line production, more goods could be produced more cheaply. [10]As a result, the price of goods was reduced significantly. [11]Naturally, more people afford to buy more items.

CONNECT FOR SUCCESS: Rewrite Fragments in Your Lecture Notes

When you take notes, you are likely to use sentence fragments as a time-saving device. After class, rewrite your lecture notes to eliminate the sentence fragments and help "set" your learning.

DEPENDENT CLAUSE FRAGMENTS

A word group can have a subject and verb but still not be a sentence because as a thought it is not sufficiently complete to stand alone. Such a word group is a **dependent clause.** A dependent clause punctuated and capitalized like a sentence is a sentence fragment. The following word groups are dependent clause fragments. They have subjects and verbs, but if you read them aloud, you will hear that they are not complete enough to stand alone as sentences.

Dependent clause fragment:	*Before our company arrives.*
Dependent clause fragment:	*When the last hamburger is cooked.*
Dependent clause fragment:	*Although we disagree with each other.*

Dependent clauses begin with words such as the following, which are **subordinating conjunctions:**

after	as though	though	whatever
although	because	unless	whether
as	before	until	while

as if	even though	when
as long as	if	whenever
as soon as	since	where

To eliminate a dependent clause fragment, join the fragment to a sentence.

Fragment and sentence: *Because you left so early. You missed the best part of the party.*

Correction: *Because you left so early, you missed the best part of the party.*

Sentence and fragment: *Harriet is a talented dancer. Who plans to study in New York.*

Correction: *Harriet is a talented dancer, who plans to study in New York.*

 GRAMMAR ALERT

Missing information does not always create a fragment. A word group can be a complete sentence in the grammatical sense even if some information is unknown.

Sentence: *We offered them a ride.* [The word group is complete and is a sentence, even though we do not know who "we" and "them" are.]

6.6 ACTIVITY

In each pair, underline the fragment that results from lack of completeness, and then rewrite to eliminate the fragment. One pair is already correct.

EXAMPLE   Whenever I read about dumb criminals. I marvel at their stupidity.

Whenever I read about dumb criminals, I marvel at their

stupidity.

1. Even though I thought I had heard it all. A recent news report surprised me.

_____

_____

2. Convenience store robbers often wear ski masks. Since they want to hide their faces.

_____

_____

3. Because one criminal was not thinking ahead. He made a serious error.

_____

_____

4. When he held up a convenience store. He used a clear plastic bag instead of a ski mask.

_____

_____

_____

5. Since he did not have a disguise. Upon entering the store, he grabbed a transparent garbage bag.

_____

_____

_____

6. Before he really thought things through. He put the bag over his head.

_____

_____

7. After putting the bag over his head. The thief robbed the store of less than a hundred dollars.

_____

_____

_____

8. When he tried to break into a house later. The police arrested him.

_____

_____

9. The garbage bag bandit told police he was a crack addict. As soon as they arrested him.

_____

_____

_____

10. Prosecution should not be too difficult. Because the store robbery was recorded on the security camera, the evidence against the man is strong.

_____

_____

6.7 ACTIVITY

Find and eliminate the dependent clause fragments.

EXAMPLE   Although he may be best remembered as the first African American Secretary of State. Colin Powell has many notable achievements.

¹The son of Jamaican immigrants, Colin Powell was born in Harlem in New York City in 1937. ²Although he was a lackluster student in high school. ³Powell did well at the City College of New York. ⁴He became a member of the Reserve Officers Training Corps (ROTC). ⁵While he attended City College. ⁶After college graduation, he entered the military as second lieutenant.⁷ He became a career officer and served with distinction in Vietnam. ⁸From 1987 to 1989, Powell was the highest ranking African American in the Reagan administration. ⁹When he served as a presidential assistant for national security. ¹⁰After that, he was the first African American to serve as chairman of the Joint Chiefs of Staff. ¹¹After he was confirmed by the Senate in 2001. ¹²Colin Powell became the first African-American secretary of state.

CONNECT FOR SUCCESS: Avoid Fragments in Formal Writing

You may find yourself using sentence fragments in informal writing situations, particularly in casual e-mail to friends, lecture notes, shopping lists, and the like. Remember, though, that in formal business, academic, and personal writing—including e-mail to professors and coworkers—you should edit to eliminate fragments.

TIPS FOR FINDING FRAGMENTS

1. You can easily overlook fragments if you simply read over your draft. A better way is to study each sentence for five to ten seconds, checking for subjects, verbs, and completeness.

2. Try slowly reading your draft backwards, from last sentence to first. Listen for lack of completeness.

3. Be sure that every sentence with an *-ing* form for the main verb (*eating, sleeping, driving,* etc.) also includes a helping verb (*is eating, was sleeping, were driving,* etc.).

4. Read aloud word groups beginning with *because, when, while, unless, if, although,* and *since* to be sure they are complete enough to be sentences.

5. Fragments cannot be made into questions, so if you are unsure whether a word group is a fragment, try changing it to a question. If it cannot be done, you have found a fragment.

Composing at the computer

If you like to compose at the computer, you may find the following strategies helpful for finding and eliminating fragments.

1. REFORMAT YOUR PAPER INTO A LIST OF SENTENCES. With your writing in list form, you may find it easier to detect fragments. When you are finished checking, reformat your writing into paragraph form.

2. USE YOUR WORD-PROCESSING PROGRAM'S GRAMMAR CHECK—WITH CAUTION. For the most part, these programs do a good job of finding fragments, but they *do* make mistakes. Double-check to be sure each word group flagged is really a fragment, and look for fragments the program might miss.

IF ENGLISH IS NOT YOUR FIRST LANGUAGE

1. In some languages, a sentence does not require a subject. However, in English, a sentence must have a subject. A word group that does not have a subject is a fragment. The exception to this rule is commands. A sentence that gives a command does not always have a stated subject: *Give me the keys.*

2. In some languages, a sentence does not have a verb. However, in English, a sentence must have a verb. A word group that does not have a verb is a fragment.

3. Sometimes a verb form that needs a helping verb is spelled the same way as the verb form that does not need a helping verb. This can cause confusion and lead to sentence fragments. Just remember that, if the subject performs the action of the verb, then a helping verb is *not* required. However, if the subject receives the action of the verb, then a helping verb *is* required.

Sentence: *The fire <u>burned</u> my finger.* [The subject performs the action.]

Fragment: *My finger <u>burned</u> by the fire.* [The subject receives the action.]

Sentence: *My finger <u>was burned</u> by the fire.* [The subject receives the action.]

6.8 CHAPTER REVIEW ACTIVITY

The following paragraph has seven fragments. First underline the fragments. Then make corrections above the line to eliminate the fragments.

EXAMPLE   Giving speeches is uncomfortable for some people. They ~~becoming~~ *become* nervous.

¹Although knowing when to speak is often easy. ²Learning how and when to pause is a challenge for people who must give speeches. ³Even a moment of silence can seem like an eternity. ⁴As speakers gain more confidence, however. ⁵They discover how useful the pause can be. ⁶It can signal the end of a thought and give an idea time to sink in. ⁷Or lend drama to a statement. ⁸As Mark Twain said, "The right word may be effective, but no word was ever as effective a rightly timed pause." ⁹The most important factor is timing. ¹⁰Which Twain knew. ¹¹For one audience, the pause will be short. ¹²For another, a little longer. ¹³Developing a sense of timing is partly a matter of common sense, partly a matter of timing. ¹⁴Inexperienced speakers will not get their pauses just right at first. ¹⁵But should keep trying. ¹⁶They should listen to experienced speakers. ¹⁷To see how they use pauses.

Source: Adapted from Stephen E. Lucas, *The Art of Public Speaking,* 7th ed. (New York: McGraw-Hill) 2001, p. 291. Copyright © 2001 The McGraw-Hill Companies. Used by permission of The McGraw-Hill Companies.

6.9 CHAPTER REVIEW ACTIVITY

The following paragraph has seven fragments. First underline the fragments. Then make corrections above the line to eliminate the fragments.

EXAMPLE   Friendship is an important part of a child's socialization. <u>How a child socializes</u> ~~being~~ *is* <u>a function of his or her age.</u>

¹Even babies enjoy friendships. ²By the time they are one. ³Most children enjoy peekaboo and simple games with their peers. ⁴They enjoy social situations and sustained interaction. ⁵Many children even showing a clear preference for certain children. ⁶Two-year-old friends fighting over toys but also playing cooperatively with each other. ⁷By the time they are three, children use their friendships as bargaining tools. ⁸If they don't get what they want. ⁹They shout, "You're not my friend anymore." ¹⁰The age of three can be a stormy period for peer relationships. ¹¹By five, children recognize that friendship means more than playing together. ¹²Children at this age solve problems and make plans together. ¹³By eight, choice of friends depending on common interests and compatibility. ¹⁴Girls are likely to have one or two friends. ¹⁵Whereas boys are more likely to play in groups. ¹⁶In

addition, girls and boys resolve conflicts differently. [17]Boys argue about the rules. [18]However, they usually resolve the conflict. [19]And go on playing. [20]Girls tend to end the game. [21]By the time they are preteens, both sexes have developed skills for settling conflicts with a minimum of fuss. [22]As teenagers, however, young people enter a new period of turbulence. [23]As a result, friendships and alliances can shift.

6.10 CHAPTER REVIEW ACTIVITY

The following paragraphs have seven fragments. First underline the fragments. Then make corrections above the line to eliminate the fragments.

EXAMPLE   Some states have names with particular meaning. Some of them
are
~~being~~ very interesting.

[1]The names of most states have some kind of meaning. But not so for Idaho. [2]The name really is a form of gibberish. [3]The name *Idaho* was first popularized by mine owners. [4]Who thought it would be a good name for the Pikes Peak mining country. [5]The mine owners claimed that the word was Apache for "Comanche," who were the dominant tribe in the area. [6]The story was believed, and Congress was set to approve the name. [7]When it was discovered that *Idaho* meant nothing in Apache or any other language. [8]It was a hoax. [9]As a result, the area was named Colorado at the last minute.

[10]However, the name *Idaho* refusing to die. [11]The same year the name began cropping up in the Pacific Northwest. [12]Now it was said to derive from a Shoshone phrase. Meaning [13]"Behold the sun coming down on the mountains." [14]Others claimed it meant "gem of the mountains." [15]While still others said it meant "salmon eaters." [16]Despite the conflicting reports, a county in Washington Territory was officially named Idaho. [17]In 1863, one of the senators who had blocked the use of the name two years earlier now supported it. [18]Congress then going along with the name and dubbing the territory Idaho.

6.11 CHAPTER REVIEW ACTIVITY

The following paragraphs contain eight sentence fragments. First underline the fragments. Then make corrections above the line to eliminate the fragments.

[1]Lyme disease is a perplexing illness. [2]Caused by the bite of a bloodsucking tick the size of a pencil point. [3]The tick is so small that a child playing in the woods might not notice its bite. [4]Or its presence on his or her body.

[5]Lyme disease usually attacks the skin, heart, nervous system, and joints. [6]The symptoms are usually triggered by a red rash. [7]That appears near the site

of a tick bite. [8]The rash may appear from one to thirty-two days after the bite. [9]And last from two months to a year.

[10]Since early detection and treatment of this mysterious disease usually prevent major complications. [11]It is important to be alert to the symptoms of Lyme disease. [12]If untreated, it can cause chronic arthritis, heart problems, blindness, and even death. [13]As with most bacterial infections. Lyme disease is usually treated with antibiotics. [14]Most children recover quickly. [15]However, pregnant women must be particularly careful. [16]Because Lyme disease causes birth defects. [17]Still, there is no reason to panic. [18]Since the ticks that carry Lyme disease are relatively rare.

6.12 COLLABORATIVE CHAPTER REVIEW ACTIVITY

Find five sentence fragments. They can be ones you have written in items such as e-mails or to-do lists, or they can be ones you have seen somewhere, perhaps in advertisements or on street signs. Rewrite the fragments to make them sentences. Then exchange fragments with a classmate and rewrite the ones you are given to make them sentences. How are the sentences you wrote similar to the ones your classmate wrote? How are they different?

GETTING IN GEAR: IDEAS FOR WRITING

The photo shows portrait artist Gilbert Stuart's unfinished portrait of George Washington, which he began in 1796. It is this portrait that served as the model for Washington's likeness on the dollar bill. To learn about ten unfinished works of art, visit www.trivia-library.com/10-famous-unfinished-works-from-art-to-architecture/index.htm.

writing topic: Word groups are fragments because they are incomplete in some way—they lack subjects, parts or all of verbs, or sufficiently complete thought. That is, they are incomplete, just as the painting of Washington is incomplete. Write about a time when you experienced incompleteness. It might be a time you were unable to finish a job or complete a goal or say good-bye the way you wanted. Tell what happened and how you felt as a result.

suggestions for prewriting
- Look at the portrait and freewrite for ten minutes on the subject of incompleteness. How does the portrait make you feel? How does incompleteness in general make you feel? What events in your life are incomplete?
- For additional ideas, answer these questions: What happened? When did it happen? Why did it happen? How were you affected?

suggestions for drafting
- Your thesis or topic sentence (depending on whether you are writing an essay or a paragraph) can mention the event and indicate how the event made you feel or how it affected you.
- If you are telling a story about incompleteness, write your details in the order they occurred.

suggestions for revising: Write three questions that reflect revising concerns you have about your draft. Give your draft, along with those questions, to a reliable reader and ask that person to respond.

suggestions for editing: Edit one extra time, checking for sentence fragments. Linger over every word group you are calling a sentence and check for a subject, a complete verb, and a sufficiently complete thought.

RECHARGE: Lesson Summary

1. In order to be a **sentence**, a word group must have
   - a subject.
   - a complete verb.
   - sufficient completeness to stand independently.

   A word group lacking one of these elements is a **sentence fragment**, even if it begins with a capital letter and ends with a period.

2. To eliminate a fragment that results from a missing subject, add the subject or join the fragment to a sentence.

   Fragment: *I put the pasta on a high heat. And forgot about it for an hour.*
   Sentence: *I put the pasta on a high heat. I forgot about it for an hour.*
   Sentence: *I put the pasta on a high heat and forgot about it for an hour.*

3. To eliminate a fragment that results from a missing subject and verb, add the missing subject and verb or join the fragment to a sentence.

   Fragment: *The hybrid car is fuel efficient. Also environmentally friendly.*
   Sentence: *The hybrid car is fuel efficient. Also, it is environmentally friendly.*
   Sentence: *The hybrid car is fuel efficient and environmentally friendly.*

RECHARGE: Lesson Summary Continued

4. To eliminate a fragment that results from an incomplete verb, add a missing helping verb or change the verb form.

Fragment: *The expensive vase broken.*

Sentence: *The expensive vase is broken.*

Sentence: *The expensive vase broke.*

5. To eliminate a dependent clause fragment, join the fragment to a sentence.

Fragment: *Although the traffic is heavy. Everyone is traveling the speed limit.*

Sentence: *Although the traffic is heavy. everyone is traveling the speed limit.*

CHAPTER 7

Improving Sentences with Coordination

Which sentence do you like better, A or B?

A. The Berlin Wall once separated free Berlin from Communist Berlin. The wall fell in 1989.
B. The Berlin Wall once separated free Berlin from Communist Berlin, but the wall fell in 1989.

Most readers prefer B for two reasons. First, A sounds choppy; second, B shows how ideas relate to each other. Writers need ways to connect ideas both to avoid choppiness and to show how ideas relate to each other. This chapter will show you how to use *coordination* to achieve those goals.

RECOGNIZING INDEPENDENT CLAUSES

Any word group that can stand as a sentence is an **independent clause.**

Independent clause:	*the photographer checked the lighting*
Sentence:	*The photographer checked the lighting.*
Independent clause:	*the phone company raised its rates*
Sentence:	*The phone company raised its rates.*

A sentence can be made up of just one independent clause, like this:

Ringtones can personalize cell phones with snippets of music.

A sentence can also be made up of two or more independent clauses. The proper joining of two or more independent clauses in one sentence is called **coordination,** and the sentence created is a **compound sentence.** When you join independent clauses with coordination, the independent clauses are equal in importance. (Co- means "equal.")

Independent clause:	*ringtones can personalize cell phones with snippets of music*
Independent clause:	*you can choose different songs for different callers*

113

Compound sentence: *Ringtones can personalize cell phones with snippets of music, and you can choose different songs for different callers.*

Independent clause: *users can play bowling and poker on their cell phones*

Independent clause: *mobile versions of Tony Hawk Pro-Skater are also popular*

Compound sentence: *Users can play bowling and poker on their cell phones, but mobile versions of Tony Hawk Pro-Skater are also popular.*

Troubleshooting

If you need to review compound subjects and compound verbs, see pages 78 and 87.

GRAMMAR ALERT

Sentences with compound subjects or compound verbs, or both, are not necessarily made up of more than one independent clause.

The <u>daffodils</u> and the <u>crocuses</u> are already in bloom. [one independent clause with a compound subject]

The police officers <u>cleared</u> the area and <u>closed</u> the street. [one independent clause with a compound verb]

7.1 ACTIVITY

In the following sentences, place brackets around each independent clause. In the blank before each sentence, write the number of independent clauses in the sentence. (One of the sentences has only one independent clause.)

EXAMPLE _____2_____ [In a monopoly, there is only one seller for a product or service,] so [the price may rise.]

1. _____ In the United States, laws prohibit monopolies, but some monopolies were approved.

2. _____ The legal system did permit monopolies in public utilities, including gas, water, and electric power.

3. _____ Public utilities commissions monitored these monopolies, so the consumer was protected.

4. _____ Recently, legislation ended the monopoly status of utilities, so consumers can choose among utility providers.

5. _____ Some say the legislation will lead to fewer utility companies, and these companies will be larger.

JOINING INDEPENDENT CLAUSES WITH A COORDINATING CONJUNCTION

To achieve coordination, you can join independent clauses in the same sentence with one of the following:

, and , nor , so
, but , for , yet
, or

The words in the preceding list are **coordinating conjunctions.** Coordinating conjunctions join sentence elements of equal importance. (Remember, *co*-means "equal.") Coordinating conjunctions can be used with commas to join independent clauses.

Independent clause: *the band stopped playing at eleven*

Independent clause: *we danced until midnight*

Coordination: *The band stopped playing at eleven* ⟨ *, but* ⟩ *we danced until midnight.*

Be sure you use the coordinating conjunction that expresses the meaning you are after.

1. Use **, and** to show addition:

   The mechanic changed the oil ⟨ *, and* ⟩ *he rotated the tires.*

2. Use **, but** or **, yet** to show contrast:

   The bus was late ⟨ *, but* ⟩ *I made it to work on time.*
   The bus was late ⟨ *, yet* ⟩ *I made it to work on time.*

3. Use **, or** to show an alternative:

   You can come with me ⟨ *, or* ⟩ *you can wait here.*

4. Use **, nor** to give a negative alternative:

   The children may not see this movie ⟨ *, nor* ⟩ *may they watch cartoons.*

5. Use **, for** to mean "because":

   The southern town was paralyzed by the snowfall ⟨ *, for* ⟩ *it owned no snowplows.*

6. Use **, so** to mean "as a result":

   Class was canceled ⟨ *, so* ⟩ *I went to the library.*

> ➤ **GRAMMAR AND PUNCTUATION ALERT**
>
> A comma by itself *cannot* join independent clauses. A coordinating conjunction must be used with the comma.
>
> No: *The cars collided, there was no damage.*
> Yes: *The cars collided, but there was no damage.*

7.2 COLLABORATIVE ACTIVITY

Look through a book, magazine, or newspaper and copy five sentences that use a comma and a coordinating conjunction to join independent clauses. Underline the commas and coordinating conjunctions. Then trade sentences with a classmate. For each sentence, write an explanation of why the particular conjunction was used.

7.3 ACTIVITY

Using a comma and a logical coordinating conjunction, join each of the pairs of sentences to make one sentence.

EXAMPLE   Rowdy parents and coaches have too long disrupted children's athletic events.
It is past time that something was done.

Rowdy parents and coaches have too long disrupted children's athletic events, so (and) it is past time that something was done.

1. The people on the sidelines were silent one Sunday.
Thousands of parents had to obey a one-day noise ban instituted by the Northern Ohio Girls Soccer League.

   _____

   _____

2. Parents had to keep mum.
Coaches had to keep quiet.

   _____

   _____

3. Parents sucked hard on lollipops.
Some even put duct tape over their mouths.

   _____

   _____

4. Except for an occasional spontaneous cheer, most parents kept quiet.
They were still able to communicate their enthusiasm.

   _____

   _____

5. Parents let their homemade signs encourage the players.
They used hand and arm gestures to convey their emotion.

   _____

   _____

6. The players were allowed to encourage each other vocally.
No one else was permitted to do so.

   _____

   _____

7. The players had a great time.
   They could make decisions on their own without being questioned or yelled at.

   _____

   _____

8. The ban was a national first.
   It is unknown how popular it can be on a larger scale.

   _____

   _____

9. League officials do not plan to make silence a permanent policy.
   They are considering another day of silent games for 3,800 girls, aged eight to fourteen.

   _____

   _____

10. Some parents love the ban.
    Others dislike it intensely.

    _____

    _____

7.4 ACTIVITY

Fill in the blanks with independent clauses. Be sure your additions are complete enough that they can stand alone as sentences.

EXAMPLE   I left in plenty of time, but *I arrived late for the*
concert.

1. I carefully opened the closet door, and _____

   _____

2. Chris tried backing into the parking space, but _____

   _____

3. We can go to the movie at the Metro, or _____

   _____

4. Waldeen can no longer play tennis, for _____

   _____

5. Dr. Shaheen explained the assignment carefully, so _____

   _____

6. The program was funny, yet _____

   _____

7. I do not enjoy animated movies, nor _____

   _____

8. The new tornado alert system worked perfectly, so _____

_____

9. More research is being done online, but _____

_____

10. The heavy rains washed out the back roads, and _____

_____

7.5 ACTIVITY

On a separate sheet, compose five sentences, each with a different coordinating conjunction (*and, but, or, nor, for, so,* or *yet*). Be sure the conjunctions join independent clauses, and remember to use a comma before each conjunction.

JOINING INDEPENDENT CLAUSES WITH A CONJUNCTIVE ADVERB

Troubleshooting

The words in the conjunctive adverb list are only "conjunctive" when they are positioned between two independent clauses. In that case, they are used with the semicolon and comma. Other times, the words are ordinary adverbs and used without semicolons.

You can join independent clauses in the same sentence with one of the following:

; consequently,	; meanwhile,	; otherwise,
; furthermore,	; moreover,	; therefore,
; however,	; nevertheless,	; thus,
; instead,	; nonetheless,	

The words in this list are **conjunctive adverbs.** Conjunctive adverbs can be used with semicolons and commas to join independent clauses.

Independent clause:	*we ordered a pepperoni pizza*
Independent clause:	*meatball sandwiches were delivered*
Coordination:	*We ordered a pepperoni pizza; however, meatball sandwiches were delivered.*

Notice that the semicolon comes first, the conjunctive adverb comes second, and the comma comes third, to form this pattern:

; conjunctive adverb,
; therefore,
My back aches; therefore, I cannot lift anything.

Be sure you use the conjunctive adverb that expresses the meaning you are after.

1. Use ; however, ; nevertheless, or ; nonetheless, to show a contrast, as follows:

The Civil War is over [*; however,*] *some people will not forget it.*
The Civil War is over [*; nevertheless,*] *some people will not forget it.*
The Civil War is over [*; nonetheless,*] *some people will not forget it.*

2. Use ; furthermore, or ; moreover, to mean "in addition."

This car dealership offers a variety of models [*; furthermore,*] *it offers an excellent buyer-protection plan.*
This car dealership offers a variety of models [*; moreover,*] *it offers an excellent buyer-protection plan.*

3. Use <u>; therefore,</u> <u>; thus,</u> and <u>; consequently,</u> to mean "as a result."

   Daylight savings time begins tonight | *; therefore,* | *we lose an hour of sleep.*

   Daylight savings time begins tonight | *; thus,* | *we lose an hour of sleep.*

   Daylight savings time begins tonight | *; consequently,* | *we lose an hour of sleep.*

4. Use <u>; meanwhile,</u> to mean "at the same time."

   I left for Virginia at noon | *; meanwhile,* | *Alice was on her way to Ohio.*

5. Use <u>; otherwise,</u> to indicate an alternative.

   You must study your history notes | *; otherwise,* | *you will not pass the test.*

6. Use <u>; instead,</u> to mean "in place of."

   I did not sleep last night | *; instead,* | *I thought about all my problems.*

PUNCTUATION ALERT

Be sure to use a semicolon before and a comma after any conjunctive adverb that joins independent clauses.

No: *I gave Charlie the book, however, he had already read it.*

No: *I gave Charlie the book however he had already read it.*

No: *I gave Charlie the book however, he had already read it.*

Yes: *I gave Charlie the book; however, he had already read it.*

CONNECT FOR SUCCESS: Notice Conjunctions and Conjunctive Adverbs to Improve Comprehension

When you read your textbooks or other important material, notice the coordinating conjunctions and conjunctive adverbs. They will help you understand how ideas connect to each other by indicating relationships such as addition, similarity, and contrast. Noting these relationships will improve your reading comprehension.

7.6 ACTIVITY

Use a semicolon, a well-chosen conjunctive adverb, and a comma to join each pair of sentences into one sentence.

EXAMPLE   The Spanish came to the New World to find wealth. They were looking for conquest.

   The Spanish came to the New World to find wealth;

   moreover, they were looking for conquest.

1. Reports of vast wealth in the New World reached Spain.
   The world began to change almost immediately.

   _____

   _____

2. Hernán Cortés completed his conquest and destroyed the culture of Mexico between 1519 and 1522.
   The Aztec people, led by Montezuma, had hailed Cortés as a god.

   _____

   _____

   _____

3. The Aztecs were terrified by Cortés's cannon.
   They were frightened by his men's spirited horses.

   _____

   _____

4. Cortés destroyed the Aztec capital.
   He built the Spanish capital Mexico City in its place.

   _____

   _____

5. Cortés expected to find gold mines or cities built of gold.
   That did not happen.

   _____

   _____

6. Cortés and his men contented themselves with confiscating the treasures of the native people.
   They melted down the treasures to send home.

   _____

   _____

7. The Spanish ruled the vast territory from the Isthmus of Panama to beyond the Rio Grande.
   They ruled as far west as the Pacific.

   _____

   _____

8. About 1540, Spanish explorer Francisco Coronado marched north, looking for El Dorado, the fabled Seven Cities of Gold.
   He found a sparse scattering of adobe huts.

   _____

   _____

   _____

9. The adobe huts belonged to the Zuni people.
Coronado had to give up his quest.

_____

_____

10. The Spanish also created the first permanent settlement in the United States at St. Augustine, Florida.
The French were trying to get a foothold in Florida at the same time.

_____

_____

Source: Adapted from Wayne Craven, _American Art: History and Culture_ (New York: McGraw-Hill, 1994), p. 16. Copyright © 1994 The McGraw-Hill Companies. Used by permission of The McGraw-Hill Companies.

7.7 ACTIVITY

Fill in the blanks with independent clauses. Be sure your additions can stand as sentences.

EXAMPLE   Michael developed a stress fracture; therefore, _he was forced to quit the track team._

1. The stray dog looked harmless; however, _____

_____

2. My new car gets excellent gas mileage; nevertheless, _____

_____

3. You must turn off the electricity before installing the new ceiling fan; otherwise,_____

_____

4. Trash collectors remain on strike for the second week; meanwhile, _____

_____

5. Clifford has the highest grade point average in the class; furthermore, _____

_____

6. More than half of the student body has the flu; therefore, _____

_____

7. The spring rains have flooded the main roads; thus, _____

_____

8. Lee's car was damaged in an accident on Main Street; consequently, _____

_____

9. Americans are becoming more concerned about what they eat; moreover,

_____

10. You should not take Route 5; instead, _____

_____

7.8 ACTIVITY

On a separate sheet, write five sentences that use a semicolon, a conjunctive adverb, and a comma to join independent clauses. Try to use a different conjunctive adverb (*however, nevertheless, nonetheless, meanwhile, furthermore, therefore, thus, otherwise, consequently, moreover,* or *instead*) in each sentence.

JOINING INDEPENDENT CLAUSES WITH A SEMICOLON

You can use a semicolon to join independent clauses in the same sentence. Use this method of coordination when a conjunction is not needed to show the relationship between clauses.

Independent clause:	*some people like convertibles*
Independent clause:	*other people hate them*
Coordination:	*Some people like convertibles; other people hate them.*

PUNCTUATION ALERT

When you use a semicolon, be sure you have an independent clause on *both* sides.

No:	*The sun brightened my day; and raised my spirits.*
Explanation:	An independent clause appears before the semicolon but not after it.
Yes:	*The sun brightened my day and raised my spirits.*
Yes:	*The sun brightened my day; it raised my spirits.*

7.9 ACTIVITY

Add semicolons where they are needed to join two independent clauses. Remember, an independent clause must appear on both sides of the semicolon. (Two sentences do not need a semicolon, because they are correct as they are.)

EXAMPLE   The stock market is difficult to predict; people should not invest money they cannot afford to lose.

1. People try many crazy things to make money in the stock market most of them never work out.

2. I thought I had heard everything then I read about an investing yucca plant.

3. The plant was an investor on the Stockholm stock exchange it issued buy and sell orders on sixteen of the most active stocks.

4. Swedish artist Ola Pehrson attached electrodes to the plant sensors connected the plant to a computer.

5. The sensors charted the plant's growth the computer linked the growth to stock market performance.

6. When the yucca's stock recommendations performed better than the general stock index, the plant was given water and light.

7. Sometimes the plant failed to deliver profits then it stayed dry and in the dark.

8. The yucca was part of an exhibition by seven Swedish artists and not a serious investment scheme.

7.10 ACTIVITY

In each item, follow the independent clause with a semicolon and another independent clause. Be sure the words you add are complete enough to stand alone as a sentence.

EXAMPLE   I do not like to eat beef *; Margery does not like to eat chicken.*

1. I turned on the hot water _____

2. Some people have trouble telling the truth _____

3. We waited over an hour for Dave _____

4. The electricity went out at noon _____

5. The presidential candidate promised to bring jobs to our area _____

7.11 ACTIVITY

In each of the following sets, only two word groups are independent clauses. Decide which word groups are independent clauses. Circle those word groups, and then write a sentence using the circled independent clauses joined by a semicolon.

EXAMPLE   because we are concerned about emerging diseases caused by parasites
we are concerned about emerging diseases caused by parasites
these are diseases such as AIDS and ebola
although these are diseases such as AIDS and ebola

We are concerned about emerging diseases caused by parasites;

these are diseases such as AIDS and ebola.

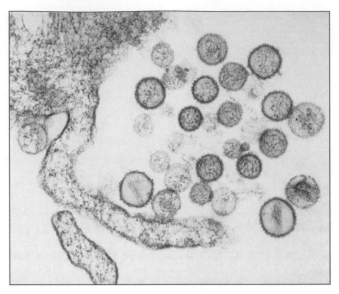

Virus viewed under a microscope.

1. when diseases emerge from their natural host
   emerging diseases emerge from their natural host
   they cause illness in humans
   when they cause illness in humans

   _____

   _____

2. the hantavirus strain emerged from the common deer mouse in 1993
   after the hantavirus strain emerged from the common deer mouse in 1993
   about sixty young people were killed in the Southwest
   since sixty young people were killed in the Southwest

   _____

   _____

3. because an unusually mild winter and wet spring caused piñon trees to
   bloom well
   whereas the trees provided more pine nuts to mice
   an unusually mild winter and wet spring caused piñon trees to bloom well
   the trees provided more pine nuts to mice

   _____

   _____

4. the increasing deer mouse population came in contact with humans
   as the increasing deer mouse population came in contact with humans
   the hantavirus leaped easily from mice to humans
   when the hantavirus leaped easily from mice to humans

   _____

   _____

5. global warming will likely upset normal weather cycles
   whereas global warming will likely upset normal weather cycles

since outbreaks of emerging diseases, including hantavirus, malaria, and cholera, will result

outbreaks of emerging diseases, such as hantavirus, malaria, and cholera, will result

_____

_____

6. the connection between global warming and emerging diseases is significant because the connection between global warming and emerging diseases is significant

steps to slow global warming should be taken

while steps to slow global warming should be taken

_____

_____

Source: Adapted from Sylvia S. Mader, *Biology,* 7th ed. (New York: McGraw-Hill, 2001), p. 109. Copyright © 2001 The McGraw-Hill Companies. Used by permission of The McGraw-Hill Companies.

 IF ENGLISH IS NOT YOUR FIRST LANGUAGE

1. The relationship between independent clauses is spelled out by the coordinating conjunction or conjunctive adverb you choose. To be sure you convey the desired relationship, consult the following chart of frequently used coordinating conjunctions and conjunctive adverbs.

Meaning	Coordinating Conjunction	Conjunctive Adverb
addition	, and	; furthermore,
		; moreover,
contrast	, but	; however,
	, yet	; nevertheless,
		; nonetheless
alternative	, or	; instead,
	, nor [negative]	; otherwise,
result	, so	; therefore,
		; consequently,
		; thus,
because	, for	

2. When *nor* connects independent clauses, the verb comes before the subject in the second clause.

          V S
I cannot go, nor do I want to.

                              V   S
The stove does not work, nor does the refrigerator.

7.12 CHAPTER REVIEW ACTIVITY

Join the two sentences into one, using the method of coordination indicated.

EXAMPLE   Use a comma and a coordinating conjunction:
America's early newspapers were funded by political parties.
The news they reported was partisan.

America's early newspapers were funded by political parties,

so the news they reported was partisan.

1. Use a semicolon:
America's early leaders were quick to recognize the importance of the press.
At Alexander Hamilton's urging, the *Gazette of the United States* was founded to promote the policies of George Washington's administration.

_____

_____

_____

2. Use a comma and a coordinating conjunction:
Hamilton was secretary of the treasury.
He supported the *Gazette of the United States* by granting it Treasury Department printing contracts.

_____

_____

3. Use a semicolon, a conjunctive adverb, and a comma:
Thomas Jefferson was secretary of state at the time.
He opposed the newspaper's politics.

_____

_____

4. Use a comma and a coordinating conjunction:
He arranged to start the *National Gazette* as an opposition newspaper.
He had to find a way to finance the paper.

_____

_____

5. Use a semicolon:
Jefferson found a way for the government to fund the paper.
He authorized it to print State Department documents.

_____

_____

6. Use a semicolon, a conjunctive adverb, and a comma:
Newspapers at the time were very expensive.
The cost of a copy was beyond the reach of ordinary citizens.

_____

_____

7. Use a comma and a coordinating conjunction:
Leading newspapers had fewer than 1,500 subscribers.
They could not have survived without political party support.

_____

_____

8. Use a semicolon, a conjunctive adverb, and a comma:
Not surprisingly, the "news" the papers printed was party propaganda.
The papers came to be called partisan press.

_____

_____

9. Use a semicolon:
President James K. Polk once persuaded a leading publisher to fire an editor.
The individual had been critical of Polk's policies.

_____

_____

10. Use a comma and a coordinating conjunction:
Technological changes eventually led to cheaper printing processes.
The partisan press gave way to self-supporting newspapers.

_____

_____

11. Use a semicolon, a conjunctive adverb, and a comma:
Cheaper papers increased circulation.
They did not lead to objective reporting.

_____

_____

12. Use a comma and a coordinating conjunction:
In the late nineteenth century, a form of sensationalism called yellow journalism became popular.
Eventually, objective reporting became the model.

_____

_____

Source: Adapted from Thomas E. Patterson, *We the People* (New York: McGraw-Hill, 2004), p. 305. Copyright © 2004 The McGraw-Hill Companies. Used by permission of The McGraw-Hill Companies.

7.13 CHAPTER REVIEW ACTIVITY

Read aloud the following paragraph, and you will notice how choppy it sounds. To eliminate this choppiness with coordination, rewrite the entire paragraph according to the directions given. Then read the revision and notice the improvement the coordination makes.

A. Join sentences 1 and 2 with a comma and *but*.
B. Join sentences 3 and 4 with a comma and *and*.
C. Join sentences 5 and 6 with a semicolon.

D.   Join sentences 7 and 8 with a semicolon, *furthermore,* and a comma.
E.   Join sentences 10 and 11 with a comma and *for.*
F.   Join sentences 12 and 13 with a comma and *yet.*

¹Most people know that the breakfast drink Tang resulted from space research. ²Few people know about other discoveries and inventions that came from space-related research. ³The Dustbuster got its start when Black and Decker was asked to develop cordless tools for sampling lunar soil. ⁴The heart-rate monitors on exercise machines were developed to keep track of astronauts' exertion levels. ⁵A particular kind of solar cell powers the $1.5 billion Hubble space telescope. ⁶It is the same kind of cell that powers a $5 calculator. ⁷The fabric used for Apollo space suits now covers the Georgia Dome in Atlanta. ⁸It covers airport terminals in Denver. ⁹Also, the Golden Gate Bridge and the Statue of Liberty are protected from corrosion by the same coatings that protect launch pads. ¹⁰The coating developed to protect plastic spacecraft parts has another application as well. ¹¹It is used as the scratch-resistant coating for plastic eyeglass lenses. ¹²Some people think that the space program has no practical applications. ¹³That is just not the case.

7.14 CHAPTER REVIEW ACTIVITY

Use the methods of coordination explained in this chapter to improve the following paragraph.

EXAMPLE   Walt Disney's movie studio played an important role in World War II*; however, people* ~~People~~ do not think of the studio as a patriotic institution.

¹Most people associate Walt Disney with Mickey Mouse, theme parks, and children's movies. ²Few people realize the role the Disney Studio played in World War II. ³ After the bombing of Pearl Harbor, the Lockheed aircraft plant in California had to be protected. ⁴Hundreds of U.S. soldiers took over the Disney Studio in Burbank, California. ⁵The soldiers lived and trained in the studio for eight months. ⁶Disney made other contributions to the war effort as well. ⁷The studio created hundreds of insignia for military units. ⁸From 1942–1943, Disney made many films for the U.S. government. ⁹A particularly notable film was *The New Spirit,* a cartoon that encouraged Americans to pay their income taxes to support the war economy. ¹⁰Americans understood that their government needed money to fight the war. ¹¹Many people still did not pay their taxes.

[12]Sixty million people saw *The New Spirit*. [13]After viewing the movie, 37 percent of them paid their taxes more willingly. [14]The next time you think of Disney, you can think of Mickey Mouse, Disneyland, and *The Lion King*. [15]You should also think of the contribution Disney Studio made to the war effort in the 1940s.

GETTING IN GEAR: IDEAS FOR WRITING

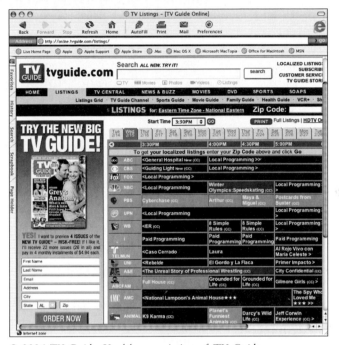

© 2006 *TV Guide*. Used by permission of *TV Guide*.

The screenshot from the *TV Guide* website gives one evening's programming. Some of the programs are wildly popular, some attract a modest following, and some are doomed to cancelation. Unfortunately for the network and cable programmers, it is impossible to be sure which programs will be popular. To read more about current programs and those from the past, you can visit *TV Guide*'s site at www.tvguide.com.

writing topic: Write about a television program that is currently popular or that was popular at one time. Try to explain why the program is or was so popular. As an alternative, try to explain the popularity of a particular entertainer.

suggestions for prewriting
- For a program to write about, consider the programs on the *TV Guide* web site or look at the programs listed in *TV Guide* or your local newspaper's television section.
- Watch one or more episodes of the program and take notes as you do.

suggestions for drafting
- Your thesis or topic sentence (depending on whether you are writing an essay or a paragraph) can mention the program and indicate either how popular it is or with whom it is popular.

- Before drafting, write an informal outline that lists the reasons for the program's popularity from least to most significant. (Informal outlines are explained on page 28.)

suggestion for revising
- Read your draft aloud. If you hear any choppiness, revise some sentences to include coordination.

suggestion for editing
- Edit one extra time to be sure you have used commas and semicolons according to the rules given in this chapter.

RECHARGE: Lesson Summary

Coordination is the correct joining of two or more **independent clauses** in the same sentence. There are three methods of coordination. Each is illustrated with these independent clauses:

Independent clause: *Congress passed a trade bill*
Independent clause: *the president vetoed it*

- Join the independent clauses with a comma and **coordinating conjunction.**
  Coordination: *Congress passed a trade bill, but the president vetoed it.*
- Join the independent clauses with a semicolon, **conjunctive adverb,** and comma.
  Coordination: *Congress passed a trade bill; however, the president vetoed it.*
- Join the independent clauses with a semicolon.
  Coordination: *Congress passed a trade bill; the president vetoed it.*

CHAPTER 8

Improving Sentences with Subordination

CHAPTER GOALS

By the end of this chapter, you will learn to

Recognize dependent clauses

Join dependent clauses to independent clauses two ways

In Chapter 7, you learned how to use coordination to eliminate choppiness and show how ideas relate to each other. This chapter will show you a second way to achieve those goals—by using *subordination*.

RECOGNIZING DEPENDENT CLAUSES

You learned in Chapter 7 that a word group with a subject and verb that can stand as a sentence is an **independent clause.**

Troubleshooting

If you need to review independent clauses, see page 113. If you need to review dependent clauses, see page 103.

> Independent clause: *the first clock was a sundial*
>
> Sentence: *The first clock was a sundial.*

You learned in Chapter 6 that a word group with a subject and verb that *cannot* stand as a sentence because it lacks a complete enough thought is a **dependent clause.** If you read a dependent clause like the following ones aloud, you can hear the lack of completeness.

> Dependent clause: *when the whistle blew*
>
> Dependent clause: *after the music stopped*
>
> Dependent clause: *since the first clock was a sundial*

Did you find yourself asking "What?" or "What then?" That's because the word groups are incomplete. Dependent clauses cannot stand as sentences.

A sentence *can*, however, be made up of a dependent clause that is attached to an independent clause. The proper joining of a dependent and an independent clause is called **subordination**, and the sentence created is a **complex sentence.** When you use subordination to join an independent clause and a dependent clause, the dependent clause gets less emphasis than the independent clause. (*Sub-* means "below.") Therefore, you should place the idea you consider more important in the independent clause.

> Dependent clause: *when Congress considered extending daylight savings time*
>
> Independent clause: *the airline industry complained.*

Complex sentence: *When Congress considered extending daylight savings time, the airline industry complained.*

Dependent clause: *after he spoke a profanity on the air*
Independent clause: *the newscaster was suspended indefinitely*
Complex sentence: *The newscaster was suspended indefinitely after he spoke a profanity on the air.*

8.1 ACTIVITY

All the following word groups are clauses because they have subjects and verbs. If the word group is an independent clause because it can stand as a sentence, write IC on the blank. If it is a dependent clause because it lacks the completeness to stand as a sentence, write DC on the blank. If you are unsure, read the clause aloud to listen for completeness.

EXAMPLES   _____*IC*_____ Cherrapunji, in India, holds the record for the most rain in one month.

_____*DC*_____ When it got 30.5 feet of rain in July 1861.

1. _____ Cherrapunji also had the most rain in one year.

2. _____ When it received an astounding 86.8 feet in 1861.

3. _____ Cherrapunji earned the title of the wettest place on earth.

4. _____ Although Mount Waiale'ale in Hawaii has the most rainy days a year, a whopping 350.

5. _____ On the other hand, the Atacama Desert in northern Chile is considered the driest place on earth.

6. _____ Since it holds the record for going the longest without rainfall.

7. _____ In 1971, the first rain for 400 years fell on the Atacama Desert.

8. _____ The hottest place on earth is Al'Aziziyah in the Sahara Desert.

9. _____ Where a shade temperature of 58 degrees centigrade is recorded.

10. _____ Even though Death Valley, here in the United States, has come close to that temperature.

JOINING INDEPENDENT AND DEPENDENT CLAUSES WITH A SUBORDINATING CONJUNCTION

Many dependent clauses begin with one of the following words, which are called **subordinating conjunctions.**

after	because	until
although	before	when
as	even though	whenever
as if	if	where
as long as	since	whereas
as soon as	though	wherever
as though	unless	whether
		while

Dependent clause:	*before you go*
Subordinating conjunction:	*before*
Dependent clause:	*whenever the humidity is high*
Subordinating conjunction:	*whenever*
Dependent clause:	*as soon as dinner is over*
Subordinating conjunction:	*as soon as*

You can make an independent clause a dependent clause if you add a subordinating conjunction.

Independent clause:	*my back hurts*
Dependent clause:	*because my back hurts*
Subordinating conjunction:	*because*
Independent clause:	*the rain finally stopped*
Dependent clause:	*after the rain finally stopped*
Subordinating conjunction:	*after*
Independent clause:	*Charlie sings the blues*
Dependent clause:	*whenever Charlie sings the blues*
Subordinating conjunction:	*whenever*

➤ GRAMMAR ALERT

Some words can be subordinating conjunctions in some sentences and prepositions (words that show how things relate in time or space) in other sentences.

Subordinating conjunction:	*I never understood Shakespeare's language <u>until</u> I read it aloud.*
Preposition:	*The new supermarket will not open <u>until</u> Tuesday.*

To achieve subordination, you join an independent clause and a dependent clause that begins with a subordinating conjunction. The dependent clause with the subordinating conjunction will be emphasized less than the independent clause. (Remember, *sub-* means "below.") The dependent clause can come either before or after the independent clause.

Independent clause:	*we could not sleep*
Dependent clause:	*because the radio was blaring*
Subordination:	*We could not sleep because the radio was blaring.*
Subordination:	*Because the radio was blaring, we could not sleep.*

Independent clause: *Jan gets a headache*

Dependent clause: *when the humidity is high*

Subordination: *Jan gets a headache when the humidity is high.*

Subordination: *When the humidity is high, Jan gets a headache.*

PUNCTUATION ALERT

Place a comma after a dependent clause that comes at the beginning of a sentence.

Comma: *If I were you, I would go.*

Explanation: The comma comes after the opening dependent clause.

8.2 ACTIVITY

Fill in the blank in each sentence with a logical subordinating conjunction. (See the list of subordinating conjunctions on page 133 for possibilities.) Then underline each independent clause and place brackets around each dependent clause.

EXAMPLE   *[When* Harvard's football team played Carlisle Institute's team in 1908,] the coaches of both teams used sneaky tactics.

1. The coach of Harvard was Percy Haughton, _____ the coach of Carlisle was "Pop" Warner.

2. Warner had used a sneaky trick _____ he played Syracuse the week before.

3. _____ he wanted to outsmart Syracuse, Warner had pads sewn into his players' jerseys.

4. _____ the pads were the same size, shape, and color as a football, the opposing team had trouble determining which player had the ball.

5. Warner got away with his scheme _____ the pads were not against the rules.

6. _____ he knew Warner would try the trick again, Coach Haughton devised his own strategy.

7. _____ Warner and Haughton met on the field to pick the game football, Warner reached into his bag and pulled one out.

8. He had dyed all the footballs red, to match his team's jerseys _____ the game was to begin.

9. _____ they had remarkable vision or supernatural powers, Carlisle's players would not be able to tell who had the ball.

10. _____ it was not against the rules, the red balls gave Harvard an unfair advantage, allowing them to win.

8.3 ACTIVITY

The following sentences are made up of one independent clause and one dependent clause. Sometimes the dependent clause comes first, and sometimes the independent clause comes first.

A. Underline the independent clause once.
B. Underline the dependent clause twice.
C. Circle the subordinating conjunction that begins the dependent clause.
D. Notice that opening dependent clauses are followed by commas.

EXAMPLE   If you think Chef Boyardee is a fictitious character associated with spaghetti, you are wrong.

1. There really is a Chef Boyardee, even though his name is not spelled the same.

2. When he was only seventeen, Hector Boiardi came to the United States from Italy.

3. He soon got a job as a chef at the prestigious Plaza Hotel in New York City, where his brother worked as a waiter.

4. After Boiardi moved to Cleveland, he developed a recipe for spaghetti and meatballs.

5. Boiardi opened his own restaurant while he was in Cleveland.

6. Because his pasta sauce was so good, customers would ask for bottles of it to take home.

7. Since his sauce was so popular, Boiardi moved into full-time pasta making.

8. He adopted the name "Boyardee" because it was easier for Americans to spell.

9. As soon as he sold his pasta and sauce business to International Home Foods, Boiardi became a consultant to the company.

10. In fact, the chef worked as an advisor to International Home Foods until his death in 1985 at the age of eighty-seven.

8.4 ACTIVITY

Join each pair of sentences into one sentence by changing one of the independent clauses to a dependent clause beginning with a subordinating conjunction (see the list on page 133). First write the sentence with the dependent clause placed first. Next rewrite the sentence with the dependent clause placed last. Remember to use a comma after an opening dependent clause. (Sentence 2 can be written only with the dependent clause last.)

EXAMPLE   Most of the world drives on the right side of the road.
A quarter of the world's countries drive on the left.

Although a quarter of the world's countries drive on the left,

most of the world drives on the right side of the road.

Most of the world drives on the right side of the road, although

a quarter of the world's countries drive on the left.

1. So many countries still drive on the left.
    There must be a logical explanation for the practice.

    _____

    _____

    _____

    _____

2. The practice of driving on the left can be traced back to feudal England.
    Most knights were right-handed and carried their lances under their right arms.

    _____

    _____

    _____

    _____

3. The knights naturally wanted to protect themselves.
    They cautiously traveled on the left to keep their sword arm on the right
    between themselves and strangers they passed.

    _____

    _____

    _____

    _____

4. Up to the late 1700s, everybody traveled on the left.
    It was the sensible option for feudal, violent societies.

    _____

    _____

    _____

    _____

Troubleshooting

Read your writing out
loud. If it sounds choppy
or singsongy, try adding
some sentences with sub-
ordination and some with
coordination to achieve a
more pleasing style.

5. The drive-on-the-right policy was adopted by the United States.
    The country was eager to cast off all ties with its British colonial past.

    _____

    _____

    _____

    _____

8.5 ACTIVITY

On a separate sheet, write six sentences that join dependent and independent
clauses. Three of the sentences should have the dependent clause at the beginning,
and three should have the dependent clause at the end. Remember to place a
comma after an opening dependent clause.

8.6 COLLABORATIVE ACTIVITY

Find five sentences with subordination in newspapers, magazines, or textbooks. Copy the sentences and underline each independent clause once and each dependent clause twice. Then circle the subordinating conjunctions. Trade sentences with a classmate. For each sentence you receive, explain whether it would be possible to express the same ideas without using dependent clauses. If so, indicate what changes would have to be made.

JOINING INDEPENDENT AND DEPENDENT CLAUSES WITH A RELATIVE PRONOUN

A particular kind of dependent clause begins with one of the following words, which are called **relative** *pronouns.*

who whose which sthat

A dependent clause that begins with one of these relative pronouns is called a **relative clause.**

Relative clauses can be joined with independent clauses to form sentences:

Sentence:	*Anita, who is my best friend, got the highest grade on the algebra test.*
Independent clause:	*Anita got the highest grade on the algebra test*
Relative clause:	*who is my best friend*
Relative pronoun:	*who*
Sentence:	*The man whose car is stalled has called the automobile club.*
Independent clause:	*the man has called the automobile club*
Relative clause:	*whose car is stalled*
Relative pronoun:	*whose*
Sentence:	*The question, which I do not understand, is worth 10 points.*
Independent clause:	*the question is worth 10 points*
Relative clause:	*which I do not understand*
Relative pronoun:	*which*
Sentence:	*The sweater that I gave you is all wool.*
Independent clause:	*the sweater is all wool*
Relative clause:	*that I gave you*
Relative pronoun:	*that*

 GRAMMAR ALERT

Who and *whose* refer to people. *Which* refers to things and animals. *That* refers to people and things.

No: *He is the person <u>which</u> gave me the letter.*

Yes: *He is the person <u>who</u> gave me the letter.*

A relative clause can appear in the middle of or at the end of the independent clause.

Relative clause
in the middle: *The woman <u>who is running for mayor</u> is currently a teacher.*

Relative clause
at the end: *This is the painting <u>that I want to buy</u>.*

There are two kinds of relative clauses. The first kind is necessary for identifying who or what is referred to:

The child who lives across the street is adorable. [*Who lives across the street* is necessary for identifying which child is adorable. Without the clause, we do not know which child is being referred to.]

The second kind of relative clause is *not* necessary for identifying who or what is referred to:

Kelly O'Hara, who lives across the street, is adorable. [The person is identified by her name, so *who lives across the street* is not necessary for identifying who is being referred to.]

Troubleshooting

To check whether a clause is necessary or not, try dropping it out of the sentence. What's lost? Is the person or thing referred to still clearly identified?

PUNCTUATION ALERT

How you punctuate a relative clause depends on whether or not the clause is necessary for identifying who or what is referred to. If the clause is *not* necessary for identification, set it off with commas. If it *is* necessary for identification, do not use commas.

Necessary for
identification: *The person who studies hard will get good grades.*

Unnecessary for
identification: *My roommate, who studies hard, will get good grades.*

8.7 ACTIVITY

Underline the relative clause in each of the following sentences, and circle the relative pronoun.

EXAMPLE This is the dog (that) bit Mohan yesterday.

1. I am the one who told you the truth.
2. I spoke to Frank, who helped me solve the problem.
3. This side of town, which is very old, is being restored.
4. A restaurant that has high prices will not survive in a college town.
5. Gregory, who hurt his back, had to give up track.
6. Carlotta, whose poetry has been published in local anthologies, is very talented.

7. The board of education voted to close South High School, which is the oldest high school in the city.

8. This is the store that has so many good bargains.

9. The child whose dog was lost cried all night.

10. The person who gave me directions was very polite.

8.8 ACTIVITY

Join each pair of sentences into one sentence by changing the second sentence to a relative clause beginning with *who, whose, which,* or *that*. You will need to eliminate one or more words in the second sentence. Remember that *who* and *whose* refer to people, *which* refers to things and animals, and *that* refers to people and things. Also remember that clauses not necessary for identification are set off with commas.

EXAMPLE Benjamin Franklin is responsible for an astonishing number of inventions and discoveries.
Benjamin Franklin did not have a great deal of formal schooling.

Benjamin Franklin, who did not have a great deal of formal schooling, is responsible for an astonishing number of inventions and discoveries.

1. Benjamin Franklin can be credited with many inventions and discoveries His inventions had a lasting influence on science.

   _____ _____

   _____

2. Franklin discovered the nature of electricity.
   The discovery of the nature of electricity is the discovery he is best known for.

   _____

   _____

3. Franklin invented bulkheads to make ocean voyages safer.
   The bulkheads were watertight.

   _____

   _____

4. He invented the Franklin stove.
   The stove allowed people to heat their homes safely with less wood.

   _____

   _____

5. Franklin created the first pair of bifocals.
   Franklin had poor eyesight.

   _____

   _____

6. Franklin never stopped trying to help others.
   Franklin's helpful inventions include the volunteer fire department and fire insurance.

   _____

   _____

7. Franklin also came up with the idea of daylight savings time.
   Franklin believed people should use daylight productively.

   _____

   _____

8. Franklin created the first political cartoon.
   The cartoon combined his wit with his political beliefs.

   _____

   _____

9. As postmaster, he invented the odometer.
   The odometer kept track of the distance of postal routes.

   _____

   _____

10. Benjamin Franklin was one of the most creative and prolific Americans. Franklin's inventions and discoveries also include swim fins, the catheter, and the charting of the Gulf Stream.

_____

_____

8.9 ACTIVITY

Add a relative pronoun to the following sentences, being sure to use commas correctly. Remember, *who* and *whose* refer to people; *which* refers to things and animals; *that* refers to people and things.

EXAMPLE   Inez ‸ _who_____ loves milk‸ is allergic to dairy products.

1. This is the restaurant _____ features vegetarian meals.

2. Cigarette smoking _____ causes heart and lung disease is banned in all state government buildings.

3. Joseph _____ short stories regularly appear in the school literary magazine hopes to become a journalist.

4. Lillian _____ has a wacky sense of humor can always cheer me up.

5. Officer Stein is the police officer _____ rescued two people from a burning car.

8.10 ACTIVITY

On a separate sheet, write five sentences with relative clauses. Remember to use commas to set off clauses unnecessary for identifying who or what is referred to.

CONNECT FOR SUCCESS: Notice Subordinating Conjunctions to Improve Comprehension

When you read your textbooks and other important material, notice the subordinating conjunctions. They will help you understand how ideas connect to each other by indicating relationships such as time, cause, and contrast. Noting these relationships will improve your reading comprehension.

IF ENGLISH IS NOT YOUR FIRST LANGUAGE

1. The relationship between an independent clause and a dependent clause is made clear by the subordinating conjunction you choose. To be sure you convey the desired relationship, consult the following chart of frequently used subordinating conjunctions.

IF ENGLISH IS NOT YOUR FIRST LANGUAGE CONTINUED

Relationship	Subordinating Conjunction
time	after, as soon as, before, until, when, whenever, while
cause	as, because, since
condition	if, unless, as long as
contrast	although, even though, though
location	where, wherever
choice	whether

Notice how the underlined subordinating conjunction changes the relationship between the clauses in the following examples:

<u>When</u> I am on a diet, I cannot eat sugar. [time]

<u>Because</u> I am on a diet, I cannot eat sugar. [cause]

If I am on a diet, I cannot eat sugar. [condition]

2. When a relative clause comes in the middle of the sentence, do not use a pronoun to repeat the subject of the independent clause.

No: *My sister, who is getting married this weekend, <u>she</u> is very nervous.*

Yes: *My sister, who is getting married this weekend, is very nervous.*

8.11 CHAPTER REVIEW ACTIVITY

Join each pair of sentences into one sentence, according to the directions given.

EXAMPLE   Make the second sentence a dependent clause and place it at the end of the first sentence:
Insects have been present for about 350 million years.
Humans have been around for only 10,000 years.

<u>Insects have been present for about 350 million years,</u>

<u>whereas humans have been around for only 10,000 years.</u>

1. Make the first sentence a dependent clause and place it at the beginning of the second sentence:
Ants are small.
They can lift and carry more than fifty times their own weight.

_____

_____

2. Make the first sentence a dependent clause and place it at the beginning of the second sentence:
Monarch butterflies are very light.
It takes about 100 of them to weigh an ounce.

_____

_____

3. Make the second sentence a relative clause and join it to the first sentence:
Houseflies find sugar with their feet.
Their feet are 10 million times more sensitive than human tongues.

_____

_____

4. Make the second sentence a relative clause and join it to the first sentence:
To survive the cold of winter months, many insects replace their body water with a chemical called glycerol.
Glycerol acts as an antifreeze.

_____

_____

5. Make the first sentence a dependent clause and place it before the second sentence:
The droppings of millions of cattle started ruining the land in Australia.
Dung beetles were imported to reduce the problem.

_____

_____

6. Make the second sentence a relative clause and join it to the first sentence after _mosquitoes:_
Male mosquitoes do not bite humans.
Male mosquitoes live on plant juices and other natural liquids.

_____

_____

7. Make the first sentence a dependent clause and place it after the second sentence:
A newly married couple was provided with enough honey wine to last for a month.
The term _honeymoon_ comes from the Middle Ages.

_____

_____

8. Make the second sentence a relative clause and join it to the first sentence after _Wasps:_
Wasps have been known to get "drunk" and pass out.
Wasps feed on fermenting juice.

_____

_____

9. Make the first sentence a dependent clause and place it at the beginning of the second sentence:
Honeybees make about 10 million trips to collect enough nectar for production of one pound of honey.
They can be considered a very determined species.

_____

_____

10. Make the second sentence a relative clause and join it to the first sentence after *beans:*
Mexican jumping beans actually have a caterpillar of a bean moth inside.
Mexican jumping beans are sometimes sold commercially.

_____

_____

8.12 CHAPTER REVIEW ACTIVITY

Read aloud the following paragraph and notice how choppy it sounds. To eliminate this choppiness with subordination, rewrite the paragraph according to the directions given. Then read the revision and notice the improvement that subordination makes. Remember to use commas after opening dependent clauses and to set off relative clauses unnecessary for identification.

A. Make sentence 2 a relative clause and join it to sentence 1, after *Drew.*
B. Make sentence 4 a dependent clause beginning with *where,* and join it to the end of sentence 3.
C. Make sentence 6 a dependent clause beginning with *until,* and join it to the end of sentence 5.
D. Make sentence 8 a dependent clause beginning with *after,* and join it to the beginning of sentence 9.
E. Make sentence 12 a relative clause and join it to sentence 13 after *Drew.*
F. Make sentence 15 a dependent clause beginning with *where,* and join it to the end of sentence 14.

[1]Charles Drew grew up in a poor family in a Washington, DC, ghetto. [2]He discovered the modern processes for preserving blood for transfusions. [3]His intelligence and athletic skill won him a scholarship to Amherst College. [4]He was captain of the track team, starting halfback on the football team, and an honors student. [5]After graduation, Drew taught and coached at Morgan College in Baltimore. [6]He earned enough money to go to the medical school at McGill University in Montreal. [7]There he became increasingly interested in the general field of medical research and in the specific problems of blood transfusion. [8]He graduated from McGill in 1932. [9]He eventually joined the faculty of Howard University and was appointed the head of surgery. [10]During World War II, he was appointed head of the National Blood Bank program. [11]At the time, the official government policy mandated that whites' and African Americans' blood be given only to members of their respective races. [12]Drew became furious with the official government policy. [13]Drew resigned from his post and returned to Howard University. [14]In 1944, he became chief of surgery at Freedman's Hospital, in Washington, DC. [15]His presence encouraged young African Americans to enter medicine. [16]Drew died in a car crash in 1950.

8.13 CHAPTER REVIEW ACTIVITY

On a separate sheet, revise the following paragraph using the methods of subordination explained in this chapter.

; created by a damaged coil in an oxygen tank

EXAMPLE   An explosion on *Apollo 13* created a harrowing situation. ~~The explosion was caused by a damaged coil in an oxygen tank.~~

¹In 1970, *Apollo 13* experienced an explosion in one of its oxygen tanks. ²Apollo 13 was in flight toward the moon. ³Astronauts Jim Lovell, Jack Swigert, and Fred Haise heard a loud bang. ⁴They noticed their oxygen tank was empty. ⁵The astronauts reported to Mission Control, "OK, Houston, we've had a problem." ⁶That transmission was an understatement. ⁷What followed was an incredibly tense drama. ⁸The crew moved into the small lunar module. ⁹The Lunar Module was designed to keep two men alive for only two days. ¹⁰However, the astronauts were four days from earth. ¹¹NASA engineers worked furiously to get the crew back safely. ¹²They devised a number of strategies, including lowering the temperature to 38 degrees Fahrenheit to conserve oxygen and electricity. ¹³The module splashed down in the Pacific, just slightly before oxygen failure. ¹⁴The world watched and waited during splashdown. ¹⁵The mission could have been a complete disaster. ¹⁶All three astronauts survived the mission. ¹⁷*Apollo 13* never reached its destination, but it made it back to earth safely.

GETTING IN GEAR: IDEAS FOR WRITING

This photograph of a member of the Himba people of Namibia. You can visit this Web site maintained by the Institute of Cognitive Neuroscience in Britain: www.icn.ucl.ac.uk/Experimental-Techniques/Cross-cultural-studies/cross-cultural.htm. There you will learn about the institute's study of the Himba and its other cross-cultural research into how cultures differ.

writing topic: Explain one aspect of your culture for a person who knows little about it. For example, you could explain how Thanksgiving is celebrated, how online dating works, or what "hanging out" is.

suggestions for prewriting

- For topic ideas, talk to an international student on your campus or someone in your community who has recently arrived from another country. Ask that person what he or she would like to better understand about our culture. (If you are an international student, ask an American student what he or she would like to learn about your culture.)
- If you are writing a paragraph, develop an informal outline (see page 28). If you are writing an essay, complete an outline map (see page 63).

suggestion for drafting: Your thesis or topic sentence (depending on whether you are writing an essay or a paragraph) can mention your topic and why it is interesting or important, something like this: *In the United States, Instant Messaging is the primary means of communication among young people.*

suggestion for revising: Read your draft aloud. If you hear any choppiness, revise some sentences to include subordination.

suggestions for editing

- If you have a tendency to write sentence fragments, look for dependent clauses punctuated as sentences, and connect these to independent clauses to achieve subordination.
- Edit one extra time to be sure you have used commas and semicolons according to the rules given in this chapter.

RECHARGE: Lesson Summary

1. **Subordination** is the correct joining of an **independent clause** and a **dependent clause** in the same **complex sentence**.

Independent clause:	*we will not have our grades until next week*
Dependent clause:	*because the computer is down*
Complex sentence:	*We will not have our grades until next week because the computer is down.*
Complex sentence:	*Because the computer is down, we will not have our grades until next week.*

2. In the first method of subordination, the dependent clause begins with a **subordinating conjunction**.

   <u>When</u> the crocuses bloom, I know it is spring.
   Asbestos must be removed from the structure before renovations begin.

RECHARGE: Lesson Summary Continued

Place a comma after a dependent clause that comes at the beginning of a sentence.

If you leave on vacation, you should unplug the appliances.

3. In the second method of subordination, a dependent clause called a **relative clause** begins with a **relative pronoun** (*who, whose, which, that*) and is joined with an independent clause.

The car, which has a hundred thousand miles on it, needs new tires.

If the relative clause is necessary for identifying who or what is referred to, do not set it off with commas.

The firefighter who saved the child was honored by the press.

If the relative clause is not necessary for identifying who or what is referred to, set it off with commas.

The captain of the firefighters, who saved the child, was honored by the press.

CHAPTER GOALS

By the end of this chapter, you will learn to

Recognize run-on sentences and comma splices

Find run-on sentences and comma splices in your own writing

Eliminate run-on sentences and comma splices from your writing

Troubleshooting

If you need to review independent clauses, see page 113.

CHAPTER 9

Eliminating Run-On Sentences and Comma Splices

Run-on sentences and *comma splices* occur when independent clauses are not properly separated. This chapter will help you avoid these sentence errors.

RECOGNIZING RUN-ON SENTENCES AND COMMA SPLICES

A word group that can stand as a sentence is an **independent clause.**

Independent clause:	*your library books are overdue*
Sentence:	*Your library books are overdue.*
Independent clause:	*you must pay a fine*
Sentence:	*You must pay a fine.*

A **run-on sentence** is a problem that occurs when two independent clauses are not correctly separated.

Independent clause:	*your library books are overdue*
Independent clause:	*you must pay a fine*
Run-on:	*Your library books are overdue you must pay a fine.*
Independent clause:	*a truck overturned on the turnpike*
Independent clause:	*the right lane is closed for 10 miles*
Run-on:	*A truck overturned on the turnpike the right lane is closed for 10 miles.*

A **comma splice** is a problem that occurs when independent clauses are separated only by a comma.

Independent clause:	*your library books are overdue*
Independent clause:	*you must pay a fine*
Comma splice:	*Your library books are overdue, you must pay a fine.* [A comma separates the independent clauses.]

148

Independent clause: *a truck overturned on the turnpike*
Independent clause: *the right lane is closed for 10 miles*
Comma splice: *A truck overturned on the turnpike, the right lane is closed for 10 miles.*

9.1 ACTIVITY

If the word group is a run-on sentence because there is no separation between independent clauses, write RO on the blank; if it is a comma splice because only a comma separates the independent clauses, write CS on the blank; if it is correct, write C on the blank.

EXAMPLES   *RO* _____ Musical taste is shaped by our environment we tend to like music familiar to us.

CS _____ Familiar music can delight us, music from other cultures can seem strange.

1. _____ Music plays an important role in developed countries throughout the world, it plays an equally important role in underdeveloped societies.

2. _____ Music in non-Western cultures can have a value as profound as in Western culture such music may be as involved and cultivated as Western music.

3. _____ Music exists in other cultures for a wide variety of reasons, frequently for reasons that are not common to our own experience.

4. _____ Any culture or nation has its regional variations, its music would reflect these variations in stylistic diversity.

5. _____ Music in other cultures may sound unfamiliar to our Western ears people in different parts of the world enjoy different melodies and rhythms.

6. _____ Popular music in all cultures is influenced by traditional songs and dances and environmental factors present from birth.

Source: Adapted from David Willoughby, *The World of Music*, 4th ed. (New York: McGraw-Hill, 1999), p. 145. Copyright © 1999 The McGraw-Hill Companies. Used by permission of The McGraw-Hill Companies.

CORRECTING RUN-ONS AND COMMA SPLICES WITH A PERIOD AND CAPITAL LETTER

To correct run-on sentences and commas splices, you can use a period and a capital letter to make each independent clause a separate sentence.

Run-on: *Bilal was a camp counselor last summer he enjoyed working with young children.*
Correction: *Bilal was a camp counselor last summer. He enjoyed working with young children.*

Troubleshooting

Do not think in terms of long and short. Something very short can be a run-on or comma splice: "We left they didn't." Something long can be correct: "Peter, one of the most dynamic characters in the novel, demonstrates his complexity in the way he handles power and in the surprising way he expresses compassion at unexpected moments."

Comma splice:	*Alligators are not picky eaters, they eat turtles with the shells on.*
Correction:	*Alligators are not picky eaters. They eat turtles with the shells on.*

9.2 ACTIVITY

Use periods and capital letters to eliminate the run-on sentences and comma splices. Some sentences are correct as they are. The first one is done as an example, so you must find and correct five errors.

[1]The author of *The Cat in the Hat* is known as Dr. Seuss, Theodor Geisel was the author's real name. [2]Theodor Geisel wrote many children's books he wrote using the name Dr. Seuss. [3]Seuss was actually Geisel's middle name he began using the name in college. [4]*The Cat in the Hat* is Geisel's most famous book it was written in response to a 1957 report about children struggling to read. [5]The report said that children responded to illustrations. they also retained more from "fun" books. [6]A publisher hired Geisel to write a book from a list of 220 words. [7]When Geisel realized that the words *cat* and *hat* on the list rhymed, he built a story around them. [8]He spent nine months writing the story, and it has been a favorite with children ever since. [9]Another favorite Geisel book is *Yertl the Turtle*. this book was based on Adolf Hitler. [10]*Marvin K. Mooney, Will You Please Go Away Now?* is based on another historical figure, former President Richard Nixon. [11]It might be interesting to learn on what other people Geisel based his humorous characters.

CORRECTING RUN-ONS AND COMMA SPLICES WITH COORDINATING CONJUNCTIONS

To correct run-on sentences and comma splices, you can separate independent clauses with one of the following words, which are called **coordinating conjunctions,** and a comma:

, and   , nor   , so
, but   , for   , yet
, or

Run-on:	*The secretary put me on hold she forgot to get back to me.*
Correction:	*The secretary put me on hold $\boxed{, but}$ she forgot to get back to me.*
Comma splice:	*First whip the cream into stiff peaks, then fold it into the chocolate mixture.*
Correction:	*First whip the cream into stiff peaks $\boxed{, and}$ then fold it into the chocolate mixture.*

Troubleshooting

If you need to review coordinating conjunctions and coordination, see Chapter 7.

Using a coordinating conjunction and a comma to separate independent clauses is a form of **coordination.**

GRAMMAR ALERT

A comma by itself cannot separate independent clauses. The comma must appear with *and, but, or, nor, for, so,* or *yet.*

No (comma splice):   *The Kennywood Tigers won the Little League tournament, their coach took them for ice cream.*

Yes: *The Kennywood Tigers won the Little League tournament │ , so │ their coach took them for ice cream.*

9.3 ACTIVITY

Use commas and coordinating conjunctions to eliminate the run-on sentences and comma splices. Some sentences are correct. The first one is done as an example, so you must correct six errors.

[1]A blind contestant once appeared on *Jeopardy!* [2]The contestant had special
   , but
needs producers had to make only a few changes to accommodate him. [3]Eddie
Timanus of Reston, Virginia, was the contestant. [4]A sportswriter for *USA Today,* he is totally blind. [5]Timanus appeared October 20, 1999, he won $14,400. [6]The show agreed to make a few changes to accommodate Timanus, all the changes were minor. [7]The producers eliminated purely visual components of the show, including video daily doubles and video-based clues. [8]These minor adjustments were the only alterations, no other changes were made. [9]Timanus was given a Braille card with the category names, along with a computer keyboard. [10]The computer keyboard was an accommodation Timanus needed to type his wagers and Final Jeopardy answer. [11]Timanus became an undefeated champion he was invited to the Million Dollar Masters playoff in New York. [12]Timanus's appearance was noteworthy, he was not the first of his family to appear on the show. [13]His mother, who was a contestant in 1991, was the first family member to appear on the program. [14]She did not win her son became an undefeated champion.

CORRECTING RUN-ONS AND COMMA SPLICES WITH CONJUNCTIVE ADVERBS

You can correct run-on sentences and comma splices by separating independent clauses with one of the following **conjunctive adverbs**, combined with a semicolon and a comma:

; consequently,	; meanwhile,	; otherwise,
; furthermore,	; moreover,	; therefore,
; however,	; nevertheless,	; thus,
; instead,	; nonetheless,	

Troubleshooting

If you need to review conjunctive adverbs and coordination, see page 118.

Using a semicolon, conjunctive adverb, and comma to separate independent clauses is another form of **coordination**.

Run-on:	*Very few people bought tickets the band canceled their performance.*
Correction:	*Very few people bought tickets* $\boxed{; therefore,}$ *the band canceled their performance.*
Comma splice:	*The band hoped to reschedule their performance, they could not promise to do so.*
Correction:	*The band hoped to reschedule their performance* $\boxed{; however,}$ *they could not promise to do so.*

→ **PUNCTUATION ALERT**

And, but, or, nor, for, so, and *yet* are the only conjunctions that can be used with just a comma to separate independent clauses. Conjunctive adverbs must be used with a semicolon and comma to separate independent clauses.

No (comma splice):	*I enjoy math, however, Joey does not.*
Yes:	*I enjoy math* $\boxed{, but}$ *Joey does not.*
Yes:	*I enjoy math* $\boxed{; however,}$ *Joey does not.*

9.4 ACTIVITY

If the sentence is correct, write "correct" on the blank. If the sentence is a run-on or comma splice, write the correction using a semicolon, an appropriate conjunctive adverb, and a comma.

EXAMPLE   Charges of discrimination have been lodged against schools, these charges have brought education to court.

Charges of discrimination have been lodged against schools;

further more, these charges have brought education to court.

1. Court action has often provided an avenue for federal involvement in schools, this involvement is particularly evident in <u>Brown v. the Board of Education of Topeka.</u>

2. In 1954 in <u>Brown v. the Board of Education of Topeka,</u> the Supreme Court reversed its doctrine of "separate but equal" it concluded that separate educational facilities are inherently unequal.

3. Race segregation has a negative psychological and educational impact on children of all races, even in schools with facilities seemingly equal.

_____

_____

_____

4. By the 1970s, courts had ruled that discrimination based on gender is a violation of the U.S. Constitution discrimination directed at students with disabilities was ruled a similar violation.

_____

_____

_____

5. Some educational issues are immune from federal influence our Congress has a long history of involvement in education.

_____

_____

_____

6. In 1972, Congress passed Title IX of the Education Amendments prohibiting discrimination on the basis of sex for any education activity receiving federal funds.

_____

_____

_____

7. Title IX prohibits sexual discrimination in sports it prohibits sexual discrimination in financial aid, counseling, admissions, and other areas.

_____

_____

_____

8. Title IX is an important piece of legislation its enforcement is sometimes lax.

_____

_____

_____

9. The 1975 Individuals with Disabilities Education Act funds education for the nation's 8 million children with disabilities, these students might be ignored.

_____

_____

_____

10. The Individuals with Disabilities Education Act provides free education for students and financial assistance for school districts.

_____

_____

_____

Source: Myra Pollack Sadker and David Miller Sadker, *Teachers, Schools, and Society,* 5th ed. (New York: McGraw-Hill, 2000), pp. 296–297. Copyright © 2000 The McGraw-Hill Companies. Used by permission of The McGraw-Hill Companies.

CORRECTING RUN-ONS AND COMMA SPLICES WITH SEMICOLONS

You can correct a run-on sentence or a comma splice by separating the independent clauses with a semicolon. You can use this method of correction when you do not need a conjunction to show how the independent clauses relate to each other.

Run-on:	*An accident occurred on Interstate 90 traffic was backed up for miles.*
Correction:	*An accident occurred on Interstate 90* [;] *traffic was backed up for miles.*
Comma splice:	*A truck with hazardous material overturned, a hazardous materials team had to be called to the scene.*
Correction:	*A truck with hazardous material overturned* [;] *a hazardous materials team had to be called to the scene.*

Using a semicolon to separate independent clauses is another form of **coordination**.

Troubleshooting

If you need to review using semicolons for coordination, see page 122.

PUNCTUATION ALERT

Before using a semicolon to eliminate a run-on or comma splice, be sure you have an independent clause on *both sides* of the semicolon.

No: *I stopped watching television after six o'clock; to devote more time to studying.* [An independent clause does not occur after the semicolon.]

Yes: *I stopped watching television after six o'clock to devote more time to studying.*

CONNECT FOR SUCCESS: Determine the Relationship between Independent Clauses

Unlike coordinating conjunctions, semicolons do not indicate the specific relationship between independent clauses. When you read your textbooks and other important material, be sure to determine how the ideas in the clauses relate to each other. Doing so will improve your reading comprehension.

9.5 ACTIVITY

Correct the run-sentences and comma splices by adding semicolons. Some of the sentences are correct.

EXAMPLE People enjoy watching the Academy Awards each year few of those people know much about the history of the ceremony.

1. The first Academy Awards ceremony was held in 1929 only 250 people attended.

2. Each of the 250 people who attended paid $10 to attend the ceremony and enjoy the accompanying banquet.

3. The affair was held at the Hollywood Roosevelt Hotel, but the public was unable to see or hear it.

4. The ceremony the following year was broadcast on a Los Angeles Radio station, only an hour segment of the ceremony was broadcast.

5. The first television broadcast of the event did not occur until 1953.

6. The oldest person to be nominated for an acting Oscar was Gloria Stuart at age eighty-seven, the oldest person to win the Oscar was Jessica Tandy, who won at age eighty-one for *Driving Miss Daisy*.

7. At age eight Justin Henry was the youngest person nominated, and at age ten Tatum O'Neal was the youngest to win.

8. No one knows for sure how the statuette Oscar got its name a popular story says that Academy librarian Margaret Herrick is responsible.

9. Herrick said the statuette resembled her Uncle Oscar, and the name stuck.

10. The Academy itself never used the name Oscar officially until 1939 the name has been popular ever since.

CORRECTING RUN-ONS AND COMMA SPLICES WITH DEPENDENT CLAUSES

Troubleshooting

If you need to review sub-ordination and subordi-nating conjunctions, see Chapter 8.

To correct run-ons and comma splices, you can change one of the independent clauses to a dependent clause and connect it to the remaining independent clause. (A **dependent clause** is a word group with both a subject and a verb that is not sufficiently complete to stand alone.) To turn the independent clause into a dependent clause, add a **subordinating conjunction**, such as the following, to the appropriate independent clause:

after	as soon as	even though	unless	where
although	as though	if	until	where as
as	because	since	when	wherever
as if	before	though	whenever	while
as long as				

Run-on: *Hurricane Floyd threatened the East Coast state governors ordered the largest evacuation in peacetime history.*

           subordinating conj.   dependent clause

Correction: *When Hurricane Floyd threatened the East Coast, state governors ordered the largest evacuation in peacetime history.*

Comma splice: *Traffic jams occurred from Florida to Virginia, too many people were on the highways at the same time.*

                              subordinating conj.

Correction: *Traffic jams occurred from Florida to Virginia because*

                        dependent clause

          too many people were on the highways at the same time.

Connecting a dependent clause to an independent clause with a subordinating conjunction is a form of **subordination.**

 GRAMMAR ALERT

Do not place a period after the new dependent clause, or you will create a problem called a **sentence fragment,** as explained in Chapter 6.

Run-on: *A cold front out of Canada plunged the East Coast into a deep freeze subzero temperatures threatened the citrus crop.*

No (fragment): *When a cold front out of Canada plunged the East Coast into a deep freeze. Subzero temperatures threatened the citrus crop.*

Correction: *When a cold front out of Canada plunged the East Coast into a deep freeze, subzero temperatures threatened the citrus crop.*

PUNCTUATION ALERT

Place a comma after a dependent clause that comes at the beginning of a sentence.

Because the city's population has declined⊙ten safety workers must be laid off.

9.6 ACTIVITY

Correct the run-on sentences and comma splices by changing one of the independent clauses to a dependent clause and connecting it to the remaining independent clause. Be sure to use an appropriate subordinating conjunction. Also, place a comma after a dependent clause that comes at the beginning of a sentence.

The Remington-Rand Calculating Machine "UNIVAC" (Universal Automatic Computer)

EXAMPLE IBM made one pivotal decision in the 1950s it dramatically changed the fortune of the company.

When IBM made one pivotal decision in the 1950s,

it dramatically changed the fortune of the company.

1. The first computers were developed in the late 1940s, Univac Corporation dominated the computer industry.

   _____

   _____

2. Univac held about 60 percent of the world computer market by the mid-1950s a company called IBM held only about 10 percent of the market.

   _____

   _____

3. The directors at Univac thought there was no future in business markets they decided to concentrate on scientific data processing.

   _____

   _____

4. IBM was not a major player in computers it made a momentous decision.

   _____

   _____

5. Univac focused on scientific computing, IBM concentrated on business computing.

   _____

   _____

6. IBM's decision seemed risky at the time, it set the course for future phenomenal growth.

   _____

   _____

Source: Adapted from Joe Cortina, Janet Elder, and Katherine Gonnet, *Comprehending College Textbooks*, 3rd ed. (New York: McGraw-Hill, 1996), p. 132. Copyright © 1996 The McGraw-Hill Companies. Used by permission of The McGraw-Hill Companies.

9.7 ACTIVITY

Make corrections above the line to eliminate the run-ons and comma splices. The first one is done as an example. Four corrections remain to be made.

[1]Corporate culture can go a long way toward making a small company a
success or ~~failure, just~~ *failure. Just* ask Amy Miller. [2]Amy's ice cream parlors in Austin and Houston, Texas, attract a great many customers because of their offbeat corporate culture. [3]On any given night, servers might be juggling with their serving spades. [4]They might be tossing scoops of ice cream to each other sometimes they might even be seen dancing on the freezer top. [5]If there is a long line, servers pass out samples to customers who will sing, dance, or otherwise entertain those in line. [6]Employees might be wearing pajamas for sleep-over night they might be wearing masks for Star Wars night. [7]Lighting may be provided by candles for romance night, or strobe lights might be in evidence for disco night. [8]It's fun at Amy's. [9]It's fun for the employees, it's fun for the customers. [10]Work does not have to be drudgery, the employees at Amy's can testify to that.

Source: Adapted from William G. Nickels, James M. McHugh, and Susan M. McHugh, *Understanding Business*, 5th ed. (New York, McGraw-Hill, 1999), p. 250. Copyright © 1999 The McGraw-Hill Companies. Used by permission of The McGraw-Hill Companies.

9.8 ACTIVITY

Make corrections above the line to eliminate run-ons and comma splices. The first one is done as an example. Five corrections remain to be made.

[1]The amount of sleep a person needs is related to age. [2]Babies sleep about
twenty hours a ~~day, kids~~ *day. Kids* need ten or eleven hours a night up to their teenage years.
[3]Most adults sleep seven or eight hours many people over fifty sleep even less.

[4]Some people can get by with very little sleep, for example, high school student Randy Gardner didn't sleep for 264 hours as part of a science fair project. [5]On the last night, he was alert enough to play 100 games on a baseball machine in a penny arcade. [6]When Randy finally went to bed, he needed less than fifteen hours of sleep to catch up. [7]He felt fine after the experiment, however, he is unusual. [8]In similar experiments, people who stayed awake began to hallucinate.

[9]No one knows for sure what sleep does, some researchers think that sleeping and dreaming help the brain develop. [10]Certainly, more research is needed we still have much to learn about the exact role of sleep.

9.9 ACTIVITY

Make corrections above the line to eliminate the run-ons and comma splices in the following passage. The first one is done as an example.

[1]Researchers from the University of Washington have made a controversial
claim. According
~~claim, according~~ to them, a three-minute heated discussion between spouses reveals whether a marriage will fail. [2]Their findings are based on videotapes of couples arguing. [3]The researchers studied 124 couples for six years each couple had been married under nine months when the study began.

[4]Researchers began discussions on such hot topics as communication, money, and in-law problems, then they asked the couples to resolve the problems on their own. [5]The videotaped discussions were later classified according to facial expressions, voice tone, and speech content. [6]Seventeen couples later divorced. [7]The researchers realized something interesting about these couples. [8]The spouses related to each other in a particular way. [9]In both happy and unhappy marriages, women began the discussions. [10]However, women in unhappy marriages began with criticism and character attacks, happier couples minimized their problems. [11]The husbands' responses were very important. [12]Husbands in happy marriages asked for clarification of the problem, however, they did not necessarily take blame for the problem.

[13]The point of the study is not diagnosing couples in three minutes it is more significant than that. [14]Couples need to learn to disagree in ways that do not jeopardize their marriages. [15]They can do that if they ask themselves an important question during disagreements: "Does the marriage win, or do I win?"

TIPS FOR FINDING RUN-ONS AND COMMA SPLICES

1. Determine how many independent clauses you have in every word group you are calling a sentence. If you have more than one, be sure they are correctly separated.

2. Check your commas. If you have independent clauses on *both* sides of a comma, be sure to include a coordinating conjunction (*and, but, or, nor, for, so, yet*).

3. Check your sentences for the conjunctive adverbs in the following list. If independent clauses appear on *both* sides of these words, be sure you have a semicolon before the conjunctive adverb and a comma after it. Commas alone will not do the job.

consequently	meanwhile	otherwise
furthermore	moreover	therefore
however	nevertheless	thus
instead	nonetheless	

COMPOSING AT THE COMPUTER

If you like to compose at the computer, you may find the following strategies helpful for finding and eliminating run-ons and comma splices.

1. USE THE "FIND" FUNCTION TO LOCATE CONJUNCTIVE ADVERBS. Once you have found these words, check for independent clauses on both sides. Wherever you find independent clauses on *both* sides, be sure you have a semicolon for separation.

2. REFORMAT YOUR PAPER INTO A LIST OF SENTENCES. With your writing in list form, you may find it easier to detect run-ons and comma splices. When finished, reformat your writing into its paragraph form.

3. USE YOUR WORD-PROCESSING PROGRAM'S GRAMMAR CHECK—WITH CAUTION. For the most part, these programs do a good job of finding run-ons and comma splices, but they *do* make mistakes. Double-check to be sure each word group flagged is really a run-on or comma splice, and look for ones the program might miss.

IF ENGLISH IS NOT YOUR FIRST LANGUAGE

In many languages, commas can legitimately separate independent clauses. If you speak one of these languages—such as Spanish or Vietnamese—double-check everything you write in English to be sure that your independent clauses are separated correctly: by a period and a capital letter, by a comma used with a coordinating conjunction, by a semicolon, or by a semicolon used with a conjunctive adverb and comma.

9.10 CHAPTER REVIEW ACTIVITY

Make corrections above the line to eliminate the five run-ons and comma splices.

EXAMPLE   The Egyptian pyramids fascinate us; their construction and longevity are an ongoing topic of study.

[1]Egypt's pyramids are the oldest stone buildings in the world, they were built about 5,000 years ago. [2]These ancient tombs are also among the world's largest structures. [3]The biggest is taller than a forty-story building, furthermore, it covers an area greater than that of ten football fields. [4]The average weight of one pyramid stone is 2½ tons that's the weight of two midsize cars. [5]To complete one of these giant structures, 100,000 people worked for twenty seasons.

[6]More than eighty pyramids still stand today. [7]Inside their limestone surfaces, there are secret passageways, hidden rooms, ramps, bridges, and shafts, most have concealed entrances and false doors. [8]Each pyramid housed a pharaoh's preserved body it also held the goods needed to live well in the next life.

[9]The pyramids were monuments to the pharaoh's power, but today they stand as reminders of a creative ancient civilization.

9.11 CHAPTER REVIEW ACTIVITY

Make corrections above the line to eliminate the seven run-ons and comma splices.

EXAMPLE   Some food discoveries were accidental, and some were the result of research.

[1]When it comes to inventions and discoveries, people do not often think of the food industry, but they should. [2]Many foods we take for granted were discoveries at one time. [3]Consider margarine, for example. [4]Napoleon III was upset, the butter his soldiers carried on long trips always spoiled. [5]In 1869, he held a contest to see if anyone could make a butter substitute, something that would last longer. [6]Hippolyte Mege-Mouries responded to the challenge, he mixed beef fat, water, and milk. [7]The result was oleomargarine he won the prize.

[8]The first person to think of the ice cream cone may have been Ernest Hamwi. [9]Hamwi was selling wafflelike pastry at the 1904 World's Fair it was called *zalabia*. [10]Next to him was a man selling dishes of ice cream. [11]Business was good, and the man soon ran out of dishes. [12]Hamwi got an idea he would roll zalabia into cones and put ice cream inside. [13]The cones were an instant success.

[14]The story of chewing gum is also interesting. [15]*Chicle* is a kind of dried tree sap, it is also the stuff the first gum was made from. [16]Thomas Adams

brought some chicle to the United States in 1872. [17]He wanted to use it as a cheap substitute for rubber. [18]Fooling around one day, Adams put some chicle in his mouth. [19]He convinced others that chewing the stuff was pleasant, chewing gum was born.

9.12 COLLABORATIVE CHAPTER REVIEW ACTIVITY

Find a seven- or eight-sentence paragraph in a magazine or newspaper and rewrite it, omitting all the periods and capital letters marking sentence boundaries. Trade rewritten paragraphs with a classmate and edit to eliminate the run-ons and comma splices.

GETTING IN GEAR: IDEAS FOR WRITING

Separation is not just a grammatical concept—it is important in many aspects of life. In his poem "Mending Wall," Robert Frost was speaking to the concept of separation when he wrote this line: "Good fences make good neighbors." To read "Mending Wall," visit this site: www.writing.upenn.edu/~afilreis/88/frost-mending.html.

writing topic: In this chapter, you learned ways to separate independent clauses, but what about separation in other aspects of life? Do you agree with Robert Frost that "Good fences make good neighbors"? Agree or disagree with the observation in Frost's poem, and explain why you believe as you do.

suggestions for prewriting: Look at the photograph and freewrite for ten minutes on the subject of separation between neighbors. What are the advantages of separation? The disadvantages?

suggestions for drafting
- Your thesis or topic sentence (depending on whether you are writing an essay or a paragraph) can mention separation or fences between neighbors and your claim about the separation or about fences between neighbors.
- Give the reasons for your claim, from least to most significant, so you have a progressive order.

suggestions for revising
- Check for coherence by making sure your details are in a logical order and that you have used transitions. (See page 43 on coherence.)
- Double-check to be sure that all your details are related, so you do not have a unity problem. (Unity is explained on page 47.)

suggestion for editing: Edit one extra time, checking for run-ons and comma splices. Linger over every word group you are calling a sentence and count the number of independent clauses. If you have more than one, be sure they are separated by a comma and coordinating conjunction; by a semicolon, conjunctive adverb, and comma; or by a semicolon.

RECHARGE: Lesson Summary

1. A **run-on sentence** occurs when two **independent clauses** (word groups that can be sentences) are not separated. A **comma splice** occurs when two **independent clauses** are separated by nothing more than a comma.

   Independent clause: *the airlines began a fare war*
   Independent clause: *ticket prices have dropped dramatically*
   Run-on: *The airlines began a fare war ticket prices have dropped dramatically.*
   Comma splice: *The airlines began a fare war, ticket prices have dropped dramatically.*

2. You can correct run-ons and comma splices in the following ways:
   - Use a period and capital letter to make each independent clause a sentence.

     The airlines began a fare war. Ticket prices have dropped dramatically.
   - Separate the independent clauses with a comma and **coordinating conjunction** (*and, but, or, nor, for, so, yet*).

     The airlines began a fare war, so ticket prices have dropped dramatically.
   - Separate the independent clauses with a semicolon, conjunctive adverb, and comma.

     The airlines began a fare war; consequently, ticket prices have dropped dramatically.
   - Separate the independent clauses with a semicolon.

     The airlines began a fare war; ticket prices have dropped dramatically.

RECHARGE: Lesson Summary Continued

• Change one of the independent clauses to a **dependent clause** (word group with a subject and verb that *cannot* stand as a sentence) and join it to the remaining independent clause.

Because the airlines began a fare war, ticket prices have dropped dramatically.

PART TWO REVIEW

Editing for multiple errors

A. Read the passage and notice how choppy it sounds because it lacks coordination and subordination. Next revise by adding the needed coordination and subordination. (You do not have to change every sentence, and you can take out and add words.) Read your revision and notice the improvement coordination and subordination make in the flow.

[1]Harriet Tubman, was called the Moses of her people. [2]She was a conductor on the Underground Railroad. [3]She became a legend in her own time. [4]She led approximately 300 slaves to freedom in ten years. [5]Born a slave, she had no real childhood or formal education. [6]She labored in physically demanding jobs as a woodcutter and field hand. [7]She had heard that some masters were kind. [8]She never experienced any. [8]She decided to escape slavery. [9]She was twenty-nine. [10]She set out with only the North Star to guide her. [11]She made her way to freedom in Pennsylvania. [12]She returned to Baltimore a year later to rescue her sister. [13]She then began guiding others to freedom. [14]A new Fugitive Slave Law was passed in 1850, making her travels more difficult. [15]Rewards offered by slaveowners for her capture totaled $40,000. [16]She was still not deterred.

[17]Tubman's heroism was highlighted between 1862 and 1865. [18]She was sent to the South as a spy and scout for the Union Army. [19]Her knowledge of geography and sense of direction were an asset. [20]She explored the countryside in search of Confederate fortifications. [21]She received official commendation from Union officers. [22]She was never paid for her services.

[23]The war ended. [24]She established a home for poor, elderly blacks. [25]She became involved in a number of causes, including women's suffrage. [26]Her death brought obituaries. [27]They showed her fame throughout the United States and Europe. [28]She was buried with military rites.

B. Revise to eliminate the fragments, run-ons, and comma splices.

[1]Many phrases that we speak and hear often have interesting histories, for example, you may have used or heard the phrase "to be in the doldrums." [2]Which means to be depressed or in low spirits. [3]The phrase has an interesting origin. [4]The doldrums is a name given by early sailors to a zone at the equator. [5]At this site, winds are often light, their direction is uncertain. [6]As a result, sailing ships were often becalmed. [7]For sailors in sailing ships, the doldrums were a great contrast to the trade winds, which blow steadily in the zone between the Tropics and the equator. [8]The northeast and southeast trade winds converge on the equator. [9]Where pressure is low and the air rises. [10]Because the air rises at the equator. [11]There is plenty of rain. [12]Sudden squalls and thunderstorms occur frequently. [13]Sailing in such conditions is difficult the ship is not carried along in any particular direction. [14]The exact location of the doldrums moves with the seasons. [15]In June, they are about 5 degrees north of the equator, in December they are about 5 degrees south.

[16]Another expression that you may have used or heard is "spitting image." [17]There are many stories about the origin of this phrase. [18]Most of them related to literal spitting. [19]In some cultures, spit was associated with conception, so a woman who wanted to have a child would drink water containing her husband's saliva. [20]In the 1600s, children in England who resembled a parent were said to look like they had been "spit out of" that parent's mouth. [21]Over the years, the phrase appeared as "spit and image," this probably happened because it sounds so much like "spitting image." [22]Today, however, "spitting image" being the most common form of the phrase.

READING AND WRITING IN RESPONSE TO TEXTBOOKS

The following textbook excerpt explains an important cultural difference.

[1]As a culture, people in the United States are goal-oriented. [2]They want to get their work done efficiently, and they assume that everyone else does, too. [3]They think they're improving things if they can figure out a way for two people using modern methods to do the same work as four people using the "old way." [4]In countries such as India and Pakistan, where unemployment is high, creating jobs is more important than working

efficiently. [5]Executives in these countries would rather employ four workers than two, and their values influence their actions.

Source: Adapted from Joe Cortina, Janet Elder, and Katherine Gonnet, *Comprehending College Textbooks,* 3rd ed. (New York: McGraw-Hill, 1996), p. 263. Copyright © 1996 The McGraw-Hill Companies. Used by permission of The McGraw-Hill Companies.

1. Which sentences include coordination? What is the coordinating conjunction?

   _____

   _____

2. Which sentence includes subordination? What is the subordinating conjunction?

   _____

   _____

3. How do coordination and subordination make it easier for students to comprehend this textbook passage?

   _____

   _____

writing topic: The textbook excerpt explains that cultural differences can account for the fact that different societies value efficiency differently. Use examples to demonstrate that people in the United States value efficiency.

Understanding Verbs

Verbs are the action words of the language and the most important. Turn to any passage on any page of a successful novel and notice the high percentage of verbs.

—novelist William Sloan, author of *To Walk the Night* and *The Edge of Running Water*

Reflection: Why do you think Sloan considers verbs to be the most important words? Is it solely because of the "high percentage" of them?

WHAT YOU WILL LEARN

How to use singular subjects with singular verbs and plural subjects with plural verbs

How to form the present tense, the past tense, the perfect tenses, and the progressive tenses

How to use the past participle and present participle forms of verbs

How to use active and passive voices

How to use tenses consistently

WHY YOU WILL LEARN IT

so that you can use the present tense correctly

so that your writing can show different times

so that you can form the perfect tenses correctly

so that you can write sentences with the subject performing the action or being acted upon

so that you can avoid inappropriate, confusing shifts in time sequence

167

CHAPTER 10

Using the Present Tense and Achieving Subject-Verb Agreement

CHAPTER GOALS

By the end of this chapter, you will learn to

Make subjects and verbs agree in the present tense

Verbs are very important, because they allow writers and speakers to indicate time frames. In this chapter, you will learn that, when your time frame is the present, your verb can indicate singular and plural but to do so correctly it must work with the subject.

UNDERSTANDING THE PRESENT TENSE AND NUMBER

A sentence must have a verb. One of the characteristics of verbs is that they can show past, present, or future time (known as **tense**). A verb in the **present tense** shows that something is happening *now*. It can also show that something happens *regularly*. Here are two examples:

Something happening now: *The basement <u>is flooded.</u>*

Something that happens regularly: *The spring rains <u>arrive</u> in early May.*

In addition to showing tense (time), another characteristic of verbs it that, in the present tense, they can also have **number** (singular or plural). **Singular** refers to one, and **plural** refers to more than one.

Singular verb: *The store <u>is</u> crowded this time of year.*

Plural verb: *The stores <u>are</u> crowded this time of year.*

Troubleshooting

If you need to review subjects and verbs, see Chapter 5.

In addition to having a verb, a sentence must have a subject. That subject can be a **noun,** which names a person, a place, an object, an emotion, or an idea. Nouns are words such as *parent, Chicago, carpet, love,* and *thought.* The subject can also be a **pronoun,** which is a word that substitutes for a noun or refers to a noun. Subject pronouns are *I, you, he, she, it, we,* and *they.*

One of the characteristics of nouns and pronouns is that they can be either singular or plural. They are **singular** when they name only one thing; they are **plural** when they name more than one. Here are a few examples:

Singular Nouns	Plural Nouns	Singular Pronouns	Plural Pronouns
child, city, hat	children, cities, hats	I, you, he, she, it,	we, you, they

Note: You can be either singular or plural, but it is always used with a plural verb.

MAKING SUBJECTS AND VERBS AGREE IN THE PRESENT TENSE

In the present tense, subjects and verbs must agree in number. That is, a singular subject must have a singular verb, and a plural subject must have a plural verb. **Subject-verb agreement** is a consideration primarily with present tense verbs.

To achieve subject-verb agreement, you need to know that sometimes a present tense verb ends in –s or –es and sometimes it does not.

Present tense with -s:	*This shoe feels tight.*
Present tense without -s:	*These shoes feel tight.*
Present tense with -es:	*Dad always watches the sunset.*
Present tense without -es:	*Mom and Dad always watch the sunset.*

The subject of the sentence determines whether or not a present tense verb takes an -s or -es ending. When you match the correct verb form to the subject, you have **subject-verb agreement**.

When the subject is *he, she, it,* or a *singular noun*, add an –s or –es ending to the verb.

He sleeps until noon every Saturday.

She watches too much television.

It appears to be broken.

The hospital employs 2,000 people.

When the subject is *I, we, they, you,* or a *plural noun*, leave off the –s or –es ending.

I expect a raise next month.

We celebrate Thanksgiving in an untraditional way.

They join me in thanking you for your help.

You hold this end of the rope.

Firefighters deserve our respect.

Troubleshooting

Do not decide on verb endings according to how a sentence sounds, as sound is not a reliable test. Instead, identify the subject and select the verb form accordingly. If you need help identifying subjects, see Chapter 5.

WITH THESE WORDS	USE THESE FORMS	EXAMPLES
he	add -s or -es	He watches.
she	add -s or -es	She eats.
it	add -s or -es	It stops.
singular noun	add -s or -es	A baby sleeps.
I	omit -s or -es	I run.
we	omit -s or -es	We watch.
they	omit -s or -es	They talk.
you	omit -s or -es	You study.
plural noun	omit -s or -es	Birds fly.

CONNECT FOR SUCCESS: Use the Present Tense When Appropriate in Your Classes

You will use the present tense often in college writing. For example, use the present tense in a paper for a political science class that compares the campaign styles of two candidates currently running for office. Also use the present tense to respond to a biology examination question that asks you to explain how plants convert carbon dioxide into oxygen. When you discuss literature, use the present tense even when the author is long dead or the action is long past. Thus, say, "Hemingway often *explores* the theme of death," even though Hemingway is dead.

10.1 ACTIVITY

Rewrite the sentences, changing the underlined past tense verbs to the present tense.

EXAMPLE   It <u>started</u> with your breath.

It starts with your breath.

1. As you <u>exhaled,</u> a trail of carbon dioxide <u>wafted</u> away from you like a ribbon.

2. A lucky mosquito <u>stumbled</u> across it, <u>zigzagged</u> back and forth, and <u>moved</u> in on it.

3. As the mosquito <u>maneuvered</u> closer, she <u>picked</u> up on other clues, such as a warm, sweaty body.

4. If she <u>considered</u> the clues appealing, the insect <u>landed,</u> and you <u>turned</u> into dinner.

5. Experiments <u>showed</u> that mosquitoes <u>liked</u> people on the basis of body chemistry and body temperature.

6. In a group of ten people exposed to mosquitoes, three <u>tended</u> to be bitten many times, four <u>faced</u> being bitten only once or twice, and three <u>escaped</u> being bitten at all.

_____

_____

_____

7. Thus, people <u>attracted</u> mosquitoes on the basis of uncontrollable factors.

_____

_____

8. I <u>appreciated</u> knowing this because it <u>explained</u> why I <u>attracted</u> mosquitoes and my husband <u>repelled</u> them.

_____

_____

_____

9. I <u>wondered</u> why I always <u>scratched</u> my way through camping trips but he <u>suffered</u> no such problem.

_____

_____

10. We <u>realized</u> that something <u>marked</u> us as different and <u>recognized</u> what it is: I <u>smelled</u> better to bugs.

_____

_____

10.2 ACTIVITY

Write a sentence using each of the following verb forms. Choose your subjects from this list (you do not have to use all the subjects):

I	we
he	she
they	you
the young child	the growing teenager
the young children	the growing teenagers

EXAMPLE   like _The young children like ice cream._ _____

_____

1. eat _____

_____

2. eats _____

_____

3. give _____

_____

4. gives _____

_____

5. see _____

_____

6. sees _____

_____

10.3 ACTIVITY

Write a sentence using each of the following subjects. Choose your verbs from this list (you do not have to use all the verbs):

remind	estimate	work
reminds	estimates	works
taste	smell	worry
tastes	smells	worries

EXAMPLE   New parents *worry about everything.*_____

1. The NASA scientist _____

_____

2. The NASA scientists _____

_____

3. Homemade banana cream pie _____

_____

4. Homemade banana cream pies _____

_____

5. The firm's new attorney _____

_____

6. The firm's new attorneys _____

_____

Am/is/are (forms of *be*)

In the present tense, the verb *be* has two singular forms and one plural form. *Am* and *is* are the singular forms; *are* is the plural form.

1. Use the singular form *am* to form the present tense when your subject is *I*:

I am late for work.

2. Use the singular form *is* to form the present tense when your subject is *he, she, it,* or a singular noun

> *He is not here.*
> *She is the top salesperson.*
> *It is too early for dinner.*
> *The decision is final.*

3. Use the plural form *are* when your subject is *you, we, they,* and plural nouns.

> *You are my best friend.*
> *We are almost home.*
> *They are an hour early.*
> *These boys are hospital volunteers.*

Troubleshooting

If you need to review helping verbs, turn back to page 85.

Helping Verbs

Am, are, and *is* are often helping verbs. That is, they are often used with other verbs to form the complete verb.

> *I am going with you.*
> *You are sitting in my chair.*
> *Jan is expecting an A in history.*

Contractions

Is and *are* can be combined with *not* to make shortened forms called **contractions.**

> *is + not = isn't*
> *are + not = aren't*

Notice that an apostrophe replaces the *o* in *not.*

> *Mickey isn't afraid of failure.*
> *The leaves aren't changing color yet.*

WITH THESE WORDS	USE	EXAMPLES
I	am	I am late.
he, she, it, the child	is (isn't)	He (She, It, The child) is late. He (She, It, The child) isn't late.
we, you, they, the children	are (aren't)	We (You, They, The children) are late. We (You, They, The children) aren't late.

 GRAMMAR ALERT

Be is often heard in place of *are* and *am.* This usage should be avoided in college and business writing.

No: *You be late.*   No: *They be late.*
Yes: *You are late.*   Yes: *They are late.*

Troubleshooting

Ain't is never correct in formal usage.

No:	We be late.	No:	The guests be late.
Yes:	We are late.	Yes:	The guests are late.
No:	I be late.	No:	He/she/it be late.
Yes:	I am late.	Yes:	He/she/it is late.
No:	Donna be late.		
Yes:	Donna is late.		

10.4 ACTIVITY

Fill in the blanks with the correct present tense form: *am, is,* or *are.* The first one is done as an example.

[1]Traditions for celebrating birthdays _are_____ different in different parts of the world, but I _____ surprised to learn they _____ similar in many ways as well. [2]For example, a birthday candle _____ used in many parts of the world; its purpose _____ to carry wishes up to heaven. [3]Also, in many regions of the world, birthday pats _____ given for good luck. [4]Other birthday traditions _____ specific to particular regions. [5]In Africa, for instance, tribes hold initiation ceremonies, in which children _____ taught the laws and customs of the tribe. [6]In Argentina, a child _____ likely to receive one pull on the earlobe for each year of life, which I _____ sure is similar to birthday pats in other regions. [7]In China, friends _____ invited to lunch, and it _____ customary to serve noodles. [8]If you _____ in Denmark, you will see a flag flying outside the window of a person celebrating a birthday, but in Nepal you _____ more likely to see a mark on the birthday person's forehead. [9]Although in the United States we _____ in the habit of making birthday cakes, Russians _____ more likely to make birthday pies. [10]Interestingly, in Ecuador, when a girl turns fifteen, she _____ given a pink dress to wear to a big celebration. [11]As you _____ learning, birthday celebrations may vary around the world, but each celebration has one thing in common: it _____ meant to honor the person turning a year older.

10.5 ACTIVITY

Rewrite the sentences, changing the underlined past tense forms of *to be* to present tense forms. Choose from *am, is,* and *are.*

EXAMPLE   Sociology majors <u>were</u> employed in many fields.

_Sociology majors are employed in many fields._____

_____

1. I <u>was</u> thinking about majoring in sociology.

2. An undergraduate degree in sociology <u>was</u> not just an excellent preparation for graduate work; it <u>was</u> valuable for many jobs.

3. Because employers <u>were</u> always looking for people knowledgeable about diverse groups, they <u>were</u> hiring sociology graduates.

4. If you <u>were</u> a graduate with a sociology major, you <u>were</u> able to work in many environments.

5. A graduate with a sociology major <u>was</u> able to work in human services, education, business, and commerce.

6. Sociology students <u>were</u> advised to take courses appropriate to their career interests.

7. Internships for sociology majors <u>were</u> helpful because you <u>were</u> more likely to find a job after completing one.

8. For example, a student hoping to become a health planner <u>was</u> advised to take medical sociology.

Source: Adapted from Richard T. Shaefer, *Sociology*, 7th ed. (New York: McGraw-Hill, 2001), p. 29. Copyright © 2001 The McGraw-Hill Companies. Used by permission of The McGraw-Hill Companies.

Have/has

The verb **to have** has two present tense forms: **have** and **has.** Use *have* with *I, you, we, they,* and plural nouns.

I have two dogs and a cat.

You have the nicest lawn on the street.

We have your best interests in mind.

They have a good idea.

The scouts have a new summer camp.

Use *has* with *he*, *she*, *it*, and singular nouns.

He has a new job.

She has enough money for the trip.

It has to be eight o'clock by now.

Carla has the flu.

Helping verbs

Have and *has* can be helping verbs. That is, they can appear with other verbs to form the complete verb.

He has left for the semester.

The tomatoes have shriveled on the vine.

Contractions

Have and *has* can be combined with *not* to make shortened forms called **contractions.**

have + *not* = *haven't*

has + *not* = *hasn't*

Notice that an apostrophe replaces the *o* in *not*.

I haven't selected a major.

The bus hasn't left yet.

WITH THESE WORDS	USE	EXAMPLES
I, you, we, they, the children	have (haven't)	I have an idea. I haven't any idea.
he, she, it, the child	has (hasn't)	The child has an idea. The child hasn't any idea.

10.6 ACTIVITY

Fill in the blanks with the correct present tense form: *have* or *has*.

¹*Has*_____ this happened to you? You ²_____ just finished working in the library, and you ³_____ to get back to your room. When you step outside, you realize that it ⁴_____ become dark. Nervously, you walk across campus as quickly as you can. We can all remember a time when we ⁵_____ felt nervous at night. And we ⁶_____ good reason

to fear the dark on campus. In fact, campus crime ⁷_____ increased. Many college campuses ⁸_____ the highest crime rates in their communities. It ⁹_____ not been widely publicized, but students ¹⁰_____ a high risk of being victims of crime. Therefore, they should ¹¹_____ crime prevention as one of their priorities. Students can be lax about crime prevention. They ¹²_____ often left their rooms or fallen asleep without locking their doors. One student I know ¹³_____ often opened the door without first checking to see who is there. We all ¹⁴_____ a responsibility to prevent crime. Lock your doors, and be careful about whom you let into the dorm.

10.7 ACTIVITY

Rewrite the sentences, changing the underlined past tense forms of *to have* to present tense forms. Choose either *have* or *has*.

EXAMPLE   I had a present for your birthday.

I have a present for your birthday.

1. I had the department chair's permission to take that course.

    _____

    _____

2. You had the worst case of the flu I had ever seen.

    _____

    _____

3. Every year, the Spanish Club had a car wash to help raise money for a trip to Mexico.

    _____

    _____

4. To end the hostilities, the countries had agreed to peace talks.

    _____

    _____

5. We had plans for the evening, so we had to refuse your invitation.

    _____

    _____

6. You had to drive because Jan had an appointment, but she had no car.

    _____

    _____

10.8 ACTIVITY

On a separate sheet, write two sentences using *haven't* and two sentences using *hasn't*.

Do/does

The verb **to do** has two present tense forms: **do** and **does**. Use *do* with I, *you*, *we*, *they*, and plural nouns.

> I *do* a hundred situps a day.
>
> You *do* beautiful work.
>
> We *do* whatever we can.
>
> They *do* more than enough.
>
> Teachers *do* their jobs for little pay.

Use *does* with he, she, it, and singular nouns.

> He always *does* the right thing.
>
> She *does* the work of two people.
>
> It *does* not make sense.
>
> The machine *does* the job quickly.

Helping verbs

Do and *does* can be helping verbs. That is, they can appear with other verbs to form the complete verb.

> I *do* believe your explanation.
>
> Lilly *does* enjoy Mexican food.

Contractions

Do and *does* can be combined with *not* to make shortened forms called **contractions.**

> do + not = don't
>
> does + not = doesn't

Notice that an apostrophe replaces the *o* in *not*.

> Many people *don't* agree with you.
>
> This problem *doesn't* have a solution.

WITH THESE WORDS	USE	EXAMPLES
I, you, we, they, the children	do (don't)	They do pushups in the gym. They don't do pushups in the gym.
he, she, it, the child	does (doesn't)	He does not do pushups in the gym. He doesn't do pushups in the gym.

10.9 ACTIVITY

Fill in the blanks with the correct present tense form: *do* or *does*.

EXAMPLE If you _*do*_____ have something to buy or sell, consider using eBay.

1. EBay _____ bring together buyers and sellers.

2. The buyers and sellers _____ browse through listed items in a fully automated way.

3. I _____ like eBay because it _____ allow me to purchase items I _____ not otherwise have access to.

4. Browsing and bidding are free, but sellers _____ pay certain charges.

5. If you sell on eBay, you _____ pay an "insertion fee," determined by the seller's opening bid.

6. A seller also _____ pay a fee to promote the item being sold.

7. When people sell items on eBay, they also _____ pay a fee based on the final selling price.

8. We _____ not always think of eBay when we have items to buy or sell, but people _____ find this online auction service both fun and useful.

10.10 ACTIVITY

Rewrite the sentences, changing the underlined past tense forms of *to do* to present tense forms. Choose either *do* or *does*.

EXAMPLE They <u>did</u> go to Myrtle Beach every year.

*They do go to Myrtle Beach every year.*_____

1. The fire department <u>did</u> inspect houses to check for faulty wiring.

   _____
   _____

2. The children <u>did</u> love to play with their play station for hours at a time.

   _____
   _____

3. On vacation, we <u>did</u> expect to gain at least 5 pounds.

   _____
   _____

4. I <u>did</u> all the baking for the annual family reunion.

_____

_____

5. You <u>did</u> well on the math portions of standardized tests, and Marco <u>did</u> well on the verbal portions.

_____

_____

6. He <u>did</u> hope to win a scholarship for his senior year.

_____

_____

10.11 REVIEW ACTIVITY

Fill in the blanks in the passage with the correct present tense forms. Make your selections by choosing a verb for the first blank from number 1 in the list, a verb for the second blank from number 2, and so forth. The first blank is filled in as an example.

1. am/is/are	6. take/takes	11. am/is/are
2. offer/offers	7. have/has	12. bring/brings
3. begin/begins	8. start/starts	13. draw/draws
4. close/closes	9. have/has	14. am/is/are
5. am/is/are	10. doesn't/don't	15. do/does

Florida's Daytona International Speedway [1]_____*is*_____ a year-round attraction. It [2]_____ world-class racing events throughout the year. The races [3]_____ in early February with the Busch Clash and Sun Bank 24 Hour race. They [4]_____ in February with the Super Bowl of Stock Car Racing, the Daytona 500. Several races [5]_____ scheduled in between.

Many races [6]_____ place in March, but the highlight [7]_____ been the Annual Daytona 200 Formula 1 Championship Race. In July, the Independence Day celebration [8]_____ early with the S.C.C.A. Paul Revere 250. This race [9]_____ Camaros, Corvettes, and other Trans Am Series cars racing at night. However, the biggest event [10]_____ come until Independence Day itself. This event [11]_____ the Firecracker 400, a Nascar Grand National Stock Car Race. November [12]_____ the Pro-Am Superbike Finals, and December brings the World Enduro Championship. This December race [13]_____ over 1,000 entries in classes of racing go-carts.

It ^{14}_____ the biggest meeting of its kind in the world. The race can be fast because the quickest carts ^{15}_____ go over 130 mph.

10.12 COLLABORATIVE REVIEW ACTIVITY

With two classmates, complete each sentence by supplying a present tense verb and any other words you want to add. You can use a verb from the list or one of your own.

EXAMPLE   This television program *is very popular with teenagers.*_____

is	think	nap	have
are	thinks	naps	has
does	study	walk	believe
do	studies	walks	believes

1. Many movie fans _____

_____

2. My best friend _____

_____

3. In the afternoon, he _____

_____

4. Every summer, they _____

_____

5. An elderly woman _____

_____

6. You _____

_____

7. To get better grades, we _____

_____

8. In my opinion, she _____

_____

MAKING SUBJECTS AND VERBS AGREE IN SPECIAL SITUATIONS

In most cases, you will have little trouble making your subjects and verbs agree. However, a few special situations can be a little tricky.

Troubleshooting

When you have a noun subject with a phrase, you may find it easier to check agreement by changing the noun and phrase to a pronoun. "The box near the shelves is empty" becomes "It is empty."

Troubleshooting

If you need to review subjects with phrases, see page 76.

Subjects with phrases

A **phrase** is a group of words that does not have both a subject and a verb. Phrases like the following often appear in the complete subject:

at first	in the evening	next to the shoes
beside me	of the cake	toward the hall
by the lake	on top of	with a friend
for a while	near the doors	under the couch

When deciding which present tense verb to use, rule out any phrases that appear in the complete subject.

Which is it?   *A pile of papers is in the corner.*
or
A pile of papers are in the corner.

Rule out the phrase: *of papers*
Now which is it?   *A pile is in the corner.*
or
A pile are in the corner.

Correct verb: *is*
Correct sentence: *A pile of papers is in the corner.*

10.13 ACTIVITY

Cross out the phrase in the complete subject of each sentence, and then write the correct verb in the blank.

EXAMPLE   (dates/date) The origin ~~of Oreos~~ _____*dates*_____ to 1912.

1. (am/is/are) The most popular cookie of all American cookies _____ Nabisco's Oreo Chocolate Sandwich Cookie.

2. (doesn't/don't) The people at Nabisco _____ know how the cookie got its name.

3. (has/have) The basic design for the immensely popular Oreos _____ not changed for more than fifty years.

4. (measures/measure) Today's version of this most popular of American treats _____ 1¾ inches across.

5. (takes/take) Most people with average-size mouths _____ a mere two or three bites.

6. (frosts/frost) The cream filling in a year's worth of Oreos _____ all the wedding cakes served in the United States in one year.

7. (has/have) Over 362 billion Oreos across the world _____ been sold to date.

8. (equals/equal) A stack of all the Oreos sold _____ the height of 9.8 million Sears Towers. (The Sears Tower is 1,454 feet tall.)

9. (encircles/encircle) These cookies in a row _____ the earth 381 times at the equator.

10. (am/is/are) Forty-two million gallons of milk _____ needed for all the Oreos dunked in a year.

10.14 ACTIVITY

Complete each of the following sentences with the correct verb and any other words you want to add.

EXAMPLE   (am/is/are) Your points of view *are always carefully thought out.*
_____

1. (was/were) The first of my problems _____
_____

2. (have/has) The yellow sweater in the pile of old clothes _____
_____

3. (am/is/are) Three professors at this college _____
_____

4. (cost/costs) These clothes on the sale table _____
_____

5. (play/plays) One of my brothers _____
_____

6. (sway/sways) The trees in the front of my house _____
_____

7. (am/is/are) The reaction to the current new movies _____
_____

8. (cause/causes) The trash along the roads _____
_____

9. (do/does) The words of this song _____
_____

10. (taste/tastes) The apples in the baskets _____
_____

Compound subjects

A **compound subject** is made up of two or more simple subjects joined by *and*, *or*, or *nor*, like this:

Dad and Mom are moving to Nebraska.

The train or the bus can take you into town.

Neither the concert nor the movie interests me.

Troubleshooting

If you need to review compound subjects, see page 78. To review simple subjects, see page 72.

Subjects joined by *and* are considered plural. Therefore, use the same present tense form you would use for *they* or *we*.

[They   are]
The mayonnaise and the eggs are *spoiled.*

[We   love]
My parents and I love *dogs.*

If singular subjects are joined by *or* or *nor*, the subject is considered singular, and the verb must be singular. Therefore, use the same present tense form you would use for *he*, *she*, or *it*.

[It   is]
The necklace or the bracelet is *a good gift for Jenny.*

[It   looks]
Neither the chicken nor the fish looks *appealing for supper.*

If one singular subject and one plural subject are joined by *or*, use the present tense form that works with the subject closer to the verb.

Either the juice or the oranges are *a good source of vitamin C.*

To avoid an unnatural-sounding sentence when one subject is singular and the other is plural, place the plural word second.

Correct but unnatural sounding: *The musicians or the manager <u>checks</u> the sound equipment.*

Better: *The manager or the musicians <u>check</u> the sound equipment.*

10.15 ACTIVITY

Fill in each blank with the correct present tense form of the verb in parentheses.

EXAMPLE   (am/is/are) Cigarettes and alcohol _____*are*_____ not as heavily taxed as they could be.

1. (monitor/monitors) The principal or the English teachers _____ the students taking the test.

2. (perform/performs) The cheerleaders and their captain _____ a dance routine at halftime.

3. (have/has) Either the wind or the hail _____ brought the power lines down.

4. (make/makes) Apple cider and fresh corn _____ the perfect accompaniment to a fall dinner.

5. (drive/drives) Juan or his parents _____ the elderly neighbors to the store once a week.

6. (know/knows) Vanessa or Leonid _____ the directions to the hotel.

7. (plan/plans) The football coach or his assistants _____ defensive strategy.

8. (am/is/are) The books or the scarves _____ an appropriate gift.

9. (visit/visits) Either Carla or her brother _____ Grandma every day.

10. (am/is/are) Neither sugar nor salt _____ allowed on Julio's diet.

Collective noun subjects

Collective nouns name a group of people or things. They are words such as these:

band	crew	group	mob
class	crowd	herd	orchestra
committee	flock	jury	team

Most often, the sense of a collective noun is that all the people or things function as one unit. Then the collective noun is singular and appears with the same present tense forms any other singular noun uses.

The band plays spirited marches.

The committee determines the membership fee.

The jury decides the defendant's fate.

When all the members of the group are acting individually, the collective noun is plural.

The committee have talked among themselves about disbanding.

> ### Troubleshooting
>
> If you are unsure about using collective nouns, place "the members of the" before the collective noun and use a plural verb. Instead of "The family vacations in Maine," you can write "The members of the family vacation in Maine."

10.16 ACTIVITY

For each item, write a sentence using the collective noun subject and the correct present tense form of the verb in parentheses.

EXAMPLE   (to spend) The family *spends every summer at* _____

Cape May. _____

1. (to pray) At the end of the service, the congregation _____

   _____

2. (to play) For concerts, the orchestra _____

   _____

3. (to enjoy) The audience _____

   _____

4. (to rehearse) The dance company _____

_____

5. (to decide) Each year, a number of those who graduate _____

_____

6. (to practice) Every Saturday, the team _____

_____

Indefinite pronoun subjects

Some pronouns are called **indefinite pronouns**, because they do not refer to a definite person, place, object, emotion, or idea:

anybody	everybody	some
anyone	everything	somebody
each	one	someone

The following indefinite pronouns are always singular, so they are used with the same verb forms as singular nouns.

-body words:	anybody	*-one* words:	anyone
	everybody		everyone
	nobody		no one
	somebody		one
			someone
-thing words:	anything	other words:	each
	everything		either
	nothing		every
	something		neither

Everybody <u>knows</u> who you are.
Something <u>is</u> better than nothing.
Nothing <u>succeeds</u> like success.
No one <u>believes</u> you.

These indefinite pronouns are plural, so they are used with the same verb forms as plural nouns:

both	few	many	several

Both of us <u>enjoy</u> rock climbing in the western mountains.
Few <u>were</u> as happy about the election outcome as you.

These indefinite pronouns can be either singular or plural, depending on the meaning of the sentence:

all	more	none
any	most	some

Some of the manuscript <u>is</u> missing.
Some of the cookies <u>are</u> missing.

To decide whether to use a singular or plural verb with indefinite pronouns that can be either singular or plural, substitute a pronoun and then decide. "All of the pain is/are gone" becomes "It is gone." "All of the answers is/are correct" becomes "They are correct."

GRAMMAR ALERT

Remember that the simple subject will not be part of a prepositional phrase, so the correct sentence is "One of the pages *is* torn," not "One of the pages *are* torn." See page 182 for more on subjects and phrases.

Composing at the Computer

You can use your computer's search function to locate most of the singular indefinite pronouns by typing in *body, one,* and *thing.* Once you have located the pronouns, see if you have used them as subjects in sentences with present tense verbs. If you have, check to be sure the verbs are singular.

10.17 ACTIVITY

Fill in each of the following blanks with the correct verb in parentheses.

EXAMPLE (am/is/are) Everybody _____*is*_____ expected to help clean up.

1. (understand/understands; ask/asks) No one _____ the question, so somebody _____ Dr. Garcia to repeat it.

2. (appear/appears; seem/seems) Nothing _____ out of place in the living room, but something _____ wrong in the kitchen.

3. (believe/believes) All of your friends _____ you can succeed, but no one _____ it more than I do.

4. (tell/tells; have/has) Something _____ me that someone _____ been using my CD player.

5. (realize/realizes) Unfortunately, these days few _____ the importance of saving money.

6. (an/is/are) Some of the pages _____ torn.

Verbs before subjects

You have probably noticed that the subject of a sentence usually comes before the verb. This is **normal order.**

　　　　　S　　　V
My father collects coins and stamps.

Sometimes the verb comes before the subject. This is **inverted order.** With inverted order, you must know how to choose the correct present tense form.

　　When a sentence begins with *there is, there are, here is,* or *here are,* look for the subject *after* the verb before deciding whether to use *is* or *are.*

　　　　　V　　　　　S
There is a storm warning for this afternoon.
　　　　　V　　　　S
There are two answers to that question.

V   S
Here *is* *your book*.
V   S
Here *are* *the lost keys*.

When you ask a question, the verb often comes before the subject.

V   S
Are *they* your friends?
V   S
Where *is* *the newspaper*?

Sometimes the subject is between the parts of the verb.

V   S   V
Has *the mail* *arrived*?
V   S   V
Will *you* *be going* with me?

Troubleshooting

If you have trouble with inverted order, rearrange a sentence with inverted order so that it has normal order. "Here is/are your mail" becomes "Your mail is here." Rearrange a question to make a statement. "Has/have you eaten?" becomes "You have eaten."

10.18 ACTIVITY

Complete the following to form sentences.

EXAMPLE   There is *no apartment for rent.*_____

1. There is _____
   _____

2. There are _____
   _____

3. Here is _____
   _____

4. Here are _____
   _____

10.19 ACTIVITY

Fill in each blank with the correct verb in parentheses.

EXAMPLE   (am/is/are) *Am*_____ I supposed to lock up when I leave?

1. (am/is/are) _____ you leaving for work early today?

2. (have/has) Where _____ Eduardo and Todd gone now?

3. (do/does) Why _____ the birds sing so sweetly in spring?

4. (do/does) How _____ Michael keep his room so neat?

5. (have/has) How _____ your aunt been feeling?

6. (am/is/are) What _____ the meaning of that remark?

7. (have/has) _____ all the doors and windows been locked?

8. (am/is/are) _____ I the only one working the afternoon shift?

10.20 COLLABORATIVE ACTIVITY

mod

✱Write five questions you have recently heard spoken on campus in the present tense. When you write the sentences, however, place a blank where each present tense verb would go. Exchange sentences with a classmate and fill in the blanks in each other's sentences.

Who/which/that (relative pronouns)

A **relative pronoun** introduces a dependent clause and refers to another world in the sentence. *Who, which,* and *that* are the relative pronouns.

dependent clause
My sister is a person who reads constantly. [*Who* refers to *person.*]

dependent clause
Cotton pants, which shrink in hot water, are cool and comfortable.
   [*Which* refers to *pants.*]

dependent clause
This is the coat that fits me. [*That* refers to *coat.*]

> **Troubleshooting**
>
> If you need to review relative pronouns and dependent clauses, see page 137.

Relative pronouns often function with present tense verbs. The form of the verb is determined by the word the relative pronoun refers to.
   In the following sentence, which is correct—*is* or *are*?

My cousins, who _____ twins, visit me every summer.

Who refers to *cousins.* It is "cousins are" (not "cousins is"). Therefore, the correct version is

My cousins, who are twins, visit me every summer.

10.21 ACTIVITY

In each sentence, circle the relative pronoun and draw an arrow to the word it refers to. Then fill in the blank with the correct present tense form of the verb in parentheses.

EXAMPLE   (am/is/are) I prefer food that _____*is*_____ not heavily seasoned.

1. (laugh/laughs) Eric is a person who _____ easily.

2. (hope/hopes) These are the people who _____ to buy my parents' house.

3. (remember/remembers) Chris is an individual who _____ everybody's name.

4. (have/has) I am the person who _____ to solve all the problems around here.

5. (am/is/are) These are the items that _____ priced for the garage sale.

6. (contain/contains) These boxes, which _____ usable clothing, can be taken to the women's shelter.

7. (am/is/are) This plan, which _____ the best I can come up with, should solve your problem.

8. (do/does) The campus parking problem, which _____ seem to be getting worse, will be addressed by student government.

9. (make/makes) Igor is someone who _____ things more difficult than necessary.

10. (have/has) These are the volunteers who _____ offered to organize the charity dance.

 ## IF ENGLISH IS NOT YOUR FIRST LANGUAGE

1. When the complete verb is made up of two or more verbs, do not add *-s* or *-es* to the last verb.

   No: *The child does sings well.*
   Yes: *The child does sing well.*

2. Use *am* between *I* and an *-ing* verb.

   No: *I be leaving soon.*
   No: *I is leaving soon.*
   Yes: *I am leaving soon.*

3. Use *have* or *has* before *been*.

   No: *The lazy employee been fired.*
   Yes: *The lazy employee has been fired.*

   No: *The lazy employees been fired.*
   Yes: *The lazy employees have been fired.*

4. Use a singular verb with noncount nouns. **Noncount nouns** name things that are not normally counted. They are words that cannot appear with a number in front of them—words such as these:

air	food	homework	oil
baggage	furniture	honesty	sugar
fear	health	luggage	water

   No: *The baggage are still on the airplane.*
   Yes: *The baggage is still on the airplane.*

Noncount nouns are also discussed on page 309.

10.22 CHAPTER REVIEW ACTIVITY

Rewrite the sentences, using the correct present tense forms of the underlined verbs with the subjects given. In some cases, you will have to change the form of the underlined verb.

EXAMPLE   Writing center tutors <u>help</u> many people.

A. The writing center tutor *helps many people.*

B. They *help many people.*

1. The teachers <u>plan</u> to review the material before the exam.

   A. The teacher _____

   B. I _____

2. We <u>do</u> understand your need to be alone.

   A. He _____

   B. Jane and I _____

3. We <u>have</u> collected a number of interesting books you can borrow.

   A. She _____

   B. They _____

4. The children <u>are</u> hoping for a surprise treat.

   A. The child _____

   B. You _____

5. We <u>aren't</u> sure which route is the fastest way to St. Loius.

   A. Karl _____

   B. She _____

6. These boxes of papers <u>are</u> a fire hazard.

   A. That box of papers _____

B. It _____

_____

7. My collections of video and audio tapes <u>take</u> up ten shelves in my bedroom.

A. My collection of video and audio tapes _____

_____

B. It _____

_____

8. Marie and Ed <u>have</u> helped with the charity auction every year.

A. Marie or Ed _____

_____

B. I _____

_____

9. Several people <u>plan</u> homecoming activities that will appeal to as many students as possible.

A. A committee _____

_____

B. You _____

_____

10. Here <u>is</u> the letter you have been looking for all week.

A. Here _____ the letters you have been looking for all week. [Fill in the blank with *is* or *are*.]

B. Where _____ the letter you have been looking for all week? [Fill in the blank with *is* or *are*.]

10.23 CHAPTER REVIEW ACTIVITY

Change the underlined past tense verb forms to correct present tense forms. The first one is done as an example.

[1]A team of scientists w*is*~~as~~ interested in what makes people laugh. [2]They <u>were</u> interested because they <u>realized</u> that laughter <u>had</u> medicinal value. [3]In their studies, they learned that laughter <u>did</u> help sick people feel better and heal faster. [4]It also <u>helped</u> people overcome mild forms of depression. [5]The scientists who <u>were</u> involved in the research <u>did</u> not agree on the reason for laughter's benefits. [6]Whereas some researchers <u>believed</u> laughter <u>stimulated</u> the immune system, other researchers <u>had</u> offered another view. [7]They <u>suggested</u> that laughter <u>jolted</u> the body into producing pain-blocking chemicals. [8]Some scientists <u>didn't</u> accept either explanation.

[9]One doctor who <u>studied</u> laughter <u>noted</u> something interesting. [10]We <u>didn't</u> have to be sick to benefit from laughter. [11]This doctor <u>explained</u> that laughter <u>was</u> good exercise. [12]There <u>were</u> fifteen different muscles exercised in just a little smile. [13]A giggle or bigger laugh <u>tightened</u> and then <u>relaxed</u> muscles all over the body. [14]<u>Did</u> he really think that laughter <u>qualified</u> as a mini-workout?

10.24 CHAPTER REVIEW ACTIVITY

Edit the passage to eliminate the errors in subject-verb agreement. The first one is done as an example. Eleven errors remain for you to correct.

[1]I ~~be~~ *am* fascinated by insects. [2]There is so many facts to learn about insects that I never get bored. [3]For example, did you know that the variety of insects range from about 750,000 different kinds to over 1 million? [4]However, there are some experts who believes the number to be twice that. [5]About 7,000 new species of insects are identified each year, but an unknown number of insects is lost annually from the destruction of their habitats.

[6]The most interesting insects to me isn't the rare ones; they are the destructive ones. [7]The desert locust, which is the insect that is referred to in the Bible, is the most destructive insect in the world. [8]It has a habitat that range from the dry regions of Africa through Pakistan and northern India. [9]Just one of these insects eat its own weight in food each day. [10]During long migratory flights, a large swarm of locusts consume 20,000 tons of grain and vegetation a day.

[11]On the other hand, bees, flies, wasps, butterflies, and moths are among the beneficial insects. [12]In fact, any insect that pollinate plants is helpful. [13]Many fruits and vegetables depends on these pollinators for seed production. [14]Also, many insects are an important food source for birds, fish, and other animals. [15]In fact, insects such as termites, caterpillars, ants, and bees are eaten by people. [16]An insect predator, including the mantises and lady bug, feed on other harmful insects.

10.25 CHAPTER REVIEW ACTIVITY

Edit the passage to eliminate the errors in subject-verb agreement. The first one is done as an example. Eight errors remain for you to correct.

[1]The police ~~has~~ *have* used polygraphs (lie detectors) since 1924 to help determine the guilt or innocence of suspected criminals. [2]These machines measure blood pressure, pulse rate, and respiration simultaneously by means of a pneumograph tube around the subject's chest and a pulse cuff around the arm. [3]Impulses from

the subject is picked up and traced on graph paper. [4]The theory is that respiration, blood pressure, and pulse be affected by the person's emotional state. [5]Fluctuations from the norm signifies emotional tumult—and, hence, a lie. [6]These tests are not mistake-proof, however. [7]Their accuracy depends, in part, upon the expertise and sound judgment of the person who administer the test.

[8]The test requires the administrator to ask a series of control questions. [9]These are questions such as "What is your name?" and "Did you ever steal anything in your entire life?" [10]If the subject answer no to the latter question, he or she likely be lying, and a change in pulse or breathing will be observed. [11]Then when the key question about a crime is asked, chances is good that the administrator can tell if the truth is being told. [12]This is done by comparing the degree of change in the line on the graph with the lines corresponding to the answers to the control questions.

[13]Because the outcome of lie detector tests depend on the skill of the test giver, polygraphs are forbidden in court and cannot be used as testimony. [14]Psychologists are not convinced of the validity of polygraphs, but the police consider them an invaluable aid.

GETTING IN GEAR: IDEAS FOR WRITING

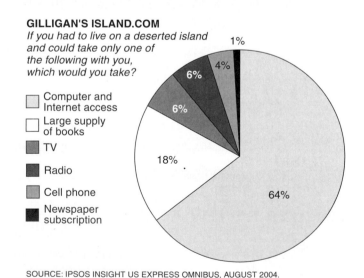

GILLIGAN'S ISLAND.COM
If you had to live on a deserted island and could take only one of the following with you, which would you take?

☐ Computer and Internet access
☐ Large supply of books
▨ TV
▨ Radio
▨ Cell phone
■ Newspaper subscription

1%
4%
6%
6%
18%
64%

SOURCE: IPSOS INSIGHT US EXPRESS OMNIBUS, AUGUST 2004.
BASE = 1000 ONLINE HOUSEHOLDS

© IPSOS Insight. Used by permission.

The pie chart gives the responses to the question "If you had to live on a deserted island and could take only one of the following [computer and Internet access, large supply of books, TV, radio, cell phone, newspaper subscription] with you, which would you take?" Do you find the responses surprising? Alarming? Comforting? To learn more about how Americans actually spend their leisure time, visit the Bureau of Labor Statistics's American Time-Use Survey at www.bls.gov/news.release/atus.t09.htm.

writing topic: Answer the question next to the pie chart for yourself and give reasons for your choice.

suggestions for prewriting: List what you would take. Give the reasons each of the items is important to you. Which item has the most compelling reasons for it?

suggestions for drafting
- Your thesis or topic sentence (depending on whether you are writing an essay or a paragraph) can mention the item you would take and why the item matters to you.
- Give the reasons for taking the item from least to most significant, so you have a progressive order.

suggestion for revising: To make your writing more concise, look for any repetition and wordiness that you can eliminate. (Concise word choice is discussed on page 49.)

suggestion for editing: If you use the present tense, edit one extra time, checking your subject-verb agreement.

RECHARGE: Lesson Summary

1. A verb can show past, present, or future tense (time).
2. A verb in the **present tense** shows that something is happening now or that something happens regularly.
3. To achieve **subject-verb agreement,** use singular present tense verbs with singular subjects and plural present tense verbs with plural subjects.
   - Add an *-s* or *-es* ending with these subjects: *he, she, it,* singular nouns.

     It always <u>rains</u> on my vacations.
   - Omit the *-s* or *-es* with these subjects: *I, we, they, you,* plural nouns.

     Five students <u>expect</u> an A on the exam.
   - The verb *to be* has three present tense forms: *am* and *is* are singular; *are* is plural.
   - The verb *to have* has two present tense forms: *has* is used with *he, she, it,* and singular nouns; *have* is used with *I, we, you, they,* and plural nouns.
   - The verb *to do* has two present tense forms: *does* is used with *he, she, it,* and singular nouns; *do* is used with *I, we, you, they,* and plural nouns.

RECHARGE: Lesson Summary Continued

4. To decide on whether to use a singular or plural verb, rule out phrases that appear with the subject.

   My collection of antique vases is valuable.

5. A **compound subject** is two or more subjects joined by *and, or,* or *nor.*

   • Use a plural verb with subjects joined by *and.*

   My dog and my cat play well together.

   • With subjects joined by *or,* use the verb that agrees with the closer subject.

   The pasta or the potatoes provide carbohydrates.

   The potatoes or the pasta provides carbohydrates.

6. A **collective noun** names a group of people or things. Use a singular verb when the people or things function as one unit and a plural verb when they function individually.

   The faculty makes its decision.

   The faculty regularly disagree about the value of tests.

7. An **indefinite pronoun** does not refer to a specific person, place, object, emotion, or idea. Some indefinite pronouns are always singular and take singular verbs; some are always plural and take plural verbs; some can be either singular or plural, depending on the meaning of the sentence.

   Someone is talking too loudly on a cell phone.

   Both of the toys are broken.

8. When a sentence has **inverted order**, the verb comes before the subject.

   Where are the necessary forms?

   There is no reason to panic.

9. With the **relative pronouns** *who, which,* and *that,* choose the verb that agrees with the word the relative pronoun refers to.

   Chris is a person who believes in superstition.

CHAPTER 11

Using the Past Tense

In Chapter 10, you learned that verbs indicate time. You also learned about the present tense and the need to achieve subject-verb agreement when you use that tense. This chapter will continue the explanation of tense by focusing on the past tense of verbs.

UNDERSTANDING THE PAST TENSE

A verb in the **past tense** shows that something took place before now. Here are two examples:

> *Last spring, Jeffrey <u>celebrated</u> his graduation with a party for his closest friends.* [Jeffrey celebrated before now, so the underlined verb is in the past tense.]
>
> *The streets <u>flooded</u> after the heavy spring rains.* [The streets flooded before now, so the underlined verb is in the past tense.]

FORMING THE PAST TENSE OF REGULAR VERBS

A large group of verbs, called **regular verbs,** form the past tense by adding *-d* or *-ed* to the base form. Here are some examples:

BASE FORM	PAST TENSE	EXAMPLES
bake	baked	Yesterday I <u>baked</u> cookies.
climb	climbed	Yesterday I <u>climbed</u> a tree.
help	helped	Yesterday I <u>helped</u> you.
jump	jumped	Yesterday I <u>jumped</u> over a fence.
slap	slapped	Yesterday I <u>slapped</u> him.
walk	walked	Yesterday I <u>walked</u> five miles.

In Chapter 10, you learned that, in the present tense, the form of the verb is determined by whether the subject is singular or plural.

> Singular subject and verb: *The <u>plant</u> in the kitchen <u>needs</u> water.*
> Plural subject and verb: *The <u>plants</u> in the kitchen <u>need</u> water.*

In the past tense, the situation changes. The same verb form is used, regardless of whether the subject is singular or plural.

Troubleshooting

In speech, you do not hear the *-d* or *-ed* ending when it comes before a *-t*. Thus, "I *used* to own a dog" sounds like "I *use* to own a dog," and "I was *supposed* to go" sounds like "I was *suppose* to go." Remember that you must write *used* and *supposed*—the *-ed* or *-d* must appear in the past tense.

I <u>needed</u> *something.*   *We* <u>needed</u> *something.*
You <u>needed</u> *something.*   *They* <u>needed</u> *something.*
He <u>needed</u> *something.*   *The child* <u>needed</u> *something.*
She <u>needed</u> *something.*   *The children* <u>needed</u> *something.*
It <u>needed</u> *something.*

SPELLING ALERT

In some verbs ending in a vowel-consonant (such as *slap*), the last letter is doubled before the *-ed* is added. When you are unsure, see Chapter 24 for the rule on when to double or consult a dictionary to check spelling.

CONNECT FOR SUCCESS: Use the Past Tense When Appropriate in Your Classes

You will use the past tense often in college writing. For example, a history paper about the events that caused World War I will rely on the past tense, as will an essay examination answer in a media class about the origins of the World Wide Web.

11.1 ACTIVITY

Above the line, change the underlined present tense verbs to past tense verbs, so the entire paragraph is in the past tense. The first one is done as an example.

In 1989, history in the West abruptly [1]<u>shifts</u> ^shifted course. The communist regimes in Eastern Europe [2]<u>end</u>, severing these nations' ties to the Soviet Union. This ending [3]<u>sparks</u> unprecedented political and economic reforms. Two years later, the Soviet Union itself [4]<u>disintegrates</u>. The Cold War [5]<u>concludes</u> and so [6]<u>finishes</u> a sharply defined historical era that [7]<u>stretches</u> back to 1914. The end of the Cold War [8]<u>renews</u> the commitment to democracy and capitalism in the West. It also [9]<u>accelerates</u> the existing movement toward unification in Europe. However, the transition in Eastern Europe and the Soviet Union [10]<u>proves</u> rocky. As people around the world [11]<u>interact</u> more and more, cultures [12]<u>mingle</u>, producing conflict and convergence. How well the West embraces the challenges remains to be seen.

Source: Adapted from Dennis Sherman and Joyce Salisbury, *The West in the World* (New York: McGraw-Hill, 2006), pp. 878–79. Copyright © 2006 The McGraw-Hill Companies. Used by permission of The McGraw-Hill Companies.

11.2 ACTIVITY

Fill in the blanks in the following sentences with the correct past tense forms of the regular verbs in parentheses.

Cdv

EXAMPLE   (to respect) Coach Earl Blaik's football players

_____*respected*_____ him.

1. (to maintain) Football coach Earl Blaik of Army always _____
strict discipline.

2. (to play) Once Army _____ against an inexperienced team.

3. (to score; to cause) Army_____ so many points that they
_____ the other team to feel humiliated.

4. (to order) Coach Blaik _____ his players to take it easy on
the team.

5. (to try; to turn) The team _____ to follow their coach's
orders, but fate _____ the tables.

6. (to fumble) The opposition _____ the ball.

7. (to scoop; to remember) A West Point player _____ up the
loose ball, but then he _____ the coach's orders.

8. (to stop; to look) The player _____ in his tracks and
_____ fearfully at Coach Blaik on the sidelines.

9. (to place) Then he _____ the ball down on the 1-yard line.

10. (to fear) Clearly, he _____ crossing into the end zone.

11.3 ACTIVITY

On a separate sheet, write sentences using the past tense forms of the regular verbs given.

1. to play
2. to graduate
3. to discuss
4. to lift
5. to wonder
6. to hope

FORMING THE PAST TENSE OF IRREGULAR VERBS

A group of verbs, called **irregular verbs**, does not form the past tense by adding -*d* or -*ed*. Instead, it forms the past tense in a variety of ways, as the following examples show.

Present: *Today I sing in the choir.*
Past: *Yesterday I sang in the choir.*

Present: *Today I fly home at noon.*

Past: *Yesterday I flew home at noon.*

Present: *Today I run my first marathon.*

Past: *Yesterday I ran my first marathon.*

The same past tense form is used, regardless of whether the subject is singular or plural.

I fell down.	*We fell down.*
You fell down.	*They fell down.*
He fell down.	*The child fell down.*
She fell down.	*The children fell down.*
It fell down.	

You already know the past tense forms of many irregular verbs. You can check the forms you do not know in the dictionary. Different dictionaries list verb forms in different ways, but typically the second form given is the past tense. Thus, if you look up *fly,* you will see these forms: *fly, flew, flown.* The second form (*flew*) is the past tense. Sometimes the *-ing* form (*flying*) is also given. If no verb forms are given, the verb is regular and forms its past tense by adding *-d* or *-ed,* as explained on page 197.

You can also check the past tense form of many irregular verbs by consulting the chart "Representative Irregular Verbs—Past Tense Forms."

REPRESENTATIVE IRREGULAR VERBS— PAST TENSE FORMS

BASE FORM	PAST TENSE	BASE FORM	PAST TENSE
be	was; were	hear	heard
become	became	hide	hid
begin	began	hold	held
blow	blew	hurt	hurt
break	broke	keep	kept
bring	brought	know	knew
build	built	lay [meaning	laid
buy	bought	"place"]	
catch	caught	lead	led
choose	chose	leave	left
come	came	lend	lent
cut	cut	let	let
dive	dove	lie [meaning	lay
do	did	"rest"]	
draw	drew	lose	lost
drink	drank	make	made
drive	drove	mean	meant
eat	ate	meet	met
fall	fell	pay	paid
feed	fed	put	put
feel	felt	quit	quit
fight	fought	read	read
find	found	ride	rode
fly	flew	ring	rang

REPRESENTATIVE IRREGULAR VERBS— PAST TENSE FORMS *(CONTINUED)*

BASE FORM	PAST TENSE	BASE FORM	PAST TENSE
forbid	forbad [or forbade]	rise	rose
		run	ran
forget	forgot	say	said
forgive	forgave	see	saw
freeze	froze	sell	sold
get	got	send	sent
give	gave	set	set
go	went	shake	shook
grow	grew	shine [meaning "give light"]	shone
hang [a picture]	hung		
hang [meaning "execute"]	hanged	shine [meaning "polish"]	shined
have	had	sing	sang
sit	sat	throw	threw
stand	stood	understand	understood
steal	stole	wake	woke
swim	swam	wear	wore
take	took	win	won
teach	taught	wind	wound
tell	told	write	wrote
think	thought		

11.4 ACTIVITY

Rewrite the sentences, changing the underlined present tense verbs to past tense verbs. Consult the chart or a dictionary if you are unsure of the correct form.

EXAMPLE   The Beatles' last concert <u>takes</u> place in San Francisco in 1966.

The Beatles' last concert took place in San Francisco in 1966.

1. On August 29, 1966, the Beatles <u>have</u> their last performance before 25,000 people in San Francisco's Candlestick Park.

2. Although they still <u>come</u> together to record until 1970, they <u>do</u> not play live in concert after 1966.

3. San Francisco also <u>gives</u> rise to the United Nations in 1945; however, because many Europeans <u>think</u> the city too far to travel to, officials <u>choose</u> to move the site to New York.

4. Interestingly, the term "sandlot baseball" also <u>begins</u> in San Francisco.

_____

5. The term comes from the 1860s, when a cemetery <u>stands</u> where the Civic Center sits.

_____

_____

6. City leaders <u>rebuild</u> the cemetery into a park, leveling a sand hill when they <u>do</u> so.

_____

7. As a result, the 17-acre park <u>becomes</u> known as the "sandlots."

_____

8. "Sandlot" quickly <u>finds</u> its way into our vocabulary as a synonym for "ball park."

_____

11.5 ACTIVITY

Fill in the blanks with the correct past tense forms of the irregular verbs in parentheses. If you are unsure of the correct forms, check the list beginning on page 200 or your dictionary.

EXAMPLE   (to give; to find) Georges de Mestral _____*gave*_____ us an

alternative to zippers and buttons when he _____*found*_____
a new way to fasten things.

1. (to go; to see)   One day in 1948, de Mestral _____ into the

woods to walk with his dog, and he _____ the way burrs
fastened themselves to his dog's coat and his own clothing.

2. (to put; to take)   Curious, de Mestral _____ a bit of burr

under a microscope and _____ a close look.

3. (to seek)   Looking closely at the burr, he _____ to
understand how it worked.

4. (to understand; to have)   He _____ that the burr

_____ barbed, hooklike seed pods, which meshed perfectly
with the looped fibers in the clothes.

5. (to think; to stand)   De Mestral then _____ that the

discovery could lead to a fastening system that _____
a chance of competing with the zipper.

6. (to come; to give)   He _____ up with a way to reproduce

the hooks and loops in woven nylon and _____ the
invention the name Velcro, from the French words *velours* and *crochet*.

11.6 ACTIVITY

Refer to the chart of irregular verbs beginning on page 200 and select five verbs whose past tense forms you are unsure about. On a separate sheet, compose sentences using the past tense forms of the five verbs.

11.7 ACTIVITY

Fill in the blanks with the correct past tense forms of the irregular verbs in parentheses. Consult the list beginning on page 200 or your dictionary if you are unsure of the correct forms. The first one is done as an example.

[1]A native of South Carolina (to tell) _told_____ me a popular coastal myth about Alice Belin Flagg. [2]It all (to begin) _____ in 1849 on a beautiful plantation in Murrells Inlet, South Carolina. [3]Alice (to go) _____ to live there with her widowed mother and overprotective brother, Dr. Flagg. [4]While attending school in Charleston, Alice (to fall) _____ in love with a wealthy young man, who (to give) _____ her a beautiful engagement ring. [5]When she (to let) _____ her brother see the ring, he (to become) _____ enraged and (to forbid) _____ her to wear it. [6]He (to feel) _____ the man was beneath Alice and (to give) _____ her orders never to see him. [7]Heartbroken, Alice secretly (to wear) _____the ring on a ribbon around her neck.

[8]A few days before the May Ball of 1849, Alice (to grow) _____ ill with a fever. [9]When Dr. Flagg (to make) _____ his medical examination of his sister, he (to find) _____ the ring and (to throw) _____ it into the waters of Murrells Inlet. [10]Soon after that, Alice died, crying out for her ring. [11]According to legend, Alice still roams the halls of the plantation, searching for her ring. [12]Recent and past visitors there (to say) _____ they (to see) _____ her and (to feel)_____ her pull on their wedding bands as she looked for her own. [13]Long after they (to leave) _____ the island, many of these visitors (to think) _____ they (to hear) _____ Alice sobbing quietly.

11.8 COLLABORATIVE ACTIVITY

Pair up with a classmate and quiz each other on the past tense forms of the irregular verbs beginning on page 200. Make a list of any forms you miss and study the list regularly.

MAKING SUBJECTS AGREE WITH *WAS* AND *WERE*

To be is the only verb with more than one past tense form. Its forms are *was* (singular) and *were* (plural). These forms must agree with their subjects in the same way that present tense verbs need to agree with their subjects.

Troubleshooting

If you need to review subject-verb agreement (using singular subjects with singular verbs and plural subjects with plural verbs), return to Chapter 10.

WITH THESE WORDS	USE	EXAMPLES
I	was	I was late.
he	was	He was late.
she	was	She was late.
it	was	It was late.
singular noun	was	The child was late.
we	were	We were late.
you	were	You were late.
they	were	They were late.
plural noun	were	The children were late.

Helping verbs

Troubleshooting

Helping verbs are discussed in more detail on page 85.

Was and *were* are often **helping verbs.** That is, they are often used with another verb to form a complete verb.

I $\boxed{was}$ *studying all afternoon.*
The clothes $\boxed{were}$ *drying on the line.*

Contractions

Was and *were* can be combined with *not* to make shortened forms called **contractions.**

> *was + not = wasn't*
>
> *were + not = weren't*

Notice that the apostrophe replaces the *o* in *not*.

The coat <u>wasn't</u> expensive
The antiques <u>weren't</u> for sale.

When you are unsure whether to use *was* or *were*, consult this list:

I, he, she, it, the child	was (wasn't)
you, we, they, the children	were (weren't)

 GRAMMAR ALERT

Many frequently heard forms should be avoided in college and business writing.

No:	*You was late.*		No:	*We was late.*
Yes:	*You were late.*		Yes:	*We were late.*
No:	*They was late.*		No:	*The band members was late.*
Yes:	*They were late.*		Yes:	*The band members were late.*
No:	*He/she/it weren't late.*			
Yes:	*He/she/it wasn't late.*			

11.9 ACTIVITY

Rewrite the following sentences, changing the underlined present tense forms of *to be* to past tense forms. (Use *was* or *were*.)

EXAMPLE   The storm <u>is</u> moving inland.

The storm was moving inland.

1. Area theaters <u>are</u> raising their ticket prices because their operating expenses <u>are</u> increasing.

2. Mr. Tong <u>is</u> worried because his job <u>is</u> in jeopardy.

3. Red and orange <u>aren't</u> Keisha's favorite colors.

4. The problem <u>isn't</u> the expense of golf; it <u>is</u> the time involved.

5. You <u>are</u> right about Carlo; he <u>is</u> the best person for the job.

6. He <u>is</u> the person they <u>are</u> talking about.

7. I <u>am</u> uncomfortable because my shoes <u>are</u> too tight.

8. The couple <u>is</u> planning a small wedding because the bride and groom <u>are</u> saving their money for tuition.

9. We <u>are</u> working while they <u>are</u> on vacation.

10. The employees <u>aren't</u> very courteous, so the store <u>is</u> losing business.

11.10 ACTIVITY

Write sentences by following each subject with *was* or *were* and any other words that make a logical sentence.

EXAMPLE   At midnight, I _was hungry for a turkey sandwich._____

1. The faded curtains _____

_____

2. My new car _____

_____

3. He _____

_____

4. It _____

_____

5. After dinner, they _____

_____

6. Last week, I _____

_____

7. In my opinion, you _____

_____

8. You _____

_____

IF ENGLISH IS NOT YOUR FIRST LANGUAGE

1. The past tense is used for actions that began and ended in the past. Time expressions are often used with the past tense; these are expressions such as *last week, a year ago, yesterday,* and *in May.*

    Last week, I _adopted_ a stray cat.
    Louisa _lost_ her driver's license yesterday.

2. Do not add a *-d* or an *-ed* ending to the past tense form of an irregular verb.

    No: *The choir _sanged_ all our favorite hymns.*
    Yes: *The choir _sang_ all our favorite hymns.*

11.11 CHAPTER REVIEW ACTIVITY

"Protecting the Herd," created in 1907 from the Library of Congress: #LC-USZ62-99358

can

Fill in the blanks with the correct past tense forms of the verbs in parentheses. Some of the verbs are regular, and some are irregular. The first one is done as an example.

Frederic Remington (1861–1909) (to paint) [1] *painted* the rugged life he (to see) [2]_____ in the West, although he (to come) [3]_____ from the East. Born in Canton, New York, Remington (to study) [4]_____ art at Yale University and at the Art Students League in New York City. In 1880, when he (to be) [5]_____ nineteen, he (to move) [6]_____ to the West, where he (to begin) [7]_____ to paint the life around him. Remington (to have) [8]_____ contact with the U.S. Cavalry, which (to bring) [9]_____ him near battles between the North American Indians and U.S. soldiers. He (to paint) [10]_____ many of these battles. In his work, Remington also (to depict) [11]_____ what he (to feel) [12]_____ and (to notice) [13]_____: men relaxing by the warmth of a campfire, the alert expression of an Indian scout, the sweat of a racing horse rider. Thus, the Wild West lives on in Remington's painting.

11.12 CHAPTER REVIEW ACTIVITY

On a separate sheet, rewrite the following passage by changing the verbs from present tense to past tense. Some of the verbs are regular, and some are irregular. The first one is done as an example.

¹In 1879, when Ivory soap ~~is~~ developed by Procter and Gamble, it sinks, just like any other brand. ²The soap's "floatability" comes about by accident.

³One day, a worker goes to lunch and leaves the machine on that mixes the solution of soap. ⁴When he returns, he discovers a curious, frothy mixture. ⁵Several workers examine the mixture and decide it is still usable. ⁶Soon, the soap hits the market, and the manufacturer gets letters from excited consumers who want more "floating soap."

⁸The company traces the soap to the frothy solution and realizes that, if they beat air into the mixture as it is being made, the soap becomes lighter than water. ⁹That is what they do, and as a result the soap floats.

11.13 CHAPTER REVIEW ACTIVITY

Fill in the blanks with the correct past tense forms of the verbs in parentheses. Some of the verbs are regular and some are irregular. The first one is done as an example.

A number of pieces of historic legislation have shaped labor-management relationships in this country. In 1932, the Norris-LaGuardia Act (to prohibit) ¹_prohibited_____ courts from issuing injunctions against nonviolent union activities and (to outlaw) ²_____' yellow-dog contracts. Yellow-dog contracts (to be) ³_____ forced on employees. These contracts (to make) ⁴_____ not joining a union a condition of employment.

The National Labor Relations Act of 1935 (to award) ⁵_____ employees the right to form and join labor unions, and it (to allow) ⁶_____ such labor activities as strikes, boycotts, and picketing. The act also (to establish) ⁷_____ the National Labor Relations Board, which (to oversee) ⁸_____ labor practices. This act (to give) ⁹_____ considerable impetus to the labor movement. The Labor-Management Relations Act of 1947 (to altered) ¹⁰_____ the National Labor Relations Act, because it (to permit) ¹¹_____ states to prohibit compulsory union membership.

In 1938, the Fair Labor Standards Act (to set) ¹²_____ minimum and maximum hourly wages in interstate commerce industries. In 1959, The Labor-Management Reporting and Disclosure Act (to change) ¹³_____ earlier laws and (to guarantee) ¹⁴_____ the rights of union members to vote for union leaders and to participate in union meetings. This law (to help) ¹⁵_____ clean up union corruption.

Source: Adapted from William G. Nickels, James M. McHugh, and Susan M. McHugh, *Understanding Business*, 5th ed. (New York: McGraw-Hill, 1999), p. 351. Copyright © 1999 The McGraw-Hill Companies. Used by permission of The McGraw-Hill Companies.

GETTING IN GEAR: IDEAS FOR WRITING

© Liza Donnelly. Used by permission.

Autobiographies come in many forms, and they are a significant source of information for historians. For a particularly interesting collection of first-person narratives available online, see the Library of Congress's Born in Slavery site, which contains more than 2,300 first-person accounts of slavery and 500 black-and-white photographs of former slaves. Visit www.loc.gov and type "born in slavery" in the search box.

writing topic: Assume that, like the woman in the cartoon, you are writing an autobiographical novel. Tell one story from your life that you would be sure to include in that novel. The story can come from your childhood or from a more recent time. It may have occurred in any context, such as with your family, at school, in your neighborhood, with your friends, during a sporting event, in your home, or on vacation.

suggestions for prewriting

- List five memorable events in your life. Indicate why each one is memorable.
- Pick one of the events and answer these questions: What happened? How did it happen? Who was involved? Why did it happen? When did it happen? Where did it happen?

suggestions for drafting

- Write the story in chronological order, starting with what happened first and moving to what happened next, and so on to the last event.
- Emphasize the most important answers to the what, how, who, why, when, where questions you answered during prewriting.

suggestion for revising: Add details to describe people or scenes to help your reader visualize the events.

suggestion for editing: Because your story will be written in the past tense, check all your past tense verb forms carefully, paying particular attention to irregular verbs. If you are unsure of a past tense form, check your dictionary.

RECHARGE: Lesson Summary

1. A **past tense verb** indicates that something took place before the present time.

2. A **regular verb** forms the past tense by adding *-d* or *-ed*.

    Phyllis <u>asked</u> three questions in class.

3. An **irregular verb** forms the past tense a variety of ways. Correct past tense forms can be checked in a dictionary or in the list on page 200.

    The swimmers <u>dove</u> into the cold lake.

4. The verb **to be** has two past tense forms—*was* (singular) and *were* (plural)—which must agree with their subjects.

    The teacher <u>was</u> proud of her class.
    The teachers <u>were</u> proud of their classes.

CHAPTER 12

Using the Perfect Tenses and the Active and Passive Voices

In Chapter 10, you learned about using the *base form* of a verb to make the *present tense;* in Chapter 11, you learned about using the *past tense form* of a verb to make the past tense. In this chapter, you will learn about using the *past participle form* to make the *perfect tenses.*

UNDERSTANDING THE PERFECT TENSES AND THE PAST PARTICIPLE

The **perfect tenses** are made with a form of the verb combined with *have* or *has,* like this:

have eaten	have asked	have felt	have thought
had eaten	had asked	had felt	had thought

You learned in Chapter 10 that *have* and *has* are helping verbs. To form one of the perfect tenses, these helping verbs are combined with a form of the verb called the **past participle.** The two perfect tenses you will learn about in this chapter are the **present perfect tense** and the **past perfect tense.**

For regular verbs, the past participle is the same as the past tense form. It is made by adding *–d* or *–ed* to the base form. Here are some examples:

BASE FORM	PAST TENSE	PAST PARTICIPLE
dance	danced	danced
move	moved	moved
plant	planted	planted
want	wanted	wanted

Irregular verbs do not form the past participle by adding *-d* or *-ed*. Instead, they form the past participle in a variety of ways, as the examples in the chart "Representative Irregular Verbs—Past Tense and Past Participle Forms" show. You

Troubleshooting

If you need to review helping verbs, see page 85.

Troubleshooting

If you need to review regular verbs, see page 197.

211

already know the past participle forms of many irregular verbs. You can check the forms you do not know in the chart or in a dictionary. Different dictionaries list verb forms in different ways, but typically the last form given is the past participle. Thus, if you look up *fly* and find *fly, flew, flown*, you know that *flown* is the past participle. If no verb forms are given, the verb is regular and makes its past participle by adding *-d* or *-ed* to the base form.

Troubleshooting

If you need to review irregular verbs, see page 199.

REPRESENTATIVE IRREGULAR VERBS—PAST TENSE AND PAST PARTICIPLE FORMS

BASE FORM	PAST	PAST PARTICIPLE
be	was; were	been
become	became	become
begin	began	begun
blow	blew	blown
break	broke	broken
bring	brought	brought
build	built	built
buy	bought	bought
catch	caught	caught
choose	chose	chosen
come	came	come
cut	cut	cut
dive	dove	dived
do	did	done
draw	drew	drawn
drink	drank	drunk
drive	drove	driven
eat	ate	eaten
fall	fell	fallen
feed	fed	fed
feel	felt	felt
fight	fought	fought
find	found	found
fly	flew	flown
forbid	forbad; forbade	forbidden
forget	forgot	forgotten
forgive	forgave	forgiven
freeze	froze	frozen
get	got	gotten; got
give	gave	given
go	went	gone
grow	grew	grown
hang [a picture]	hung	hung

REPRESENTATIVE IRREGULAR VERBS—PAST TENSE AND PAST PARTICIPLE FORMS (CONTINUED)

BASE FORM	PAST	PAST PARTICIPLE
hang [meaning "execute"]	hanged	hanged
have	had	had
hear	heard	heard
hide	hid	hidden
hold	held	held
hurt	hurt	hurt
keep	kept	kept
know	knew	known
lay [meaning "place"]	laid	laid
lead	led	led
leave	left	left
lend	lent	lent
let	let	let
lie [meaning "rest"]	lay	lain
lose	lost	lost
make	made	made
mean	meant	meant
meet	met	met
pay	paid	paid
put	put	put
quit	quit	quit
read	read	read
ride	rode	ridden
ring	rang	rung
rise	rose	risen
run	ran	run
say	said	said
see	saw	seen
sell	sold	sold
send	sent	sent
set [on a table]	set	set
shake	shook	shaken
shine [meaning "give light"]	shone	shone
shine [meaning "polish"]	shined	shined
sing	sang	sung
sit (in a chair)	sat	sat
stand	stood	stood
steal	stole	stolen
swim	swam	swum
take	took	taken

REPRESENTATIVE IRREGULAR VERBS—PAST TENSE AND PAST PARTICIPLE FORMS *(CONTINUED)*		
BASE FORM	**PAST**	**PAST PARTICIPLE**
teach	taught	taught
tell	told	told
think	thought	thought
throw	threw	thrown
understand	understood	understood
wake	woke	woken; waked
wear	wore	worn
win	won	won
wind	wound	wound
write	wrote	written

The principal parts of verbs

The **principal parts** of verbs are the base, past, and past participle forms. Learning the principal parts is important, because the present tense, past tense, and perfect tenses are formed from them, as the following chart illustrates.

THE PRINCIPAL PARTS OF VERBS		
Base Makes the present tense	**Past** Makes the past tense	**Past Participle** Makes the present perfect and past perfect tenses with helping verbs
Be *I am late.* [present]	**Was; Were** *I was late.* [past] *We were late.* [past]	**Been** *I have been late.* [present perfect] *I had been late.* [past perfect]
Cook *I cook dinner.* [present]	**Cooked** *I cooked dinner.* [past]	**Cooked** *I have cooked dinner.* [present perfect] *I had cooked dinner.* [past perfect]
Do *I do it.* [present]	**Did** *I did it.* [past]	**Done** *I have done it.* [present perfect] *I had done it.* [past perfect]

Remember, the past and past participle forms of *regular verbs* look alike. They are made by adding *-d* or *-ed* to the base form. (See *cook* in the chart "The Principle Parts of Verbs.") You can find the past and past participle forms of *irregular verbs* by checking the chart beginning on page 212 or by consulting a dictionary.

12.1 ACTIVITY

Fill in the following blanks with the principal parts of the verbs given. Some of the verbs are regular, and some are irregular. If you need help with the irregular verbs, consult the chart beginning on page 212 or your dictionary.

EXAMPLES	Verb	Base	Past	Past Participle
	to eat	*eat*	*ate*	*eaten*
	to dance	*dance*	*danced*	*danced*

Verb	Base	Past	Past Participle
1. to bake			
2. to try			
3. to teach			
4. to type			
5. to bring			
6. to stand			
7. to steal			
8. to drink			
9. to enjoy			
10. to help			

12.2 COLLABORATIVE ACTIVITY

Pair up with a classmate and quiz each other on the principal parts of the irregular verbs beginning on page 212. Make a list of any forms you miss and study the list regularly.

The present perfect tense

The **present perfect tense** has three uses:

1. to show that something began in the past and continues into the present time

    Already we have studied an hour.

2. to show that something began in the past and just recently ended

    The hospital has completed its new wing.

3. to show that something occurred at an unspecified time in the past

    I have eaten chocolate covered ants before.

CONNECT FOR SUCCESS: Use the Present Perfect Tense When Appropriate in Your Classes

You will have many opportunities to use the present perfect tense in your classes, particularly to discuss a trend that began in the past and continues into the present. In an economics class, for example, you might write "The unemployment rate *has declined* steadily for the past three years." In a nutrition class you might write "Because of the Atkins and South Beach diets, in the past five years adults *have eaten* more protein and fewer carbohydrates."

Notice that the present perfect tense is a two-word verb form. It is made by combining the helping verb *have* or *has* with the past participle.

have + past participle	has + past participle
have + eaten	has + jumped
I have eaten.	*She has jumped.*

The past participle form does not change, but be sure that the helping verb *has* or *have* agrees with the subject.

I have left.	*We have left.*
You have left.	*They have left.*
He has left.	*The child has left.*
She has left.	*The children have left.*
It has left.	

Sometimes the helping verb and the past participle are separated, like this:

I have already left.

Troubleshooting

If you need to review when to use *have* and when to use *has,* see page 175.

Troubleshooting

If you gave trouble recognizing the present perfect tense, remember that it often includes a time indicator such as "since," "recently," "already," or "for the past few days." Here is an example: "*For three weeks*, the temperature has been below normal."

GRAMMAR ALERT

Be sure to use *have* or *has* with the past participle.

No: *We gone with you every year.*
Yes: *We have gone with you every year.*

Remember to use the -*d* or -*ed* ending with the past participle forms of regular verbs.

No: *We have enjoy ourselves.*
Yes: *We have enjoyed ourselves.*

Be sure you are using the past participle form and not the past tense form.

No: *We have went with you every year.*
Yes: *We have gone with you every year.*

12.3 ACTIVITY

In each pair of sentences, one sentence has a verb in the present perfect tense, and one does not. Place a check mark next to the sentence with the verb in the present perfect tense.

EXAMPLE _____ I cooked chicken for supper.

_____✔_____ I have cooked chicken for supper.

1. _____ The bands have warmed up for an hour.

_____ The bands will warm up for an hour.

2. _____ Greg has read three novels this summer.

_____ Greg read three novels this summer.

3. _____ Caroline enjoys the summer band concerts in the park.

_____ Caroline has enjoyed the summer band concerts in the park.

4. _____ The movie has begun ten minutes early.

_____ The movie began ten minutes early.

5. _____ The union members will vote on the new contract.

_____ The union members have voted on the new contract.

6. _____ The road crew has resurfaced the highway.

_____ The road crew resurfaces the highway.

7. _____ Carlotta lived in California all her life.

_____ Carlotta has lived in California all her life.

8. _____ The flooding has destroyed the corn crop.

_____ The flooding destroyed the corn crop.

12.4 ACTIVITY

Complete the present perfect tense by filling in the blanks with the past participle form of the verb in parentheses. If you need help with the forms for irregular verbs, consult the chart beginning on page 212 or your dictionary.

EXAMPLE (to change) Technology has _changed_ the way we view movies at home.

1. (to become) The digital versatile disc (DVD) has _____ enormously popular.

2. (to establish) In fact, the DVD has _____ itself as the hottest-selling consumer electronics device.

3. (to put) Many movie studios have _____ extra features on DVDs.

4. (to release) Studios have sometimes _____ new movies on DVDs first.

5. (to be; to provide) DVDs have _____ capable of higher picture resolution than VCR tapes and have _____ a stable storage environment, too.

6. (to make) For the most part, this format has _____ the VCR close to obsolete.

12.5 ACTIVITY

Complete the present perfect tense by filling in the blanks with *have* or *has*.

EXAMPLE Radio _____*has*_____ remained one of the most competitive of the electronic media businesses.

1. Judging by the number of radio stations and the number of radios in homes, the medium _____ survived the threat of televison.

2. Once stations were family owned, but now they _____ merged into groups owned by corporations.

3. Fueled by relaxed ownership regulations, these corporations _____ led the consolidation of the radio business.

4. Station owners _____ turned to format programming because of intense competition.

5. This trend _____ resulted in the franchising and depersonalization of the medium.

6. National Public Radio _____ been the most influential noncommercial radio station, although it _____ suffered from decreased federal funding.

7. The newest form _____ been satellite radio.

8. Begun in 2002, this new form _____ grown rapidly.

12.6 ACTIVITY

In each pair of sentences, one verb should be a past tense form, and the other should be a present perfect tense form. Using meaning as your guide, fill in each blank with either the correct past tense or present perfect tense of the verb in parentheses. Be prepared to explain how the meaning differs for each sentence in the pair.

EXAMPLE (to practice) The team _____ foul shots last week.

Since early this morning, the team _____ foul shots.

1. (to be)   Since 1989, James _____ your best friend.

               Until 1989, James _____ your best friend.

2. (to enter)   Last week, George _____ his terrier in the dog show.

               Every year since I've known him, George

               _____ his terrier in the dog show.

3. (to eat)   I _____ lunch in this restaurant almost every day since it opened.

               I _____ lunch in this restaurant almost every day until it closed.

4. (to wear)   Marcus is easily recognized by his handlebar mustache;

               he _____ it for years.

               Marcus was easily recognized by his handlebar mustache;

               he _____ it for years.

5. (to vacation)   The family _____ in the mountains when the children were young.

               Since the children were young, the family

               _____ in the mountains.

6. (to run)   I _____ a mile a day since my recovery from surgery.

               I _____ a mile a day until my surgery.

12.7 ACTIVITY

Fill in the blanks with the correct past tense or present perfect tense of the verb in parentheses, whichever is appropriate.

EXAMPLE   (to be) Tea _____*has been*_____ popular for a long time.

From the time you have been old enough to drink caffeine, you probably (to enjoy) [1]_____ tea many times, but you probably (to think) [2]_____ little about its origins. The Chinese (to discover) [3]_____ tea around 2700 B.C. By the 1400s, the tea ceremony had become part of the culture of Japan, but tea (to be) [4]_____ available in the West only since the 1600s.

In today's dollars, the tea of the 1600s (to sell) [5]_____ for $100 a pound. It (to be) [6]_____ so expensive that the teapots made in the seventeenth and eighteenth centuries (to be) [7]_____ small. Each pot (to hold) [8]_____ about two cups of tea, and tea was kept in a locked tea caddy. Sugar and milk (to be) [9]_____

added ingredients only since around 1665. Interestingly, people (to drink)
10 _____ iced tea only since the 1880s, and they (to enjoy)
11 _____ the convenience of tea bags since the first one was
made in New York City in 1908.

The custom of serving afternoon tea (to start) 12 _____ in the
late 1600s and (to remain) 14 _____ popular in many countries to
this day. Now in many places, tea parties (to become) 13_____
fashionable once again.

The past perfect tense

The **past perfect tense** shows that one thing occurred in the past before another
thing occurred in the past. Thus, when you are writing in the past tense, you can
use the past perfect to show that something occurred in the *more distant* past.
Here are two examples:

    past   *more distant past*
I [*believed*] *you* [*had made*] *a mistake.*

      past   *more distant past*
She [*said*] *that Michael* [*had left*] .

To form the past perfect tense, use the helping verb *had* with the past
participle.

had + past participle
had + fallen

I had fallen.   *We had fallen.*
You had fallen.   *They had fallen.*
He had fallen.   *The child had fallen.*
She had fallen.   *The children had fallen.*
It had fallen.

Troubleshooting

If you are unsure of the
past participle form for an
irregular verb, consult the
list beginning on page 212
or your dictionary.

GRAMMAR ALERT

Remember to use the past participle with *had*.

    No: *The children eaten their lunch.*
    Yes: *The children had eaten their lunch.*

Be sure to use the *-d* or *-ed* ending with the past participle of regular verbs.

    No: *They had play all day.*
    Yes: *They had played all day.*

Be sure to use the past participle form, not the past tense form, with *had*.

    No: *I had began at noon.*
    Yes: *I had begun at noon.*

The sequence of tenses

Knowing when to use the present perfect tense and when to use the past perfect tense can be tricky when a single sentence has more than one verb in more than one tense. In general, use the present perfect tense with the present tense and the past perfect tense with the past tense.

> *present perfect*   *present*
> After I <u>have finished</u> a book, I <u>lend</u> it to someone.

>   *past perfect*   *past*
> Because my boss <u>had given</u> me several assignments, I <u>was</u> busy.

CONNECT FOR SUCCESS: Use the Past Perfect Tense in Story Telling

The past perfect tense can be important when you are telling a story, and the order of events is critical. For example, in a business administration class, you might write the story of a businessperson's success and include a sentence like this: "In 2002, the sandwich shop Martin *had opened* ten years earlier was a profitable franchise."

12.8 ACTIVITY

Each of the following sentences has a part that refers to the past and a part that refers to the more distant past. Draw one line under the part that refers to the past and two lines under the part that refers to the more distant past.

EXAMPLE   <u><u>After I had eaten,</u></u> <u>I became ill.</u>

1. Molly had applied four times before she entered the police academy.
2. When I went to sleep last night, I had decided to quit my job.
3. After Benjamin had explained his problem, his advisor helped him.
4. Because you had broken your leg, you were on crutches.
5. Before Sheila left for school, she already had worked five hours in the diner.
6. When I arrived, you had finished painting the ceiling.

12.9 ACTIVITY

Rewrite the sentences, changing the underlined verbs to past perfect forms.

EXAMPLE   I <u>will drive</u> the 300 miles to Detroit.

I had driven the 300 miles to Detroit _____

1. Perry <u>has prepared</u> a special dinner to celebrate Mom and Dad's anniversary.

_____

_____

2. The dental hygienist <u>cleaned</u> my teeth last week.

_____

_____

3. We <u>expect</u> you to pick us up at six o'clock.

_____

_____

4. Jean and Marilyn <u>applied</u> for the same management position at Dillards Department Store.

_____

_____

5. We <u>hope</u> to visit Boston on our trip down the eastern seaboard.

_____

_____

6. The school board <u>has chosen</u> a new superintendent to replace Dr. Lu.

_____

_____

7. The wind <u>will blow</u> steadily from the north throughout the morning.

_____

_____

8. I <u>saw</u> your sister studying in the library.

_____

_____

12.10 ACTIVITY

Fill in the blanks with the present perfect or past perfect forms of the verbs in parentheses. Use the present perfect with the present tense and the past perfect with the past tense.

EXAMPLES   (to sleep)   After she ___*had slept*___ eight hours, Anne felt better.

(to eat)   After he ___*has eaten*___ breakfast, Noam is more alert.

1. (to make)   Once Daria _____ up her mind, she never changes it.

2. (to figure out)   Before Lorenzo finished the mystery, he _____ who committed the murder.

3. (to take)   The Union forces won the Battle of Gettysburg because they _____ the high ground.

4. (to study) June and Luis _____, so now they are ready for their algebra final.

5. (to live) I _____ in apartments all my life, and I like them.

6. (to explain) You _____ your opinion five times, but I still do not understand it.

7. (to learn) Jamie _____ conversational Spanish before he left for Mexico.

8. (to tell) You _____ me what I need to know.

UNDERSTANDING THE ACTIVE AND PASSIVE VOICES

When the subject of a sentence *acts*, the sentence is in the **active voice.** When the subject of the sentence is *acted upon*, the sentence is in the **passive voice.**

	subj.
Active voice (the subject acts):	Carpenter ants destroyed the front porch.
	subj.
Passive voice (the subject is acted upon):	The front porch was destroyed by carpenter ants.

In addition to helping form the perfect tenses, the past participle serves another purpose—it helps form the passive voice. To form the passive voice, use the past participle form of the verb with a form of the helping verb *to be (am, is, are, was, were).* Here are some examples of passive voice, with the verb underlined as a study aid:

I *am honored* to meet you.
The cause of the accident *is believed* to be wet pavement.
The children *are expected* to join us for dinner.
The tree *was uprooted* by hurricane-force winds.
The tree *had been uprooted* before the hurricane.
We *were annoyed* by the rude behavior of the couple seated behind us.

Active voice emphasizes the *performer* of the action; passive voice emphasizes the *receiver* of the action. Ordinarily, you should use active voice to give sentences more energy. However, when you do not know who performed an action or when the performer is unimportant, use passive voice.

Weak passive voice (who did the scolding?):	The children were scolded for being late.
Active voice (the subject identifies the person who did the scolding):	The principal scolded the children for being late.
Passive voice (when you do not know who performed the action):	The car was broken into in the middle of the night.

Composing at the computer

Your word-processing program's style checker may automatically flag every use of passive voice. Often, you will want to follow the style checker's recommendation and rewrite the sentence in the active voice. However, evaluate these flagged sentences carefully, because you should use the passive voice when you want to emphasize the receiver of the action.

CONNECT FOR SUCCESS: Evaluate the Passive Voice

When you read material, particularly material on controversial issues, be suspicious when the writer uses the passive voice to hide information. For example, a person who says, "I *was told* that the governor accepted illegal campaign contributions" may not want to reveal the source of the information—or may not really have a source.

12.11 ACTIVITY

For each sentence, first underline the verb. Then write an A if the sentence is in the active voice and P if it is in the passive voice.

EXAMPLE _____*A*_____ The Iditarod, an 1,150-mile dog sled race, <u>occurs</u> once a year.

1. _____ Once, the Iditarod was called "The Last Great Race on Earth."

2. _____ Each team of twelve to sixteen dogs and their mushers race from Anchorage, Alaska, to Nome in ten to seventeen days.

3. _____ The races are run over the roughest, most beautiful terrain in the state, perhaps in the world.

4. _____ The course includes jagged mountain ranges, a frozen river, dense forest, desolate tundra, and miles of windswept coast.

5. _____ In addition, temperatures fall far below zero.

6. _____ Often, a complete loss of visibility is caused by high winds.

7. _____ Finally, long hours of darkness and treacherous hills add to the difficulty.

8. _____ This is not just a dog sled race.

9. _____ It is best described as a challenge to the stamina and conditioning of well-trained humans.

10. _____ Mushers enter from all walks of life.

11. _____ Fishers, lawyers, doctors, miners, artists—both male and female—have their own reasons to take the challenge.

12.12 ACTIVITY

Three sentences in the paragraph are in the passive voice. Identify them and rewrite them to be in the active voice.

EXAMPLE   The Iditarod trail was begun as a supply route to coastal towns.

The Iditarod trail began as a supply route to coastal towns.

[1]The Iditarod is now a National Historic Trail. [2]This trail began as a mail and supply route from the coastal towns of Seward and Knik to the interior mining camps and beyond to the West Coast. [3]Mail and supplies were brought in by dog sleds. [4]On the return trip, gold was taken out by them. [5]In 1925, part of the Iditarod Trail became a life-saving highway. [6]Diphtheria threatened to devastate the population. [7]Serum was needed by the victims. [8]Again, intrepid dog mushers and their faithful, hard-driving dogs saved the day because they got the necessary medicine to the region. [9]Today's Iditarod race is a commemoration of this past—a past Alaskans view with understandable pride.

 IF ENGLISH IS NOT YOUR FIRST LANGUAGE

1. Certain words are often used with the present perfect tense to show that something began in the past and continues into the present. These words are *since, for, until now, so far, now,* and *these days.*

    Eduardo <u>has been</u> a boy scout leader <u>since</u> 1985.
    Katie <u>has worked</u> for a professional photographer <u>for</u> ten years.
    No one <u>has done</u> that job <u>until now.</u>
    <u>These days</u> the pollen count <u>has been</u> high.

2. Certain other words are often used with the present perfect tense to show that something just recently ended. These words are *just, already,* and *recently.*

    The movie <u>has just ended.</u>
    The instructor <u>has already passed out</u> the test papers.
    A new project director <u>has recently joined</u> the firm.

3. In many languages, particularly Asian languages, the present, past, and perfect tenses do not exist. If you speak one of these languages, be patient with yourself until you get a feel for the perfect tenses. You are more likely to see these tenses in writing than to hear them spoken, so be sure to study the forms when you see the perfect tenses in your English reading.

12.13 CHAPTER REVIEW ACTIVITY

Fill in the blanks with the correct present perfect or past perfect forms of the verbs in parentheses.

EXAMPLE   Once I (to review) *had reviewed* my draft, I realized I needed more description.

[1]After I looked over my essay, I no longer liked what I (to write)

_____. [2]Whenever I am unsure about my writing, I ask Luis to

read it, because in the past he (to give) _____ me excellent advice.

[3]This time was no exception. [4]He told me I (to rush) _____

through the supporting details. [5]As a result, I (to develop) _____

my points inadequately. [6]For the better part of today, I added examples to

support my points. [7]I thought I (to provide) _____ enough

details, but now I see that I had not. [8]I feel much better about the piece,

now that I (to illustrate)_____ my points. [9]I (to work)

_____ harder on this essay than any other one this term.

12.14 CHAPTER REVIEW ACTIVITY

Fill in the blanks with the correct present perfect or past perfect forms of the verbs
in parentheses. The first one is done as an example.

Although sociologists (to give) [1] _have given_____ a great deal of

attention to "old boy networks," there (to be) [2] _____ growing

interest in the social networks created by women. Sociologist Pierette

Hondagneu-Sotelo (to study) [3] _____ Hispanic women who are

domestic workers. These women (to create) [4] _____ strong

social networks in various social settings, such as baby showers, church events,

and gatherings at women's homes. Hondagneu-Sotelo discovered that these

women share cleaning tips, remedies for work-related ailments, and advice for

dealing with employers.

In addition, networking (to help) [5] _____ the A Team, a social

network of female health care professionals in Boston. The A Team began in 1977

through a series of casual lunches. Soon it (to evolve) [6] _____ to

a network for helping women advance in a predominantly male work

environment. By 1984, many members (to advance) [7] _____

to middle management and, by 1995, many members (to make)

[8] _____ it to top executive posts in health care institituions.

Source: Adapted from Richard T. Shaefer, *Sociology*, 7th ed. (New York: McGraw-Hill, 2001),
p. 127. Copyright © 2001 The McGraw-Hill Companies. Used by permission of The McGraw-Hill
Companies.

12.15 CHAPTER REVIEW ACTIVITY

Correct the errors with present perfect tense, past perfect tense, and passive voice
by crossing out and writing above the line. The first correction is made as an
example. You will need to make nine corrections.

cdm In the United States, some of our wilder television programs are adaptations of shows from other countries. For example, in 1999 in the Netherlands, people were glue to their television sets to watch a wildly popular program called *Big Brother*. For the show, every minute of the participants' days was videotaped and played live on television and the Internet. The show lasted a hundred days before it cancelled.

The show, which was name for the "Big Brother" in George Orwell's classic novel *1984*, simulated the ever-present Big Brother of the book with the 24 cameras and 59 microphones that were place throughout the house—even in the bathroom. Before the 100-day run of the show ended, millions of viewers have followed the real-life soap opera on television and the program's website. They watched as participants engaged in conversation, conducted their affairs, made tea, took out the garbage, and so forth.

At regular intervals, viewers were gave the opportunity to vote on their favorite participants. Those with fewest votes were vote off the program. The last to leave the show were men named Bart, Ruud, and Willem. By the time they were finish with the show, the three had been rocketed to stardom. At the end of the run, viewers had the final say on their favorite character, with the $120,000 top prize going to Bart, twenty-three. Participants' surnames were not maked public.

Big Brother is the program that began the reality TV craze that had been so popular recently.

GETTING IN GEAR: IDEAS FOR WRITING

Source: © Arcadia University. Used by permission.

When Beaver College changed its name to Arcadia College in 2001, applications to the school doubled. Apparently, a college called Arcadia fosters a different set of expectations than one called Beaver. Visit your college's website. What impression is it likely to create for prospective students? Does your school's name contribute to that impression?

writing topic: For good or ill, how has college been different from what you expected? Write about one way college has not met your expectations.

suggestions for prewriting
- Try mapping. In the center of a page, write "college expectations," and draw a circle around it. Branch off ideas from that circle by following the mapping instructions on page 9. (Think about your classes, your workload, your teachers, other students, your living conditions, your social life, and your activities outside the classroom.)
- Select one or more ideas from your map and write two lists—one labeled "What I Thought College Would Be Like" and one labeled "What College Is Really Like."
- You might also generate ideas about why you had the expectation you did.

suggestions for drafting
- Your thesis or topic sentence (depending on whether you are writing an essay or a paragraph) can mention your expectation for college and the reality, something like this: "I thought college would be _____, but it was really_____." Remember to limit yourself to one aspect of college.

- Your thesis or topic sentence can also note why you had your expectation, something like this: "Because the university's brochures pictured ethnically diverse students and teachers, I expected more cultural diversity on this campus."
- First write out what you expected college to be like; then write out what it really is like.

suggestion for revising: Since your writing will include contrast, these transitions and conjunctions may be helpful for coherence: *in contrast, on the other hand, however, in reality, yet, nevertheless.*

suggestion for editing: You may have opportunities to use the present and past perfect tenses. For example, you may write sentences similar to these: "Although I thought I would be lonely, I *have met* many people" and "I *had hoped* to study nutrition, but I changed my major to early childhood education." Edit one extra time, checking for correct forms of the perfect tense and past participle.

RECHARGE: Lesson Summary

1. The **past participle** form of a regular verb is identical to the past tense. It is made by adding *-d* or *-ed* to the base form.

    talk + ed = talked   cook + ed = cooked

2. The **past participle** form of an irregular verb is formed in a variety of ways.

    become   begun   felt

3. Use the past participle with the helping verb *have* or *has* to form the **present perfect tense.** The present perfect tense shows one of the following:

    - that something began in the past and continues into the present

        The play has run for forty-nine weeks.

    - that something began in the past and recently ended

        The workers have negotiated a new contract.

    - that something occurred at an unspecified time in the past

        The rabbits have eaten the vegetables in the garden.

4. Use the past participle with *had* to form the **past perfect tense.** The past perfect tense shows that one thing occurred in the past before another thing occurred in the past.

    We realized that you had eaten already.

5. **Active voice** means that the sentence subject performs the action. **Passive voice** means that the sentence subject is acted upon. To form the passive, use the past participle with the helping verb *am, is, are, was,* or *were.*

    Active voice: *The dog hid the bone.*
    Passive voice: *The bone was hidden by the dog.*

CHAPTER 13

Using the Progressive Tenses

CHAPTER GOALS

By the end of this chapter, you will learn to

Understand the present participle form

Use the present progressive tense correctly

Use the past progressive tense correctly

Troubleshooting

If you need to review helping verbs, see page 85.

In Chapter 10, you learned how to use the *base form* of a verb to make the *present tense*; in Chapter 11, you learned how to use the *past tense form* of a verb to make the past tense; in Chapter 12, you learned how to use the *past participle form* of a verb to make the *perfect tenses*. Now you will learn how to use the *present participle form* to make the *progressive tenses*.

UNDERSTANDING THE PROGRESSIVE TENSES AND THE PRESENT PARTICIPLE

The **progressive tenses** are made with *am, is, are, was,* or *were* combined with the *–ing* form of the verb. *Am, is, are, was,* and *were* are **helping verbs.** The *–ing* form of the verb is the **present participle.**

HELPING VERB	+	PRESENT PARTICIPLE	=	PROGRESSIVE TENSE
am		eating		am eating
is		feeling		is feeling
are		going		are going
was		sleeping		was sleeping
were		doing		were doing

When you combine the present participle with *am, is,* or *are,* you form the **present progressive tense.** When you combine the present participle with *was* or *were,* you form the **past progressive tense.**

Present progressive tense: *Kim is wondering where you are.*

Past progressive tense: *Kim was wondering where you are.*

 SPELLING ALERT

Sometimes the last letter is doubled before *-ing* is added (*swim* becomes *swimming*), and sometimes the last letter is dropped before adding *-ing* (*love* becomes *loving*). These rules are discussed on pages 383 and 384. If you are unsure of the spelling of a present participle, check your dictionary.

230

The present progressive tense

The **present progressive tense** shows that an action is in progress *right now*. Here are two examples:

> *Janet is sleeping late.*
> *The leaves are changing color.*

Unlike the simple present, the present progressive always shows that something is occurring at the time the sentence is being spoken or written.

Present Progressive	**Simple Present**
Janet is sleeping late.	*Janet sleeps late.*
The leaves are changing color.	*The leaves change color.*

You will often hear sportscasters using the present progressive tense to explain the ongoing action of an event, like this: "Tiger Woods *is approaching* the tee."

The present progressive can also show that something will take place in the future.

> *Tomorrow I am leaving for Maine.*
> *Soon you are going home.*

Be sure your helping verb agrees with the subject. To form the present progressive, use the correct helping verb *am*, *is*, or *are* with the present participle.

am + present participle	is + present participle	are + present participle
am + eating	is + eating	are + eating
I am eating.	*He is eating.*	*You are eating.*
	She is eating.	*We are eating.*
	It is eating.	*They are eating.*
	The child is eating.	*The children are eating.*

Troubleshooting

If you need to review when to use *am, is,* and *are* to achieve subject-verb agreement, see page 172.

→ GRAMMAR ALERT

Be sure to use *am*, *is*, or *are* with the *-ing* form to make the present progressive.

No:	*I going to the store now.*
Yes:	*I am going to the store now.*
No:	*My mother going to the store now.*
Yes:	*My mother is going to the store now.*
No:	*We going to the store now.*
Yes:	*We are going to the store now.*

CONNECT FOR SUCCESS: Use the Present Progressive Tense When Appropriate in Your Classes

There will be times in your classes when you will need to use the present progressive tense to clarify that an action is ongoing in the present time. For example, in a paper about education reform, you might write "School systems *are examining* the impact of 'No Child Left Behind' policies on their curricula." In a homework response explaining why the president is having difficulty appointing federal judges, you might write "Senators *are using* the filibuster to block the appointment of the most conservative judges."

13.1 ACTIVITY

Rewrite the sentences, changing the underlined present tense verbs to present progressive forms.

EXAMPLE   Joyce <u>hopes</u> to join your softball team.

Joyce is hoping to join your softball team.

1. The firefighters <u>battle</u> the three-alarm blaze.

   _____

   _____

2. Ilya <u>hopes</u> to win a scholarship for his sophomore year.

   _____

   _____

3. For extra protein, we <u>eat</u> turkey sandwiches for lunch.

   _____

   _____

4. Because of the excessive heat, I <u>drink</u> extra fluids.

   _____

   _____

5. You <u>spend</u> too much time on unimportant matters.

   _____

   _____

6. At this time, he <u>works</u> out in the gym for two hours.

   _____

   _____

7. All the neighbors <u>complain</u> because the children <u>play</u> the radio very loudly.

   _____

   _____

8. When you leave for school, I <u>plan</u> to rent your room.

   _____

   _____

9. She wants to work this afternoon if it <u>rains.</u>

   _____

   _____

10. She <u>explains</u> the problem, but she also <u>offers</u> a solution.

   _____

   _____

Pair up with a classmate, and each of you select a different pair of original and rewritten sentences from Activity 13.1. Together, do the following and be prepared to report your conclusions to the class.

- Decide how the meaning changes when the tenses change from the present to the present progressive.
- Decide when you are likely to use each tense.

The past progressive tense

The **past progressive tense** is used to show that something was ongoing in the past. Here are two examples:

> The telephone <u>was ringing</u>.
>
> I <u>was hoping</u> to go to Florida.

The difference between the simple past and the past progressive is this: The simple past shows that something began and ended in the past, but the past progressive stresses that an action was continuing across past time.

Past Progressive	Simple Past
The dog <u>was barking</u> all night.	The dog <u>barked</u> all night.
I <u>was working</u> in the library.	I <u>worked</u> in the library.
We <u>were telling</u> you the truth.	We <u>told</u> you the truth.

The past progressive is often used to show that one thing was going on *before* another thing happened, *at the same time* another thing happened, or *after* another thing happened.

Here is an example of one thing going on before another thing happened.

> This happened second.   This happened first.
>
> Before my dinner guests arrived, I <u>was searching</u> for extra napkins.

In this example, one thing was going on at the same time another thing happened.

> Both events happened at the same time.
>
> The performer took a bow while the audience <u>was clapping</u>.

Here, one thing was going on after another thing happened.

> This happened first.   This happened second.
>
> After the storm ended, the children <u>were splashing</u> in the puddles left in the street.

To form the past progressive, use the helping verb *was* or *were* with the present participle. Be sure the helping verb agrees with the subject.

was + present participle	were + present participle
was + going	were + going
Helen was going home.	We were going home.
I <u>was going</u>.	We <u>were going</u>.
The child <u>was going</u>.	They <u>were going</u>.
He <u>was going</u>.	You <u>were going</u>.
She <u>was going</u>.	The children <u>were going</u>.
It <u>was going</u>.	

Troubleshooting

If you need to review when to use *was* and *were*, see page 204.

GRAMMAR ALERT

Be sure to use *was* or *were* with the *-ing* form of a verb to make the past progressive.

No: *Mark leaving early.*

Yes: *Mark was leaving early.*

No: *They leaving early.*

Yes: *They were leaving early.*

Composing at the computer

If you omit *was* or *were* from the past progressive, or if you omit *am, is,* or *are* from the present progressive, your word-processing program's grammar check is likely to flag the error as a sentence fragment. When you correct, be sure to add the verb (*am, is, are, was,* or *were*) that agrees with the subject.

CONNECT FOR SUCCESS: Use the Past Progressive Tense in Story Telling

The past progressive tense can be important when you are telling a story, and you must show that one event was occurring before another. For example, in a paper about business ethics for a business administration class, you might write "The company's executives *were cashing* in their stock options just before third quarter losses were announced."

13.3 ACTIVITY

Rewrite the sentences, changing the underlined past tense forms to past progressive forms.

EXAMPLE Western Europe <u>lost</u> its colonial empires before the outbreak of World War II.

Western Europe was losing its colonial empires before the

outbreak of World War II.

1. Before World War II, national liberation movements around the globe <u>gathered</u> momentum.

_____

_____

2. Europe's control over its colonial territories <u>weakened</u>.

_____

_____

3. At the beginning of the war, Germany <u>defeated</u> imperial nations, such as France and the Netherlands, and Japan <u>conquered</u> Western holdings in the Pacific.

4. At the end of the war, countries in the United Nations <u>pressed</u> the view that colonialism denied human rights.

_____

_____

5. They, therefore, <u>contributed</u> to the anticolonial view.

_____

_____

6. Despite the intensity of these sentiments, many European settlers <u>felt</u> they had lived in the colonies too long to give up control to local populations.

_____

_____

7. After the war, national liberation revolts <u>threatened</u> the British empire in southern Asia.

_____

_____

8. In India, Mohandas Gandhi <u>led</u> the independence movement.

_____

_____

9. He <u>used</u> passive resistance and civil disobedience to pressure British officials to grant Indian independence.

_____

_____

10. Gandhi succeeded and soon British colonial rule <u>came</u> to an end.

_____

_____

Source: Adapted from Dennis Sherman and Joyce Salisbury, *The West in the World* (New York: McGraw-Hill, 2006), p. 828. Copyright © 2006 The McGraw-Hill Companies. Used by permission of The McGraw-Hill Companies.

 IF ENGLISH IS NOT YOUR FIRST LANGUAGE

1. The following verbs are rarely used in a progressive tense.

appreciate	hate	mind	recognize
be	know	need	understand
believe	like	prefer	want
dislike			

IF ENGLISH IS NOT YOUR FIRST LANGUAGE CONTINUED

No: *I am appreciating your help.*
Yes: *I appreciate your help.*

2. The following verbs rarely appear in a progressive tense, unless they are describing a specific action or they are part of certain expressions.

appear   look   seem   sound
hear   see   smell   taste

I am hearing something in the distance. [a specific action]
I hear the church bells.
Your plan is sounding better all the time. [an expression]

3. The following verbs almost never appear in a progressive tense.

belong to   own
cost   possess

No: *As a teenager, I was owning a dog.*
Yes: *As a teenager, I owned a dog.*

4. The progressive form of *have* is used with a form of *be* to mean "be experiencing," "be eating," or "be drinking."

I am having trouble with my English homework.
Dana is having soup for lunch.
We are having wine with dinner.

5. In a progressive tense, *think* refers to a mental process. In a simple tense, it refers to a conclusion or an opinion that has been reached.

I was thinking of changing my major. [a mental process]
I think we should leave now. [a conclusion]

13.4 CHAPTER REVIEW ACTIVITY

In each of the following pairs of sentences, place a check mark next to the sentence with the correct tense.

EXAMPLE   _____   At the moment, Darla eats supper.

   ___✓___   At the moment, Darla is eating supper.

1. _____   Most of the time, we shop at the corner market.

   _____   Most of the time, we are shopping at the corner market.

2. _____   When we visited Toronto, we enjoyed the zoo.

   _____   When we visit Toronto, we were enjoying the zoo.

3. _____   By the time I am graduating, I will have two minors.

   _____   By the time I graduate, I will have two minors.

4. _____   Chris leaves Boston to work in Chicago.

   _____   Chris is leaving Boston to work in Chicago.

5. _____ You ate dinner when the phone rang.

_____ You were eating dinner when the phone rang.

6. _____ Laura explained her point when you interrupted her.

_____ Laura was explaining her point when you interrupted her.

7. _____ Finally, we take control of our lives.

_____ Finally, we are taking control of our lives.

8. _____ Dr. Moritz always answers any questions we ask.

_____ Dr. Moritz is always answering any questions we ask.

9. _____ They sleep late this morning.

_____ They are sleeping late this morning.

10. _____ She worked on her computer when the electricity went off.

_____ She was working on her computer when the electricity went off.

13.5 CHAPTER REVIEW ACTIVITY

On a separate sheet, rewrite the following passage, changing the underlined past and present tense verbs to the corresponding progressive forms. The first one is done as an example.

is having

[1]Georgie has trouble deciding what he wants to do. [2]At first, he considered traveling across the country. [3]Then he thought about joining the navy. [4]Now he wonders whether he should quit school. [5]If he does not decide what he wants soon, he will turn thirty with no sense of direction. [6]I hope he considers seeing a counselor, because he needs to speak to someone who can help him set goals and direct his life. [7]Unfortunately, at the moment he resists that idea.

13.6 CHAPTER REVIEW ACTIVITY

Edit the paragraph to correct the four mistakes with progressive tense.

EXAMPLE In the seventeenth century, Isaac Newton ~~is~~ *was* pondering an important force of nature.

One night in 1665, English physicist Isaac Newton is sitting in his garden. He trying to figure out why the moon circled the earth. From the corner of his eye, he saw an apple fall from a tree. Newton began wondering why the apple fell down instead of up. He wondered whether the earth were causing the apple to fall. Then he began wondering whether the moon is circling the earth because it wasn't close enough to fall. These thoughts moved Newton in the right direction, but he did not finish working out his laws until 1682. Even then, he was so shy that he did not want to publish his findings. It took his friends three years to persuade him to make his discoveries public.

GETTING IN GEAR: IDEAS FOR WRITING

theatre

An increasing number of people are complaining that watching a movie in a theater is no longer enjoyable. Commercials, discourteous patrons, and overly long trailers are commonly cited as annoyances that detract from the experience. Is watching a movie in a theater is usually an enjoyable experience for you? If not, you can sign the petition for the Movie Goers' Bill of Rights at www.petitononline.com/a101/petition.html.

writing topic: Write about a pleasant or an unpleasant movie-going experience you have had. Explain why the experience was good or bad.

suggestions for prewriting
- List the last three to six movies you watched in the theater. Next to each one, indicate whether your experience was positive or negative.
- Select one movie experience from your list to write about.
- Answer these questions: Why was the experience pleasant or unpleasant? What people helped make it so? What events helped make it so?

suggestion for drafting: Using chronological order, write out what happened and who was involved.

suggestion for revising

- Add descriptive details that help your reader understand why the experience was pleasant or unpleasant.
- Ask a reader with good judgment about writing to read your draft and tell you whether it is clear why the experience was pleasant or unpleasant.

suggestion for editing: You may have opportunities to use the progressive tenses in this writing. For example, you may write sentences similar to these: "The child *was opening a potato chip bag and making a great deal of noise.*" Edit one extra time, checking for correct forms of any progressive tenses you use.

RECHARGE: Lesson Summary

1. The **present participle** is the *–ing* form of the verb:

   dancing   singing   laughing   walking   thinking

2. Use the present participle with the helping verb *am, is,* or *are* to form the **present progressive tense.** The present progressive tense shows one of the following:

   - that something is occurring at the time the sentence is being spoken or written

     The concert is running late.

   - that something will take place in the future

     Next week, I am moving to a new apartment.

3. Use the present participle with the helping verb *was* or *were* to form the **past progressive tense.** The past progressive tense shows one of the following:

   - that something was going on in the past

     They were expecting us for dinner.

   - that one thing was going on before another

     Before I hit the telephone pole, I was trying to change the radio station.

   - that something was going on at the same time another thing was happening

     The performers were dancing while they were singing the song.

CHAPTER 14

Eliminating Inappropriate Tense Shifts

CHAPTER GOALS

By the end of this chapter, you will learn to

Recognize inappropriate tense shifts

Eliminate inappropriate tense shifts from your writing

Troubleshooting

To review the present tense, refer to Chapter 10; to review the past tense, refer to Chapter 11; to review the perfect tenses, refer to Chapter 12; to review progressive tenses, refer to Chapter 13.

As you know from earlier chapters in this part, verbs have different forms—called **tenses**—to show present and past times.

Present:	*Kerry plays guitar in a local band.*
Past:	*Kerry played guitar in a local band.*
Present perfect:	*Kerry has played guitar in a local band.*
Past perfect:	*Kerry had played guitar in a local band.*
Present progressive:	*Kerry is playing guitar in a local band.*
Past progressive:	*Kerry was playing guitar in a local band.*

Sometimes it is appropriate to shift from one of these tenses to another, but sometimes it is not. In this chapter, you will learn how to avoid inappropriate tense shifts.

RECOGNIZING INAPPROPRIATE TENSE SHIFTS

Sometimes writers must legitimately move from one tense to another to show a change in time.

Move from past to present:
past
Last year, I worked at Hamburger Heaven,
present
but now I am tutoring in the math lab.

If you move from one tense to another without a valid reason, you create a problem called **tense shift.** An inappropriate tense shift is a problem, because it confuses the time frame of your writing.

Confusing tense shift:
past
After I stepped on the gas pedal, the light
present
turns red.

Correction:
past
After I stepped on the gas pedal, the light
past
turned red.

Confusing tense shift: *present*
Lee <u>is</u> cooking cabbage for dinner. The smell
past
<u>was</u> making me ill.

Correction: *present*
Lee <u>is</u> cooking cabbage for dinner. The smell
present
<u>is</u> making me ill.

→ GRAMMAR ALERT

Watch out for confusing tense shifts when you are telling a story. Here is an example:

Confusing tense shift: *past*   *past*
I <u>walked</u> into my morning class and <u>found</u> a

past   *past*
seat. The instructor <u>began</u> lecturing, so I <u>took</u>

present   *present*
notes. Then I <u>realize</u> that I <u>am</u> in the wrong
class.

Correction: *past*   *past*
I <u>walked</u> into my morning class and <u>found</u> a

past   *past*
seat. The instructor <u>began</u> lecturing, so I <u>took</u>

past   *past*
notes. Then I <u>realized</u> that I <u>was</u> in the wrong
class.

SHIFTING TENSES WITH *WILL* OR *CAN* AND WITH *WOULD* OR *COULD*

In a complex sentence, if the dependent clause is in the present tense, the independent clause uses *will* or *can*.

dep. cl. in pres. tense   ind. cl.
When you <u>finish</u> the job, you <u>will</u> get paid.

dep. cl. in pres. tense   ind. cl.
When Lottie's dog <u>runs</u> away, Henry <u>can</u> always find him.

If the dependent clause is in the past tense, the independent clause uses *would* or *could*.

dep. cl. in past tense   ind. cl.
When the baby <u>laughed</u>, she <u>would</u> wave her arms.

dep. cl. in past tense   ind. cl.
Although Henri <u>practiced</u> daily, he <u>could</u> not learn the piano concerto.

To avoid inappropriate tense shifts, most often you will use *will* or *can* with the present tense and *would* or *could* with the past tense.

Inappropriate tense shift: Lisa <u>graduates</u> in June. Then she <u>could</u> get a
job.

Correction: Lisa <u>graduates</u> in June. Then she <u>can</u> get a job.

Troubleshooting

If you need to review complex sentences, see page 131; to review independent and dependent clauses, see pages 113 and 131.

Inappropriate tense shift: *I often <u>locked</u> myself out of the apartment. However, the apartment manager <u>will</u> always let me in for a fee.*

Correction: *I often <u>locked</u> myself out of the apartment. However, the apartment manager <u>would</u> always let me in for a fee.*

CONNECT FOR SUCCESS: Avoid Tense Shifts in Notetaking

When you take notes in class, be careful to keep your tenses straight. Inappropriate shifts can create problems. For example, you do not want to write "In the seventeenth century, only 200,000 people could vote in England; the government <u>is</u> staffed by the elite," when your instructor said, "In the seventeenth century, only 200,000 people could vote in England; the government <u>was</u> staffed by the elite." If you make this inappropriate tense shift, you might mistakenly think that the English government is run by the elite *today*.

14.1 ACTIVITY

Circle the verbs in the following sentences. Then write TS in the blank if there is a confusing tense shift. If there is no tense shift, or if the shift is appropriate to show a time change, write OK in the blank.

EXAMPLE _____TS_____ Megen (answered) the phone, and then she (sits) down for a long conversation.

1. _____ I mixed the flour, water, and eggs into a dough, which I shaped into a loaf. Then I bake it at 350 degrees.

2. _____ The mechanic explained to Gary that the car needed a new radiator.

3. _____ The soccer team hopes that next season they can win more games.

4. _____ Last week I wanted my own apartment, but now I am happy in a dormitory.

5. _____ The sky darkened as huge storm clouds rolled in. Then the lightning begins .

6. _____ After lunch, the children play in the schoolyard. When the bell rings, they returned to their classrooms.

7. _____ Douglas was certain that he would make the Dean's List this term.

8. _____ Before I leave on vacation, I checked the map and I fill my gas tank.

9. _____ When I buy a new car, I could take you to work.

10. _____ Because my key was bent, I could not get into my house.

Fill in each blank with the verb form from the following list that does not create an inappropriate tense shift. (Some tense shifts are appropriate.)

The first one is done as an example.

1. designs/designed	**5.** is/was	**9.** is/was
2. calls for/called for	**6.** is/was	**10.** visit/visited
3. see/saw	**7.** is/was	**11.** find/found
4. am/was	**8.** is/was	

When she was an undergraduate architecture student at Yale, Maya Lin

¹ _designed_____ the National Vietnam War Memorial. Her original design

² _____ two walls of polished black granite that met in a V, with

the names of the 57,662 Americans killed in Vietnam between 1959 and 1973

inscribed on it. I ³ _____ the wall when I ⁴ _____

in Washington, DC, in 2004. It ⁵ _____ a very moving experience,

because the monument ⁶ _____ so powerful. Minimalist in

its simplicity, the design ⁷ _____ dignified and eloquent. It

⁸ _____ hard to believe that this beautiful monument

⁹_____ controversial at first. When I ¹⁰_____

the memorial on my recent trip, I ¹¹_____ it a fitting tribute.

Source: Adapted from Wayne Craven, *American Art: History and Culture* (New York: McGraw-Hill, 1994), pp. 618–19. Copyright © 1994 The McGraw-Hill Companies. Used by permission of The McGraw-Hill Companies.

14.3 ACTIVITY

The following passage contains a number of tense shifts, but only seven of them are inappropriate. Cross out the incorrect verbs and write the correct ones above them.

EXAMPLE   Cell phones are a fact of life that few of us think we ~~could~~ can live without.

¹Cell phones mean fast communication from almost any location. ²Those little devices in our briefcases, pockets, and purses mean we could conduct business while shopping at the mall, arrange a dinner date while waiting in the dentist's office, and make an airline reservation while pushing a shopping cart through the grocery store. ³More important, the phones offer a measure of safety. ⁴For example, a flat tire on a deserted highway is less alarming with a cell phone on the front seat.

⁵However, despite the safety and convenience they provide, cell phones can be very annoying. ⁶Diners in restaurants complained regularly because their dinners are disturbed by cell phone chats at the next table. ⁷Often we are talking face-to-face with someone, only to have the conversation interrupted by the ring of the person's cell phone. ⁸Worst of all is the inability to escape cell phone interruptions. ⁹Because phones are portable, they interrupted us everywhere—on the beach, in our cars, on the tennis court—few places are unreachable by cell phone. ¹⁰However, no cell phone interruption is more incredible than one that occurs in a Hong Kong hospital.

¹¹A patient complained that a surgeon uses a cell phone during an operation. ¹²Taxi driver Chung Chi-cheong says he heard the phone conversation while he is under local anesthetic for surgery to remove a polyp in his intestine. ¹³"During the operation, I found the doctor talking. ¹⁴I was surprised because the conversation had nothing to do with my medical condition," Chung said. ¹⁵"The conversation was about buying a car and how much the car cost." ¹⁶Clearly, technology can be taken too far.

 ## IF ENGLISH IS NOT YOUR FIRST LANGUAGE

When you write a direct quotation, a shift in tenses is often appropriate.

Appropriate tense shift: *Jamal __said__, "I __enjoy__ winter sports."*
(past)   (present)

14.4 CHAPTER REVIEW ACTIVITY

The following passage has eight inappropriate tense shifts. Cross out the incorrect verbs and write the correct forms above them.

EXAMPLE   In 1961, baseball player Sandy Koufax made the record books when he ~~leads~~ *led* the National League in strikeouts.

[1]On August 13, 1959, in a baseball game against the Giants, Los Angeles Dodger Sandy Koufax struck out 18 batters. [2]This sets a National League record that equaled the great Bob Feller's Major League triumph. [3]In the game before, Koufax had struck out 13 Philadelphia Phillies batters. [4]His strikeouts for the two games total 31, which creates a Major League record.

[5]However, Koufax's greatest day came two years later. [6]On May 29, 1961, in a night game against the St. Louis Cardinals, Sandy Koufax strikes out 13 batters and becomes the first National League player to win six games and to lead the league in strikeouts.

[7]By the middle of the 1961 season, Koufax had struck out 128 batters in 119 innings. [8]Even more amazing is the fact that in only seven seasons he strikes out 811 players in 811 innings, to average one strikeout for every inning he played. [9]By the end of 1961, Koufax again ties Bob Feller's record by striking out 18 batters in one game. [10]In 1962, Koufax's earned run average of 2.54 leads the National League. [11]Truly, Sandy Koufax was one of baseball's greatest players.

GETTING IN GEAR: IDEAS FOR WRITING

Friendships change as we age, as society changes, and as our circumstances change. For example, not too long ago, we never would have envisioned the kind of friendship that is fostered by the Internet at sites such as www.friendster.com. Take a look at this site and consider the quality of the friendships likely to be formed and maintained on the Internet.

writing topic: Write a story about a friend or about friendship. For example, you can tell a story about meeting or losing a friend, about something you did with a friend, or about how you learned the meaning of friendship. Your story can come from childhood or from a more recent time.

suggestions for prewriting

- To find your writing topic, use the photographs for inspiration and complete two maps, one about your childhood friendships and one about your friendships as an adult. (See page 9 on mapping.) Select as your topic one item from one of your maps.
- For ideas to develop your draft, answer these questions: What happened? How did it happen? Who was involved? Why did it happen? When did it happen? Where did it happen?

suggestions for drafting

- Write the story in chronological order, starting with what happened first, moving to what happened next, and so on to the last event.
- Emphasize the most important answers to the what, how, who, why, when, where questions you answered during prewriting.

suggestion for revising: Look for opportunities to describe people or scenes to give your reader a clear mental image.

suggestion for editing: Edit one extra time to check your verb tenses. Anytime you switch from one tense to another, be sure the shift is appropriate. If you are unsure whether the switch is appropriate, check with your instructor or a writing center tutor.

RECHARGE: Lesson Summary

1. An **inappropriate tense shift** occurs when you move from one verb tense to another without a valid reason.

    Inappropriate tense shift: *First I <u>called</u> 911, and then I <u>leave</u> the apartment.*

    Correction: *First I <u>called</u> 911, and then I <u>left</u> the apartment.*

2. In a complex sentence, if the dependent clause is in the present tense, the independent clause uses *will* or *can*. If the dependent clause is in the past tense, the independent clause uses *would* or *could*.

    If I <u>learn</u> CPR, I <u>can</u> apply for a job as a teacher's aide.
    When Joe <u>had</u> chicken pox, he <u>would</u> wear gloves to avoid scratching.

3. Use *will* or *can* with the present tense and *would* or *could* with the past *tense.*

    The tropical storm <u>threatens</u> to move ashore, so we <u>will</u> prepare for heavy winds.
    I <u>planted</u> my garden with care. Nonetheless, the plants <u>would</u> not thrive.

PART THREE REVIEW
Editing for multiple errors

A. The following passage has five subject-verb agreement errors, three tense shifts, two unnecessary passive voices, and two incorrect verb forms. Cross out the errors and write the corrections above the line.

[1]In 1958, Bank of America introduced the first credit card and creates the modern consumer. [2]The availability of credit has transform how Americans shop and budget their finances. [3]In fact, the average American consumer hold more than $2,000 in credit.

[4]"Charge cards" predated Bank of America's Bank Americard, but they were store-specific and offered credit only at a particular chain of gas stations or department stores. [5] Consumers themselves were provided credit by Bank of America's innovation. [6]Also, the retailer was given assurance of bill payment by it .

[7]At first, the Bank Americard (which later becomes VISA) was available in California only. [8]However, by 1970 it and MasterCharge (which later becomes MasterCard) was issuing cards across the country.

[9]Credit cards can be a convenience, but they can also create problems. [10]In particular, one group of people at risk are college students. [11]Credit card companies send students unsolicited cards. [12]Lured by the "buy-now-pay-later" philosophy, students run up big bills and later discover they be unable to pay. [13]Often, by the time these users of a credit card discovers they have a problem, they are so far in debt that it takes years for them to recover. [14]Even worse, their credit rating can be ruined, creating a problem that plague them for life.

B.   The following passage has five subject-verb agreement errors, three tense shifts, two incorrect verb forms, and one unnecessary passive voice. Cross out the errors and write the corrections above the line.

[1]Long ago, there was no regular firefighters. [2]If a house caught fire, everybody becomes a firefighter. [3]People formed bucket brigades to fight fires. [4]That changed in 1666, when London had a fire that burned down 13,000 buildings, including St. Paul's Cathedral. [5]The English then begin to develop hand-operated pumps, so firefighters could spray water through a hose. [6]Citizens begun to join together in volunteer companies. [7]They promised to drop everything and rush to a fire whenever it breaked out.

[8]In Philadelphia, Benjamin Franklin founded the first department of volunteer firefighters in the United States. [9]It replaced the bucket brigades that had existed up to then. [10]In 1835, the first paid fire patrol was established by New York City. [11]There were 4 members, who was paid $250 a year. [12]The following year, there were 40 members, who was known as the Fire Police. [13]Then in 1855, New York City organizes the first firehouse.

[14]Today, in the United States, there is about 1,000 fire departments staffed by fully paid professional firefighters. [15]In addition, more than 15,000 other departments include both paid and volunteer firefighters. [16]The proud group of paid firefighters include over 80,000 people. [17]The ranks of volunteers number over 800,000.

READING AND WRITING IN RESPONSE TO TEXTBOOKS

The following textbook excerpt tells about the origin of the Environmental Protection Agency.

[1]Rachel Carson published her book *Silent Spring* in 1962. [2]In it, she predicted the harmful effects of pesticides on animal life. [3]Soon thereafter, pesticides were found to cause the thinning of eggshells in bald eagles. [4]As a result of this thin-

ning, the eagles' eggs were breaking, and the chicks were dying. [5]Additionally, populations of terns, gulls, cormorants, and lake trout declined after they ate fish contaminated by high levels of environmental toxins. [6]The concern was so great that the United States Environmental Protection Agency came into existence. [7]The efforts of this agency and civilian environmental groups have brought about a reduction in pollution release and a cleanup of emissions. [8]Even so, we are now aware of more subtle effects that pollutants can have.

Source: Adapted from Sylvia S. Mader, *Biology,* 7th ed. (New York: McGraw-Hill, 2001), p. 307. Copyright © 2001 The McGraw-Hill Companies. Used by permission of The McGraw-Hill Companies.

1. Which sentence is in the present tense? _____

2. In what tenses are the following sentences written?

    A. sentences 1, 2, and 5 _____

    B. sentence 4 _____

    C. sentence 7 _____

3. There are a number of tense shifts in the paragraph. Are any of those shifts

    inappropriate? Explain. _____

    _____

4. Why is *were* used in sentence 3 and *was* in sentence 6? _____

    _____

5. Which sentence is in the passive voice? Why is the passive voice used?

    _____

    _____

writing topic: The textbook excerpt explains that, following the publication of *Silent Spring,* we began understanding the harmful effects of both pesticides and pollution. Although the efforts of the Environmental Protection Agency are crucial, individuals can also help in many ways, including by buying hybrid cars and chemical-free organic foods. Unfortunately, such cars and foods are significantly more expensive than their traditional counterparts. Are you willing to spend more money for one or more of these items? Explain why or why not.

Understanding Pronouns

You write with ease to show your breeding /
But easy writing is cursed hard reading.
—Inventor, statesman, author, and
publisher, Benjamin Franklin

Reflection: Has your experience shown
Franklin to be correct or incorrect? Explain.

WHAT YOU WILL LEARN	WHY YOU WILL LEARN IT
How to recognize and use subject, object, possessive, reflexive, and intensive pronouns	so that you can write correct sentences
How to use singular and plural pronouns	so that you can write correct sentences
How to use nonsexist pronouns	so that you can avoid sexist sentences and have a pleasing style
How to avoid person shifts	so that you can write correct sentences
How to use demonstrative pronouns	so that you can write correct sentences
How to avoid unnecessary pronouns	so that you can write correct sentences
How to avoid reference problems	so that you can avoid confusing sentences

CHAPTER 15

Using Pronouns

CHAPTER GOALS

by the end of this chapter, you will learn to

Recognize subject, object, possessive, reflexive, and intensive pronouns

Recognize the words pronouns substitute for (their antecedents)

Use subject, object, possessive, reflexive, and intensive pronouns correctly

Without pronouns, you would be forced into unpleasant repetition, like this:

> *Harry asked where <u>Harry's</u> coat was so <u>Harry</u> could go home.*

With pronouns, however, you can avoid the unpleasant repetition:

> *Harry asked where <u>his</u> coat was so <u>he</u> could go home.*

In this chapter, you will learn a great deal about different kinds of pronouns and how to use them.

RECOGNIZING NOUNS AND PRONOUNS

A **noun** names a person, a place, an object, an emotion, or an idea. Nouns are words such as these:

Person	Place	Object	Emotion	Idea
cousin	city	car	anger	belief
Delores	lake	Chevy	fear	concept
man	Memphis	foot	joy	democracy
teacher	world	hat	love	freedom

A **pronoun** is a word that substitutes for a noun.

> *The <u>chair</u> is broken, so do not sit in <u>it</u>.*

> *<u>Louise</u> won a prize for <u>her</u> metal sculpture.*

The following words are pronouns and therefore can substitute for nouns.

> I, me, my, mine
> you, your, yours
> he, him, his
> she, her, hers
> it, its
> we, us, our, ours
> they, them, their, theirs

The noun a pronoun substitutes for is called its **antecedent.**

Kimberly made her decision.

Pronoun: *her*
Antecedent: *Kimberly*

The teachers wrote their lesson plans.

Pronoun: *their*
Antecedent: *teachers*

Bev and Raul said that they enjoy sociology.

Pronoun: *they*
Antecedents: *Bev. Raul*

Troubleshooting

If you need to review sentence subjects, see page 72.

USING PRONOUNS AS SUBJECTS

A pronoun often functions as the subject of a sentence, as in these examples:

They gave the cab driver a generous tip.
He is my best friend.

Subject pronouns

I	it
you	we
he	they
she	

USING PRONOUNS AS OBJECTS

A pronoun can also function as the *object of the verb* or the *object of a preposition.*

Object pronouns

me	it
you	us
him	them
her	

Objects of verbs

When a pronoun receives a verb's action, it is the **object of the verb.** To find the object of a verb, ask "whom or what?" after the verb, like this:

Chris threw it across the room.

Verb: *threw*
Ask: threw whom or what?
Answer: *it*
Object of verb: *it*

GRAMMAR ALERT

The object of a verb is sometimes called the **direct object.**

Objects of prepositions

A pronoun can come after a preposition (a word such as *in, on, to, of, near, at, for,* or *by*). In this case, the pronoun is the **object of a preposition.**

In the following examples, the preposition is circled and the pronoun is underlined.

Uri lives near *me.*
Olivia has faith in *you.*
The cat sleeps beside *him.*

Sometimes the preposition is not written out. Instead, it is the unstated *to* or *for.* Here are two examples:

Unstated *to:*   *Chris gave her bad advice.* [Chris gave bad advice to her.]

Unstated *for:*   *Chester bought them a wedding gift.* [Chester bought a wedding gift for them.]

Troubleshooting

If you need to learn more about prepositions, turn to Chapter 20.

GRAMMAR ALERT

The object of a preposition is sometimes called the **indirect object.**

USING PRONOUNS AS POSSESSIVES

Pronouns can show possession (ownership), like this:

The students handed in their essays. [The essays belong to the students.]

The woman caught her hem on the heel of her shoe. [The hem and the shoe belong to the woman.]

Possessive pronouns

my	hers
mine	its
your	our
yours	ours
his	their
her	theirs

GRAMMAR ALERT

The possessive pronoun is *its*, not *it's*, which is the contraction form for "it is" or "it has."

Possessive: *The floor has lost its shine.*
Contraction: *It's too early to call Judy.*

COMPARING SUBJECT, OBJECT, AND POSSESSIVE PRONOUNS

As you have learned so far in this chapter, you choose a pronoun depending on whether it is used as a subject, an object, or a possessive. If you are ever unsure about which pronouns are used as subjects, which are used as objects, and which are used as possessives, consult the following list.

Subject Pronouns
Use as the subject of a sentence.

Singular

I	*I like pizza.*
you	*You are a good friend.*
he	*He is late.*
she	*She dances well.*
it	*It does not work.*

Plural

we	*We cannot go.*
you	*You all should leave.*
they	*They understand calculus.*

Object Pronouns
Use as the object of a verb or as the object of a preposition.

Singular

me	*Give the book to me.*
you	*Juanita likes you.*
him	*Louis told him to leave.*
her	*Ask her that question.*
it	*Karl will leave it here.*

Plural

us	*Doris lent us the notes.*
you	*I like all of you.*
them	*Dad bought a car for them.*

Possessive Pronouns
Use to show ownership.

Singular

my	*I lost my keys.*
mine	*These books are mine.*
your	*Your ideas are important.*
yours	*The job is yours.*
his	*His car is stalled.*
her	*Her temper is short.*
hers	*This idea was hers.*
its	*The idea has its advantages.*

Plural

our	*Our vacation was canceled.*
ours	*These problems are ours to solve.*
your	*You students must do your homework.*
yours	*These handouts are yours to keep.*
their	*Their anger is understandable.*
theirs	*The fault is theirs.*

GRAMMAR ALERT

You and *it* are used as both subjects and objects. *You your, and yours* are both singular and plural.

15.1 ACTIVITY

Rewrite the sentences, changing the underlined nouns to pronouns. Be sure to use subject, object, and possessive pronouns correctly. Then label each pronoun you use S for subject, O for object, or P for possessive. Check the preceding list if you are unsure.

EXAMPLE   <u>Some prisoners</u> did not like <u>soft jailers.</u>
                          S   O
                They did not like them.

                                    _____

Remove

1. <u>Some English criminals</u> found <u>a private prison</u> too soft.

    _____

    _____

2. <u>These criminals</u> believed <u>the criminals'</u> guards treated <u>the criminals</u> too nicely.

    _____

    _____

3. <u>The guards</u> treated <u>the prisoners</u> as fellow human beings.

    _____

    _____

4. <u>This treatment</u> came as a shock to <u>the criminals.</u>

    _____

    _____

Remove

5. Chief Inspector of Prisons Sir David Ramsbotham reported <u>the phenomenon</u>
    in a report.

    _____

    _____

6. According to <u>Ramsbotham</u>, <u>prisoners</u> were on a first-name basis with <u>the
    prisoners'</u> guards and shared meals with <u>the guards.</u>

    _____

    _____

7. <u>Prisoners</u> experienced "culture shock" at the prison because the jail did not
    offer the <u>prisoners</u> a sufficiently threatening environment.

    _____

    _____

8. To <u>the criminals</u>, <u>a jail</u> was not comfortable if <u>the jail</u> was too comfortable.

    _____

    _____

CHOOSING SUBJECT AND OBJECT PRONOUNS IN PROBLEM SITUATIONS

Selecting the correct subject or object pronoun is not always easy, and the
problem situations are explained next. Fortunately, as you read the next sections,
you will see that there are helpful strategies for dealing with the problem
situations.

Pronouns in compounds

And, or, or *nor* can join a pronoun with a noun to form a **compound,** like one of these:

Lionel and I	my dog and me	Phyllis or she	neither Henri nor he
the boy and him	my friend or he	the child and her	neither Greg nor him

To decide whether a subject or an object pronoun is needed in a compound, rule out everything in the compound except the pronoun. Here are two examples:

Which is correct?   *My friend and I left early.*
or
My friend and me left early.

Rule out everything in the compound except the pronoun.

~~My friend and~~ *I left early.*
~~My friend and~~ *me left early.*

Now you can tell that the correct pronoun is *I.*

I left early.

Therefore, the correct compound is this:

My friend and I left early.

Which is correct?   *Lesley invited Antonio and I.*
or
Lesley invited Antonio and me.

Rule out everything in the compound except the pronoun.

Lesley invited ~~Antonio and~~ *I.*
Lesley invited ~~Antonio and~~ *me.*

Now you can tell that the correct sentence is this:

Lesley invited Antonio and me.

 GRAMMAR ALERT

In a compound, the pronoun is placed *after* the noun.
No: *Dr. Huang gave the answer to me and Jeff.*
Yes: *Dr. Huang gave the answer to Jeff and me.*

15.2 ACTIVITY

In each of the following pairs of sentences, rule out everything in the compound except the pronoun. Then place a check mark next to the correct sentence.

EXAMPLE   ___✓___ ~~Harry and~~ I lost our library books.
   _____ ~~Harry and~~ me lost our library books.

1. _____ Louisa asked the boys or he to stay.

   _____ Louisa asked the boys or him to stay.

2. _____ The track coach showed Frankie and I the proper way to stretch.

   _____ The track coach showed Frankie and me the proper way to stretch.

3. _____ For our anniversary, my parents gave Jack and me a beautiful tablecloth.

   _____ For our anniversary, my parents gave Jack and I a beautiful tablecloth.

4. _____ In the morning, my brothers and I will leave for Chicago.

   _____ In the morning, my brothers and me will leave for Chicago.

5. _____ The lab assistant or she will conduct the experiment.

   _____ The lab assistant or her will conduct the experiment.

6. _____ Stavros gave the directions to Lee and he.

   _____ Stavros gave the directions to Lee and him.

7. _____ Dr. Hernandez asked Sheila and they to look up the answer.

   _____ Dr. Hernandez asked Sheila and them to look up the answer.

8. _____ The governor and them studied the legislation.

   _____ The governor and they studied the legislation.

15.3 ACTIVITY

On a separate sheet, write sentences using each of the following compounds correctly.

EXAMPLE   your uncle and him *I gave the keys to your uncle and him.*

1. Bob or us   4. my friends and I

2. Katrina or them   5. the teacher and her

3. my family and me   6. neither Angelo nor he

Pronouns in comparisons

Than and *as* can be used to show **comparisons**, like this:

> *Sanjeen runs faster than Mike.* [compares the running ability of Sanjeen and Mike]
> *Lynette is as talented as Joan.* [compares the talent of Lynette and Joan]

When *than* or *as* is used to compare, some words are unstated.

> *Sanjeen runs faster than Mike [runs].*
> *Lynette is as talented as Joan [is].*

To choose the correct subject or object pronoun, mentally add the missing words.

> Which is it?   *Darlene studies more than me.*
>
> or
>
> *Darlene studies more than I.*

To decide, add the missing words:

Darlene studies more than me study.
Darlene studies more than I study.

Now you can tell that the correct sentence is this:

Darlene studies more than I.

Which is it?   *The teacher praised Dale as much as me.*
or
The teacher praised Dale as much as I.

Add the missing words:

The teacher praised Dale as much as he praised me.
The teacher praised Dale as much as he praised I.

Now you can tell that the correct sentence is this:

The teacher praised Dale as much as me.

GRAMMAR ALERT

Sometimes pronoun choice affects meaning. Consider the following sentences, for example.

I like surfing more than he. [This sentence means that I like surfing more than he does.]

I like surfing more than him. [This sentence means that I like surfing more than I like him.]

15.4 ACTIVITY

Rewrite each sentence, adding the unstated words. Then write the correct subject or object pronoun in the blank.

Troubleshooting

In informal speech, you often hear an object pronoun after a form of *to be* (*am, is, are, was, were*). For example, people often say on the telephone, "This is her," and you often hear "It's me." In formal situations, however, use a subject pronoun after *to be*: "This is she." Although we hardly ever hear "It is I" anymore, in the strictest, most formal contexts, it is still correct.

EXAMPLES   (I, me) Hugh enjoys stock car racing more than _____*I*_____ .

Hugh enjoys stock car racing more than I do.

(I, me) The honor belongs to Julio as much as _____*me*_____ .

The honor belongs to Julio as much as it belongs to me.

1. (I, me) Nick is as good a carpenter as _____ .

    _____

    _____

2. (he, him) Spicy food bothers Helen as much as _____ .

    _____

    _____

3. (she, her) Santha began working in the library later than _____ .

    _____

    _____

4. (we, us)   Learning languages is easier for Brett than _____ .

   _____

   _____

5. (they, them)   No one is happier for you than _____ .

   _____

   _____

6. (they, them)   Taking risks is less stressful for Jonathan than _____ .

   _____

   _____

7. (I, me)   This plan should help you as much as _____ .

   _____

   _____

8. (we, us)   Lonnie always felt they were stronger swimmers than _____ .

   _____

   _____

When the antecedent follows immediately

Sometimes a pronoun is followed immediately by its **antecedent,** as in the following examples.

> *We students support the tuition increase.*
>
>   Pronoun: *we*
>   Antecedent: *students*
>
> *The police officer told us pedestrians to cross the street.*
>
>   Pronoun: *us*
>   Antecedent: *pedestrians*

To decide whether a subject or an object pronoun is needed, rule out the antecedent.

>   Which is it?   *We students must stick together.*
>   or
>   *Us students must stick together.*

Rule out the antecedent.

> *We ~~students~~ must stick together.*
> *Us ~~students~~ must stick together.*

Now you can tell that the correct choice is this:

> *We students must stick together.*

Here is another example:

>   Which is it?   *Some of we band members practice three hours a day.*
>   or
>   *Some of us band members practice three hours a day.*

Rule out the antecedent.

Some of we ~~band members~~ practice three hours a day.
Some of us ~~band members~~ practice three hours a day.

Now you can tell that the correct choice is *us*, because an object pronoun is needed as the object of the preposition *of*.

15.5 ACTIVITY

Combine each pair of sentences into one sentence by following the correct pronoun with its antecedent.

EXAMPLE   Many of the seniors live in apartments.
We are the seniors.

Many of us seniors live in apartments.

1. We are required to take a writing course.
   We are new students.

   _____

   _____

2. All of the volunteer firefighters have had extensive training.
   We are the volunteer firefighters.

   _____

   _____

3. The university does not allow sophomores to have cars on campus.
   We are the sophomores.

   _____

   _____

4. The volunteers decided to raise money for the food bank.
   We are the volunteers.

   _____

   _____

5. Cross-country skiers need considerable upper body strength.
   We are cross-country skiers.

   _____

   _____

6. None of the students knew that answer.
   We are the students.

   _____

   _____

15.6 COLLABORATIVE ACTIVITY

Photocopy one page from a textbook from one of your other courses and do the following.

A. Circle the first ten pronouns.

B. Draw an arrow from each pronoun to its antecedent.

C. Above each circled pronoun, write S, O, or P to label each as a subject, an object, or a possessive pronoun.

D. Trade pages with a classmate and check each other's work. Consult with your instructor if you disagree about any of the circles, arrows, or labels.

Remove

CONNECT FOR SUCCESS: Substitute Words for Numbers in Math and Science

Just as pronouns substitute for nouns, numbers substitute for words in math and science formulas. This means that, as a study aid in math and science, you can write formulas out in words to test your understanding and help you remember them. For example, you can write out the Pythagorean theorem ($a^2 + b^2 = c^2$) like this: If you take the lengths of the two shorter sides of a triangle, square them, and add those numbers together, you get the square of the length of the longest side.

USING REFLEXIVE AND INTENSIVE PRONOUNS

Reflexive pronouns and **intensive pronouns** end in *-self* in the singular and *-selves* in the plural. The reflexive and intensive pronouns are given in the following list.

Reflexive and intensive pronouns

Singular	Plural
myself	ourselves
yourself	yourselves
himself	themselves
herself	
itself	

Reflexive pronouns often indicate that the subject of the sentence did something to or for itself.

Janie helped herself to another cookie.

The child taught himself to ride a bike.

Reflexive pronouns can also express the idea of being alone or doing something without help.

We did our algebra homework ourselves.

Liam prefers to sit by himself.

Intensive pronouns can emphasize the words they refer to.

I myself never eat sugar.

The doctors themselves did not know what to do.

GRAMMAR ALERT

Never use *hisself* and *theirselves*.

No: *The boy locked hisself out of the house.*
Yes: *The boy locked himself out of the house.*

No: *They asked theirselves the same question.*
Yes: *They asked themselves the same question.*

 GRAMMAR ALERT

Do not use a reflexive pronoun without a word it can refer to.

No: *Jerri and myself left early.*
Yes: *Jerri and I left early.*

15.7 ACTIVITY

Write sentences using the reflexive and intensive pronouns given.

EXAMPLE (reflexive pronoun *myself*) <u>*I was so hungry that I ate an entire apple pie myself.*</u>

1. (reflexive pronoun *yourself*) _____

   _____

2. (intensive pronoun *yourself*) _____

   _____

3. (reflexive pronoun *myself*) _____

   _____

4. (intensive pronoun *ourselves*) _____

   _____

 IF ENGLISH IS NOT YOUR FIRST LANGUAGE

1. Two different sentence patterns can be used to express the same idea, one with *to* or *for* written out and one with *to* or *for* unstated. (Notice that the order of the pronouns is reversed when *to* or *for* is omitted.)

   Karen lent <u>it</u> to <u>him</u> yesterday.
   Karen lent <u>him it</u> yesterday.

   Luis made <u>it</u> for <u>her</u> already.
   Luis made <u>her it</u> already.

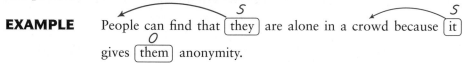

IF ENGLISH IS NOT YOUR FIRST LANGUAGE CONTINUED

2. Remember that *yourself* is a singular form and *yourselves* is a plural form.

You yourself know the answer. [One person knows.]

You yourselves know the answer. [More than one person knows.]

15.8 CHAPTER REVIEW ACTIVITY

Circle each pronoun and draw an arrow to its antecedent. Above each circled pronoun, write S, O, or P to identify each as a subject, an object, or a possessive pronoun.

EXAMPLE People can find that [they] are alone in a crowd because [it] gives [them] anonymity.

[1]A group has the power to arouse its members, but it also can render them unidentifiable. [2]The snarling crowd hides the snarling basketball fan. [3]A lynch mob enables its members to believe they will not be prosecuted. [4]They perceive the action as the *group's*. [5]Rioters are made faceless by the mob, so they are freed to loot. [6]Researcher Brian Mullen researched lynch mobs in 1986. [7]His findings reveal that, the bigger the lynch mob, the more its members lose self-awareness and become willing to commit atrocities.

Source: Adapted from David G. Myers, *Exploring Social Psychology,* 2nd ed. (New York: McGraw-Hill, 2000), pp. 154–55. Copyright © 2000 The McGraw-Hill Companies. Used by permission of The McGraw-Hill Companies.

15.9 CHAPTER REVIEW ACTIVITY

The following passage has nine errors in pronoun usage. Cross out the incorrect pronouns and write the correct ones above them.

EXAMPLE If you take a cruise, I hope you have as much fun as ~~us~~ *we* did.

More and more families are taking cruises together, and now that I have cruised with my family, I understand why. There is something for everyone on a cruise. Us adults could relax all we wanted, while the children could amuse theirselves with a wide range of activities, including Ping-Pong, treasure hunts, dances, swimming, and arcade games. My husband and me particularly appreciated the adult entertainment provided by the casino, Las Vegas–style shows, and bingo. We never worried about the children, because they were enjoying themselves as much as us. In fact, my son told me hisself that he wants to cruise again with his father, brother, and me I .

Perhaps the best part of a cruise is it's food. My husband and me gained 5 pounds on six-course meals served six times a day. Of course, cabin service is available twenty-four hours a day. The food is truly elegant. In fact, my children, my husband, and I ate food we had only heard of before, including escargots.

I recommend a cruise to all families. It is surprisingly affordable, and I don't think any other vacationing family had as much fun as us on our cruise.

GETTING IN GEAR: IDEAS FOR WRITING

The Earth Calendar Web site at www.earthcalendar.net/index.php lists holidays by date, country, and religion. Browse the site and read about an unfamiliar holiday. Do you find the holiday appealing? Why or why not?

writing topic: Write about the best or worst holiday or birthday celebration you have experienced, being sure to explain what made it so pleasant or unpleasant.

suggestion for prewriting: Do two freewritings, one on birthday celebrations and one on a specific holiday celebration, such as Thanksgiving, Independence Day, Kwanza, Easter, or Chanukah.

suggestions for drafting
- Your thesis or topic sentence (depending on whether you are writing an essay or a paragraph) can mention the celebration and your reaction to it, something like this: "For my tenth birthday, my parents threw me a surprise party that I will never forget."
- Some or most of this writing will be a story, so arrange your details in chronological order.

suggestions for revising

- To make your writing vivid, look for opportunities to describe people and scenes.
- Give your draft to a trustworthy reader and ask that person if he or she can tell what made the celebration so pleasant or unpleasant. If your reader cannot tell this, you need to add details.

suggestion for editing: Edit one extra time, checking for correct subject, object, possessive, reflexive, and intensive pronouns.

RECHARGE: Lesson Summary

1. A **pronoun** substitutes for a **noun** (a word that names a person, a place, an object, an emotion, or an idea). The noun a pronoun substitutes for is the **antecedent.**

2. **Subject pronouns** can function as sentence subjects; **object pronouns** can function as objects of verbs or objects of prepositions; and **possessive pronouns** can show ownership.

   - To choose the correct pronoun in a compound, rule out everything except the pronoun.
   - To choose the correct pronoun in a comparison, add the unstated words.
   - To choose the correct pronoun when its antecedent follows immediately, rule out the antecedent.

3. **Reflexive pronouns** indicate that sentence subjects did something to or for themselves. They also express the idea of being or acting alone.

4. **Intensive pronouns** emphasize the words they refer to.

CHAPTER **16**

Achieving Pronoun-Antecedent Agreement

CHAPTER GOALS

By the end of this chapter, you will learn to

Use singular and plural pronouns correctly

Refer correctly to people in general

Avoid sexist pronoun usage

In Chapter 10, you learned about making verbs agree with their subjects. In this chapter, you will learn about another important kind of grammatical agreement—the agreement between pronouns and the words they refer to (their antecedents).

RECOGNIZING SINGULAR AND PLURAL PRONOUNS

When nouns name only one person, place, object, emotion, or idea, they are **singular.** When nouns name two or more people, places, objects, emotions, or ideas, they are **plural.** Here are some examples:

	Singular		**Plural**
	doctor		doctors
	dog		dogs
one	feeling	two or more	feelings
	lake		lakes
	religion		religions
	toy		toys

Some pronouns are *singular* because they substitute for singular nouns. Some pronouns are *plural* because they substitute for plural nouns.

Singular Pronouns	**Plural Pronouns**
I	we
me	us
my, mine	our, ours
he, she, it	they
him, her	them
his, hers, its	their, theirs

Pronouns That Are Both Singular and Plural
you

your, yours

Troubleshooting

The noun a pronoun replaces is called an **antecedent**. If you need to review antecedents, see page 253.

MAKING PRONOUNS AGREE WITH THEIR ANTECEDENTS

To achieve **pronoun-antecedent agreement,** you must use singular pronouns to substitute for singular noun antecedents and plural pronouns to substitute for plural noun antecedents. Here are some examples:

Singular pronoun and antecedent: *Dinah lost her car keys.*

Plural pronoun and antecedent: *The students opened their test booklets.*

Above each underlined pronoun in the following passage, write the pronoun's noun antecedent. Also, write an S if the pronoun and antecedent are singular and a P if the pronoun and antecedent are plural. The first one is done as an example.

¹Large, round, flat stones were the first money. ²Because these stones were
hard to find, they [*stones-P*] were valuable. ³The larger the stone, the more valuable it was.
⁴A smaller stone, which was the size of a dinner plate, might buy a fish or vegetables. ⁵Because the larger stones were so heavy, slaves carried them when their masters went shopping. ⁶The richest people had stones too big to carry, so they left them in front of their houses to show everyone how rich they were.

⁷People on the coasts used red, black, and white shells for their money. ⁸The woman in a household broke the shells into little pieces, polished them, and strung them on strings. She could use one string to buy food and a hundred strings to buy a cow.

⁹Some people made bricks out of salt to use as money. ¹⁰Salt money was not heavy, like stone, or hard to find, like shells. ¹¹However, during a rain shower, it melted.

¹²Eventually, people began using metal money. ¹³It is better than most other things that have been tried, but it is heavy and takes up a lot of space, which explains why people also use paper money.

ACHIEVING AGREEMENT IN SPECIAL SITUATIONS

In most cases, you will have little trouble making your pronouns and antecedents agree. However, a few special situations can be a little tricky. These situations are discussed next.

Phrases after the antecedent

Do not let a phrase after the antecedent trick you into choosing the wrong pronoun. To be sure that you choose correctly, eliminate the phrase. Here is an example:

Which is it?   *A packet of letters is missing from its folder.*

or

A packet of letters is missing from their folder.

Eliminate the phrase: *of letters*

Troubleshooting

Remember that *its* is a possessive pronoun, so it shows ownership. *It's* is a contraction, meaning "it is" or "it has." When tempted to use *it's,* try replacing it with "it is" or "it has." If the substitution does not make sense, you want *its,* as at the right.

Troubleshooting

If you need to review phrases, see page 182.

Now which is it?   *A packet is missing from its folder.*

or

A packet is missing from their folder.

Correct pronoun: *its* [singular pronoun to substitute for singular *packet*]

Correct sentence: *A packet of letters is missing from its folder.*

16.2 ACTIVITY

In each sentence, cross out the phrase after the antecedent, circle the antecedent, and then fill in the blank with the correct pronoun. Choose your pronoun from this list: *its, his, her, their.*

EXAMPLE   The proud ⟮father⟯ ~~of the puppies~~ wagged _____*his*_____ tail.

1. Six scouts in the troop lost _____ leader.

2. The members of the football team improved _____ grades this semester.

3. The workers in the union wanted _____ contract improved.

4. The box of souvenirs fell off _____ shelf in the closet.

5. One of the mothers took _____ child to a play group each day.

6. The can of vegetables has passed _____ expiration date.

7. A large bottle of pills sat on _____ side on the bathroom counter.

8. Police officers at the scene gave _____ account of the accident.

9. A government of the people gets _____ support from an informed electorate.

10. The opinions of the mayor have lost _____ influence with the city council.

Compound antecedents

A two-part antecedent is called a **compound antecedent.** Here is an example:

Francis and Alphonso lost their way on Route 80.

Pronoun: *their*

Compound antecedent: *Francis, Alphonso*

If the antecedents are joined by *and*, use a plural pronoun.

The young girl and her older brother played catch in their backyard.

If the antecedents are joined by *or* or *nor*, choose the pronoun that agrees with the antecedent closer to it.

Singular: *Either Helene or Nikki will bring her tape recorder.* [Nikki is closer.]

Plural: *Neither the teacher nor the students will bring their tape recorder.* [*Students* is closer.]

For a more natural-sounding sentence, place the plural part of a compound antecedent second.

Correct: *Either the pillows or the sofa lost its stuffing.*

Correct but more natural sounding: *Either the sofa or the pillows lost their stuffing.*

16.3 ACTIVITY

Following the directions given, combine each pair of sentences to form one sentence with a compound antecedent and correct pronoun.

EXAMPLE   Combine using *and*:
Henry cannot try his in-line skates yet.
Pablo cannot try his in-line skates yet.

Henry and Pablo cannot try their in-line skates yet.

1. Combine using *and*:
   Lionel brought his dogs to the concert in the park.
   Dimitri brought his dogs to the concert in the park.

   _____

   _____

2. Combine using *or*:
   Chloe will win the award for her design.
   My brothers will win the award for their design.

   _____

   _____

3. Combine using *and*:
   My car keys may not be in their usual place.
   My wallet may not be in its usual place.

   _____

   _____

4. Combine using *or*:
   The band director will compose her own music for the concert.
   The assistant director will compose her own music for the concert.

   _____

   _____

5. Combine using *or*:
   Jerry will lend Barry his biology notes.
   Terry will lend Barry his biology notes.

   _____

   _____

6. Combine using *and:*
   Evelyn left her gloves in the car.
   Leo left his gloves in the car.

   _____

   _____

Collective noun antecedents

Collective nouns name a group of people or objects. They are words such as these:

audience	committee	group	mob
band	flock	jury	team

Usually, a collective noun is singular, because all the people or objects function as *one* unit. Thus, a collective noun usually takes a *singular* pronoun.

The crowd made its displeasure known.

Sometimes a collective noun is plural because the people or objects act *individually*. Then the collective noun takes a *plural* pronoun.

The class argued their opinions about the issue.

Sometimes collective nouns can be either singular or plural, depending on the intended meaning.

The steering committee announced its plans.

The steering committee announced their plans.

CONNECT FOR SUCCESS: Learn the Important Collective Nouns in Other Subjects

Think about your major, your career field, and the subjects you are taking this term, and learn their important collective nouns. Are these terms usually singular, plural, or either? For example, in math, *set* is common, as in a "set of numbers," and it is always singular. In law, *jury* is used, and it can be either singular or plural.

16.4 ACTIVITY

Circle the collective noun antecedent in the following sentences taken from academic disciplines you might study in college. Then fill in the blanks with the correct singular or plural pronouns.

EXAMPLE   Music: The ⟦Stan Kenton Band⟧ frequently demonstrated

   its _____ jazz, bebop, and swing virtuosity
   in a single arrangement.

1. Sociology: To be successful, a culture must be organized so that

   _____ members can transmit a common heritage and culture.

2. Business: The Knights of Labor lost _____ prominence after being blamed for exploding a bomb at a labor rally in Chicago in 1886.

3. Psychology: The experimenter told the control group to record _____ responses to the various stimuli.

4. Electronic media: The American public changed _____ leisure habits as a result of television.

5. Philosophy: An ethical population accepts responsibility for the behavior of _____ citizens.

6. Education: A panel of artists, educators, and business representatives presented _____ standards for the arts curriculum.

16.5 ACTIVITY

Underline the collective noun and circle the pronoun that refers to it. If the pronoun is correct, do nothing. If it is incorrect, cross it out and write the correct pronoun above the line.

EXAMPLE The sheep <u>herd</u> is losing ~~their~~ *its* grazing land.

1. The Student Services staff spent the afternoon planning its annual holiday party.
2. The family of rabbits lost their home when the lawn mower ran across it.
3. On the first Wednesday of every month, the membership committee has their meeting.
4. After taking a final curtain call, the cast of the play retired to their dressing rooms.
5. The trio is known for their folk songs and intricate musical arrangements.
6. The governor's staff could not make up its minds about the best legislative initiative.
7. The audience shouted its approval to the speaker.

Indefinite pronoun antecedents

Indefinite pronouns do not refer to specific persons, places, objects, emotions, or ideas. They are words such as these:

anybody	everybody	some
anyone	everything	somebody
each	one	someone

Indefinite pronouns can be antecedents for other pronouns.

Everything has fallen from its shelf.

Antecedent: *everything*
Pronoun: *its*

The following indefinite pronouns are always singular, so they are used with singular pronouns.

-body words	*-one* words	*-thing* words	other words
anybody	anyone	anything	each
everybody	everyone	everything	either
nobody	no one	nothing	every
somebody	some one	something	neither
	one		

Nothing is in its place.

Somebody left her purse on the table.

Each of the priests took his vows.

The following indefinite pronouns are plural, so they are used with plural pronouns:

both   few   many   several

Few of the girls remembered their coats.
Several squirrels fought over their acorns.

The following indefinite pronouns are either singular or plural, depending on the meaning expressed.

all   any   more   most   none   some

When singular in meaning, they are used with singular pronouns. When plural in meaning, they are used with plural pronouns.

Singular in meaning: *Some of the book is ripped from its binding.*
Plural in meaning: *Some of the students have quit their jobs.*

Composing at the computer

To help you edit for pronoun-antecedent agreement, type *body, one, thing,* and *each* into your computer's search function. This procedure will help you find singular indefinite pronouns.

CONNECT FOR SUCCESS: Be Wary of Indefinite Pronouns in Examination Questions

Answers to true-false questions with the indefinite pronouns *everyone, everything,* and *no one* are usually false, because a single exception is all it takes to disprove the statement in the question.

Avoiding sexist pronoun usage

Some pronouns in English are gender-specific. *She, her,* and *hers* are feminine, and *he, him,* and *his* are masculine. In earlier times, writers routinely used masculine pronouns to refer to singular indefinite pronouns.

Everybody should receive his registration materials by Monday.

Troubleshooting

Frequent use of "he or she" can be cumbersome, so whenever possible use the plural: "When *people* eat too little fat, *they* can have health problems."

This usage is still grammatically correct. However, writers are now more aware that, when the indefinite pronoun antecedent can refer to both males and females, other options are available:

Use both a male and a female pronoun.

Everybody should receive *his or her* registration materials by Monday.

Make both the antecedent and the pronoun plural.

All students should receive *their* registration materials by Monday.

Eliminate the gendered pronoun, if possible.

Everybody should receive registration materials by Monday.

GRAMMAR ALERT

Informally, people often use *they* or *their* to refer to singular indefinite pronouns ("Nobody has their book in class today"). However, in formal college and business writing, use singular pronouns to refer to singular indefinite pronouns.

Often heard informally: *Everyone should have their vacation requests submitted by the first of the month.*

Formal: *Everyone should have his or her vacation requests submitted by the first of the month.*

References to people in general

When you refer to people in general, you have several choices. Here are some examples:

When people hurry, they make mistakes.
When a person hurries, he or she makes mistakes.
When we hurry, we make mistakes.
When someone hurries, he or she makes mistakes.
When anybody hurries, he or she makes mistakes.

Be sure to match the pronoun to the word you use to mean "people in general."

No: *If a person eats too much fat, they may get heart disease.* [*Person* is singular, and *they* is plural.]

Yes: *If a person eats too much fat, he or she may get heart disease.* [*Person* and *he or she* are both singular.]

Yes: *If people eat too much fat, they may get heart disease.* [Both *people* and *they* are plural.]

No: *When someone asks for help, we must give it to them.* [*Someone* is singular, but *them* is plural.]

Yes: *When someone asks for help, we must give it to him or her.* [*Someone* and *him or her* are both singular.]

CONNECT FOR SUCCESS: Use Indefinite Pronouns in Business Writing

Indefinite pronouns are common in business writing. An e-mail to employees from the human resources department might say, "*Anyone* who submits a sick leave form . . . ." A marketing report might state, "*Everyone* who responded to the survey . . . ."

16.6 ACTIVITY

Fill in the blanks with the correct pronoun: *he or she, its,* or *their.*

EXAMPLE   Anybody can wallpaper a room if ___*he or she*___ has patience and the right tools.

1. Most of the group jumped to _____ feet to applaud the orchestra's performance.

2. The travel instructions explained that everyone who crosses the border must have _____ passport.

3. I'm not sure what it is, but something in this room is not in _____ proper place.

4. Before time was up, all of them had answered _____ exam questions.

5. The police officer said that no one was leaving the scene of the accident without showing _____ driver's license.

6. Each nun was given _____ new missionary assignment.

7. Some of the doors in this apartment are off of _____ hinges.

8. Anybody who misplaces _____ registration materials will be charged $5.00 for replacement documents.

9. If a person wants to volunteer to monitor the sea turtle nests, _____ should attend the training session tomorrow at noon.

10. One of the stores on Main Street is having _____ annual sidewalk sale.

16.7 COLLABORATIVE ACTIVITY

With one or two classmates, compose sentences that begin with each of the following openers. Be sure that each sentence also includes a pronoun that substitutes for the indefinite pronoun.

EXAMPLE   Each child should have his or her immunizations by now.

A. Anyone   E. Each girl

B. Something   F. Every person

C. Somebody   G. Some of the clothes

D. Nothing

16.8 ACTIVITY

The following sentences refer to people in general. Cross out the incorrect pronouns and write the correct ones above them. Two sentences are correct.

EXAMPLE   Before a person reveals personal information, ~~they~~ *he or she* should have an established relationship.

1. A person practicing openness, empathy, and effective problem-solving techniques will find their interpersonal relationships more successful.

2. A close friend may share their secrets with you.

3. People who intentionally disclose sensitive information are comfortable revealing their secrets.

4. When someone wants to reduce uncertainty in relationships, they may disclose personal information.

5. A person does not disclose their life story early in a relationship.

6. A person who reveals too much personal information too soon may make his or her acquaintances uncomfortable.

7. If a person reveals personal information incrementally, they will make others more comfortable.

8. When someone seeks information about others, they will disclose personal information first.

Source: Adapted from Judy Pearson et al., *Human Communication*, 2nd ed. (New York: McGraw-Hill, 2006), pp. 136–37. Copyright © 2006 The McGraw-Hill Companies. Used by permission of The McGraw-Hill Companies.

IF ENGLISH IS NOT YOUR FIRST LANGUAGE

The indefinite pronouns *some* and *any* are used in a generic sense.

> *Do you have any paper?* [No specific kind of paper is asked for.]
> *Do you have my paper?* [Specific paper is asked for.]

> *Juan needs some help.* [The help can come from anyone.]
> *Juan needs your help.* [The help must come from a specific person.]

16.9 CHAPTER REVIEW ACTIVITY

Cross out incorrect pronouns or sexist pronoun usage, and write the correction above the line. If the sentence is correct, do nothing.

EXAMPLE   One of the girls lost ~~their~~ *her* shoe.

1. Every teacher has their own specialty.

2. A three-part series on local corruption won their author a journalism award.

3. The child and her mother lost their way in the park.

4. Each employee should bring his health records.

5. Someone put their car in my parking space.

6. The cooperation by area labor leaders proved its effectiveness when unemployment dropped in the region.

7. The class was pleased to learn that their assignment was postponed for a week.

8. Every lawyer hopes that his or her future holds a big, splashy case that makes the headlines.

9. Everyone has his reasons for going to college.

10. Either Nicholas or my brothers will bring his ladder.

11. The restaurant's offer of free french fries served its purpose, because business improved.

12. Everybody agreed that their time was well spent.

13. Anyone who wants his car inspected should report to the police station on Saturday.

14. My file of financial records is missing from their drawer.

15. Some of the flowers in the arrangement are losing their leaves.

16.10 CHAPTER REVIEW ACTIVITY

Fill in the blanks in the following passage with the correct pronouns, and circle their antecedents. The first one is done as an example.

[1]Elephants are very interesting animals. [2]Both the African elephant and the Asiatic elephant can run with amazing speed when *they* want to: up to 24 miles an hour. [3]Surprisingly, the heaviest animal of all land animals actually walks on _____ toes, which is possible because large toe pads act as cushions. [4]The trunk of an elephant is the longest nose of any living animal. [5]_____ has 40,000 muscles and tendons. [6]_____ make the trunk flexible and strong so _____ can pluck a single flower or lift a heavy log. [7]Big tusks help elephants find _____ food. [8]An elephant can plow up the ground with _____ tusks to find roots, or _____ can pry open tree trunks to get the soft wood inside. [9]When water is scarce, the tusks of an elephant can drill into dry riverbeds to dig up water.

[10]Elephants are very social and stay together in herds. [11]A herd of elephants chooses _____ leader from among the old females. [12]Female elephants

in the herd are affectionate; _____ nuzzle each other frequently. [13]Male elephants, however, are unpredictable—gentle and friendly one minute and violent and dangerous the next. [14]Everybody who works in a zoo makes sure _____ is careful when working with the males.

[15]Elephants have been subject to attack for a long time, but today a herd of elephants may be facing _____ greatest danger. [16]Illegal hunters are killing these animals for _____ ivory tusks. [17]Also, population increases limit the amount of land elephants can feed on, leading to starvation. [18]Each local government or conservation group must use _____ influence to save these magnificent beasts.

GETTING IN GEAR: IDEAS FOR WRITING

The promotion of gender equality is an important social movement. Those who support this movement try to avoid traditional stereotypes, such as the idea that business executives (like the one in the above advertisement) must be male. One small way to foster gender equality is to use the nonsexist pronouns explained in this chapter. Another way is to learn more about the issues facing women by visiting the website for the National Organization for Women at www.now.org/.

writing topic: Select one issue related to men and/or women that you think our society faces, such as employment opportunities, gender roles, or childcare, and explain why you think that issue matters.

suggestion for prewriting: Freewrite on these questions: What are the biggest issues facing men and women today? Are their issues similar or different?

suggestions for drafting
- Your thesis or topic sentence (depending on whether you are writing an essay or a paragraph) can mention the topic (the issue) and your claim (why the issue is important).
- You can arrange your ideas in a progressive order, saving your most compelling reason for last.

suggestion for revising: Have someone read your draft to you. Listen carefully and make notes about problems you hear and changes you should make. Listen, in particular, for whether your supporting details show rather than merely tell.

suggestions for editing: Edit an extra time, checking pronoun-antecedent agreement. The following tips may help.
- Do not let phrases after the antecedent trip you up. Mentally cross them out.
- Remember that *body, one,* and *thing* are singular, so indefinite pronouns ending with these suffixes are also singular.
- If you have referred to people in general, check for agreement between your singular and plural forms.
- Be sure you have avoided sexist pronouns.

RECHARGE: Lesson Summary

1. To achieve **pronoun-antecedent agreement**, use **singular pronouns** to refer to **singular nouns** (nouns that name one person, place, object, emotion, or idea) and **plural pronouns** to refer to **plural nouns** (nouns that name more than one person, place, object, emotion, or idea). Remember the following for correct pronoun-antecedent agreement.

   - Rule out phrases after the antecedent.
   - Use a plural pronoun with antecedents joined by *and.*
   - When antecedents are joined by *or,* use the pronoun that agrees with the closer antecedent.
   - Use a singular pronoun with a singular **collective noun** antecedent and a plural pronoun with a plural collective noun antecedent.
   - **Indefinite pronouns** can be antecedents. Some indefinite pronouns are singular, some are plural, and some are either singular or plural, depending on the meaning.

2. Avoid sexist pronoun usage.

CHAPTER **17**

CHAPTER GOALS

By the end of this chapter, you will learn to

Avoid inappropriate person shifts

Use *this, that, these,* and *those* correctly

Avoid unnecessary pronouns

Avoid unclear antecedents

Avoid unstated antecedents

Troubleshooting

If you have trouble with person shift, remember that *I, we,* and *you* do not substitute for nouns. *I* and *we* refer to the speaker or writer, and *you* refers to the listener or reader.

Eliminating Common Pronoun Errors

As you know, pronouns substitute for nouns. As substitutes, pronouns have a built-in potential to be confusing. Some pronoun errors can be particularly confusing, and in this chapter you will learn how to eliminate them. In particular, you will learn how to avoid problems with *person shift, unnecessary pronouns, demonstrative pronouns, unclear antecedents and unstated antecedents.*

AVOIDING INAPPROPRIATE PERSON SHIFT

To write or speak about yourself, use these **first person** pronouns: *I, we, my, mine, our, ours, me,* and *us.*

> *I can bring <u>my</u> tent on the camping trip.*

To write or speak directly to your reader or listener, use these **second person** pronouns: *you, your,* and *yours.*

> <u>*You*</u> *can bring <u>your</u> tent on the camping trip.*

To write or speak about anyone or anything that does not include yourself or your reader or listener, use these **third person pronouns:** *he, him, his, she, her, hers, it, its, they, their, theirs,* and *them.*

> <u>*They*</u> *can bring <u>their</u> tent on the camping trip.*

Use *you, your,* and *yours* only when you want to address your reader or listener directly, like this:

> <u>*You*</u> *always were a patient person.*
> *I understand <u>your</u> point.*
> *These books are <u>yours</u>.*

If you use *I, we,* or a noun, do not shift to *you,* or you will create a problem called **person shift.**

Shift from I to *you*:	*I prefer to study on the top floor of the library. <u>You</u> can really concentrate there.*
Correction:	*I prefer to study on the top floor of the library. <u>I</u> can really concentrate there.*

280

Shift from *we* to *you*:	*We have found hypnosis to be a helpful relaxation technique.* *You can also use it for self-improvement.*
Correction:	*We have found hypnosis to be a helpful relaxation technique.* *We can also use it for self-improvement.*
Shift from a noun to *you*:	*Seniors should visit the campus career center. You can learn* *about a variety of job options there.*
Correction:	*Seniors should visit the campus career center. They can* *learn about a variety of job options there.*

17.1 ACTIVITY

The passage includes eight inappropriate person shifts. To eliminate the shifts, cross out each *you* that is used incorrectly, and write the correct pronoun above it.

EXAMPLE   If students need academic help, they can visit the tutoring center,

and if they need financial help, ~~you~~ *they* can visit the financial aid

office.

¹Most colleges have many support services available to students. ²If students need help with a particular subject, they can visit the writing center, the reading lab, or the math lab. ³In addition, you can go to the tutoring center for help in other subjects. ⁴Colleges offer other services as well. ⁵Students who are unsure about what to major in can visit the career services office, where you can learn about marketable majors. ⁶You can also see a counselor in the counseling center and take some interest and aptitude tests to learn what you would be good at. ⁷In fact, I have an appointment there this week, because you want to learn something about yourself and your interests. ⁸One of the most valuable resources for students is the academic advisor, who can help you with difficult decisions. ⁹Thus, students are not alone. ¹⁰They have many people and many resources waiting to help them.

AVOIDING PROBLEMS WITH DEMONSTRATIVE PRONOUNS

This, that, these, and *those* are **demonstrative pronouns,** used to point out specific people, places, objects, emotions, or ideas. Use *this* and *these* for something nearby and *that* and *those* for something farther away. In the following examples, notice that the antecedent comes *after* the verb.

Singular Nearby: *this*	**Plural** Nearby: *these*
This is the scariest book I ever read.	*These are not important papers.*
Farther away: *that*	Farther away: *those*
That is the best diner in town.	*Those are not my gloves.*

GRAMMAR ALERT

Do not use *here* or *there* with a demonstrative pronoun.

No:	*This here is my car.*
Yes:	*This is my car.*
No:	*That there is an expensive store.*
Yes:	*That is an expensive store.*

Also, do not use *them* as a demonstrative pronoun.

No:	*Them are the shoes I want.*
Yes:	*Those [These] are the shoes I want.*

17.2 ACTIVITY

Correct the sentences by crossing out the incorrect word and writing the correct demonstrative pronoun above the line, if necessary. (In one case, more than one correction is possible.) If the sentence is correct, do nothing.

EXAMPLE   ~~That~~ *This* [nearby] is the car I want to buy.

1. Them are the children who collected clothes for the homeless.

2. Those [near] are the shoes that hurt my feet, so I am returning them.

3. If you ask me, these here are the more difficult math problems, not those there.

4. These [near] are the sweaters that are on sale.

5. Those [far away] are beautiful flowers on the hill.

6. This [near] is the algebra problem we must complete for homework.

7. That [nearby] is the person I want you to meet.

ELIMINATING UNNECESSARY PRONOUNS

It is unnecessary (and incorrect) to use a pronoun immediately after its antecedent. Instead, use either the pronoun *or* the antecedent—not both.

No:	*My <u>mother, she</u> told me to be careful.*
Yes:	*My mother told me to be careful.*
Yes:	*She told me to be careful.*

Notice that the comma between the antecedent and the pronoun is eliminated.

17.3 ACTIVITY

Cross out the unnecessary pronouns in the following passage.

EXAMPLE   Our senators and representatives ~~they~~ appropriate money for billions of dollars of projects.

[1]Our government, it spends so much money that we are accustomed to hearing that billions of dollars are being spent on something. [2]We are so accustomed, in fact, that we may not realize just how much a billion it really is. [3]To help you appreciate the magnitude of a billion, consider this. [4]If you wanted to count a billion dollars, one dollar at time, it would take you thirty-two years if you counted one dollar every second, day and night, without stopping. [5]We know that because thirty-two years it is composed of 1 billion seconds. [6]We should publish this information in the newspaper, so people they would have a true appreciation for how much money a billion dollars is. [7]Then, maybe citizens like us, we would be more interested in how our legislators spend money.

AVOIDING UNCLEAR ANTECEDENTS

Confusion occurs when a reader cannot tell which of two antecedents a pronoun refers to. To solve the problem, change one of the pronouns to a noun. Here are two examples:

> *Cal was talking to Raul when __he__ noticed the missing wallet.* [Who noticed the missing wallet, Cal or Raul?]

> Correction 1: *Cal was talking to Raul when Raul noticed the missing wallet.*

> Correction 2: *Cal was talking to Raul when Cal noticed the missing wallet.*

> *When I placed the bowl on the glass shelf, __it__ broke.* [What broke, the shelf or the bowl?]

> Correction 1: *When I placed the bowl on the glass shelf, the bowl broke.*

> Correction 2: *When I placed the bowl on the glass shelf, the shelf broke.*

CONNECT FOR SUCCESS: Eliminate Unclear Antecedents in Business Writing

Unclear antecedents can cause confusion in business writing. For example, consider the problem these sentences would cause in a report: "The district manager favors consolidating the sales force, and the marketing manager does not. I am certain he is right." Who is right, the district manager or the marketing manager?

17.4 ACTIVITY

Rewrite the following sentences to solve problems of unclear antecedents. You will have to decide which word you want to be the antecedent. There is more than one correct answer.

EXAMPLE   When Tom told Greg the truth, he became very angry.

When Tom told Greg the truth, Greg [Tom] became very

angry.

1. Mother told Aunt Sue that her opinion was carefully thought out.

    _____

    _____

2. Julia wanted to borrow Eleni's skirt and sweater, but she couldn't because it was at the cleaners.

    _____

    _____

3. When Daria saw Lizette across the math class, she smiled.

    _____

    _____

4. Senator Rodriguez introduced a fair trade bill and an education reform bill, but it had little chance of getting out of committee.

    _____

    _____

    _____

5. The doctor urged Dad to quit smoking, but he did not think the lecture would work.

    _____

    _____

6. The exterminators removed all the furniture from the attic and sprayed it to kill the fleas.

    _____

    _____

AVOIDING UNSTATED ANTECEDENTS

A pronoun's antecedent must be written out, or a problem called **unstated antecedent** occurs.

Unstated antecedent occurs when *they* or *it* appears without a stated antecedent. To solve the problem, substitute a noun for the pronoun.

> *When I went to the Admissions Office, they said that the new catalogs were not ready yet.*

Who are *they*? Without an antecedent, we do not know, so we have a problem of *unstated antecedent*. To correct the problem, substitute a noun for the pronoun.

> Correction: *When I went to the Admissions Office, the secretary said that the new catalogs were not ready yet.*
>
> *On the lid of my washer, it says not to overload the machine.*

What is *it?* Without an antecedent, we do not know, so we have a problem of *unstated antecedent.* To correct the problem, substitute a noun for the pronoun.

> Correction: *On the lid of my washer, <u>the warning</u> says not to overload the machine.*

Unstated antecedent also occurs when the antecedent is a *form* of the intended word but is not the word itself. To correct the problem, substitute the intended form for the pronoun.

> *Jerry is highly motivated. <u>It</u> will help him succeed.*

The intended antecedent is *motivation,* but this word does not appear; *motivated* does. To correct the problem, substitute *motivation* for the pronoun.

> Correction: *Jerry is highly motivated. <u>His motivation</u> will help him succeed.*

> *In Hemingway's novels, <u>he</u> writes about death.*

The intended antecedent is *Hemingway,* but this word does not appear; *Hemingway's* does. To correct the problem, rewrite the sentence with an antecedent that is not a possessive noun.

> Correction: *In his novels, Hemingway writes about death.*

Composing at the computer

Use your computer's search function to find each use of *you, they,* and *it.* Then check each *you* to be sure you do not have a person shift and each *they* and *it* to be sure you do not have unstated antecedent.

17.5 ACTIVITY

Rewrite the following sentences to correct problems with unstated antecedent.

EXAMPLE Jason was very angry. It caused him to say things he did not mean.

> <u>*Jason was very angry. His anger caused him to say things he did not mean.*</u>

1. Juanita has always been ambitious. It is the reason she is so competitive.

2. When I visited the homeless shelter, they explained that many homeless people were once part of the middle class.

3. In Elton John's new CD, he plays less piano than usual.

4. In the restaurant, it says that no smoking is allowed.

5. Because exams begin next week, all my friends are tense. It is causing us to argue with each other.

    _____

    _____

6. When I went to the health center, they advised me to get a flu shot.

    _____

    _____

 IF ENGLISH IS NOT YOUR FIRST LANGUAGE

Sometimes, the use of *this*, *that*, *these*, and *those* depends on whether you are speaking in the present or the past tense.

Present tense: *I believe <u>this</u> is important.*
Past tense: *I believed <u>that</u> was important.*

Present tense: *I understand <u>these</u> math problems.*
Past tense: *I understood <u>those</u> math problems.*

17.6 CHAPTER REVIEW ACTIVITY

Cross out the five pronoun errors. If corrections are needed, write them above the line.

EXAMPLE   With cooperative learning, students ~~they~~ work in groups.

[1]In cooperative learning, students work on activities in small, diverse groups, and you often receive rewards based on the overall group performance. [2]Although cooperative learning can be traced back to the 1920s, it seems new because most classrooms they remain competitive. [3]The competitive structure and the cooperative structure are very different, because it produces winners and losers, and usually only a small number of *A*s are possible. [4]In a cooperative structure, however, everyone can get an *A*. [5]According to researchers, cooperative learning groups work best when they are small, perhaps limited to two to six members. [6] It is an important characteristic, since face-to-face contact is necessary for the success of group members. [7]Because this here research shows that students make higher achievement gains in a cooperative environment, more schools may try cooperative learning.

Source: Adapted from Myra Pollack Sadker and David Miller Sadker, *Teacher, Schools, and Society,* 5th ed. (New York: McGraw-Hill, 2000), p. 73. Copyright © 2000 The McGraw-Hill Companies. Used by permission of The McGraw-Hill Companies.

GETTING IN GEAR: IDEAS FOR WRITING

Conflicts between individuals, between groups of people, between nations, and between cultures can create serious difficulty. To learn more about the conflicts people experience, along with creative ways to resolve those conflicts, visit the Conflict Resolution Information Source at http://v4.crinfo.org/.

writing topic: The pronoun problems explained in this chapter can create confusion, misunderstanding, and even minor conflicts. For example, in the following sentence, you can't tell what the pronoun *it* refers to, so you can't tell what broke, the vase, the candle, or the table: "When I moved the vase and candle to dust the table, it broke." Explain and illustrate one factor that creates confusion and misunderstanding in communication. Can that factor lead to conflict? You might consider circumstances such as poor listening skills, thoughtless word choice, distractions, and cultural, age, or gender differences.

suggestion for prewriting: Freewrite about a time you misunderstood someone or someone misunderstood you. The misunderstanding could have involved an argument similar to the one in the photograph, or it could have involved another problem. What happened? Why did it happen? How serious were the consequences?

suggestions for drafting
- Develop an informal outline to guide your draft.
- Write your draft in one sitting, skipping troublesome parts. You can go back to those later.

suggestions for revising

- The fewer examples you use, the more detailed each one should be. Check whether you need more examples or more detailed examples.
- Look for general words that you can revise to be more specific. For example, if you have written "Celia became upset," you might be able to change it to "Celia's face tightened with rage."

suggestions for editing

- Check each use of *you* to be sure you do not have a person shift.
- Check each *it* and *they* for stated antecedents.

RECHARGE: Lesson Summary

1. A **person shift** occurs when you shift from using a noun, *I,* or *we* to using *you.*

   Shift: *Skiers must have strong ankles, or you could hurt yourself.*
   Correction: *Skiers must have strong ankles, or they could hurt themselves.*

2. The **demonstrative pronouns** are *this, that, these,* and *those.*
3. Avoid using a pronoun immediately after its antecedent.

   No: *The firefighters, they deserve a pay increase.*
   Yes: *The firefighters deserve a pay increase.*

4. To avoid **unclear antecedents,** be sure a pronoun's antecedent is obvious.

   No: *The children asked their parents whether they were leaving.*
   Yes: *The children asked their parents whether the parents were leaving.*

5. To avoid unstated **antecedent,** be sure a pronoun's antecedent is written out.

   No: *I called the customer service department, and they said I could get a refund.*
   Yes: *I called the customer service department, and a representative said I could get a refund.*

PART FOUR REVIEW

Editing for multiple errors

A. The following passage has one incorrect possessive pronoun form, one incorrect pronoun used with a renaming word, one incorrect reflexive form, three errors in pronoun-antecedent agreement, two person shifts, two problems with demonstrative pronouns, and one unclear antecedent. Cross out the errors, and write the corrections above the line. (Changing the pronoun will require changing the verb in one case.)

[1]Everyone in the United States says, "Hello" when they answer the telephone. [2]In fact, this here greeting is so common that most people assume it has always been used. [3]You would be surprised to learn that the greeting is newer than you think. [4]The use of "hello" as a telephone greeting has their first recorded use in 1883. [5]Even then, it was not a shoo-in for the greeting. [6]It competed with other options. [7]Alexander Graham Bell hisself favored "ahoy."

[8]The term "hello" has it's origins in the form "hallo," which dates to 1840 and is a cry of surprise. [9]"Hallo," in turn, is related to "halloo," a cry to urge on hunting dogs. [10]Us frequent users of "hello" may be interested in the fact that "halloo" dates to about 1700, but a variant, "aloo," appears in Shakespeare's *King Lear* a century earlier than that. [11]It has an earlier variant—in 1588, Shakespeare used "hollo" in *Titus Andronicus*. [12]The word group that predates "hello" also has their cognates in Germanic languages, and them may be words that also form part of the history of "hello."

[13]The next time you greet someone on the phone, think about the history of the word you use to do so.

B. The following passage has one pronoun used incorrectly in a comparison, six errors in pronoun-antecedent agreement, one sexist pronoun, one incorrect demonstrative pronoun, one unnecessary pronoun, and one problem with unstated antecedent. Cross out the errors and make the corrections above the line. (Twice, changing the pronoun requires changing the verb.)

[1]Perhaps you know more about state laws than me, but if not, you will be surprised to learn some of the wacky laws on the books. [2]For example, in Vermont, everyone must take one bath a week—on Saturday night (whether they need it or not). [3]Furthermore, people, they cannot whistle underwater. [4]In Michigan, a woman is not allowed to cut their own hair without their husband's permission. [5]Also, any person over the age of twelve may own a handgun as long as he has not been convicted of a felony. [6]In Alaska, they may not view moose from an airplane or push a live moose from a plane. [7]In California, women in housecoats may not drive her cars, nor may any vehicles without a driver have their speed exceed 60 miles per hour. [8]In North Carolina, neither men nor women can plow his or her fields with elephants or sing off key. [9]A woman with a sweet tooth may want to move to Idaho, where a man may not give their sweetheart a box of candy under 50 pounds. [10]This is some bizarre laws, I must say.

READING AND WRITING IN RESPONSE TO TEXTBOOKS

This textbook excerpt explains the interplay between media and culture.

[1]Because people depend on the mass media to inform them, the media play a major role in shaping our culture. [2]Consider the influence of televised football on the American culture. [3]The sense of "maleness" and competition that surround football supports the belief that men are supposed to be big, tough, and macho. [4]The game subtly reinforces the notion that people can be anything they want, if only they try hard enough, a distinct belief of the American culture. [5]Indeed, as early as the nineteenth century, cheap paperback novels promoted the American virtues of hard work, education, and rugged individualism. [6]Such values have been repeated in radio programs, magazine stories, and television situation comedies so often they have become a part of our social fabric.

Source: Judy Pearson et al., *Human Communication,* 2nd ed. (New York: McGraw-Hill, 2006), p. 272. Copyright © 2006 The McGraw-Hill Companies. Used by permission of The McGraw-Hill Companies.

1.   Name the pronouns in the first sentence, and label them as subject, object, or possessive pronouns.

     _____

     _____

2.   Why is *our* used in the first sentence, instead of *their*?

     _____

     _____

3.   Assume sentence 4 were rewritten to begin this way: "The game subtly reinforces the notion that *a person* . . . ." Since the paragraph is about football, maleness, and the image of men, could you complete the sentence using the pronoun *he*? Or is *he or she* needed? Explain.

     _____

     _____

     _____

     _____

4.   In sentence 6, what is the antecedent of *they*?

     _____

     _____

writing topic: In the textbook excerpt, televised football is cited as an example of one way that the media shape American culture. Explain and illustrate another way television or another form of media shapes our culture.

Understanding Modifiers and Prepositions

If any personal description of me is thought desirable, it may be said, I am, in height, six feet, four inches, nearly; lean in flesh, weighing, on an average, one hundred and eighty pounds; dark complexion, with coarse black hair, and grey eyes—no other marks or brands recollected.

—Abraham Lincoln (1809–1865), U.S. president

Reflection: Does Lincoln do a good job of describing himself? Explain.

WHAT YOU WILL LEARN

How to use adjectives and adverbs

How to avoid double negatives

How to use the comparative and superlative forms of adjectives and adverbs

How use participles and infinitives to describe

How to avoid dangling modifiers

How to use prepositional phrases

WHY YOU WILL LEARN IT

so that you can describe to express yourself more precisely

so that you can write correct sentences

so that you can compare two or more items

so that you can express yourself more precisely

so that you can write correct sentences

so that you can express yourself more precisely

291

CHAPTER 18

Using Adjectives and Adverbs

CHAPTER GOALS

By the end of this chapter, you will learn to

Use adjectives and adverbs correctly

Avoid double negatives

Use comparative and superlative forms correctly

Imagine how dull a travel brochure, a novel, or a paragraph telling a story would be without a description of people or scenes. Imagine how hard it would be to write an e-mail to a friend about your new apartment if you could not include a description of what the place looks like. In this chapter, you will learn how to use descriptive words correctly so you can express yourself more readily.

UNDERSTANDING MODIFIERS

Adjectives and *adverbs* are the words that writers and speakers use to describe. Because adjective and adverbs "modify" meaning by describing other words, they are a class of words called **modifiers**. As modifiers, adjectives and adverbs are important because they allow writers and speakers to shade their meaning to express their ideas with precision. Consider these sentences and notice that the addition of the underlined descriptive word modifies meaning in an important way:

> *Frederico refuses to watch movies.*
> *Frederico refuses to watch <u>violent</u> movies.*

USING ADJECTIVES

Adjectives describe nouns and pronouns.

> *<u>Spicy</u> chili is my <u>favorite</u> food.* [Spicy is an adjective because it describes the noun *chili*. *Favorite* is an adjective because it describes the noun *food*.]
>
> *He is <u>hot</u> and <u>thirsty</u>.* [Both *hot* and *thirsty* are adjectives because they describe the pronoun *he*.]

Is is a linking verb, and linking verbs cannot be described. Therefore, *hot* and *thirsty* must describe *he*.

Troubleshooting

If you need to review linking verbs, return to page 84.

18.1 ACTIVITY

Fill in each blank in the following sentences with an adjective. Then draw an arrow to the noun or pronoun it describes.

EXAMPLE   The _____green_____ car belongs to Chris.

1. That _____ vase has been in our family for five generations.

2. My _____ brother attends school in Michigan.

3. Carla gave David a(n) _____ sweater for his birthday.

4. You are very _____

5. I cooked a(n)_____ dinner, which included

_____ chicken and _____ potatoes.

18.2 COLLABORATIVE ACTIVITY

With two classmates, list on a separate sheet every word you can think of to describe *child* (words such as *young, happy,* and *crying*). The words in your list will be adjectives.

Demonstrative adjectives

When they describe nouns, *this, that, these,* and *those* are **demonstrative adjectives.** *This* and *that* are used with singular nouns, and *these* and *those* are used with plural nouns. Use *this* and *these* for people and objects that are nearby. Use *that* and *those* for people and objects that are farther away.

Singular	**Plural**
Nearby: *this*	Nearby: *these*
Farther away: *that*	Farther away: *those*

Singular: *This coat* [nearby] *is too small, but that coat* [farther away] *is fine.*

Plural: *These crackers* [nearby] *are fresh, but those cookies* [farther away] *are stale.*

> **Troubleshooting**
>
> *This, that, these,* and *those* can also be **demonstrative pronouns.** If you are unsure when these words are used as adjectives and when they are used as pronouns, see page 281.

→ GRAMMAR ALERT

Them does not substitute for *this, that, these,* or *those.*

No: *Them shoes are an unusual color.*

Yes: *These shoes are an unusual color.*

Yes: *Those shoes are an unusual color.*

18.3 ACTIVITY

Write a sentence combining *this, that, these,* or *those* with the word or words given. Use *this, that, these,* and *those* one time each.

EXAMPLE   tree *This tree offers excellent shade.*

1. child _____

_____

2. houses _____

_____

3. movie _____

_____

4. people _____

_____

5. news report _____

_____

Articles—*A, An*, and *The*

A, an, and *the* are special adjectives called **articles.** Use *a* and *an* to mean *one* or when you do not know the specific identity of the noun. Use *the* when you know the specific identity of the noun.

> Specific identity unknown: *I found a key.*
>
> Specific identity known: *I found the key.*

Use *an* before a word that begins with a vowel sound (*a, e, i, o,* and *u*). Use *a* before a word that does not begin with a vowel sound. Here are some examples:

Vowel Sound	No Vowel Sound
an orange	a bat
an apple	a deer
an eagle	a pizza
an old scar	a new umbrella

Sometimes the letter *u* has a vowel sound, and sometimes it does not have one. Use *a* and *an* accordingly.

Vowel Sound	No Vowel Sound
an umpire	a unicorn
an uncle	a union
an understanding	a unit

Use *a* when the letter *h* is pronounced and *an* when it is silent.

Vowel Sound	No Vowel Sound
an honor	a heart
an hour	a helmet

18.4 ACTIVITY

Place *a* or *an* (whichever is correct) in front of each of the following words or phrases, and use the phrase in a sentence.

EXAMPLE ___*an*___ island *Most people know that Manhattan is an island.*

1. _____ ironing board _____

_____

2. _____ book _____

_____

3. _____ uncertain future _____

_____

4. _____ honest person _____

_____

5. _____ unique experience _____

_____

6. _____ ugly coat _____

_____

7. _____ hard problem _____

_____

8. _____ university _____

_____

USING ADVERBS

Adverbs describe verbs, adjectives, or other adverbs. Many adverbs end in *-ly*.

An adverb describing a verb:	*You sing beautifully.*
An adverb describing an adjective:	*Your suit is extremely attractive.*
An adverb describing another adverb:	*Sheila speaks very loudly.*

Many adverbs tell *how, when,* or *where.*

An adverb telling *how:*	*Your dress is very short.* [*Very* tells how short.]
An adverb telling *when:*	*Jack arrived late.* [*Late* tells when Jack arrived.]
An adverb telling *where:*	*I fell down.* [*Down* tells where I fell.]

Many descriptive words have both an adjective form and an adverb form. The adverb form ends in *-ly.*

Adjective—Describes Nouns and Pronouns	**Adverb**—Describes Verbs, Adjectives, and Adverbs
slow: *The slow dance ended.*	slowly: *We walked slowly.*
happy: *She is a happy girl.*	happily: *He smiled happily.*
angry: *The father was angry.*	angrily: *I motioned angrily.*

quick: *Let's make a quick stop.*   quickly: *She ran quickly.*

loud: *Turn down the loud music.*   loudly: *You speak loudly.*

GRAMMAR ALERT

Be sure to use the adverb (*-ly*) form to describe verbs.

No: *Jan drove careful down the icy road.*

Yes: *Jan drove carefully down the icy road.*

18.5 COLLABORATIVE ACTIVITY

With two classmates, list on a separate sheet every word you can think of to describe *walking* (words such as *slowly, briskly,* and *clumsily*). These words will be adverbs.

18.6 ACTIVITY

Circle each adverb in the following sentences, and draw an arrow to the verb, adjective, or adverb it describes. Then, in the blank, write whether the adverb tells *how, when,* or *where.*

EXAMPLE   Unsterilized milk will spoil [quickly,] causing people to become [seriously] ill. *when; how*

1. Drinking unsterilized milk can be very dangerous. _____

2. French chemist Louis Pasteur finally discovered a way to sterilize milk. _____

3. Pasteur's process later became known as pasteurization. _____

4. Pasteurized milk still has bacteria, but in extremely low concentrations. _____

5. Refrigeration keeps the bacteria from further growth. _____

6. The milk sold there is often unpasteurized, so I never drink it. _____

18.7 ACTIVITY

Circle the descriptive words in the following sentences and draw arrows to the words they describe. Above each descriptive word, write ADJ if the word is an adjective or ADV if the word is an adverb.

EXAMPLE   *ADJ* [Loud] thunder frightens me [greatly.] *ADV*

1. Happy children are playing outside.

2. Rare books were discovered yesterday.

3. You are extremely talented.

4. Someone is playing music too loudly.

5. She politely asks very difficult questions.

6. Excellent grades earned you valuable scholarships.

18.8 ACTIVITY

In each sentence, if a noun or pronoun is described, fill in the blank with the first form in parentheses, which is an adjective. If a verb, an adjective, or an adverb is described, fill in the blank with the *-ly* form, which is an adverb. Then draw an arrow to the word described.

EXAMPLE   (unfortunate, unfortunately)   Makers of video games are guilty of

_unfortunate_____ gender stereotyping.

1. (frequent, frequently)   Gender stereotyping occurs _____ in video games.

2. (recent, recently; common, commonly)   A _____ article in *Mass Communications and Society* reports on a study about

    _____ portrayals in these games.

3. (popular, popularly) Researchers focused on the clothing worn by the main

   characters in _____ Nintendo and PlayStation games.

4. (close, closely) Of the 600 characters researchers

   studied _____, more than 70 percent were men.

5. (typical, typically) For the female characters, women's clothing

   was _____ revealing.

6. (voluptuous, voluptuously) About 40 percent of the women were described

   as _____ .

7. (immediate, immediately) The attention of players was

   drawn _____ to the women's bodies.

8. (poor, poorly; quick, quickly) The _____ representation of

   women in video games can reinforce gender stereotyping _____
   among young people.

Source: Adapted from Joseph R. Dominick, Fritz Messere, and Barry L. Sherman, *Broadcasting, Cable, the Internet, and Beyond,* 5th ed. (New York: McGraw-Hill, 2004), p. 301. Copyright © 2004 The McGraw-Hill Companies. Used by permission of The McGraw-Hill Companies.

18.9 ACTIVITY

On a separate sheet, write sentences using the following adjectives and adverbs correctly.

1. loud   4. seriously
2. loudly   5. painful
3. serious   6. painfully

CHOOSING ADJECTIVES AND ADVERBS IN SPECIAL SITUATIONS

In most cases, understanding that adjectives describe nouns and pronouns, whereas adverbs describe verbs, adjectives, and other adverbs, is enough to help writers and speakers use these words correctly. However, knowing when to use *good* and when to use *well*, when to use *bad* and when to use *badly*, can be a little tricky, so these pairs will be discussed next.

Good and *well*

Many writers confuse *good* and *well*.

Good is an adjective, so it usually describes nouns.

Salvadore is a good writer. [Good describes the noun *writer.*]

A good friend is a treasure. [Good describes the noun *friend.*]

Good is often used as an adjective after the verbs *taste, feel, seem, appear,* and *look.*

This chicken tastes good. [Good describes the noun *chicken.*]

A cotton sweater always feels good. [Good describes the noun *sweater.*]

Jake looks good today. [Good describes the noun *Jake.*]

Well is an adverb, so it usually describes verbs.

Janice explains things well. [*Well* describes the verb *explains* by telling how.]

I am sure I did well on the examination. [*Well* describes the verb *did* by telling how.]

Well is also an adjective, but only when it means "healthy."

I do not feel well today.   *Harry felt well enough to join us.*

18.10 ACTIVITY

Fill in the blanks in the following sentences with *good* or *well*.

EXAMPLE   After years of practice, I play piano _____*well*_____.

1. The children behaved very _____ at the museum.

2. Carla sees _____ enough now to give up her glasses.

3. The stew tastes _____ now that you have added salt.

4. Julia speaks Spanish _____ enough to use it on her trip to Mexico.

5. After his fourth piece of fudge, Uri did not feel _____.

6. Zachary looks _____, even though he has been sick.

7. How _____ did you understand this morning's psychology lecture?

8. This is a _____ opportunity to visit Uncle Ike.

9. These new shoes feel _____ on my tired feet.

10. Sandy gets along _____ with all kinds of people.

18.11 COLLABORATIVE ACTIVITY

Write two sentences using *good*, two sentences using *well* as an adverb, and two sentences using *well* as an adjective meaning "healthy." Then trade sentences with a classmate and check each other's work.

Bad and badly

Many writers confuse *bad* and *badly*.

Bad is an adjective, so it usually describes nouns.

I have a bad feeling about how this scheme will turn out. [*Bad* describes the noun *feeling*.]

The bad news is that the governor has recommended a reduction of funding to higher education. [*Bad* describes the noun *news*.]

Bad is often used as an adjective after the verbs *taste, feel, seem, appear,* and *look.*

> The quarterback felt *bad* about fumbling the ball. [*Bad* describes the noun *quarterback.*]
>
> The roads seem *bad* because of the freezing rain. [*Bad* describes the noun *roads.*]
>
> The stew tastes *bad* because it is too salty. [*Bad* describes the noun *stew.*]

Badly is an adverb, so it usually describes verbs.

> The orchestra played the first movement of the symphony *badly.* [*Badly* describes the verb *played* by telling how.]
>
> I did *badly* on my history exam. [*Badly* describes the verb *did* by telling how.]

18.12 ACTIVITY

Fill in the blank in the following sentences with *bad* or *badly.*

EXAMPLE   The weather on the coast was _____*bad*_____ because a tropical storm was stalled offshore.

1. Keith felt _____ that he forgot his best friend's birthday.

2. My rash seems _____, but it should clear up in a week.

3. Because the roof leaks so _____, we cannot stay in our apartment.

4. Red is your color, but you do not look _____ in yellow.

5. No one could eat the chicken because it was cooked so

   _____.

6. The _____ performed play closed after three performances.

7. One _____ decision can spoil everything.

8. The wedding planner did a _____ job, so the bride and groom refused to pay her.

9. The boat was leaking _____, so I refused to get on it.

10. Because I got a _____ score on my math placement test, I decided to hire a tutor.

18.13 COLLABORATIVE ACTIVITY

Write two sentences using *bad* and two sentences using *badly.* Then trade sentences with a classmate and check each other's work.

Composing at the computer

You can use your word-processing program's search and find function to locate each use of *good* and *well* and *bad* and *badly*, so you can check to be sure you have used them correctly.

Troubleshooting

The examples to the right show that, when you eliminate one negative, you may have to change *no* to *a, any,* or *an; nothing* to *anything*; or *nowhere* to *anywhere*.

AVOIDING DOUBLE NEGATIVES

The following words are **negatives** because they communicate the idea of *no.*

no	none	hardly
not	nowhere	scarcely
no one	nobody	
never	nothing	

Contractions often include the negative *not.*

can't = cannot	don't = do not
won't = will not	wouldn't = would not
shouldn't = should not	couldn't = could not

If you use two negative words in a single clause, you create a problem called **double negative.** To avoid this problem, use only *one* negative to express a negative idea.

No (two negatives): *You <u>can't</u> bring <u>no</u> friend.*
Yes (one negative): *You <u>can't</u> bring a friend.*

No (two negatives): *I <u>won't</u> do <u>nothing</u>.*
Yes (one negative): *I <u>won't</u> do anything.*
Yes (one negative): *I will do <u>nothing</u>.*

No (two negatives): *He <u>doesn't</u> go <u>nowhere</u>.*
Yes (one negative): *He <u>doesn't</u> go anywhere.*
Yes (one negative): *He goes <u>nowhere</u>.*

→ GRAMMAR ALERT

Remember that *hardly* and *scarcely* are negatives.

No (two negatives): *I <u>can't hardly</u> hear you.*
Yes (one negative): *I can <u>hardly</u> hear you.*
Yes (one negative): *I <u>cannot</u> hear you.*

No (two negatives): *I <u>can't scarcely</u> believe it.*
Yes (one negative): *I <u>can't</u> believe it.*
Yes (one negative): *I can <u>scarcely</u> believe it.*

18.14 ACTIVITY

Rewrite the following sentences to eliminate the double negatives.

EXAMPLE   I won't do no work now.

I won't do any work now.

1. I asked a question, but I didn't get no answer.

   _____

   _____

2. These people will not never do what we ask.

   _____

   _____

3. The audience in the balcony couldn't hardly see the stage.

   _____

   _____

4. You can't go nowhere without me.

   _____

   _____

5. Since Catherine moved, I scarcely never see her anymore.

   _____

   _____

6. I don't know nothing about fixing cars.

   _____

   _____

CONNECT FOR SUCCESS: Use Adjectives and Adverbs in Your Courses and in the Workplace

Adjectives and adverbs are important in most course work and job-related writing. For example, in sociology and psychology courses and professions, adjectives and adverbs help people write case notes with precision. Behavior might be described as *agitated,* and a background might be described as *impoverished.* Dance students and critics might write a review of a ballet that describes the work as danced *brilliantly,* and finance majors and stockbrokers might describe a company's stock as climbing *too rapidly.*

USING ADJECTIVES AND ADVERBS IN COMPARISONS

Adjectives and adverbs describe.

Paul runs fast. [*Fast* describes *runs.*]

Nuha is young. [*Young* describes *Nuha.*]

However, adjectives and adverbs let writers and speakers do more than describe. They also have forms that let us show how two things compare with each other.

Comparing two things—comparative forms

Forms that compare two things are called the **comparative**. Here are two examples:

Paul runs <u>faster</u> than Nigel. [The speeds of Paul and Nigel are compared.]

Nuha is <u>younger</u> than Sue. [The ages of Nuha and Sue are compared.]

To form the comparative of one-syllable adjectives and adverbs, as well as some two-syllable adjectives and adverbs, add *-er.*

Adjective or Adverb	Comparative
tall	taller
fast	faster
filthy	filthier

SPELLING ALERT

Sometimes the last letter is doubled before *-er* is added. Thus, the comparative form of *thin* is *thinner.* If you are unsure of a spelling, check your dictionary or Chapter 24.

Use *more* to form the comparative of most adjectives and adverbs with two or more syllables.

Adjective or Adverb	Comparative
important	more important
slowly	more slowly
usual	more usual

SPELLING ALERT

Remember this exception: If a two-syllable adjective ends in *y*, change the *y* to *i* and add *-er.*

Adjective	Comparative
easy	easier
friendly	friendlier
happy	happier

GRAMMAR ALERT

Never use *-er* comparative form with *more.*

No: *I am <u>more hungrier</u> than a bear.*

Yes: *I am <u>hungrier</u> than a bear.*

No: *Be <u>more carefuler</u> next time.*

Yes: *Be <u>more careful</u> next time.*

18.15 ACTIVITY

Next to each adjective or adverb, write the correct comparative form. If you are unsure about the spelling, check a dictionary.

EXAMPLES lonely _____*lonelier*_____   important ___*more important*___

1. slow _____

2. annoyed _____

3. quickly _____

4. angry _____

5. foolish _____

6. lucky _____

7. young _____

8. awkwardly _____

9. beautiful _____

10. careful _____

11. frequently _____

12. valuable _____

18.16 ACTIVITY

Fill in each blank with the correct comparative form of the adjective or adverb in parentheses.

EXAMPLE (handsome) Lionel gets ___*more handsome*___ every time I see him.

1. (fancy) Chez Henri's is a _____ restaurant than Armando's.

2. (wide) We will never get the box through the door because the box is _____ than I thought.

3. (interesting) The senior class play is_____ than anyone thought it would be.

4. (rapidly) We arrived early because we traveled _____ than anticipated.

5. (lucky) Joel has purchased two winning lottery tickets in the last year; no one is _____ than he is.

6. (focused) Dorothy's grades improved this semester because she is _____ on her studies than she was last semester.

Comparing more than two things—superlative forms

Adjectives and adverbs have forms that are used to compare more than two things. These forms are called the **superlative.** Here are two examples:

Paul is the <u>fastest</u> runner on the team. [The speeds of more than two runners are compared.]

Nuha is the <u>youngest</u> of three children. [The ages of three children are compared.]

To form the superlative of one-syllable adjectives and adverbs, as well as some two-syllable adjectives and adverbs, add *-est*.

Adjective or Adverb	Superlative
hard	hardest
shiny	shiniest
fast	fastest

 SPELLING ALERT

Sometimes the last letter is doubled before *-est* is added. Thus, the superlative form of *thin* is *thinnest*. If you are unsure of a spelling, check a dictionary or Chapter 24.

Use *most* to form the superlative of most adjectives and adverbs with two or more syllables.

Adjective or Adverb	Superlative
freely	most freely
intelligent	most intelligent
understanding	most understanding

 SPELLING ALERT

Remember this exception: If a two-syllable adjective ends in *-y*, change the *y* to *i* and add *-est*.

Adjective	Superlative
friendly	friendliest
heavy	heaviest

 Troubleshooting

If you are unsure how to form or spell the comparative or superlative forms, look up the base form in your dictionary. If something other than *-er* or *-est* is used, those forms will be given.

 GRAMMAR ALERT

Never use the *-est* superlative form with *most*.

No: *Ian is the <u>most friendliest</u> person on campus.*

Yes: *Ian is the <u>friendliest</u> person on campus.*

No: *Biology is my <u>most importantest</u> class this term.*

Yes: *Biology is my <u>most important</u> class this term.*

CONNECT FOR SUCCESS: Compare When You Think Critically

Comparing two or more things is an important component of critical thinking and analysis, both in the classroom and in the workplace. In a management class, you may be asked to compare two management styles; in a literature class, you may need to compare two short stories; and in a nutrition class, you may be required to compare two weight loss programs. On the job, you may need to compare long distance calling plans or computer networks to determine which is the right one for your workplace, or you may need to compare job applicants to determine which person to hire.

18.17 ACTIVITY

Next to each adjective or adverb in the following list, write the correct superlative form.

EXAMPLES   easy _____easiest_____   desirable _*most desirable*_

1. angry _____

2. loudly _____

3. rapidly _____

4. important _____

5. careful _____

6. careless _____

7. happy _____

8. tired _____

9. smart _____

10. completely _____

11. cautiously _____

12. near _____

18.18 ACTIVITY

Fill in each blank in the following sentences with the correct superlative form of the adjective or adverb in parentheses.

EXAMPLE   (successful) Lou is the __*most successful*__ quarterback in the school's history.

1. (fair) Dr. Petrakis has a reputation for being one of the _____ professors on campus.

2. (deadly) The venom of the brown recluse spider is one of the _____ poisons in nature.

3. (deep) Fully clothed, the young child jumped into the _____ section of the pool.

4. (annoyed) This is the _____ I have ever seen you.

5. (ambitious) Jamal is the _____ employee in the accounting department.

6. (fiercely) Of everyone on the gymnastics squad, Gwen competes the

_____ .

Write sentences according to the directions given.

EXAMPLE   Use the comparative form of *moody:*

Helen has been moodier since Miguel left town.

1. Use the comparative form of *quiet:*

_____

_____

2. Use the comparative form of *wise:*

_____

_____

3. Use the comparative form of *cheaply:*

_____

_____

4. Use the comparative form of *important:*

_____

_____

5. Use the superlative form of *seriously:*

_____

_____

6. Use the superlative form of *clear:*

_____

_____

7. Use the superlative form of *old:*

_____

_____

8. Use the superlative form of *difficult:*

_____

_____

Irregular comparative and superlative forms

The comparative and superlative forms of *good, well, bad,* and *badly* are irregular. If you are unsure about these forms, check the following list or a dictionary when you use them.

Adjective or Adverb	Comparative	Superlative
good	better	best
I had a <u>good</u> time.	*I had a <u>better</u> time last week.*	*I had the <u>best</u> time ever.*
well	better	best
He sings <u>well</u>.	*He sings <u>better</u> than I.*	*He is the <u>best</u> singer in the choir.*
bad	worse	worst
Karl had a <u>bad</u> idea.	*Karl's idea is <u>worse</u> than mine.*	*Karl's idea is the <u>worst</u> ever.*
badly	worse	worst
My back aches <u>badly</u>.	*My back aches <u>worse</u> than yours.*	*My back aches the <u>worst</u> of all.*

 GRAMMAR ALERT

Avoid *worser* in the speech and writing you use in college and on the job.

No: *I feel <u>worser</u> today than yesterday.*

Yes: *I feel <u>worse</u> today than yesterday.*

 GRAMMAR ALERT

Do not use *more* or *most* with the comparative and superlative forms.

No: *Jake's job is <u>more better</u> than yours.*

Yes:. *Jake's job is <u>better</u> than yours.*

CONNECT FOR SUCCESS: Use Modifiers When You Study Your Textbooks

An excellent way to learn material in your textbooks is to write your reactions, insights, and questions in the margins. When you do, use adjectives and adverbs to write responses such as *"surprising* statistic," *"weak* example," and *"strongly* agree."

18.20 ACTIVITY

Fill in the blank in each of the following sentences with the correct comparative or superlative form of the adjective or adverb in parentheses.

EXAMPLE (good) Joanna likes rap music _____*better*_____ than alternative rock.

1. (good) Professor Antonucci is the _____ teacher in the psychology department.

2. (well) Mark pitches fast balls _____ than he pitches curve balls.

3. (bad) I rewrote my introduction, but I think it is _____ than the first version.

4. (badly) Carol played the guitar _____ after she sprained her wrist.

5. (good) Business is _____ now that the store has lowered its prices.

6. (bad) This production of *Hamlet* is the _____ I have ever seen.

7. (well) Of all the people in the class, Kwame translates French

   poetry _____ .

8. (good) You have always been the _____ bridge player in the group, because you never lose your concentration.

IF ENGLISH IS NOT YOUR FIRST LANGUAGE

In English, **count nouns** name persons, places, objects, emotions, or ideas that can be counted; that is, you can put a number in front of them. They include words such as these:

apple	car	girl	shoe
book	fear	hand	teacher
boy	friend	lake	tree

Yes: *one apple*
Yes: *three friends*

Noncount nouns name things that cannot be counted; that is, you cannot put a number in front of them. They include words such as these:

air	furniture	honesty	pride
cereal	health	luggage	water

1. Use *a* or *an* with a singular count noun whose specific identity is unknown to the reader, usually because it has not yet been mentioned.

   Jeff hired a tutor to help him with math. [*Tutor* is being mentioned for the first time; the specific identity is unknown.]

2. Use *the* before a singular count noun whose identity is known to the reader.

   Jeff hired Pilar to help him with math. The tutor charges $10 an hour. [The identity of the tutor is known to be *Pilar*.]

3. Never use *a* or *an* with plural nouns.

   No: *I enjoy an eggs for breakfast.*
   Yes: *I enjoy eggs for breakfast.*

4. Never use *a* or *an* with noncount nouns.

   No: *I helped Henri move a furniture.*
   Yes: *I helped Henri move the furniture.*
   Yes: *I helped Henri move furniture.*

IF ENGLISH IS NOT YOUR FIRST LANGUAGE CONTINUED

5. Use *the* with noncount nouns that name representatives of a larger group.

No: *A coffee is very good at this restaurant.*
Yes: *The coffee is very good at this restaurant.*

6. Use *the* to point out something specific.

No: *A new major in hotel management is popular.*
Yes: *The new major in hotel management is popular.*

Noncount nouns are also discussed on page 190.

18.21 CHAPTER REVIEW ACTIVITY

On a separate sheet, write sentences as directed.

1. Add adjectives and adverbs (whichever is appropriate) to describe the underlined words. Label each word you add as an adjective or adverb.

   EXAMPLE   The <u>child</u> <u>cried</u>.

               adj.   *adv.*
   The young child cried hysterically.

   A. A <u>storm</u> <u>is making</u> its way up the coast.
   B. The <u>business</u> needed a <u>loan</u> for <u>repairs</u> to its <u>plant.</u>
   C. The radio was playing <u>loudly</u> in the <u>room.</u>
   D. After the <u>concert,</u> the <u>performers</u> <u>waited</u> for their car to drive them to the <u>airport.</u>
   E. At noon, Professor Torres will give a(n) <u>lecture</u> on the results of his <u>research.</u>

2. Write sentences using the following words.

   A. *quiet*
   B. *quietly*
   C. *random*
   D. *randomly*
   E. *good*
   F. *well* (the adjective)
   G. *well* (the adverb)
   H. the comparative form of *graceful*
   I. the superlative form of *ugly*
   J. the comparative form of *good*
   K. the comparative form of *well*
   L. the superlative form of *bad*
   M. the superlative form of *badly*

18.22 CHAPTER REVIEW ACTIVITY

Cross out the twelve incorrect forms in the following passage, and where necessary make corrections above the line.

EXAMPLE   A healthy heart is one of the ~~importantest~~ aspects of physical fitness. *most important*

[1]The more healthier you are, the more better you can achieve all the objectives in your life. [2]This is the reason that the fitness industry has become a multimillion-dollar business. [3]Nonetheless, peak cardiovascular fitness may not be best for no one who wants to be a astronaut, according to a study done at the University of Texas Southwestern Medical Center in Dallas.

[4]Endurance athletes who are high trained develop hearts with different mechanical properties than those of less active people. [5]As a result, their hearts fill with and pump out blood different. [6]It seems that them endurance athletes respond worser to the reduced pressure conditions of no gravity than others do. [7]In a unusual experiment, athletes who ran 50 miles a week or cycled 250 miles a week were studied in a special tank which reduced the pressure on their lower bodies. [8]When scientists studied the preliminary data, they were very surprised. [9]The findings suggest that endurance athletes have a more larger decrease in the volume of blood pushed out with each heartbeat than less active people, which makes them unfit for space travel. [10]Thus, you won't never travel in space if you're more fitter than you need to be.

GETTING IN GEAR: IDEAS FOR WRITING

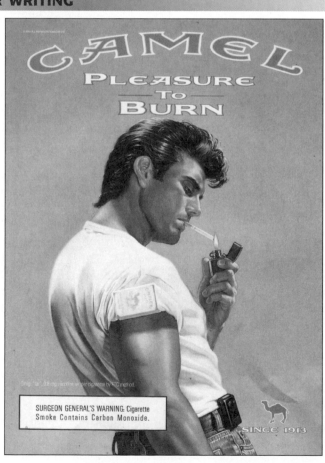

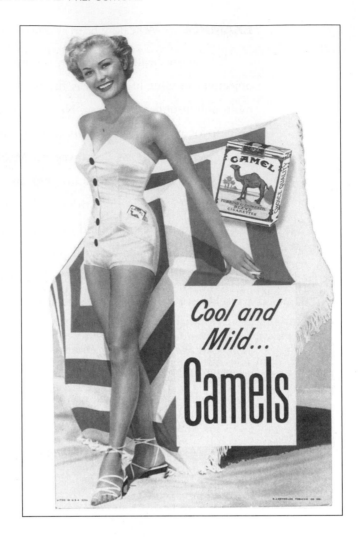

To view a collection of cigarette advertisements from the 1940s and 1950s, visit www.library.uiuc.edu/adexhibit/cigarettes.htm. Notice how superlatives are used to build a case for a product that we now know is extremely dangerous. Are similar claims made in current ads? Are the claims false or exaggerated?

writing topic: The "Pleasure to Burn" ad is recent, and the "Cool and Mild . . . Camels" ad is from the 1950s. Explain some of the ways these advertisements are alike and some of the ways they are different.

suggestions for prewriting
- Make two lists. Label one "Similarities" and one "Differences." Study the ads and list the similarities and differences between the ads. Think about how the pictures and words help the ads reach their target audiences and how the ads achieve their purpose. Are the audiences the same or different? What about the purposes?
- You do not have to discuss every similarity and difference, so look over your lists and checkmark the most important, surprising, or interesting similarities and differences. Circle the ones you want to discuss, and consider what these similarities and differences mean.

suggestion for drafting: Develop an informal outline to guide your draft. Consider discussing first the similarities and then the differences (or the reverse).

suggestions for revising
- Check your supporting details to be sure everything relates to similarities and differences.
- Be sure you have noted specific features in the ads to prove the points you make about similarities and differences.
- Use transitions such as *similarly, in like manner, however,* and *on the other hand* for coherence.

suggestion for editing: Because you are comparing and contrasting two items, you are likely to use comparative forms of adjectives and adverbs. Check to be certain these forms are correct.

RECHARGE: Lesson Summary

1. **Modifiers** are words that describe.
2. **Adjectives** are modifiers because they describe nouns and pronouns.

    The funny clown made the young children laugh.

    She is tall for her age.

3. *This, that, these,* and *those* are **demonstrative adjectives.**

    That cantaloupe is overripe.

4. *A* and *an* are special adjectives called **articles.** Use *an* before words that begin with a vowel sound, and use *a* with words that do not begin with a vowel sound.

    An old, cozy sweater is welcome on a brisk evening.

5. *Good* and *bad* are adjectives. They are often used after *taste, feel, seem, appear,* and *look.*

    You had a good idea.

    I always feel good after I exercise.

    A bad cold can be miserable.

    The storm seems bad enough to cause damage.

6. **Adverbs** are modifiers because they describe verbs, adjectives, and other adverbs. Adverbs often tell *how, when,* or *where.*

    The audience applauded enthusiastically.

    The train arrived early.

    You are too kind.

    The band played very softly.

7. *Well* is an adverb, unless it means "healthy." Then it is an adjective.

    Marta plays the piano well.

    I feel well, although I did not sleep last night.

RECHARGE: Lesson Summary Continued

8. *Badly* is an adverb.

The carpenter built the bookshelves <u>badly</u>, so they might collapse.

9. Avoid using two negatives in a single clause, so you do not create a problem called **double negative.**

Double negative: *The old building <u>doesn't</u> have <u>no</u> air conditioning.*
Correction: *The old building doesn't have any air conditioning.*
Correction: *The old building has no air conditioning.*

10. Use the **comparative form** of adjectives and adverbs to compare two items; use the **superlative form** to compare more than two items.

Comparative: *Dan is <u>taller</u> than Henry.*
Superlative: *Dan is the <u>tallest</u> player on the team.*

CHAPTER 19

Using Participles and Infinitives to Describe

Here's a riddle: When can verb forms be used as modifiers? The answer is explained in this chapter: When the verb forms are *participles* and *infinitives* and they describe other words, they are verb forms used as modifiers.

USING PARTICIPLES TO DESCRIBE

The **present participle** is the *-ing* form of a verb. Thus, present participles are words such as these:

dancing	eating	loving	swimming	wanting
doing	going	seeing	walking	winning

Although the present participle is a verb form, it can function as an adjective by describing nouns and pronouns. Here are two examples:

Whistling, Joy walked past the cemetery. [*Whistling* describes *Joy.*]

Smiling, I told a joke I heard yesterday. [*Smiling* describes *I.*]

The present participle can be combined with other words to form a phrase that describes.

Whistling a familiar tune, Joy walked past the cemetery.

Smiling broadly, I told a joke I heard yesterday.

 PUNCTUATION ALERT

As the previous examples show, you should place a comma after a participle or a participial phrase that comes at the beginning of a sentence.

315

The **past participle** is the *-ed* form of a regular verb. Thus, past participles are words such as these:

danced	helped	moved	started
feared	loved	solved	wanted

Some past participles are irregular. Instead of being formed with *-ed,* they are formed in a variety of ways. Here are some examples:

broken	found	seen	swollen
eaten	gone	spent	worn

Although the past participle is a verb form, it can function as an adjective when it describes nouns and pronouns. Here are some examples:

Helen put her <u>tired</u> feet on the sofa. [*Tired* describes *feet.*]

The child was <u>exhausted</u>. [*Exhausted* describes *child.*]

<u>Annoyed,</u> I refused to answer the question. [*Annoyed* describes *I.*]

The past participle can be combined with other words to form a phrase that describes.

Helen put her <u>very tired</u> feet on the sofa.

The child was <u>exhausted from the picnic.</u>

<u>Instantly annoyed,</u> I refused to answer the question.

➡ PUNCTUATION ALERT

Place a comma after a past participle or a past participial phrase that comes at the beginning of a sentence.

19.1 ACTIVITY

Combine the following sentence pairs into one sentence. First, change one sentence to a present participle or a present participial phrase. Then join it to the beginning of the remaining sentence. Remember to use a comma after a participle or a participial phrase at the beginning of a sentence. (The sentences can be written more than one way.)

EXAMPLES   The bride and groom danced a waltz.
They gazed into each other's eyes.

Gazing into each other's eyes, the bride and groom danced

a waltz.

or

Dancing a waltz, the bride and groom gazed into each

other's eyes.

1. The wide receiver ran into the end zone.
   He was grinning.

   _____

   _____

2. The child ran home immediately.
   He heard his mother call.

   _____

   _____

3. The storm was gathering force.
   It was approaching our town.

   _____

   _____

4. Carlos prepared to study.
   He sharpened his pencil and opened his book.

   _____

   _____

5. The puppy ran in circles.
   He chased his tail.

   _____

   _____

6. Juliane told the waiter to take back her steak.
   She complained loudly.

   _____

   _____

7. Our car turned 360 degrees.
   It was sliding on the ice.

   _____

   _____

8. Stavros and Don stood on the street corner.
   They were waiting for a bus.

   _____

   _____

19.2 COLLABORATIVE ACTIVITY

With two classmates, add a present participle or a present participial phrase at the beginning of each sentence.

EXAMPLE   _Slurping loudly_   , Sue drank her coffee.

1. _____ , Jonathan disturbed everyone nearby.

2. _____ , the car narrowly missed striking a pedestrian.

3. _____ , I strolled through the park.

4. _____ , Jan stormed out of the room.

5. _____ , the marathon runner fell across the finish line.

6. _____ , the instructor handed out the examination questions.

19.3 ACTIVITY

Combine each pair of sentences by placing the underlined past participle or past participial phrase next to the word it describes. Remember to place a comma after a past participle or a past participial phrase at the beginning of a sentence.

EXAMPLES The children found all the Easter eggs.
The Easter eggs were <u>hidden in the grass.</u>

The children found all the Easter eggs hidden in the grass.

I didn't know what to do.
I was <u>torn in two directions.</u>

Torn in two directions, I didn't know what to do.

1. I decided to take a nap.
   I was <u>tired after work.</u>

   _____

   _____

2. Frank threw the shirt away.
   The shirt was <u>torn.</u>

   _____

   _____

3. Mrs. Chung gasped.
   She was <u>surprised by what she saw.</u>

   _____

   _____

4. Diane ran out of the room.
   She was <u>embarrassed.</u>

   _____

   _____

5. We all admired the silver.
   The silver was <u>brightly polished.</u>

   _____

   _____

6. The mother soothed the child.
   The child was <u>distressed.</u>

   _____

   _____

7. The cat arched its back and hissed.
   The cat was <u>angered.</u>

   _____

   _____

8. I could not sleep.
   I was <u>worried about my job interview in the morning.</u>

   _____

   _____

19.4 ACTIVITY

Select five of the following past participles or past participial phrases. On a separate sheet, write five sentences, each using one of your selections. In each sentence, draw an arrow to the noun or pronoun described by the past participle or the past participial phrase. Remember to place a comma after a past participle or a past participial phrase at the beginning of a sentence.

EXAMPLE   exhausted

Exhausted, Lou fell asleep in the chair.

determined to improve	hidden in the bushes
disgusted	neatly written
excited by the news	overheated
frozen solid	worried about the test

USING INFINITIVES TO DESCRIBE

The **infinitive** is _to_ and the base form of the verb. Thus, infinitives are forms such as these:

to jump	to sing	to help	to run
to feel	to taste	to be	to realize

Although the infinitive is a verb form, it can function as an adjective by describing nouns and pronouns or as an adverb by describing verbs. Here are some examples:

The restaurant to try is The Lobster House. [To try describes _restaurant._]

To illustrate, I will draw you a picture. [To illustrate describes _will draw._]

The infinitive can be combined with other words to form a phrase that describes.

The restaurant to try as soon as possible is The Lobster House.

To illustrate my point, I will draw you a picture.

PUNCTUATION ALERT

Place a comma after an infinitive or an infinitive phrase that comes at the beginning of a sentence *only* when it describes.

Infinitive describes: *To avoid a penalty, pay your bill now.*

Infinitive does not describe;
it is the sentence subject: *To leave now is rude.*

19.5 ACTIVITY

Combine each pair of sentences by placing the infinitive or infinitive phrase in the second sentence at the beginning of the first sentence. Remember to use commas.

EXAMPLE   I set the alarm for six a.m.
I set the alarm to wake up early.

To wake up early, I set the alarm for six a.m.

1. Gloria hired a tutor.
She hired a tutor to get better grades.

_____

2. You must score three more points.
You must score the points to win.

_____

3. Eduardo made an appointment with his advisor.
He made the appointment to discuss changing his major.

_____

4. Mike and Catherine gave a big party.
They gave the party to celebrate their engagement.

_____

5. Fred questioned the student council candidates.
He questioned them to learn their positions on the issues.

_____

6. I painted the bedroom yellow.
I painted it to make it more cheerful.

_____

19.6 ACTIVITY

Add an infinitive or an infinitive phrase to the beginning of each of the following sentences. Remember to use commas.

EXAMPLE *To make the opening more interesting,* I revised the introduction of my essay.

1. _____ you will have to hurry.

2. _____ I must take another humanities course.

3. _____ Cassie practiced three hours every day.

4. _____ we cleaned the house thoroughly.

5. _____ the police questioned all the suspects.

AVOIDING DANGLING MODIFIERS

A participle or an infinitive at the beginning of a sentence must modify (describe) the subject of the sentence. When it does not modify the subject, the error is called a **dangling modifier,** because the modifier (the participle or infinitive) is left *dangling*—it is out there on its own, with nothing to connect to. Here are some examples of dangling modifiers:

Knowing the answer, my hand was raised. [Did *my hand* know the answer?]

Depressed, Janine's tears flowed. [Were *Janine's tears* depressed?]

To eat less, fewer snacks were in the house. [Did *fewer snacks* want to eat less?]

To eliminate a dangling modifier, rewrite so the participle or infinitive has a sentence subject it can describe sensibly. You may need to rework some sentences extensively to accomplish this. Here are three examples:

Dangling modifier
(present participle): *Knowing the answer, my hand was raised.*

Correction: *Knowing the answer, I raised my hand.* [Now the present participle can sensibly describe the subject *I.*]

Dangling modifier
(past participle): *Depressed, Janine's tears flowed.*

Correction: *Depressed, Janine cried hard.* [Now the past participle can sensibly describe the subject *Janine.*]

Dangling modifier
(infinitive): *To eat less, fewer snacks were in the house.*

Correction: *To eat less, Jack kept fewer snacks in the house.* [Now the infinitive can sensibly describe the subject *Jack.*]

CONNECT FOR SUCCESS: Eliminate Dangling Modifiers from Classroom Writing

Because dangling modifiers do not express your intended meaning, they are particularly troublesome in the classroom. For example, your biology instructor may not be sure that you understand the makeup of a cell if you write this sentence with a dangling modifier: "Containing cellulose fibrils, the composition of plant and bacterial cell walls is different." Eliminate the dangling modifier and your instructor knows you understand: "Containing cellulose fibers, a plant cell wall has a different composition than does the cell wall of bacteria."

19.7 ACTIVITY

Rewrite the following sentences to eliminate dangling modifiers. Two sentences are correct as they are. For these, write "correct" in the blanks.

EXAMPLE Riding my bike, the wheel fell off.

Riding my bike, I realized the wheel fell off.

1. Tired after work, a nap was what I wanted.

2. Walking down the street, mud was splashed on me.

3. To quit smoking, a great deal of candy was in the house.

4. Concerned about education reform, Martha decided to run for the school board.

5. Exploring the park with Carl, a lovely pond was discovered.

6. To do well in physics, a person needs good math skills.

7. Thrown into the deep underbrush, I lost the ball.

   _____

   _____

8. Chopping wood, splinters got in his eye.

   _____

   _____

IF ENGLISH IS NOT YOUR FIRST LANGUAGE

1. A participle or a participial phrase can appear before or after the word it describes.

   Pacing back and forth, Dr. Menendez delivered the lecture.

   Dr. Menendez, *pacing back and forth,* delivered the lecture.

2. Participles and participial phrases can come after linking verbs and can describe the subject.

   Cody was *frightened* by the loud noise.

   The eleven o'clock newscast was *alarming.*

19.8 CHAPTER REVIEW ACTIVITY

On a separate sheet, write three sentences using present participles or present participial phrases as modifiers, three sentences using past participles or past participial phrases as modifiers, and three sentences using infinitives or infinitive phrases as modifiers. Remember to use commas correctly, and remember to provide a nearby word for each participle or infinitive to describe.

19.9 CHAPTER REVIEW ACTIVITY

Make corrections above the line to eliminate five dangling modifiers.

                                        people try many strategies.

EXAMPLE   Not wanting to oversleep, ~~many strategies are tried.~~

[1]To avoid oversleeping, an alarm clock is used. [2]Accustomed to this practice, no thought is given to it by those of us who must wake up at a specific time. [3]However, before 1787, alarm clocks were not available. [4]It was in that year that Levi Hutchins hit upon the idea. [5]Always oversleeping, something to wake Levi up was what he needed. [6]In fact, he needed something to wake him up at the same time each day: four o'clock in the morning. [7]Struck by an idea, a clever device was envisioned. [8]Fixing a bell to the inside of one of his clocks, Levi rigged it so that, when the hands pointed to four o'clock, the bell would ring. [9]The device worked, and as far as we know, Levi never overslept again.

[10]As helpful as the alarm clock is, it did not solve one problem many of us have. [11]Turning off the alarm and rolling over, sleep overtakes us once more. To solve that problem, the snooze alarm was devised over a hundred years later. [12]Plagued by an inability to get up easily in the morning, I for one am grateful for that improvement on Levi's invention.

GETTING IN GEAR: IDEAS FOR WRITING

Over the years, we have relationships with many people who play important roles in our lives—people such as the ones depicted in the photographs. These people can affect us so profoundly that they influence our thinking and behavior for a lifetime.

writing topic: Assume that a person who has played an important role in your life is being honored at an awards banquet and that you have been asked to write a piece for the program that describes why the individual is special to you. For examples of tributes to people, visit the New York Times site that includes tributes to those who died in the attacks on the World Trade Center: www.nytimes.com/pages/national/portraits/.

suggestions for prewriting

- Using the photographs for inspiration, list ten people who have been important to you. You might consider family, friends, coaches, teachers, neighbors, and clergy.
- Select a person from the list to write about, and list as many words and phrases as you can think of to explain why he or she is important to you.

suggestions for drafting

- Your topic sentence (for a paragraph composition) or thesis (for an essay) can mention the person (that's your topic) and why that person is important to you (that's your claim about the topic).
- You might want to tell a story that shows why the person is important to you or give a few examples that demonstrate the person's importance.

suggestion for revising: To be sure your writing is well organized, outline your draft *after* it is written—even if you outlined before you drafted. Study your outline to be sure all your ideas follow logically.

suggestion for editing: If you have described the person or the person's actions, check your use of adjectives and adverbs, especially descriptive participles and infinitives.

RECHARGE: Lesson Summary

1. **Present participles** (-*ing* verb forms), **past participles** (-*ed* forms of regular verbs), and **infinitives** (*to* and the base form of verbs) can function as descriptive words.

    Present participle: *Singing, I walked across campus.*
    Past participle: *Fascinated, Jan looked more closely at the painting.*
    Infinitive: *To repeat, I completely agree with you.*

2. To avoid a **dangling modifier,** be sure the describing participle or infinitive has a stated subject to describe.

    Dangling modifier: *Running quickly, the bus passed me by.*
    Correction: *Running quickly, I missed the bus.*

CHAPTER 20

Using Prepositions

CHAPTER GOALS

By the end of this chapter, you will learn to

Use prepositions and prepositional phrases correctly

Use prepositions in common expressions

Most *prepositions* are short words, such as *in, at, from, of, on, up,* and *near.* However, do not be fooled by the fact that many prepositions are short. Their length does not mean that they are unimportant. In fact, as you will learn in this chapter, prepositions are very important, because they help writers and speakers demonstrate relationships.

UNDERSTANDING PREPOSITIONS

A **preposition** shows how a noun or pronoun relates to another word. Often the relationship is one of time or space. Here are two examples:

> *The wallet fell <u>under</u> the chair.* [*Under* is a preposition that shows how the wallet was positioned in space: It was *under* the chair.]

> *Laurie graduated <u>in</u> December.* [*In* is a preposition that shows how Laurie's graduation was positioned in time: It occurred *in* December.]

Following is a partial list of prepositions. Studying it will help you recognize prepositions in writing.

about	before	from	through
above	behind	in	to
across	beside	into	toward
after	between	like	under
against	by	of	until
along	during	off	up
among	except	on	with
at	for	over	without

USING PREPOSITIONAL PHRASES

A **prepositional phrase** is a preposition and the word or words that go with it. Here are some examples:

at first	*between* the red chairs	*in* the new car
after school	*by* now	*on* the roof
before this	*during* the night	*with* you

Prepositional phrases help a writer describe something, as the following examples show.

Troubleshooting

A good way to remember prepositions is to think of how a dog can be positioned in relation to a doghouse. The dog can be *in* the doghouse, *beside* the doghouse, *near* the doghouse, *by* the doghouse, or *on* the doghouse. Thus, *in, beside, near, by,* and *on* are prepositions. Although this test will not identify all prepositions, it will identify many of them.

I left the keys <u>in the new car</u>. [The prepositional phrase describes *left*.

The meeting <u>at school</u> is running late. [The prepositional phrase describes *meeting*.]

<u>By now</u> the game should be over. [The prepositional phrase describes *should be*.]

GRAMMAR ALERT

A preposition can be more than one word. Here are some examples:

along with	in addition to
as well as	next to

The garage is <u>next to</u> the house.

20.1 ACTIVITY

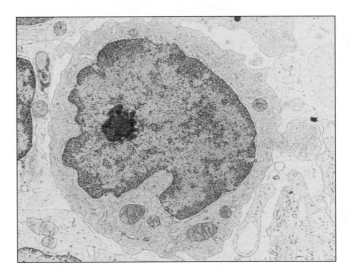

Underline each prepositional phrase and circle each preposition. A sentence can have more than one prepositional phrase.

EXAMPLE The study ⟨of⟩ cells is essentially the study ⟨of⟩ life.

1. The study of cells did not begin until the microscope's invention in the seventeenth century.

2. With the microscope came cell theory, which states that all living things are made of fundamental units called cells.

3. Cell theory also states that the cell is the basic unit of life and that new cells arise from preexisting cells.

4. A few cells, including a hen's egg or a frog's egg, are large enough to be seen by the naked eye, but most are too small to be seen without magnification.

5. The length across the surface of most cells is about 1 cubic millimeter.

6. The small size of cells is explained by surface-to-volume ratio.

7. Nutrients enter a cell, and wastes exit a cell at its surface, so larger cells require more nutrients and create more waste.

8. In other words, the volume represents how much a cell needs during its life.

9. Despite their small size, cells are responsible for many functions associated with life.

10. Cells interact with the environment, obtain chemicals and energy from their surroundings, grow, and reproduce.

Source: Adapted from Sylvia S. Mader, *Human Biology* (New York: McGraw-Hill, 2004), p. 38. Copyright © 2004 The McGraw-Hill Companies.

20.2 COLLABORATIVE ACTIVITY

Alone or with two classmates, add one or more prepositional phrases to each of the following sentences.

EXAMPLE   I went to a Dixie Chicks concert.

During spring break, I went to a Dixie Chicks concert with Liz.

1. The traffic is terrible.

_____

_____

2. Dr. Phillips explained the research assignment.

_____

_____

3. The police officer signaled me to pull over.

_____

_____

4. The fall trees are the most colorful.

_____

_____

5. The fans cheered.

_____

_____

6. I dropped my keys.

_____

_____

7. Bill told a story.

    _____

    _____

8. The City Council trimmed the budget.

    _____

    _____

20.3 ACTIVITY

Combine each group of three sentences into one sentence. To do so, add the prepositional phrases in the second and third sentences to the first sentence.

EXAMPLE   I put my sweater on.
              I put it on without looking.
              I put it on inside out.

Without looking, I put my sweater on inside out.

1. The instructor was pleased.
    She was pleased by the test scores.
    The test scores were those of her students.

    _____

    _____

2. As a child, I fished every day.
    I fished in the lake.
    The lake was near my house.

    _____

    _____

3. My car stalled.
    It stalled on the freeway.
    It stalled during rush hour.

    _____

    _____

4. Carmen gave a fascinating speech.
    His speech was about his summer trip.
    His trip was to Italy.

    _____

    _____

5. Half the audience left.
    They left during intermission.
    They left in disgust.

    _____

    _____

6. The dog jumped.
   He jumped in the air.
   He jumped for the Frisbee.

_____

_____

USING PREPOSITIONS IN COMMON EXPRESSIONS

A number of expressions customarily use certain prepositions. The following are some of these expressions, with examples.

1. Use *accompanied by* with a person; use *accompanied with* with a thing or an object.

   The actor was <u>accompanied by</u> his agent.

   The fever was <u>accompanied with</u> a sore throat.

2. Use *angry with* and *upset with* with a person; use *angry at* and *upset at* with a thing or a situation.

   Peter is still <u>angry with</u> Troy.

   I am <u>upset at</u> your stubbornness.

3. Use *between* for two things; use *among* for more than two things.

   I cannot decide <u>between</u> the black suit and the brown one.

   I cannot decide <u>among</u> the black suit, the brown one, and the navy one.

4. Use *correspond to* in a comparison; use *correspond with* to mean letter writing.

   Your facts <u>correspond to</u> mine.

   I have <u>corresponded with</u> Isaac for years.

5. Use *differ with* to mean "disagree with"; use *differ from* to mean "are unlike."

   I <u>differ with</u> you about who the best candidate is.

   This product <u>differs from</u> its picture in the magazine.

6. Use *different from*, not *different than*.

   No: *Your beliefs are <u>different than</u> mine.*
   Yes: *Your beliefs are <u>different from</u> mine.*

7. Use *disagree with* with a person; use *disagree on* with a topic or a thing.

   Julie <u>disagrees with</u> everyone.

   We <u>disagree on</u> the meaning of the novel.

8. Use *identical with*, not *identical to*.

   No: *Your shoes are <u>identical to</u> mine.*
   Yes: *Your shoes are <u>identical with</u> mine.*

9. Use *independent of*, not *independent from*.

   No: *This university is <u>independent from</u> the state.*
   Yes: *This university is <u>independent of</u> the state.*

10. Do not use *like* to mean "for example" or "such as."

No: *Stephen King has written many books, <u>like</u> <u>Christine</u>, <u>Misery</u>, and <u>Needful Things</u>.*

Yes: *Stephen King has written many books, <u>such as</u> <u>Christine</u>, <u>Misery</u>, and <u>Needful Things</u>.*

Yes: *Stephen King has written many books. <u>For example</u>, he is the author of <u>Christine</u>, <u>Misery</u>, and <u>Needful Things</u>.*

➡ **PUNCTUATION ALERT**

Do not use a comma after "such as."

11. Do not use *over to* or *over at* for *to* or *at*.

No: *We went <u>over to</u> Janine's to eat.*

Yes: *We went <u>to</u> Janine's to eat.*

No: *We met <u>over at</u> Sue's.*

Yes: *We met <u>at</u> Sue's.*

12. Use *respond with* with a reaction; use *respond to* with a procedure or an action.

<u>Responding with</u> anger will not solve the problem.

The upset child <u>responded to</u> my kindness.

13. Use *responsible for* with an action; use *responsible to* with a person.

I am <u>responsible for</u> my own behavior.

Senators must be <u>responsible to</u> the people who elected them.

14. Use *similar to*, not *similar with*.

No: *Your schedule is <u>similar with</u> mine.*

Yes: *Your schedule is <u>similar to</u> mine.*

15. Use *toward*, not *towards*.

No: *We steered the boat <u>towards</u> the shore.*

Yes: *We steered the boat <u>toward</u> the shore.*

CONNECT FOR SUCCESS: Learn Common Expressions in Your Studies

Different subjects have common expressions using prepositions. For example, in literary studies, the expression "symbolism *of*" is often used and, in advertising, the expression "demographics *for*" is often used. Make note of common expressions with prepositions in your textbooks, and listen for them in lectures. Write them down and learn them.

20.4 ACTIVITY

Place a checkmark next to the sentence in each pair that uses prepositions correctly.

EXAMPLE ____✓____ Your schedule is different from mine.

_____ Your schedule is different than mine.

1. _____ Lorenzo is working toward a degree in English.

_____ Lorenzo is working towards a degree in English.

2. _____ The students were accompanied with a chaperon on their class trip to Disneyworld.

_____ The students were accompanied by a chaperon on their class trip to Disneyworld.

3. _____ I divided the cake among the three of us.

_____ I divided the cake between the three of us.

4. _____ Rita Moreno has won many awards, such as the Tony, the Emmy, the Oscar, and the Grammy.

_____ Rita Moreno has won many awards, like the Tony, the Emmy, the Oscar, and the Grammy.

5. _____ The two candidates differ with each other about how to reduce the deficit.

_____ The two candidates differ from each other about how to reduce the deficit.

6. _____ Let's go over to the student union and see a movie.

_____ Let's go to the student union and see a movie.

7. _____ Karen is upset with herself for making a silly mistake.

_____ Karen is upset at herself for making a silly mistake.

8. _____ Authorities disagree on the significance of the research.

_____ Authorities disagree with the significance of the research.

9. _____ This apartment is similar with the one I used to rent.

_____ This apartment is similar to the one I used to rent.

10. _____ Now that I have a job, I am independent from my family.

_____ Now that I have a job, I am independent of my family.

 IF ENGLISH IS NOT YOUR FIRST LANGUAGE

1. See number 6 on page 91 for information on English verbs that are combined with prepositions and for information on when the prepositions can be separated from the verbs and when they cannot be separated.

2. Be aware of the uses of *in, on,* and *at* to show time and place.

   A. Use *in* for seasons, months, and years that do not include specific dates. Use *on* if a specific date appears.

      I was born in 1949.
      I was born on May 4, 1949.

IF ENGLISH IS NOT YOUR FIRST LANGUAGE CONTINUED

    B. Use *in* for a period of the day. Use *on* for a specific day. Use *at* for a specific time or period of the day.

> *I like to run 2 miles <u>in</u> the morning.*
> *I will run 2 miles <u>on</u> Wednesday.*
> *I like to run 2 miles <u>at</u> dawn.*

    C. Use *in* for a location that is surrounded by something else. Use *at* for a specific location.

> *I lived <u>in</u> London for a year.*
> *Join me <u>in</u> the living room.*
> *I lived <u>at</u> 518 Tod Lane.*
> *Meet me <u>at</u> the crossroads.*

3. In English, the subject of a sentence cannot appear in a prepositional phrase, so cross out prepositional phrases before trying to identify the subject of a sentence.

> *subject*
> ~~In the morning,~~ ⌐the sun⌐ *rises over the ocean.*

4. Prepositional phrases that show place come before those that show time.

> No: *Edmund worked in 1992 in Mexico.*
> Yes: *Edmund worked in Mexico in 1992.*

20.5 CHAPTER REVIEW ACTIVITY

Cross out the nine incorrect prepositions in the following passage, and write the correct ones above the line.

EXAMPLE   Some people disagree ~~with~~ *on* the Monroe Doctrine.

[1]The Monroe Doctrine is a statement of foreign policy that was issued by President James Monroe. [2]On December 1823, Monroe included in his annual message at Congress the points that became known as the Monroe Doctrine—points like the following:

[3]• The American continents can no longer be colonized by Europe.

[4]• The European political system is different than that of the United States. Therefore, efforts to extend the European system to the Western Hemisphere will be considered dangerous to the United States.

[5]• The United States will not interfere of any existing European colonies.

[6]• The United States will not be responsible to interfering in the internal affairs of European nations.

[7]Sometimes the United States does not act in a way that is identical to the principles of the Monroe Doctrine. [8]For example, Theodore Roosevelt, in what

became known as the Roosevelt Corollary, claimed for the United States "police power" in Latin America. [9]He claimed that the United States could and should intervene in the internal affairs of Western Hemisphere nations in cases of wrongdoing.

[10]Of course, many people maintain that the United States should extend the principles of the Monroe Doctrine to its behavior with non-European nations. [11]These people say that this country interferes too much on the affairs of Asian, African, and Middle Eastern nations. [12]They believe that countries are independent from each other, so we should leave countries alone to work out their own problems.

GETTING IN GEAR: IDEAS FOR WRITING

Which do you think people value more, looks or brains? Much research has been done on this topic. For a summary of one study that assesses the effects of perceived attractiveness versus academic success on popularity among 9th grades, take a look at this site: http://www.ncbi.nlm.nih.gov/entrez/query.fcgi?cmd=Retrieve& db=PubMed&List_uids=9729839&dopt=Citation.

writing topic: Which would you rather have, great physical attractiveness or superior intelligence? Be sure to give reasons for your decision.

suggestions for discovering ideas

- Use the photographs of Albert Einstein and the attractive couple to help stimulate your thinking. In addition, consider your own experiences and observations. Then make two lists, one giving the advantages and disadvantages of physical attractiveness and one giving the advantages and disadvantages of superior intelligence.
- Study your lists, make your decision, and checkmark the ideas you will include in your draft. If one reason is particularly compelling, you can focus on that reason alone, being sure you explain it in detail.

suggestions for drafting

- Your thesis or topic sentence (depending on whether you are writing an essay or a paragraph) can mention the choices and which you would choose, something like this: "Given the choice between great beauty and superior intelligence, I would choose beauty." Your thesis or topic sentence can also mention why you choose as you do: "Given the choice between physical attractiveness and superior intelligence, I would choose physical attractiveness because _____."
- It might be effective to write your reasons from least to most significant, so you have a progressive order. If you are focusing on one reason, you may also want to arrange the details that explain it in progressive order.

suggestion for revising: Look for general words and phrases that you can make more specific with the addition of prepositional phrases. For example, instead of writing "Short men have a more difficult time succeeding," you might be able to write "<u>In business</u>, men <u>under 5 feet 9 inches tall</u> often lose jobs <u>to equally qualified men</u> who are taller."

suggestion for editing: Read over your draft and linger over each preposition, checking to make sure it is used correctly. Pay particular attention to prepositions that are part of the common expressions on pages 330–331.

RECHARGE: Lesson Summary

1. **Prepositions** show how things are positioned in time or space. They are words such as *at, by, near, through,* and *under.*
2. A **prepositional phrase** includes a preposition and the word or words that function with it. They are phrases such as *at noon, by now, through the tunnel,* and *under the water.*
3. **Some expressions customarily use certain prepositions.**

PART FIVE REVIEW
Reviewing modifiers and prepositions

A. Cross out and write corrections above the line to eliminate five errors with adjectives and adverbs, one incorrect article, two dangling modifiers, one double negative, and four errors with prepositions.

[1]Almost all parts of the world celebrate something similarly to April Fools' Day. [2]This almost universal celebration is an day when practical jokes are played to friends and neighbors. [3]Although explained several ways, we are not sure how April Fools' Day began. [4]One theory of origin, however, seems more likelier than others.

[5]This theory states that April Fools' Day started with the French. [6]When the calendar was reformed, the first nation to adopt it was France. [7]Charles IX ordered, on 1564, that the year should definite begin January 1. [8]Until then, New Year's visits and the exchange with New Year's gifts had been associated with a different date, April 1.

[9]After Charles issued his decree, visits and gifts became associated with the first of January. [10]However, many people were unhappy by the change. [11]Refusing to go along with it, jokes were played on these people. [12]The jokesters made fun of them by giving them mock gifts; they pretended to visit them, and they invited them to mock New Year's celebrations—all on the first of April. [13]In other words, the jokesters made these people April Fools—people who still felt April was the more better beginning of the new year. [14]Thus, the custom of fooling people on April 1 started with the mock gifts and celebrations directed at those who would not never give in to Charles's decree.

[15]Although this explanation is only one of many, it explains the origin of April Fools' Day as good as any other one. [16]The next time you play an April

Fools' Day prank on someone, you might as well remember the thanks you owe to France's King Charles.

B. Cross out and write corrections above the line to eliminate four errors with adjectives and adverbs, three incorrect articles, two dangling modifiers, one double negative, and two errors with prepositions.

[1]Marian Anderson was the first African American to sing at the Metropolitan Opera. [2]She was known primary for her rich voice and wide range. [3]Named to the National Arts Hall of Fame, her contribution to the American performing arts cannot never be overestimated. [4]She was also cited at the first annual Kennedy Center Honors in 1978. [5]In addition to her noteworthy opera career, Anderson was acclaimed even more wide for her singing of spirituals.

[6]Anderson first sang at church choirs. [7]To obtain the training necessary for her career, her race made it necessary for her to overcome great difficulties. [8]In 1935, she sang for Arturo Toscanini, who said that she had a voice that comes once in an hundred years. [9]However, four years later, the Daughters of the American Revolution denied her access to Washington's Constitution Hall for a concert. [10]Eleanor Roosevelt then arranged her concert on the steps of the Lincoln Memorial before a audience of 75,000.

[11]After that, Anderson was named by the government as a alternate United Nations delegate. [12]She sang in the inaugural balls of Presidents Eisenhower and Kennedy. [13]She made many recordings and was noted wide for the deep timbre and style of her singing.

[14]Anderson retired after one of her most successfulest concert tours in 1965.

READING AND WRITING IN RESPONSE TO TEXTBOOKS

The following excerpt from an American history textbook opens a discussion of American Colonial resistance to British taxation imposed by The Stamp Act.

[1]On the first night of November 1765, the narrow, winding streets of New York glowed with unaccustomed light. [2]The Stamp Act was to have taken effect on that date, but the colony's stampmaster had resigned his office earlier. [3]What had frightened him into resignation could be seen in the moving shadows of men, women, and children, hundreds of them. [4]The flaring torches and flickering candles that they carried aloft through the city's crooked byways cast on storefronts and doorways dark images of a crowd protesting the "death of Liberty."

Source: Adapted from James West Davidson et al., *Nation of Nations*, 3rd ed. (New York: McGraw-Hill, 1998), p. 158. Copyright © 1998 The McGraw-Hill Companies. Used by permission of The McGraw-Hill Companies.

1. Answer the following questions about sentence 1:

    A. How many prepositional phrases are there? _____

    B. Which prepositional phrase describes *streets?*_____

C. What other words describe *streets*? Are these words adjectives or adverbs?

_____

D. Is *unaccustomed* an adjective or adverb? What word does it describe?

_____

2. In sentence 2, what word is an adverb? What does that adverb describe?

_____

3. In sentences 3 and 4, what participles describe nouns?

_____

4. In sentence 4, what word does *aloft* describe? Is *aloft* an adjective or adverb?

_____

5. How do the descriptive adjectives, adverbs, and prepositional phrases help students understand Colonial reaction to the Stamp Act?

_____

_____

writing topic: Street demonstrations, such as the one described in the textbook excerpt, are common forms of protest in this country. What other forms of protest do Americans engage in? Which of those forms are the most popular? Why? As an alternative, tell about a protest you have participated in.

Improving Sentences

Books aren't written—they're rewritten. . . . It is one of the hardest things to accept, especially after the seventh rewrite hasn't quite done it.

—Michael Crichton, bestselling author of many novels, including *Andromeda Strain, Jurassic Park, Lost World,* and *State of Fear*

Reflection: Are you like Michael Crichton in that you have trouble accepting the need to revise? Why or why not?

WHAT YOU WILL LEARN	WHY YOU WILL LEARN IT
How to place items in series and pairs in the same grammatical form	so that your sentences have a pleasing balance
How to use pairs of conjunctions	so that your sentences have a pleasing balance
How to use simple subjects and verbs that make sense together	so that you can write correct sentences
How to eliminate illogical equations	so that you can write correct sentences
How to write definitions and explanations without *is when, is where,* and *the reason is because*	so that you can write correct sentences
How to eliminate mixed sentence structures	so that you can write correct sentences
How to use a variety of sentence openers	so that you can have a pleasing style

CHAPTER **21**

Achieving Parallelism

CHAPTER GOALS

By the end of this chap-
ter, you will learn to

Recognize parallelism

Achieve parallelism with
series and pairs

Achieve parallelism with
pairs of conjunctions

Which of the following sentences is more pleasing to your ear?

> *Juan is known as an excellent swimmer, a strong runner, and he does the*
> *high jump well.*

> *Juan is known as an excellent swimmer, a strong runner, and a good high*
> *jumper.*

If you picked the second sentence, then you already recognize that a sentence with
parallelism reads better than a sentence without parallelism.

ACHIEVING PARALLELISM WITH WORDS IN SERIES AND PAIRS

Parallelism means that items that form a pair (two things) or items that form a
series (more than two things) have the same grammatical form. In the following
examples, the parallel items are underlined.

Parallel pair:	*Before bed, I like <u>watching</u> the eleven o'clock news and <u>drinking</u> milk.*
Parallel series:	*This coffee is <u>cold</u>, <u>weak</u>, and <u>bitter</u>.*

Notice how much less appeal the sentences have without parallelism.

> *Before bed, I like watching the eleven o'clock news and to drink milk.*
> *This coffee is cold, weak, and it is bitter.*

To eliminate problems with parallelism, place all the items in a series or pair
in the same form. Here are two examples:

Lacks parallelism:	*The instructor told me <u>to study more</u> and <u>that I should get a tutor</u>.*
Correction 1:	*The instructor told me <u>to study more</u> and <u>to get a tutor</u>.*
Correction 2:	*The instructor told me <u>that I should study more</u> and <u>that I should get a tutor</u>.*
Lacks parallelism:	*The movie is <u>dull</u>, <u>pretentious</u>, and <u>it is too long</u>.*
Correction 1:	*The movie is <u>dull</u>, <u>pretentious</u>, and <u>too long</u>.*
Correction 2:	*The movie is <u>dull</u>, <u>it is pretentious</u>, and <u>it is too long</u>.*

340

21.1 ACTIVITY

Circle the element in each item that is not parallel. Write the parallel form in the blank.

EXAMPLE   young
innocent
full of ambition
clever

ambitious

1. tall
athletic
feeling cheerful
intelligent

   _____

2. to sail
swimming
to ski
to fish

   _____

3. in the woods
by the stream
behind the house
lakeside

   _____

4. eating in good restaurants
small parties
political lectures
modern art museums

   _____

5. charity for the homeless
being kind to strangers
help for the ill
friendship for the lonely

   _____

6. Study daily.
Ask questions.
Take notes.
You should read assignments.

   _____

7. hair that shines
radiant skin
twinkling eyes
lovely smile

   _____

8. She explains points well.
She answers questions thoroughly.
Her sense of humor is appealing.
She enjoys students.

   _____

9. feeling alarmed by the thunder
blown by the wind
drenched by the rain
pelted by the hail

   _____

10. Stop smoking.
Reduce my salt intake.
Limit sugar.
That I should exercise daily.

   _____

21.2 ACTIVITY

In each pair of sentences, place a checkmark next to the sentence with parallelism.

EXAMPLE   ___✓___   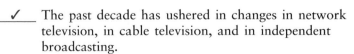 The past decade has ushered in changes in network television, in cable television, and in independent broadcasting.

   _____   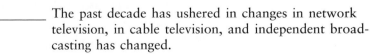 The past decade has ushered in changes in network television, in cable television, and independent broadcasting has changed.

1. _____ Television networks and cable systems face increasing competition from radio, the Internet, magazines, and they face competition from mobile pagers.

   _____ Television networks and cable systems face increasing competition from radio, the Internet, magazines, and mobile pagers.

2. _____ To respond to the competition, television news outlets might cooperate with other news outlets or working with rival cable systems and local newspapers often occurs.

   _____ To respond to the competition, television news outlets might cooperate with other news outlets or work with rival cable systems and local newspapers.

3. _____ Some of the new trends in television journalism include coventures, regional cable news, and news-on-demand is a significant trend.

   _____ Some of the new trends in television journalism include coventures, regional cable news, and news-on-demand.

4. _____ Coventuring occurs when a local network affiliate buys time on an independent station to program an alternative version of its local news and to offer a choice of different stories.

   _____ Coventuring occurs when a local network affiliate buys time on an independent station to program an alternative version of its local news and it can offer a choice of different stories.

5. _____ As part of coventuring, CNN has partnered with *Sports Illustrated,* with *Entertainment Weekly,* and it has partnered with *People* magazine.

   _____ As part of coventuring, CNN has partnered with *Sports Illustrated,* with *Entertainment Weekly,* and with *People* magazine.

6. _____ Regional cable news offers local versions of CNN, news summaries to cable viewers, and it provides twenty-four-hour coverage.

   _____ Regional cable news offers local versions of CNN, news summaries to cable viewers, and twenty-four-hour coverage.

7. _____ Regional cable is popular with smaller communities and in isolated areas.

   _____ Regional cable is popular with smaller communities, and isolated areas like it.

8. _____ News-on-demand allows a sports enthusiast to watch a steady diet of game highlights, a news junkie to watch the day's significant events, and a weather enthusiast to view the current Doppler radar report.

   _____ News-on-demand allows a sports enthusiast to watch a steady diet of game highlights, a news junkie to watch the day's significant events, and a weather enthusiast can spend an entire day watching the current Doppler radar report.

21.3 COLLABORATIVE ACTIVITY

With two classmates, fill in the blanks with a parallel word or words.

EXAMPLE   Most people like Edward because he is friendly, honest, and _funny_____.

1. Lesley no longer eats chocolate because it gives her a headache and _____.

2. If you study every day, you will keep up with your assignments, reduce stress, and _____.

3. Although she is eighty years old, Aunt Hattie is in good shape because she exercises regularly, stays active, and _____.

4. In my freshman orientation class, I learned how to add and drop classes, where to find a tutor, and _____.

5. When traveling at night, be sure to have a full tank of gas, directions to your destination, and _____.

6. After I ran five miles, my ankles hurt and _____.

7. Dr. Goldberg's lectures are always inspiring, informative, and _____.

8. You will find him in his room or _____.

21.4 ACTIVITY

The underlined element in each sentence is not parallel. Rewrite the sentences to achieve parallelism.

EXAMPLE   The first crayons consisted of charcoal and <u>oil was used.</u>
_The first crayons consisted of charcoal and oil._____

1. The first box of eight Crayola crayons included green, brown, blue, red, yellow, orange, purple, and <u>it also had basic black.</u>

    _____
    _____

2. Today Crayola makes crayons that sparkle with glitter, glow in the dark, change colors, wash off walls, and <u>ones that smell like flowers.</u>

    _____
    _____

3. Children's favorite crayon colors are red, and <u>they like to color with blue.</u>

    _____
    _____

4. Since their inception in 1903, Crayola crayons have become one of the most respected brands, one of the most recognizable products, and <u>people find it one of the most trusted children's items.</u>

_____

_____

_____

5. Smith and Binney, the company that makes Crayola crayons, early on made red pigments used for painting barns, carbon used for coating automobile tires, and <u>to make graphite for school pencils.</u>

_____

_____

_____

6. Currently, Smith and Binney makes more than 120 crayon colors, an array of creative materials, and <u>it creates art products for schools.</u>

_____

_____

7. The company that manufactures Crayola crayons now distributes its products throughout the world, in over a dozen languages, and <u>manufactures them for a variety of purposes.</u>

_____

_____

8. Honored with a U.S. postage stamp, placed in the Smithsonian, and <u>because they are used almost half an hour a day by American children,</u> Crayola crayons are <u>an American</u> business success story.

_____

_____

_____

ACHIEVING PARALLELISM WITH PAIRED CONJUNCTIONS

Conjunctions are joining words. A number of conjunctions work in pairs. Four of these paired conjunctions are

both . . . and   neither . . . nor
either . . . or   not only . . . but also

To achieve parallelism when you use paired conjunctions, follow each conjunction with the same grammatical form.

Troubleshooting

When something sounds "off" when you read your draft, you might have a problem with parallelism.

Lacks parallelism: *You must not only <u>pass</u> the test, but also <u>you must earn a high B.</u>* [*Not only* is followed by a verb, and *but also* is followed by a subject and a verb.]

Achieves parallelism: *Not only <u>must you</u> pass the test, but also <u>you must</u> earn a high B.* [*Not only* and *but also* are both followed by subjects and verbs.]

Lacks parallelism:	*I either <u>get</u> a job or <u>I drop</u> out of school.* [*Either* is followed by a verb, and *or* is followed by a subject and a verb.]
Achieves parallelism:	*Either <u>I get</u> a job or <u>I drop</u> out of school.* [*Either* and *or* are both followed by subjects and verbs.]
Lacks parallelism:	*This waffle both <u>is</u> cold and <u>soggy</u>.* [*Both* is followed by a verb and a descriptive word, and *and* is followed by just a descriptive word.]
Achieves parallelism:	*This waffle is both <u>cold</u> and <u>soggy</u>.* [*Both* and *and* are followed by descriptive words.]

21.5 ACTIVITY

In each pair of sentences, place a checkmark next to the sentence that achieves parallelism.

EXAMPLE   _____✓_____ Either we leave now or we will be late.
             _____ We either leave now or we will be late.

1. _____ The children neither watched the television nor turned it off.
_____ The children watched neither the television nor turned it off.

2. _____ Carla not only bought the hat but also the scarf to go with it.
_____ Carla bought not only the hat but also the scarf to go with it.

3. _____ Majoring in special education is both challenging and rewarding.
_____ Majoring in special education both is challenging and rewarding.

4. _____ Ruth volunteers not only at nursing homes but also at the senior citizens' center.
_____ Ruth not only volunteers at nursing homes but also at the senior citizens' center.

5. _____ Either the exam will be postponed until Tuesday or Thursday.
_____ The exam will be postponed until either Tuesday or Thursday.

6. _____ Clarice is amazing because she is both a talented painter and an accomplished musician.
_____ Clarice is amazing because she both is a talented painter and an accomplished musician.

7. _____ Recycling not only helps the environment but also saves money.
_____ Recycling helps not only the environment but also saves money.

8. _____ The candidate's speeches are either too long or too technical.
_____ The candidate's speeches either are too long or too technical.

21.6 ACTIVITY

Circle the paired conjunctions in each of the following sentences, determine what grammatical forms appear after them, and then decide whether parallelism has been achieved. If it has, write "correct" in the blank. If not, rewrite the sentence to achieve parallelism.

EXAMPLE   I [neither] enjoy handball [nor] racquetball.
I enjoy neither handball nor racquetball.

1. Candace can either play the female lead in the production, or she can be the understudy.

_____

_____

2. The new restaurant on the corner of Broad Street and Fifth Avenue is both reasonably priced and attractively decorated.

_____

_____

3. Igor was not only Dave's roommate, but also he was his best friend.

_____

_____

4. I can neither reach Joy at her home nor at her office.

_____

_____

5. Mohammed wants to live either in Los Angeles or in Houston after graduation.

_____

_____

6. The door is either bolted from the inside or the lock is broken.

_____

_____

7. This pudding is not only delicious but also fat-free.

_____

_____

8. Shopping at this store is both convenient and economical.

_____

_____

21.7 ACTIVITY

1. Find and copy down two examples of parallelism in your textbooks for other classes.

   A. _____

   _____

B. _____

_____

2. Does the parallelism make it easier for you to learn and understand the material?

   Explain. _____

_____

IF ENGLISH IS NOT YOUR FIRST LANGUAGE

Consult the following list if you need help with the meanings and uses of the paired conjunctions.

1. *Either . . . or* indicates choice.

2. *Not only . . . but also* indicates addition.

3. *Neither . . . nor* indicates negative choice.
   (*Neither . . . nor* does not usually join clauses.)

4. *Both . . . and* indicates addition.
   (*Both . . . and* does not usually join clauses.)

21.8 CHAPTER REVIEW ACTIVITY

Five of the sentences in the following passage lack parallelism. Cross out the problems and write any needed corrections above the lines.

EXAMPLE   The simple ball has been a popular toy, both in ancient times and
                          modern times.
                  in ~~times that are modern.~~

¹No one knows who invented the ball, but we do know that people have played with balls from the earliest times.²In fact, all civilizations—both early ones and ones that are existing today—have played games using some kind of ball. ³Some early people wove reeds into rounded shapes, and leather was stuffed with feathers by-others. ⁴The Greeks and Romans added a new idea—they used a blown-up leather ball to play catch.

⁵Balls have been made from many materials, depending on what was available in the region. ⁶Deer hide, wrapped tissue, and balls made with vegetable gum have been used. ⁷It was the vegetable gum ball, used by Central American Indians, that led to the present-day use of a bouncy rubber ball.

⁸Many modern ball games either began as religious or magical ceremonies. ⁹Often the games told of old beliefs about war, gods, devils, life, and about

death. [10]Ancient Egyptians, for example, used a wooden ball and sticks for a ceremonial contest between two gods. [11]Whoever knocked the ball through the opposing goal won a victory for that team's god. [12]The Egyptians were among the first to have ceremonial ball games.

GETTING IN GEAR: IDEAS FOR WRITING

Fashions change rapidly, and often when we look back at fashions we used to wear, we either wince or laugh. Explore this site to be reminded of fashion history after 1980: www.fashion-era.com/fashion_after1980.htm. Did you wear these fashions? What do you think of them now?

writing topic: Write about something that appealed to you and your peers when you were in high school but did not appeal to the rest of the population—a particular form of dress, a certain kind of music, a special television program, or a way of talking, for example. Explain why it appealed to you and your peers.

suggestions for discovering ideas
- Freewrite about things that appealed to teenagers in your high school and why those things were appealing to teens, but not to others.
- If you need additional ideas, try a second, focused freewriting and then develop an informal outline.

suggestions for drafting

- Your thesis or topic sentence (depending on whether you are writing an essay or a paragraph) can mention the element that appealed to you and why it appealed to you.
- Remember to show, rather than merely tell.

suggestion for revising: Look for opportunities to use specific words to explain the element's appeal. Rather than write "As teenagers, we would play rock music on the car radio as loudly as possible," try this: "As teenagers, we would crank up the car radio, so that the rock music's pounding drum beat and wailing guitar would drown out the world." (See page 49 on specific word choice.)

suggestions for editing

- Look for words in series and pairs. Be sure they are in parallel form.
- Looked for the paired conjunctions. Be sure you follow each conjunction with the same grammatical form.

RECHARGE: Lesson Summary

To achieve **parallelism,** be sure that elements in a series, in a pair, or after paired conjunctions have the same grammatical form.

Parallel pair:	*I like <u>running on a treadmill</u> or <u>running on a beach</u>.*
Parallel series:	*The mayoral candidate promised <u>a pay hike for police officers</u>, <u>tax incentives for new businesses</u>, and <u>road repairs</u>.*
Paired conjunctions:	*Either <u>fix the car</u> or <u>buy a new one</u>.*

CHAPTER 22

Solving Special Sentence Structure Problems

CHAPTER GOALS

By the end of this chapter, you will learn to

Use simple subjects and verbs that make sense together

Eliminate illogical equations

Eliminate problems with *is when, is where,* and *the reason is because*

Eliminate mixed sentence structures

Certain sentence structure problems can make sentences seem tangled. When that happens, the ideas you are trying to express become confused, and you do not express yourself as effectively as you would like. This chapter will help you identify and solve these special sentence structure problems.

CORRECTING SIMPLE SUBJECTS AND VERBS THAT DO NOT MAKE SENSE TOGETHER

The **simple subject** is the most important word in the complete subject. Simple subjects never appear in prepositional phrases (see page 76).

Sentence:	*The frosting on the cake is chocolate.*
Complete subject:	*the frosting on the cake*
Prepositional phrase:	*on the cake*
Simple subject:	*frosting (The <u>frosting</u> <s>on the cake</s> <u>is</u> chocolate.)*

A sentence structure problem can result when a verb works with a word in a prepositional phrase, rather than with the simple subject.

No:	*The purpose of the shot prevents the flu.* [The simple subject is *purpose. Purpose* does not prevent the flu; *shot* does. However, *shot* is part of the prepositional phrase *of the shot.*]
Correction 1:	*The <u>shot</u> <u>prevents</u> the flu.*
Correction 2:	*The <u>purpose</u> of the shot <u>is</u> to prevent the flu.*

22.1 ACTIVITY

Underline the simple subject once and the verb twice in each sentence, and then check to see if they work logically together. If they do, write "correct" on the blank. If they do not, rewrite the sentence to eliminate the problem.

EXAMPLE The <u>importance</u> of certifying prospective teachers <u>is</u> a responsiblity of individual states.

Certifying prospective teachers is a responsibility of individual states.

1. The increase in the number of state-mandated teacher competency exams is growing.

   _____

   _____

2. The movement for state-required competency tests had spread to most states by the early 1990s.

   _____

   _____

3. Initiated in 1940, the purpose of the teacher competency exam aids in teacher selection.

   _____

   _____

4. A goal of the teacher examination weeds out incompetent teachers.

   _____

   _____

5. According to some, a criticism of the examination discriminates against people of color.

   _____

   _____

6. For some people, the difficulty and familiarity of many questions are hard to answer.

   _____

   _____

7. Test results in states across the nation hope to eliminate discrimination and graduate competent teachers.

   _____

   _____

8. According to some, the current process of state licensure screens potential teachers adequately.

   _____

   _____

Source: Adapted from Sadker, Myra Pollack and David Miller Sadker, *Teachers, Schools, and Society,* 5th ed. (New York: McGraw-Hill, 2000), pp. 40–41. Copyright © 2000 The McGraw-Hill Companies. Used by permission of The McGraw-Hill Companies, Inc.

ELIMINATING ILLOGICAL EQUATIONS WITH FORMS OF *BE*

Forms of the verb *be* (*am, is, are, was, were, been,* and *being*) can act like an equals sign (=). When this is the case, the form of *be* equates the subject with a word or words after the verb.

> Jane ⬚is⬚ an excellent violinist.
> Jane = violinist
>
> My dentist ⬚was⬚ my uncle.
> dentist = uncle

A sentence structure problem occurs when a form of *be* sets up an illogical equation.

Illogical equation:	*At one time, a teacher was a career for women only.* [*teacher = career?*]
Explanation:	A "teacher" is a person, not a "career."
Correction:	*At one time, teaching was a career for women only.*
Illogical equation:	*A popular major at this school is hospitality manager.* [*major = manager?*]
Explanation:	A "major" is a thing, not a "manager."
Correction:	*A popular major at this school is hospitality management.*

To correct sentences with illogical equations, you may have to rewrite by adding words.

Illogical equation:	*My instructor's reaction to my essay was too short and choppy.*
Correction:	*My instructor's reaction to my essay was that it was too short and choppy.*

22.2 ACTIVITY

Fill in the blanks to show the equation set up with the form of *be*. Then decide whether the equation is logical. If it is not, rewrite to correct the problem. For the two sentences that are correct, write "correct" in the blank.

EXAMPLE   Real charity is a person who gives anonymously.

> *charity* _____ = *person* _____
>
> *Real charity is giving anonymously.* _____

1. The study of the lake's pollution is too high for swimming.

    _____ = _____

    _____

    _____

2. The columnist's criticism of the television show is too violent.

    _____ = _____

    _____

    _____

3. Our view of his artwork is shoddy and overpriced.

   _____ = _____

   _____

   _____

4. College instructors are a good place to ask about job opportunities in your major.

   _____ = _____

   _____

   _____

5. The most important traits of my high school guidance counselor were gentle and intelligent.

   _____ = _____

   _____

   _____

6. The most frightening part of the movie was the conclusion.

   _____ = _____

   _____

   _____

7. A necessary asset of a distance runner is enduring.

   _____ = _____

   _____

   _____

8. The most entertaining section of your essay is the beginning.

   _____ = _____

   _____

   _____

DEFINING AND EXPLAINING WITHOUT *IS WHEN*, *IS WHERE*, OR *THE REASON IS BECAUSE*

Problems with sentence structure result when writers use *is when, is where,* or *the reason is because.*

To avoid sentence structure problems, do not use *is when* or *is where* in definitions. Here are two examples:

No: *Exam anxiety is when students get so nervous about tests that they freeze up and cannot perform.* Exam anxiety is a problem, not a time, so *when* is inaccurate. To correct the sentence, rewrite it.

Correction: *Exam anxiety causes students to get so nervous about tests that they freeze up and cannot perform.*

No: *Unrestrained jealousy <u>is where</u> you can never be happy with what you have.* Unrestrained jealousy is a condition, not a place, so *where* is inaccurate. To correct the problem, rewrite the sentence.

Correction: *Unrestrained jealousy means you can never be happy with what you have.*

Because means "the reason is that." If you use "the reason is because," you will be saying, "the reason is the reason is that." To avoid sentence structure problems when explaining, avoid saying *the reason is because.*

No: *<u>The reason</u> I got the job <u>is because</u> I have good communication skills.*

Yes: *The reason I got the job is that I have good communication skills.*

Yes: *I got the job because I have good communication skills.*

CONNECT FOR SUCCESS: Use Correct Sentence Structure with Definitions

When you write definitions in your classes, avoid *is when* and *is where*. For example, in a physical therapy class or physical education class, you might be asked on a quiz to define *tendonitis*. Do not weaken your writing with incorrect structures. Rather than write "Tendonitis is when tissue connecting muscle to bone becomes inflamed," write "Tendonitis is the inflammation of tissue connecting muscle to bone."

22.3 COLLABORATIVE ACTIVITY

A. With two classmates, complete each of the following sentences by adding an explanation.

EXAMPLE The reason you lost your job is *that you were always late.*

1. The reason I got lost was _____

_____

2. One reason Harry got an *A* on his essay is _____

_____

3. The reasons everyone likes you are _____

_____

B. Alone or with two classmates, complete each of the following sentences by adding a definition.

EXAMPLE True maturity is *accepting people for who they are.*

4. Math anxiety is _____

_____

5. A blind date is _____

_____

6. Freedom of speech is _____

_____

ELIMINATING MIXED SENTENCE STRUCTURES

Here are two sentences that use different structures to convey the same idea:

Structure 1: *By switching to a better grade of gasoline, I reduced the engine noise.*

Structure 2: *Switching to a better grade of gasoline reduced the engine noise.*

If a writer begins a sentence with one sentence structure and switches to another sentence structure, a problem with **mixed sentence structures** results. Here is an example of mixed sentence structures resulting from mixing structure 1 and structure 2:

Mixed sentence structures: *By switching to a better grade of gasoline reduced the engine noise.*

To correct the problem, use one sentence structure.

Mixed sentence structures: *Because the superintendent closed the school means the test is postponed.*

Correction (structure 1): *Because the superintendent closed the school the test is postponed.*

Correction (structure 2): *The superintendent's closing of the school means the test is postponed.*

Mixed sentence structures often result when a writer begins by making a statement but switches to asking a question.

A statement: *The band director asked whether everyone remembered the music.*

A question: *The band director asked, "Does everyone remember the music?"*

Mixed sentence structures: *The band director asked does everyone remember the music.*

To correct the problem, either make a statement or ask a question.

Mixed sentence structures: *The instructor wanted to know did anyone have a question.*

Correction 1 (a statement): *The instructor wanted to know whether anyone had a question.*

Correction 2 (a question): *The instructor asked, "Does anyone have a question?"*

Composing at the computer

If you like to compose at the computer, you might like this editing tip. Use your computer's search function to see if you have used these constructions: *is when, is where,* and *the reason is because.* If your computer finds any of these, you can rewrite to eliminate them.

22.4 ACTIVITY

Cross out and rewrite above the lines to correct the sentences with mixed structure. (It is possible to rewrite more than one way.) Three sentences are correct.

EXAMPLE   People do not mean to be hurtful. However, because they act
thoughtlessly ~~damages~~ *they damage* the environment.

[1]Human beings threaten the biosphere in many ways. [2]By clearing forests or grasslands to grow crops modifies existing ecosystems. [3]People also alter ecosystems when they build houses on farmland and convert small towns into large cities. [4]Because of the development of coasts caused pollutants to make their way into the sea. [5]As human populations increase severely threatens coral reefs and tropical rain forests. [6]Many scientists have asked do people care enough to protect the environment's ecosystems. [7]After all, ecosystems must be protected to ensure the continued existence of humans.

Source: Adapted from Sylvia S. Mader, *Human Biology,* 8th ed. (New York: McGraw-Hill, 2004), pp. 4–5. Copyright © 2004 The McGraw-Hill Companies.

IF ENGLISH IS NOT YOUR FIRST LANGUAGE

1. In some languages, the subject is repeated, but in English it is not repeated.

   No: *Your new haircut, it is very attractive.*
   Yes: *Your new haircut is very attractive.*

   No: *Caffeine and nicotine, they can cause headaches.*
   Yes: *Caffeine and nicotine can cause headaches.*

2. Do not use a pronoun to refer to a word already referred to by *who, which,* or *that.*

   No: *Someone stole my wallet, which I had left it on the desk.*
   Yes: *Someone stole my wallet, which I had left on the desk.* [*Which* already refers to *wallet,* so *it* is unnecessary.]

   No: *The pill that Raymond took was difficult to swallow it.*
   Yes: *The pill that Raymond took was difficult to swallow.* [*That* already refers to *pill,* so *it* is unnecessary.]

IF ENGLISH IS NOT YOUR FIRST LANGUAGE CONTINUED

3. In English, subjects are not omitted, except in some commands and requests.

    No: *Studying takes up a great deal of time. Is what I do six hours a day.*

    Yes: *Studying takes up a great deal of time. It is what I do six hours a day.*

    No: *In the United States watch television too much.*

    Yes: *In the United States, people watch television too much.*

4. Try to think in English when you speak and write. If you think in your native language and then attempt to translate into English, you are more likely to have problems with your English sentence structure.

22.5 CHAPTER REVIEW ACTIVITY

In the following passage, seven sentences have sentence structure problems. Revise to eliminate the problems.

EXAMPLE   ~~The reason exercise~~ *Exercise* is important is because it improves cardiovascular health.

¹The best exercise program is where you begin with a three- to five-minute warm-up to increase respiration, circulation, and body temperature. ²The purpose of a warm-up also stretches muscles, tendons, and connective tissue to reduce the risk of injury. ³After the warm-up comes the conditioning period. ⁴By conditioning increases cardiovascular fitness. ⁵You should exercise at a moderate rate—not at an exhaustive level.

⁶If you exercise regularly while gradually increase the intensity level improves fitness. ⁷Your goal should be thirty to sixty minutes of conditioning at least three times a week. ⁸The reason the range is thirty to sixty minutes is because the amount of time depends on how strenuous the activity is and your general health. ⁹After exercising, cool down for a few minutes. ¹⁰Don't stand still or lie down after exercising. ¹¹If you walk around for a few minutes lets your body adjust to the decreased physical demands.

¹²Don't let exercise be a fad. ¹³Regular workouts mean cardiovascular fitness that can improve the quality of life. ¹⁴For healthy people, regular exercise is a lifetime commitment. ¹⁵If, however, you have any doubts about your ability to exercise, be sure to consult your doctor. ¹⁶Remember, the goals of any exercise program is healthy and strong.

GETTING IN GEAR: IDEAS FOR WRITING

These days, people change jobs with increasing frequency. Across a lifetime, a person might be a teacher, a musician, and a car salesperson. Most likely, you don't appreciate the full range of job choices available to you; to get a better idea, explore the *Dictionary of Occupational Titles* with its job descriptions at www.occupationalinfo.org/.

writing topic: Write about a job you have had or one you hope to have, noting and illustrating a specific skill the job requires. For example, if you write about your job as an assistant basketball coach, you might say that being a coach requires skill as a motivator. To illustrate that feature, you might tell about your attempts to persuade team members to keep trying their best when they are having a losing season.

suggestions for discovering ideas
- List all of your past jobs and the job you want after graduation.
- Select two or three of the jobs and list the skills required.
- Review your lists and select a job and skill to write about.
- Freewrite about the job and skill to discover ideas for illustrating the skill.

suggestion for drafting: Your thesis or topic sentence (depending on whether you are writing an essay or a paragraph) can mention the job and skill.

suggestion for revising: Check for unity by making sure that all your details are clearly related to your topic and your claim. (Unity is discussed on page 47.)

suggestions for editing
- Check sentences with forms of *be* to be sure you have not set up illogical equations.
- Look for and eliminate *is when, is where,* and *the reason is because* constructions.

RECHARGE: Lesson Summary

Sentence structure problems occur when

- a verb functions with a word in a prepositional phrase, rather than the simple subject.
- a form of *be* sets up an illogical equation.
- *is when, is where,* and *the reason is because* are used incorrectly.
- different sentence structures are mixed in the same sentence.

CHAPTER 23

Varying Sentence Openers

CHAPTER GOALS

By the end of this chapter, you will be learn to

Open sentences with adverbs

Open sentences with participles and participle phrases

Open sentences with prepositional phrases

Open sentences with dependent clauses

Read the following passage out loud:

> *I saw the car cross the center line and come toward me. I slammed on my brakes. I quickly went into a skid. The car weaved back and forth all over the road. It finally came to a stop. It was resting in a drainage ditch.*

Nothing is grammatically wrong with this passage, but you probably noticed how choppy it sounds because every sentence begins the same way—with the subject. To avoid such unpleasant choppiness in your own writing, follow the suggestions in this chapter for varying sentence openers. They will help you write more like this:

> *When I saw the car cross the center line and come toward me, I slammed on my brakes. Weaving back and forth all over the road, I quickly went into a skid. Finally, the car came to a stop. It was resting in a drainage ditch.*

OPEN WITH ONE OR TWO ADVERBS

Adverbs are descriptive words often ending in *-ly*. They are words such as these:

cautiously   loudly   slowly
fearfully   quickly   tenderly

Try opening some of your sentences with an adverb.

> *<u>Thoughtfully,</u> Delores read her assignment.*
> *<u>Earnestly,</u> Kevin explained the reason for his view.*

Try opening some sentences with a pair of adverbs.

> *<u>Slowly and carefully,</u> I ironed the expensive shirt.*
> *<u>Quickly but skillfully,</u> Helene painted my portrait.*
> *<u>Gently, lovingly,</u> Harry covered the sleeping infant.*

To open with an adverb, you may only need to rearrange words.

> *Dominic <u>slowly</u> pushed his shopping cart down the aisle.*
> *<u>Slowly,</u> Dominic pushed his shopping cart down the aisle.*

Troubleshooting

If you need a more complete discussion of adverbs, see page 295.

→ **PUNCTUATION ALERT**

As the preceding examples show, an opening adverb is followed by a comma.

23.1 ACTIVITY

Combine each pair of sentences into one sentence. To do so, open with the adverb or pair of adverbs given in the second sentence. Remember to use commas correctly.

EXAMPLE   Communication is hindered by cultural insensitivity.
Communication is hindered regularly.

Regularly, communication is hindered by cultural insensitivity.

1. We are exposed to people of different cultures.
   We are exposed increasingly.

2. Intercultural communication is important.
   It is frequently important.

3. Cultural barriers can be reduced by learning the norms and values of other cultures.
   Cultural barriers can, fortunately, be reduced.

4. Communication problems occur in intercultural communication as a result of stereotyping.
   The problems occur predictably.

5. People should avoid stereotypes to improve their communication competence.
   They should do so consistently and willingly.

6. People should correct stereotypical remarks made by others.
   They should correct the remarks tactfully but firmly.

7. Effective communicators open new communication channels.
They open the channels frequently and enthusiastically.

_____

_____

8. Effective communicators practice supportive communication behaviors.
They practice the behaviors uniformly.

_____

_____

Source: Adapted from Judy Pearson et al., *Human Communication,* 2nd ed. (New York: McGraw-Hill, 2006), p. 181. Copyright © 2006 The McGraw-Hill Companies.

23.2 ACTIVITY

Pick five of the following adverbs and adverb pairs, and use them to open sentences. Write the sentences on a separate sheet, and remember to use commas correctly.

cautiously	loudly and angrily
fearlessly	quickly but carefully
gently	slowly, patiently

OPEN WITH A PRESENT PARTICIPLE OR A PRESENT PARTICIPIAL PHRASE

The **present participle** is the *-ing* form of a verb. Here are some examples of present participles:

believing	eating	running
dancing	moving	seeing

The present participle can be combined with one or more words to form a **present participial phrase.** Here are some present participial phrases:

believing in you	eating lunch	running across campus
dancing slowly	moving quickly	seeing the sunset

Try opening some of your sentences with present participles and present participial phrases.

Singing, Henry walked through the park.
Singing show tunes, Henry walked through the park.
Laughing, I left the room.
Laughing loudly, I left the room.

Troubleshooting

If you need more information about present participles and present participial phrases, see pages 230 and 315. Dangling modifiers are discussed on page 321.

PUNCTUATION ALERT

As the previous examples illustrate, an opening present participle or participial phrase is followed by a comma.

→ **GRAMMAR ALERT**

Be sure your present participle or present participial phrase is followed by a simple subject the participle can sensibly describe, or you will have a **dangling modifier.**

Dangling modifier: *Sleeping peacefully, the alarm woke me up.* [Was the alarm sleeping peacefully?]

Correct: *Sleeping peacefully, I woke up to the alarm.*

23.3 ACTIVITY

Change one sentence in each pair to a present participle or a present participial phrase, and open the remaining sentence with it. Remember to use a comma after the opening participle or phrase. (The sentences can be written more than one way.)

EXAMPLES   Dad was asleep on the couch.
He snored loudly.

Snoring loudly, Dad was asleep on the couch.

or

Sleeping on the couch, Dad snored loudly.

1. Stavros walked past the cemetery at midnight.
   He whistled.

   _____

   _____

2. Jan tried to sleep.
   She was coughing.

   _____

   _____

3. Lillian played the car radio loudly.
   She drove down the highway.

   _____

   _____

4. I stirred the sauce on the stove.
   I talked on the phone.

   _____

   _____

5. Chuck dribbled the ball down the basketball court.
   He smiled at the crowd.

   _____

   _____

6. The audience jumped to its feet.
The audience was applauding enthusiastically.

_____

_____

7. The Girl Scouts were ringing doorbells in the neighborhood.
They were trying to sell cookies.

_____

_____

8. Sylvia and Juan sat on a park bench at noon.
They were eating their lunches.

_____

_____

23.4 COLLABORATIVE ACTIVITY

With two classmates, add an opening present participle or an opening present participial phrase to each of the following sentences. Follow the opening participle or phrase with a comma.

EXAMPLE   _Watching television,_____ I fell asleep on the couch.

1. _____ the students walked out of the classroom.

2. _____ Enrico jogged along the beach.

3. _____ the cat jumped from the window ledge.

4. _____ the police officer wrote Randy a ticket for speeding.

5. _____ Chu Yen stormed angrily out of the room.

6. _____ Grandma told the story of how she met Grandpa.

7. _____ we ran three blocks to get to the theater on time.

8. _____ the ten-year-old raced down the street on her new red bicycle.

23.5 ACTIVITY

Pick five of the present participles and present participial phrases listed, and use them to open sentences. Write the sentences on a separate sheet, and remember to use a comma after an opening participle or participial phrase.

chuckling	smiling broadly
humming	trying to understand the assignment
screaming	whistling a familiar tune

OPEN WITH A PAST PARTICIPLE OR A PAST PARTICIPIAL PHRASE

The **past participle** is the *-ed* form of a regular verb. Past participles are words such as these:

believed   loved   started

flirted   moved   walked

Some past participles are irregular. Instead of being formed with *-ed,* they are formed in a variety of ways. Here are some examples:

driven   given   seen

eaten   gone   written

The past participle can be combined with one or more words to form a **past participial phrase,** such as one of these:

driven home	given half a chance	seen at night
eaten quickly	gone for good	started at noon
flirted outrageously	moved across town	written on a postcard

Try opening some of your sentences with past participles and past participial phrases.

> <u>Exhausted,</u> Roy took a nap.
> <u>Exhausted after work,</u> Roy took a nap.
> <u>Confused,</u> Delia asked a question.
> <u>Confused about the assignment,</u> Delia asked a question.

Troubleshooting

If you need additional discussions of past participles, see pages 211 and 316.

 PUNCTUATION ALERT

As the preceding examples illustrate, an opening past participle or participial phrase is followed by a comma.

Troubleshooting

If you need to review dangling modifiers, see page 321.

GRAMMAR ALERT

Be sure your past participle or past participial phrase is followed by a simple subject the participle can sensibly describe, or you will have a **dangling modifier.**

Dangling modifier: *Worn out, a vacation was needed.* [Was the vacation worn out?]

Correction: *Worn out, I needed a vacation.*

23.6 ACTIVITY

Combine each pair of sentences into one sentence. To do so, open the first sentence with the past participle or past participial phrase from the second sentence. Write your sentences in the following blanks, and remember to use commas after opening participles and participial phrases.

EXAMPLE   I complained to the landlord.
I was irritated by the dripping faucet.

Irritated by the dripping faucet, I complained to the landlord.

1. Zahava laughed loudly at the joke.
   She was amused.

2. Ross changed his major to anthropology.
   He was fascinated by other cultures.

3. Ivan organized a food drive on campus.
   He was concerned about the plight of the poor.

4. Blake quit the football team before the first game.
   He was tired of the long practices.

5. Marion and Lucy moved to New York to audition for parts in the theater.
   They had been bitten by the acting bug.

6. The tractor trailer rig was blocking traffic.
   It was stalled in the middle of the highway.

7. The Jerrolds were given the city's humanitarian award.
   The Jerrolds are known for their charity work.

8. We could not tell Lee about the surprise party.
   We were sworn to secrecy.

23.7 COLLABORATIVE ACTIVITY

With two classmates, add an opening past participle or participial phrase to each of the following sentences. Be sure to use commas correctly.

EXAMPLE   *Annoyed by the loud band,* we left the party early.

1. _____ Conchetta thought about how to improve her grades.

2. _____ the doctor told me to get more rest.

3. _____ the umpire warned the first baseman to watch his temper.

4. _____ the dog began howling.

5. _____ the table server spilled the hot coffee all over the floor.

6. _____ I laughed to myself as I crossed campus.

7. _____ Dale threw the vase across the room.

8. _____ Daniel decided to take a much needed vacation.

23.8 ACTIVITY

Pick five of the past participles and past participial phrases listed, and use them to open sentences. Write your sentences on a separate sheet, and remember to use a comma after an opening past participle or past participial phrase.

amused	disgusted
angered	frightened by the movie
cooked too long	worn out from the race

OPEN WITH A PREPOSITIONAL PHRASE

A **preposition** shows how things are positioned in time or space. Prepositions are words such as these:

around	behind	during	near	to
at	by	in	of	under

I live near you. [*Near* shows position in space.]

I will leave before you. [*Before* shows point in time.]

A **prepositional phrase** is a preposition and the word or words that go with it. Here are some examples:

at noon	by the garage	in the summer
behind the couch	during May	under the table

Troubleshooting

If you need a more complete discussion of prepositions and prepositional phrases, see Chapter 20.

Try opening some of your sentences with prepositional phrases.

Before now, I never understood you.
During my lunch hour, I walk a mile.
In his pocket, Lou found a $5 bill.

To open with a prepositional phrase, you may only need to rearrange words.

Sentence: _Carlos found an abandoned kitten by the road._
Rearranged: _By the road, Carlos found an abandoned kitten._

 PUNCTUATION ALERT

As the preceding sentences illustrate, an opening prepositional phrase is usually followed by a comma.

23.9 ACTIVITY

Rewrite the following sentences by adding opening prepositional phrases. Remember to use commas correctly.

EXAMPLE   Many audience members left.
During the first act, many audience members left.

1. Jack lost his wallet yesterday.

2. The city council considered whether it should rewrite the city charter.

3. The new play opened to rave reviews.

4. The couple began arguing very loudly.

5. Voter turnout was surprisingly small.

6. The coach decided that the team needed additional practice.

23.10 ACTIVITY

On a separate sheet, write five sentences that begin with prepositional phrases. Remember to use commas correctly.

OPEN WITH A DEPENDENT CLAUSE

A **dependent clause** has a subject and a verb, but it cannot stand alone as a sentence. Here are some examples of dependent clauses:

> *when the discussions were over*
> *before you leave*
> *although I disagree with you*

Try opening some of your sentences with dependent clauses.

> *If I were you, I would find another job.*
> *Because the lead singer is ill, the concert has been canceled.*
> *Although I respect his view, I disagree with it.*

To open with a dependent clause, you may only need to rearrange words.

> *The athletic program may be eliminated, because the school levy failed.*
> *Because the school levy failed, the athletic program may be eliminated.*

Troubleshooting

If you need a more complete discussion of dependent clauses, see page 131.

PUNCTUATION ALERT

As the previous sentences illustrate, an opening dependent clause is followed by a comma.

23.11 ACTIVITY

Join each pair of sentences into one sentence. First change the second sentence into a dependent clause beginning with one of the following words.

although	before	if	while
because	even though	since	when

Then use the dependent clause you created to open the first sentence. Be sure to use a comma after the opening dependent clause.

EXAMPLE   College textbooks include a great deal of material.
The information is not all equally important.

> *Although the information is not all equally important, college textbooks include a great deal of material.*

1. College textbooks have idea density.
They have many ideas or facts packed into a single paragraph.

_____

_____

2. A great deal of technical vocabulary will be introduced in college textbooks.
   Each college subject has its own special terms.

   _____

   _____

3. There are many patterns of organization in college-level reading.
   Some patterns are more common than others.

   _____

   _____

4. You will need to to check your understanding of your reading by asking
   yourself questions about the material.
   You can be sure you comprehend your textbooks.

   _____

   _____

5. It is your responsibility to fill in the gaps in your knowledge.
   A textbook assumes you know more than you do about a subject.

   _____

   _____

6. Find simpler or clearer explanations in other textbooks.
   You must fill in the gaps in your knowledge.

   _____

   _____

7. Checking other textbooks can save you time and frustration.
   It seems like more work.

   _____

   _____

8. You will learn to cope with difficult college reading material.
   You will feel discouraged at times.

   _____

   _____

Source: Adapted from Joe Cortina, Janet Elder, and Katherine Gonnet, *Comprehending College Textbooks,* 3rd ed. (New York: McGraw-Hill, 1996), pp. 5–6. Copyright © 1996 The McGraw-Hill Companies. Used by permission of The McGraw-Hill Companies, Inc.

23.12 ACTIVITY

Use five of the following dependent clauses to open sentences. Write your sentences on a separate sheet, and remember to use a comma after each opening dependent clause.

Because students experience stress	Since registration begins soon
Before Helen begins a race	Until the votes are counted
If I were you	When I was young

IF ENGLISH IS NOT YOUR FIRST LANGUAGE

1. Varied sentence openers are less important than grammatical correctness. Thus, do not consider whether or not you need to work on sentence openers until after you are sure you have made all the necessary changes in grammar.

2. If you are not sure whether or not your sentence openings need to be varied, ask a reliable reader (perhaps a writing center tutor) to read your work out loud and help you decide.

3. If you open some of your sentences with dependent clauses, be sure you understand the meanings of any subordinating conjunctions that open the clauses. You can check these meanings by looking back to page 142.

23.13 CHAPTER REVIEW ACTIVITY

On a separate sheet, write sentences according to the directions given.

1. Open with a prepositional phrase.
2. Open with a present participle.
3. Open with a past participial phrase.
4. Open with a dependent clause.
5. Open with two adverbs.
6. Open with a present participial phrase.
7. Open with a past participle.
8. Open with one adverb.

23.14 CHAPTER REVIEW ACTIVITY

The following passage would read better with a variety of sentence openers. Rewrite the passage, rearranging word order in some sentences to vary sentence openers with adverbs, present and past participles, participial phrases, prepositional phrases, and dependent clauses. More than one satisfactory rewrite is possible, so your work will differ from your classmates' work.

EXAMPLE George Washington Carver was a great educator and agricultural
About 1864, he was born on the Moses Carver plantation
researcher. He was born about 1864 on the Moses Carver
in Diamond Grove, Missouri.
plantation in Diamond Grove, Missouri.

[1]George Washington Carver was one of the world's greatest agricultural scientists. [2]His parents were the black slaves of Moses Carver. [3]George's father died soon after George was born. [4]The baby and his mother were kidnapped by bandits a few months later. [5]Moses Carver was able to buy George back, although the mother was never found. [6]The Carvers raised George themselves.

[7]George showed a love for growing things at an early age. [8]The neighbors called him the plant doctor because he used to care for and cure sick plants. [9]He later wandered about the United States, seeking an education and performing jobs to pay for it. [10]He finally entered Iowa State College. [11]He was the first black person to graduate from the college, and he became its first black teacher.

[12]Carver, appointed head of the agriculture department, joined the staff of Tuskegee Institute in 1896. [13]He taught at Tuskegee for nearly fifty years. [14]He worked long hours, seeking ways to help the poor southern farmers. [15]He introduced the peanut, pecan, and sweet potato to enrich soil worn out by cotton farming. [16]He discovered new uses for these crops in his laboratory, including making butter, rubber, flour, coffee, and ink. [17]Carver gave his discoveries to the world, asking no profit for himself.[18]He freely advised anyone who consulted him. [19]He received many high-paying job offers. [20]He preferred to remain at Tuskegee and teach. [21]His work is carried on today through the George Washington Carver Foundation, which provides scholarships in agricultural research to black youth.

GETTING IN GEAR: IDEAS FOR WRITING

The poster, from the New York Public Library's web site, depicts animals in danger of extinction because they are losing their habitats to human development and other encroachments. When we lose species, we lose some of the diversity, some of the variety that enriches life. If you want to read more about the dangers to species and the threatened loss of diversity, visit the New York Public Library site at www.nypl.org/admin/exhibitions/endangered/whatz.html.

writing topic: In this chapter, you learned that varying sentence openers is important for creating interest in your writing and enriching your writing style. Variety is important in other areas as well. For example, the variety of animal species and habitats enriches our lives; variety in workout routines helps people maintain interest in exercise. Discuss other ways that variety is important for maintaining interest or for enriching lives.

suggestions for discovering ideas
- Freewrite about variety for about ten minutes.
- If you need additional ideas, do a second, focused freewriting or try mapping.

suggestion for drafting: Before beginning your draft, develop an informal outline or outline map.

suggestion for revising: Read your draft aloud. If you hear passages that sound either sing-songy or choppy, revise to vary the sentence openers.

suggestions for editing
- Edit a separate time, looking for each of the kinds of errors you make habitually.
- Edit again to find any other kinds of errors.

RECHARGE: Lesson Summary

To avoid choppiness, vary your sentences in the following ways.
- Open with one or two adverbs.

  Anxiously, I awaited the doctor's report.
- Open with a present participle or present participial phrase.

  Seeing my opportunity, I slipped out the door.
- Open with a past participle or past participial phrase.

  Disturbed by the violence, we left the movie.
- Open with a prepositional phrase.

  Beside the pond, two ducks sunned themselves.
- Open with a dependent clause.

  Because I need more money, I will ask for a raise.

PART SIX REVIEW

Editing for multiple errors

A. Cross out and write above the line to correct two problems with parallelism and five problems with sentence structure.

¹Have you every wondered how did some things get their names? ²By learning about word histories is a good way to enrich our knowledge of language. ³Consider "cops," which has come to mean "police officers." ⁴One theory says the reason is because in the nineteenth century many policemen wore big copper badges. ⁵People began referring to the police as "coppers" because of these badges. ⁶"Cops" was when people shortened "coppers."

⁷"Motel" is another interesting coinage. ⁸The combination of "motor" and "hotel" come together to form the word "motel." ⁹This word was coined by Arthur Heinman, who opened the first motel in California in 1925.

¹⁰"Denim," "trivia," and the word "Gypsy" also have interesting origins. ¹¹Both "denim" and "trivia" come from foreign languages. ¹²"Denim" got its name from the French town of DeNimes, where it was first made. ¹³"Trivia" comes from the Latin *trivium*, which means either "public square" or it can mean "where three roads meet." ¹⁴The plural Latin form is *trivia*, which means "street talk." ¹⁵"Gypsy" comes from the middle letters of "Egypt," since Gypsies were originally believed to be from Egypt.

B. Cross out and write above the line to correct two problems with parallelism and two problems with sentence structure. Also, eliminate choppiness by increasing the variety of sentence openings.

¹Valentine's Day is an important holiday for many people. ²The reason is because they can express their affection for those they care the most about. ³Most people do not know the origin of the holiday, although they celebrate it with enthusiasm. ⁴It actually began in ancient Rome, where February 14 was the day to honor Juno. ⁵Juno was the queen of Roman gods and goddesses, the goddess of women, and she was the goddess of marriage.

⁶The lives of young boys and girls were strictly separate in ancient Rome. ⁷Boys, however, would get to pick the names of young girls from a vase during the Lupercalia Festival. ⁸The boys became partners with the girls they chose. ⁹The pairs of children then danced with each other for the duration of the festival. ¹⁰The pairing of children sometimes lasted an entire year. ¹¹By pairing off for so long caused many to fall in love and later marry.

¹²The first valentine was created many years later. ¹³It was a poem sent in 1415 by Charles, Duke of Orleans, to his wife. ¹⁴In the United States, Esther

Howland receives credit for sending the first valentine's cards. [15]Commercial valentines were introduced in the 1800s. [16]Now the holiday has become tremendously commercialized. [17]Friends and lovers feel obliged either to send flowers or they feel they must send other gifts.

READING AND WRITING IN RESPONSE TO TEXTBOOKS

The following excerpt from an introductory business administration textbook introduces a section on the quality imperative.

[1]As this chapter mentioned earlier, one consequence of global competition is that no country dares fall behind other countries in providing high-quality products. [2]Quality production techniques have been in place for over a decade in countries such as Japan, the United States, and Germany. [3]A U.S. citizen, W. Edwards Deming, was instrumental in introducing quality concepts worldwide. [4]Using his techniques, top-quality manufacturers are able to make products with almost no defects and to make them quickly. [5]Global consumers will fast become accustomed to such quality.

[6]Quality in today's firms is defined as providing customers with goods and services that go beyond the expected. [7]At IBM, for example, quality is defined as meeting customers' demands, both inside and outside the organization, for defect-free products, services, and business processes. [8]Additionally, much of Wal-Mart's success has come because the company provides such value. [9]Companies that can't provide the combination of high quality and low price will be less able to compete in the twenty-first century. [10]Even small businesses, such as Custom Research Inc., are able to compete with large firms because of quality.

Source: Adapted from William G. Nickels, James M. McHugh, and Susan M. McHugh, *Understanding Business,* 5th ed. (New York: McGraw-Hill, 1999), p. 19. Copyright © 1999 The McGraw-Hill Companies. Used by permission of The McGraw-Hill Companies, Inc.

1. To analyze the variety of sentence openers, answer the following questions.

   A. Which sentences begin with the subject? _____

   _____

   B. Which sentence begins with a dependent clause? _____

   _____

   C. Which sentence begins with a present participial phrase? _____

   _____

    D. Which sentence begins with a prepositional phrase? _____

_____

    E. Which sentence begins with an adverb? _____

_____

2. How does varying the sentence openers help students learn the material?

_____

_____

3. How is parallelism achieved in sentences 2 and 7? _____

_____

4. How is parallelism achieved in sentence 4? _____

_____

5. How does parallelism help students learn the material? _____

_____

writing topic: The textbook exercises suggests that quality products are important. Do you agree? When you make purchases, are you more concerned about price or quality? Are you willing to pay more for higher-quality products? Explain.

Becoming a Better Speller

You can't help respecting anybody who can spell Tuesday, *even if he [or she] doesn't spell it right; but spelling isn't everything. There are days when spelling* Tuesday *simply doesn't count.*

—Winnie the Pooh, character in a children's book written by A.A. Milne

Reflection: When is spelling important and when doesn't it count?

WHAT YOU WILL LEARN

How to become a better speller

How to use several spelling rules

How to identify a number of words that are often confused for each other

WHY YOU WILL LEARN IT

so that you can spell with confidence

so that you can spell with confidence

so that you can spell frequently confused words correctly

377

CHAPTER 24

Spelling Correctly

Spelling errors can distract a reader from your ideas, and they can create a negative impression. For these reasons, in the writing you do for your classes and in the workplace, you should edit carefully to eliminate spelling errors. This chapter will help.

TEN WAYS TO BECOME A BETTER SPELLER

If you do not currently spell well, the following suggestions can help.

1. WAIT UNTIL YOU EDIT TO CHECK SPELLINGS.   If you check during drafting and revising, you may check a word that you take out later.

2. USE A DICTIONARY WHEN YOU EDIT.   Check *every* word you are unsure of. If you have even the slightest doubt, look up the word.

3. USE AN ELECTRONIC SPELL CHECKER.   Use either a handheld model or one that is part of your word-processing program. However, be sure you understand the limits of these tools. They will not flag incorrect words that are correctly spelled, so if you write *hear* instead of *ear,* the spell checker will not notice.

4. KEEP A PERSONAL SPELLING LIST.   Write the correct spellings of any words you misspell in any of your classes. Study the list every day, and have your classmates quiz you weekly. Then return the favor for them. Try underlining the troublesome parts of words, like this:

    def<u>inite</u>ly

5. SPELL BY SYLLABLES.   Long words, in particular, may be easier to spell if you sound them out syllable by syllable.

    cit∗i∗zen∗ship

6. SPELL PART BY PART.

    hand∗book   ground∗work   un∗break∗able

7. PRONOUNCE WORDS CORRECTLY.   If you do so, you are more likely to spell them correctly. For example, you may misspell *athlete* if you pronounce it incorrectly as *athelete,* with an extra syllable.

8. USE MEMORY TRICKS.   For example, you may spell *tragedy* correctly if you remember that it contains the word *rage* and that characters in a tragedy are often filled with rage.

9. EDIT VERY SLOWLY. Pause for a few seconds over every word to think about the spelling.

10. LEARN THE RULES EXPLAINED IN THIS CHAPTER. They will help you.

CONNECT FOR SUCCESS: Learn to Spell Key Terms and Names in Your Courses

Each of your courses will have important key terms and names. For example, in a business class, you might encounter the term *entrepreneurship,* and in history, you might encounter the name *Napoleon Bonaparte.* Learn to spell these key terms and names, so you do not misspell them in your papers and on your exams.

IDENTIFYING VOWELS AND CONSONANTS

To apply many of the spelling rules in this chapter, you must know the difference between vowels and consonants.

These letters are vowels:

a, e, i, o, u

All other letters, except *y,* are always consonants.

b, c, d, f, g, h, j, k, l, m, n, p, q, r, s, t, v, w, x, z

Y can be a consonant or a vowel, depending on the way it sounds.

Y as a vowel sound: *silly why company*

Y as a consonant sound: *yellow young yodel*

24.1 ACTIVITY

If the first underlined letter is a vowel, write V in the blank; if it is a consonant, write C. Then write V or C in the second blank, to indicate whether the second underlined letter is a vowel or a consonant. Remember, *y* is sometimes a vowel and sometimes a consonant.

EXAMPLE friendly ____C____ ____V____

1. yelp _____ _____

2. ruin _____ _____

3. promise _____ _____

4. lucky _____ _____

5. tired _____ _____

6. apple _____ _____

7. yesterday _____ _____

8. handle   _____   _____

9. orange   _____   _____

10. turkey   _____   _____

RULE 1. ADDING A PREFIX

A **prefix** is one or more letters added to the *beginning* of a word to create a new word with a new meaning.

Prefix	+	Word	=	New Word with New Meaning
il	+	legal	=	illegal
im	+	mature	=	immature
un	+	eaten	=	uneaten

When a prefix is added, the spelling of the base word does not change.

im + mobile = immobile   *over + run = overrun*

in + audible = inaudible   *un + nerved = unnerved*

➡ SPELLING ALERT

The prefix rule often results in double letters, as the following examples show.

immobile   *overrun*   *unnerved*

24.2 ACTIVITY

Fill in each blank with the correct spelling of the word given.

EXAMPLE   un + certain = _____*uncertain*_____

1. im + passable = _____
2. il + legible = _____
3. un + noticed = _____
4. dis + appear = _____
5. mis + spent = _____
6. over + come = _____
7. in + appropriate = _____
8. un + necessary = _____
9. in + audible = _____
10. un + discovered = _____

11. im + mortal = _____
12. un + knowing = _____
13. over + rule = _____
14. un + nerved = _____
15. dis + service = _____
16. im + partial = _____
17. mis + judge = _____
18. il + legitimate = _____
19. un + natural = _____
20. mis + spell = _____

RULE 2. ADDING ENDINGS TO WORDS WITH A FINAL -Y

When you add an ending to a word with a final -*y*, change the -*y* to an *i* if there is a consonant before the -*y*. Keep the -*y* if a vowel appears before it.

Consonant before the Final -Y: Change the -Y to I

C
cr*y* + ed = cried

C
kindl*y* + ness = kindliness

C
happ*y* + est = happiest

C
stud*y* + ed = studied

Vowel before the Final -Y: Keep the -Y

V
b*o*y + s = boys

V
pl*a*y + er = player

V
enj*o*y + ment = enjoyment

V
rel*a*y + ed = relayed

SPELLING ALERT

Here are some exceptions to the rule, for you to memorize:

day + ly = daily   pay + ed = paid
dry + ly = dryly   say + ed = said
gay + ly = gaily   shy + ly = shyly
lay + ed = laid

When you add the ending -*ing*, keep the -*y*.

employ + ing = employing   say + ing = saying
enjoy + ing = enjoying   try + ing = trying

24.3 ACTIVITY

Fill in each blank with the correct spelling of the word given.

EXAMPLES   ugly + er = *uglier*   joy + s = *joys*

1. study + ed = _____

2. tempt + ing = _____

3. cry + ed = _____

4. happy + ness = _____

5. marry + ed = _____

6. stay + ed = _____

7. deny + al = _____

8. hurry + ing = _____

9. clumsy + ness = _____

10. fly + er = _____

11. destroy + er = _____

12. delay + ed = _____

13. play + er = _____

14. eat + ing = _____

15. likely + hood = _____

16. fly + ing = _____

17. crazy + est = _____

18. pretty + est = _____

19. occupy + ed = _____

20. lonely + ness = _____

RULE 3. ADDING ENDINGS TO WORDS WITH A FINAL -*E*

When you add an ending to a word with a final -*e*, drop the -*e* if the ending begins with a vowel. Keep the -*e* if the ending begins with a consonant.

Endings Beginning with a vowel: Drop the -*E*

dine + *er* = *diner* [One -*e* is dropped.]
drive + *ing* = *driving*
love + *able* = *lovable*
move + *ed* = *moved* [One -*e* is dropped.]

Endings Beginning with a Consonant: Keep the -*E*

care + *less* = *careless*   *place* + *ment* = *placement*
false + *hood* = *falsehood*   *plate* + *ful* = *plateful*

➜ **SPELLING ALERT**

Here are some exceptions, for you to memorize:

acknowledge + *ment* = *acknowledgment*   *judge* + *ment* = *judgment*
argue + *ment* = *argument*   *mile* + *age* = *mileage*
awe + *ful* = *awful*   *nine* + *th* = *ninth*
courage + *ous* = *courageous*   *notice* + *able* = *noticeable*
                                                                      true + *ly* = *truly*

24.4 ACTIVITY

Fill in each blank with the correct spelling of the word given.

EXAMPLES   wake + ing = _____*waking*_____

                          wake + ful = _____*wakeful*_____

1. hope + ing = _____

2. create + ion = _____

3. spite + ful = _____

4. wide + ly = _____

5. advise + ing = _____

6. judge + ed = _____

7. take + s = _____

8. settle + ment = _____

9. use + less = _____

10. continue + ing = _____

11. sense + ible = _____

12. life + like = _____

13. graze + ing = _____

14. retire + ment = _____

15. relate + ion = _____   18. fine + est = _____

16. love + ly = _____   19. bake + ed = _____

17. taste + ful = _____   20. move + ment = _____

Troubleshooting

If you cannot look up a word in a dictionary because you do not know how to spell it, buy a pronunciation dictionary, which lets you find words according to the way they sound, rather than the way they are spelled.

RULE 4. DOUBLING THE FINAL CONSONANT IN ONE-SYLLABLE WORDS

When you add an ending to a one-syllable word, double the final consonant if

1. the ending begins with a vowel (*-ing, -ed, -er, -est,* and so forth) and

2. the last three letters of the word are consonant-vowel-consonant (C-V-C).

One-Syllable Word Ending in C-V-C	+	Ending Beginning with a Vowel	=	Final Consonant Doubled
CVC run	+	er	=	runner
CVC g rab	+	ing	=	grabbing
CVC s lim	+	est	=	slimmest

Do not double the final consonant when the word does not end in C-V-C.

One-Syllable Word Not Ending in C-V-C	+	Ending Beginning with a Vowel	=	Final Consonant Not Doubled
VVC cl ear	+	est	=	clearest
VVC p eel	+	ing	=	peeling
VVC f ear	+	ed	=	feared

➤ **SPELLING ALERT**

Here are some exceptions, for you to memorize:

box + ing = boxing

bus + ing = busing [*Bussing* means "kissing."]

saw + ed = sawed

24.5 ACTIVITY

Circle the last three letters of each of the following words, and label each letter C (consonant) or V (vowel). Then write in the blank the word formed with the ending given, being careful to apply the rule for doubling consonants.

EXAMPLES   *CVC* hop + ed = *hopped*   *VVC* ch eap + er = *cheaper*

1. sit + ing = _____
2. clear + er = _____
3. sad + en = _____
4. fat + en = _____
5. coil + ed = _____
6. ask + ing = _____
7. thin + est = _____
8. wet + er = _____
9. wrap + ed = _____
10. skip + ing = _____

11. dip + er = _____
12. send + ing = _____
13. cool + er = _____
14. tap + ed = _____
15. loot + ing = _____
16. tan + ed = _____
17. tall + est = _____
18. red + er = _____
19. drug + ist = _____
20. boil + ed = _____

RULE 5. DOUBLING THE FINAL CONSONANT IN WORDS WITH MORE THAN ONE SYLLABLE

When a word has more than one syllable, double the final consonant if *all three* of the following conditions are met.

1. The ending begins with a vowel (*-ed, -ing, -er, -est,* and so forth).
2. The last three letters of the word are consonant-vowel-consonant (C-V-C).
3. The accent (stress or emphasis) is on the last syllable (begín).

Two- or More Syllable Word Ending in C-V-C with Accent on Last Syllable	+	Ending Beginning with a Vowel	=	Final Consonant Doubled
CVC begin	+	er	=	beginner
CVC regret	+	ed	=	regretted
CVC permit	+	ing	=	permitting

If one or more of the three conditions is not met, do not double the final consonant.

1. If the ending does not begin with a vowel, do not double the consonant.

    commit + ment = commitment

2. If the last three letters are not C-V-C, do not double the consonant.

    befriend + ed = befriended

3. If the accent is not on the last syllable, do not double the consonant.

    visit + or = visitor

    Do not double the final consonant if the accent moves from the last syllable when the ending is added.

    > Accent on last syllable: *prefer*
    >
    > Accent moves to first syllable: *preference* [Do not double the consonant.]

➤ **SPELLING ALERT**

Here are some exceptions, for you to memorize:

cancel + ation = cancellation
equip + ed = equipped
excel + ence = excellence
excel + ent = excellent

24.6 ACTIVITY

Circle the last three letters of each of the following words, and mark each letter C for consonant or V for vowel. Next, determine which syllable is accented. Then spell the word with the given ending, being careful to double consonants according to the rule.

EXAMPLES   CVC   CVC
ad⟨mit⟩ + ed = *admitted*   la⟨bor⟩ + er = *laborer*

1. repent + ing = _____   11. labor + ed = _____

2. expel + ed = _____   12. permit + ed = _____

3. answer + ing = _____   13. ordain + ed = _____

4. begin + ing = _____   14. refer + ence = _____

5. pretend + ed = _____   15. enter + ed = _____

6. submit + ed = _____   16. occur + ed = _____

7. travel + ing = _____   17. motor + ist = _____

8. patrol + ed = _____   18. evict + ing = _____

9. accept + ance = _____   19. confer + ed = _____

10. gossip + ing = _____   20. omit + ed = _____

RULE 6. ADDING *-S* OR *-ES*

Most nouns add *-s* to form the plural.

Singular Noun	Plural Noun
girl	girls
hat	hats
shoe	shoes
umbrella	umbrellas

Most verbs add *-s* in the present tense when their subject is *he, she, it,* or a singular noun.

It
The chef
He
She
} makes, stirs, cooks, eats, sleeps, feels

If a word ends in *-s, -x, -z, -ch,* or *-sh,* add *-es.*

address + es = addresses
mix + es = mixes
waltz + es = waltzes
birch + es = birches
dish + es = dishes

If a word ends in a consonant and *-y,* change the *-y* to *-i* and add *-es.* If the word ends in a vowel and *-y,* just add *-s.*

Consonant and -Y		Vowel and -Y	
f ly	flies	t oy	toys
gup py	guppies	b oy	boys
la dy	ladies	k ey	keys

If a word ends in a consonant and *-o,* add *-es.* If the word ends in a vowel and *-o,* just add *-s.*

Consonant and -O		Vowel and -O	
he ro	heroes	pat io	patios
torna do	tornadoes	rat io	ratios

➡ SPELLING ALERT

Many words related to music add *-s.* Some of these are exceptions to the preceding rule, but some are not.

altos	radios	sopranos
pianos	solos	trios

24.7 ACTIVITY

Add -s or -es, whichever is correct.

EXAMPLES church _____churches_____ television _____televisions_____

1. puppy _____   11. do _____

2. chair _____   12. fox _____

3. wax _____   13. enjoy _____

4. potato _____   14. brush _____

5. stitch _____   15. genius _____

6. tomato _____   16. dictionary _____

7. candy _____   17. marry _____

8. crash _____   18. joy _____

9. monkey _____   19. echo _____

10. boy _____   20. miss _____

RULE 7. CHOOSING BETWEEN *IE* AND *EI*

Here is an old rhyme that can help you decide whether *ie* or *ei* is correct:

> Use *i* before *e*
> Except after *c*
> Or when sounded like *a*,
> As in *neighbor* and *weigh*.

1. Use *i* before *e*:

   achieve   chief   priest
   believe   grief   yield

2. Use *ei* after *c*:

   ceiling   deceive   receipt
   conceive   perceive   receive

3. Use *ei* when the sound is a long *a*:

   freight   sleigh   veil
   neighbor   their   weigh

4. The previous three rules apply when *ie* and *ei* are pronounced as one syllable. They do not apply when the letters are divided between two syllables. Usually when the letters are divided between two syllables, you can tell the spelling by the sound, as the following examples show.

   deity   diet   science

SPELLING ALERT

Here are some exceptions, for you to memorize:

ancient	height	protein
caffeine	leisure	seize
either	neither	weird

24.8 ACTIVITY

Fill in the blanks in the following words with *ie* or *ei*.

EXAMPLES   r __*ei*__ gn

br __*ie*__ f

1. p _____ ce

2. w _____ ght

3. s _____ ge

4. fr _____ nd

5. f _____ ld

6. dec _____ t

7. soc _____ ty

8. n _____ gh

9. f _____ rce

10. v _____ n

11. sl _____ gh

12. sh _____ ld

13. _____ ght

14. misch _____ f

15. rel _____ f

16. bel _____ f

17. b _____ ge

18. n _____ ce

19. exper _____ nce

20. aud _____ nce

SPELLING LIST

Troubleshooting

Tape a list of words you frequently misspell to your computer monitor, so you can easily check these words as you write.

The following is a list of fifty words people often misspell. Study a few of the words every day, review often, and you will be on your way to becoming a better speller.

absence	conscience	fourth	judgment
accommodate	occasion	government	knowledge
across	occurred	grammar	license
answer	disappear	harass	mathematics
athlete	embarrass	height	miscellaneous
beginning	environment	illegal	necessary
calendar	exaggerate	immediately	occasion
career	familiar	important	occurred
cemetery	February	integration	parallel
colonel	forty	jewelry	personnel

possess	rhythm	temperature	until
recipe	separate	thorough	Wednesday
reference	strength		

24.9 COLLABORATIVE

Pair up with a classmate and quiz each other on the frequently misspelled words in the preceding list. If one of you misses a word, write it down and study it.

Composing at the computer

Your computer's spell check program will flag words it judges to be misspelled and will suggest the correct spellings, but use this tool with caution. It will not flag words that are not in the computer's memory, and it may not always suggest the correct spelling. Also, the computer will not recognize a correctly spelled but incorrect word, such as *sealing* for *dealing*.

IF ENGLISH IS NOT YOUR FIRST LANGUAGE

The characteristics of your native language can make mastering English spelling difficult. For example, since Spanish has no *wh* sound, speakers of Spanish may spell *which* as *wich*. Similarly, speakers of Japanese may reverse *l* and *r*. For this reason, keeping a personal spelling list is very important. As you discover words you cannot spell, add them to your list and study them daily.

24.10 CHAPTER REVIEW ACTIVITY

A. Write the correct spellings of the following words in the blanks. If you are unsure, consult the rules in parentheses or check your dictionary.

EXAMPLE   mis + spell = *misspell*   *(rule 1)*

1. un + natural = _____ (rule 1)

2. shove + ed = _____ (rule 3)

3. bat + er = _____ (rule 4)

4. carry + ed = _____ (rule 2)

5. dip + ed = _____ (rule 4)

6. care + ful = _____ (rule 3)

7. walk + ing = _____ (rule 4)

8. feel + ing = _____ (rule 4)

9. prefer + ence = _____ (rule 5)

10. flat + en = _____ (rule 4)

11. run + ing = _____ (rule 4)

12. friendly + er = _____ (rule 2)

13. regret + ed = _____ (rule 5)

14. enchant + ment = _____ (rule 2)

15. re + evaluate = _____ (rule 1)

16. admit + ed = _____ (rule 5)

17. enjoy + able = _____ (rule 2)

18. visit + ed = _____ (rule 5)

19. mis + spoke = _____ (rule 1)

20. love + able = _____ (rule 3)

B. Write the correct spellings of the following words in the blanks. If you are unsure, check your dictionary or consult rules 6 and 7.

EXAMPLES   memo + (s or es) = _____*memos*_____

for _*ei*_ gn (*ie* or *ei*)

1. match + (s or es) = _____

2. mosquito + (s or es) = _____

3. th _____ r _____ (*ie* or *ei*)

4. fix + (s or es) = _____

5. w _____ ght _____ (*ie* or *ei*)

6. reach + (s or es) = _____

7. h _____ r _____ (*ie* or *ei*)

8. moss + (s or es) = _____

9. Cheerio + (s or es) = _____

10. perc _____ ve (*ie* or *ei*)

11. veto + (s or es) = _____

12. grow + (s or es) = _____

13. candy + (s or es) = _____

14. c _____ ling (*ie* or *ei*)

15. gr _____ ve (*ie* or *ei*)

16. dish + (s or es) = _____

17. hurry + (s or es) = _____

18. t _____ d (*ie* or *ei*)

19. pay = (s or es) = _____

20. r _____ gn (*ie* or *ei*)

24.11 CHAPTER REVIEW ACTIVITY

The following passage has ten spelling errors. Find the errors by studying each word, syllable by syllable. Cross out each misspelled word and write the correct spelling above it. If you are unsure, consult your dictionary.

EXAMPLE Our brains <del>dettermine</del> *determine* how we learn.

¹For many of us, our learning style preferences result from the kind of processing our brain "specailizes" in. ²Left-brain processing concentrates more on tasks reqiring verbal competence, such as speaking, reading, thinking, and reasoning. ³Information is processed sequentially, one bit at a time. ⁴For instance, people who are naturaly inclined to use left-brain processing might be more likely to perfer analytic learning styles, because they first like to look at individual bits of information and then put them together.

⁵On the other hand, right-brain processing tends to concentrate more on the processing of information in nonverbal domains, such as the understanding of spatial relationships, the recognition of patterns and drawings, music, and emotional expression. ⁶Furthermore, the right hemasphere tends to process information globally, considering it as a whole before focusing on individual peices of information. ⁷Consequently, people who instinctivly tend toward right-brain processing might faver relational learning styles.

Source: Adapted from Robert Feldman, *Power Learning* (New York: McGraw-Hill, 2005), p. 63. Copyright © 2005 The McGraw-Hill Companies. Used by permission of The McGraw-Hill Companies, Inc.

GETTING IN GEAR: IDEAS FOR WRITING

You have probably seen the "For Dummies" series of books, which provides a simple introduction to everything from gardening to religion. For an overview of the subjects covered by the books, visit www.dummies.com/WileyCDA/. Have you ever used such books? Why do they think they are so popular? Are there any drawbacks to learning a skill from such books?

writing topic: Maybe you do not currently spell very well (many people don't), but there are likely many other things you do well. Select something you do well, and assume you are writing the preface to a "For Dummies" book that deals with that skill. Explain the benefits of knowing how to do that thing well to motivate users of the book.

suggestions for discovering ideas
- List the things you do well, such as entertaining young children, throwing a fast ball, choosing the perfect presents, growing flowers, or baking.
- Select one of the items from your list and freewrite about the benefits associated with the activity.

suggestion for drafting: Your thesis or topic sentence (depending on whether you are writing an essay or a paragraph) can mention the activity you perform well and a general benefit, something like this: "If you learn to speak Spanish, you will always be able to find a high-paying job."

suggestion for revising: If you explain several benefits or several problems, use transitions such as these for coherence: *first, in addition, also, more important, finally.*

suggestion for editing: Point to every word and study it, syllable by syllable, for a few seconds to consider the spelling. Be sure to check your dictionary if you have even the slightest feeling that a word is misspelled.

RECHARGE: Lesson Summary

To become a better speller,
- use a dictionary or spell checker.
- learn the rules for
    - adding a prefix.
    - adding endings to words with a final -*y*.
    - adding endings to words with a final -*e*.
    - doubling the final consonant in one-syllable words.
    - doubling the final consonant in words with more than one syllable.
    - forming noun plurals.
    - using *ie* and *ei*.

Using Frequently Confused Words Correctly

By the end of this chapter, you will learn to

Use a number of words that are often confused with one another

A number of words that look or sound alike are confused for each other and used
incorrectly as a result. If you are aware of the possibilities for confusion, you will
avoid problems with these frequently confused words. This chapter will help you
do that.

A/AN

For an explanation of how to use these frequently confused words, see page 294.

A LOT/ALOT

The correct form is **a lot.**

ACCEPT/EXCEPT

1. **Accept** means "receive" or "get." It is a verb.

   Jonathan does not accept *help easily.*

2. **Except** means "excluded" or "other than." It is a preposition.

   All of the senators except *Senator Howard answered the roll call vote.*

Memory tip: To remember that *except* means "excluded," remember that both
begin with *ex-*.

A. Fill in the blanks in the following sentences with *accept* or *except*.

1. I hope you can find it in your heart to _____ my apology.

2. People are happiest when they _____ their limitations.

Copyright © 2007, The McGraw-Hill Companies, Inc.

3. I finished all the problems _____ the last one.

4. _____ for Carlos, everyone decided to attend the economics lecture in the auditorium.

5. Jane and Larry broke up because they could not _____ each other's faults.

6. Every weather forecaster _____ the one on Channel 9 is predicting snow for Christmas.

B. On a separate sheet, write two sentences using *accept* and two using *except*.

ADVICE/ADVISE

1. **Advice** is a suggestion or an opinion. It is a noun.

    If you have a problem, ask Lee for advice.

2. **Advise** means "offer a suggestion." It is a verb.

    I advise you to get your tickets early.

Memory tip: Remember that *advice* contains the word *vice*, and a person with a *vice* needs *advice*.

25.2 ACTIVITY

A. Fill in the blanks in the following sentences with *advice* or *advise*.

1. My _____ to you is to study harder.

2. I _____ you to study harder.

3. If _____ is what you want, you have come to the wrong person.

4. Imran wants Dr. Barolsky to _____ him about how to apply to a good journalism school.

5. Most people listen to David's _____ and then do the opposite of what he recommends.

6. No one can _____ you better than your own conscience.

B. On a separate sheet, write two sentences using *advice* and two using *advise*.

AFFECT/EFFECT

1. **Affect** means "influence." It is a verb.

    High humidity affects my sinuses.

2. **Effect** means "result." It is a noun.

    The effect of the tax hike is not yet clear.

3. **Effect** can also be a verb meaning "bring about."

   Congress will try to __effect__ a change in our trade agreement with Japan.

Memory tip: Remember that *effect* means "result" by remembering that the first syllable of *effect* rhymes with the first syllable of *result*.

25.3 ACTIVITY

A. Fill in the blanks in the following sentences with *affect* or *effect*.

1. The _____ of early childhood trauma can last a lifetime.

2. Psychologists have found that creativity can _____ intelligence.

3. A person's genetic makeup will _____ his or her life expectancy.

4. Cultural differences can _____ a person's ability to send and receive verbal cues.

5. Title IX legislation helped _____ a change in the status of women.

6. Disease and famine have a negative _____ on population growth.

B. On a separate sheet, write two sentences using *affect* and two using *effect*.

ALL READY/ALREADY

1. **All ready** means "all set" or "prepared."

   I am __all ready__ to go with you.

2. **Already** means "previously," "by a specific time," or "by this time." It is an adverb.

   We are __already__ an hour late for dinner.

Memory tip: To remember that *all ready* means "all set," remember that they are both two words.

25.4 ACTIVITY

A. Fill in the blanks in the following sentences with *all ready* or *already*.

1. The reporters were _____ at the scene when the police arrived.

2. I am _____ a week ahead on my reading assignments, but I want to work a little longer.

3. The plane was _____ for departure, but some of the passengers had not arrived yet.

4. Once the sound crew completes its work, we will be _____ for the light crew to begin.

5. Once Martha gets a transcript of her grades, her scholarship application will be _____ to mail.

6. Ivan _____ told you not to wait for him.

B. On a separate sheet, write two sentences using *all ready* and two using *already.*

CONNECT FOR SUCCESS: Use Mnemonics

Mnemonics, pronounced "neh-MON-ix," are tricks for remembering things. The memory tips throughout this chapter are mnemonics. Another mnemonic is the poem "Use *i* before *e*, except after *c*, or when sounded like *a*, as in *neighbor* and *weigh*," introduced in Chapter 24 to help you remember correct spelling. You can devise your own mnemonics for remembering material in all your courses. For example, to remember for your psychology class that the meaning of *sociopath* is someone with no regard for the rules and morals of society, you might see *path* coming after *socio* and think of a sociopath as someone whose *path* moves away from society and its rules and morals.

ALL RIGHT/ALRIGHT

In formal situations, do not use **alright. All right,** which means "satisfactory" or "good," is the acceptable form in college and on the job.

BEEN/BEING

1. **Been** is the past participle of *be.* To form a complete verb, *been* is used with *have, has,* or *had.*

   You *have been* my best friend since seventh grade.
   Charlie *has been* here before.
   I *had been* angry until you apologized.

   For a complete discussion of the past participle and its uses, see Chapter 12.

 GRAMMAR ALERT

Be sure to use *have, has,* or *had* with *been.*

No: *The car been parked in a tow-away zone.*
Yes: *The car had been parked in a tow-away zone.*

---

2. **Being** is the present participle (the *-ing* form) of *be.* To form the complete verb, it is used with *am, is, are, was,* or *were.*

I am being stubborn about this.
The car is being delivered this afternoon.
We are being fair to you.
He was being rude last night.
The letters were being mailed to you.

For a complete discussion of the present participle and its uses, see Chapter 13.

GRAMMAR ALERT

Be sure to use *am, is, are, was,* or *were* with *being.*

No: *You being very understanding.*

Yes: *You are being very understanding.*

25.5 ACTIVITY

A. Fill in the blanks in the following sentences with the correct form: *been* or *being.* Also, circle the helping verb (*have, has, had, am, is, are, was,* or *were*).

1. The rowdy fans were _____ asked to leave.

2. You are _____ a very good friend to Jerry.

3. Before you arrived, I had _____ cleaning the basement.

4. The children have _____ very patient.

5. If I am _____ unfair, I apologize.

6. Royce DePizzo has _____ a baseball coach for twenty-five years.

B. On a separate sheet, write two sentences using *been* and two using *being.*

BESIDE/BESIDES

1. **Beside** means "alongside."

   Put the table beside the chair.

2. **Besides** means "in addition to."

   Besides a fever, I have a sore throat.

Memory tip: To remember that *besides* means "in addition to," think of the second *s* in *besides* as functioning in addition to the first *s.*

25.6 ACTIVITY

A. Fill in the blanks in the following sentences with *beside* or *besides.*

1. _____ going to the mall, we can shop downtown.

2. Do you mind if I sit _____ you?

3. _____ the student center, the university planted a beautiful flower garden.

4. No one, _____ you, believes that the final exam will be difficult.

5. _____ studying, I have to practice my clarinet tonight.

6. The child placed her favorite doll _____ her on the couch.

B. On a separate sheet, write two sentences using *beside* and two using *besides*.

BUY/BY

1. **Buy** means "purchase." It is a verb.

   I cannot afford to <u>buy</u> those shoes.

2. **By** means "near" or "a means of." It is a preposition.

   We can travel to Toronto <u>by</u> train.

Memory tip: Remember that *buy* means "purchase" by thinking of the *u* in both words.

25.7 ACTIVITY

A. Fill in the blanks in the following sentences with *buy* or *by.*

1. When I get my paycheck, I can _____ tickets to the concert.

2. For your birthday, Josie will _____ you dinner at your favorite restaurant.

3. _____ my calculations, we will be out of money before the end of the week.

4. Wanda asked José to meet her _____ the clock tower at noon.

5. This article was written _____ a noted sociologist.

6. This month, every time you _____ a hamburger at Carl's, 2¢ will be donated to the hospital's children's ward.

B. On a separate sheet, write two sentences using *buy* and two using *by.*

CAN/COULD

Can is a present tense form used for writing about something that is happening *now.* **Could** is most often a past tense form used for writing about something that happened *before now.*

Present: *When I am bored, I <u>can</u> sleep all day.*
Past: *When I was bored, I <u>could</u> sleep all day.*

A. Fill in the blanks in the following sentences with the correct form: *can* or *could*.

1. You _____ tell that Bebe was crying, because her eyes were red.

2. If you are willing to take her advice, Inez _____ help you.

3. This morning, Professor Hyatt said that we _____ leave class early.

4. When spring arrives, I _____ notice everybody's mood improving.

5. Last semester, you _____ decide between an American and a British history class, and this semester you _____ decide between a French and a German class.

6. Now when I see chocolate, I _____ no longer resist it.

B. On a separate sheet, write two sentences using *can* and two using *could*.

> **Troubleshooting**
>
> If you often make mistakes with some of the frequently confused words, tape them—along with their definitions—to your computer screen as a reminder.

GOOD/WELL

For an explanation of how to use these frequently confused words, see page 298.

HAVE/OF

Some writers mistakenly use **of** instead of the helping verb **have.** This error most frequently occurs after one of these verbs: *could, would, should, may, must, might,* and *will,* probably because *of* sounds like *have* in phrases such as *could have. Of* is never correct in these constructions.

No: *I <u>could of</u> won the race.*
Yes: *I <u>could have</u> won the race.*

No: *She <u>must of</u> lost her way.*
Yes: *She <u>must have</u> lost her way.*

No: *Jan <u>should of</u> tried harder.*
Yes: *Jan <u>should have</u> tried harder.*

On a separate sheet, write sentences using any four of the following: *could have, would have, should have, may have, might have, must have,* and *will have.*

HEAR/HERE

1. **Hear** means "listen." It is a verb.

   We cannot <u>hear</u> you over the radio.

2. **Here** means "a nearby place." It is an adverb.

   Joseph will pick you up <u>here</u> at three o'clock.

Memory tip: Hear, which means "listen," has the word *ear* in it: h `ear` .

25.10 ACTIVITY

A. Fill in the blanks in the following sentences with *hear* or *here*.

1. Let's move up front, so we can _____ better.

2. _____ are the reports you are looking for.

3. To _____ Lionel tell it, he saved the day single-handedly.

4. Donna has lived _____ for thirty years.

5. Dane refuses to admit that he cannot _____very well.

6. An important Civil War battle was fought _____.

B. On a separate sheet, write two sentences using *hear* and two using *here*.

ITS/IT'S

1. **Its** shows ownership. It is a pronoun.

   This coat has a hole in <u>its</u> pocket.

2. **It's** is a contraction that means "it is" or "it has."

   <u>It's</u> raining again.
   <u>It's</u> been raining all day.

Memory tip: Do not use *it's* unless you can substitute *it is* or *it has*.

25.11 ACTIVITY

A. Fill in the blanks in the following sentences with *its* or *it's*.

1. A language is composed of _____systems of syntax, seman-tics, phonology, and morphology.

2. Children in all countries learn language in a similar sequence, although _____accomplished with individual variations.

3. Observations of children learning language reveal that _____ learned informally.

4. _____ been clear for many years that children master language by the time they are five or six.

5. Each language offers _____ challenges to language learners.

6. _____ easier to learn a language as a child than as an adult.

B. On a separate sheet, write two sentences using *its* and two using *it's*.

KNOW/NO AND KNEW/NEW

1. **Know** means "understand" or "have knowledge of." It is a verb.

   Juan knows CPR and first aid.

2. **No** expresses a negative idea.

   No, you may not come with me.

3. **Knew** is the past tense of *know*.

   Larry knew the answer, but he forgot it.

4. **New** means "not old."

   Sylvia's new car is sporty.

25.12 ACTIVITY

A. Fill in the blanks in the following sentences with *know, no, knew,* or *new*.

1. The _____ philosophy professor is a fascinating lecturer.

2. Eleni _____ longer works in the library.

3. I _____ you were coming, so I made more for supper.

4. We all _____ Lucy to be honest and sincere.

5. Most Americans believe that anything _____ is better.

6. Mike _____ he would have to lose 10 pounds to wrestle in the lighter weight classification.

7. I _____ what I want to say, but I can't think of the right word.

8. There is _____ reason to be angry.

B. On a separate sheet, write one sentence using each of these words: *know, no, knew,* and *new*.

LIE/LAY

1. **Lie** is an irregular verb meaning "rest on a surface." It has the following forms: *lie, lying, lay, lain.*

Present:	*lie(s)* *I* <u>lie</u> *down every day at three o'clock.*
Present participle:	*lying* *Raul is* <u>lying</u> *down for an hour.*
Past:	*lay* *She* <u>lay</u> *down for a nap an hour ago.*
Past participle:	*lain* *Margo has* <u>lain</u> *down for awhile.*

2. **Lie** is also a regular verb meaning "to not tell the truth." It has these forms: *lie, lying, lied, lied.*

Present:	*lie(s)* *If you* <u>lie</u>*, I will know it.*
Present participle:	*lying* *Dorrie can tell if I am* <u>lying</u>*.*
Past:	*lied* *He was sorry he* <u>lied</u> *to you.*
Past participle:	*lied* *The child has* <u>lied</u> *about his grade.*

3. **Lay** is an irregular verb meaning "put down" or "place." It has these forms: *lay, laying, laid, laid.*

Present:	*lay(s)* *Sheila* <u>lays</u> *her keys on the table.*
Present participle:	*laying* *You are* <u>laying</u> *that in the wrong place.*
Past:	*laid* *I thought I* <u>laid</u> *my book on the bed.*
Past participle:	*laid* *Mario has* <u>laid</u> *the tools on the bench.*

25.13 ACTIVITY

A. Fill in the blanks in the following sentences with the correct form of *lie* or *lay*.

1. Mahammed _____ down under a tree to read a book.

2. Whenever I _____ about something important, I become angry with myself.

3. Andy _____ his lunch by his schoolbooks and then left without it.

4. I fell asleep _____ on the couch.

5. When you set the table, you should _____ the forks to the left of the plates.

6. Doris has _____ about her accomplishments too often, and now nobody believes her.

7. We can't remember where we _____ our sunglasses.

8. I _____ down in the hammock and fell asleep instantly.

9. They have _____ on the grass so long that their clothes are grass-stained.

10. Mother is gently _____ the teddy bear next to the sleeping baby.

B. On a separate sheet, write two sentences using a form of the *irregular* verb *lie,* two using a form of the *regular* verb *lie,* and two using a form of the *irregular* verb *lay.*

LOOSE/LOSE

1. **Loose** means "not tight." It is an adjective.

   Because I have been exercising, my pants are loose.

2. **Lose** means "misplace" or "not win." It is a verb.

   I lose my keys once a week.

   You will lose the match if you do not concentrate more.

Memory tip: Loose has two *o*'s and *lose* has only one. You can remember that *lose* means "to misplace" if you think one *o* has been misplaced.

25.14 ACTIVITY

A. Fill in the blanks in the following sentences with *loose* or *lose*.

1. Put your registration materials in a safe place so you will not

   _____ them.

2. If we _____ this game, we will not make it to the district championship.

3. _____ clothing is more comfortable than tight clothing.

4. My credit card numbers are recorded in my drawer, in case I

   _____ my wallet.

5. The door is squeaking because a hinge is _____.

6. Have you heard the expression "_____ lips sink ships"?

B. On a separate sheet, write two sentences using *loose* and two using *lose*.

PASSED/PAST

1. **Passed** is the past tense of the verb *pass*. It means "went by" or "handed."

   The police car passed us at 80 miles an hour.
   When Rajá passed the milk, she knocked over the vase of flowers.

2. **Past** means "previous time." It also means "by."

   I am not proud of my past.
   Drive past Maurice's house to see if he is home.

Memory tip: To remember that *past* means "previous time," remind yourself of the *p* and the *t* in both *past* and *previous time.*

25.15 ACTIVITY

A. Fill in the blanks in the following sentences with *passed* or *past*.

1. Our _____ experiences influence what we become in the future.

2. The speeding car _____ us in the inside lane.

3. In the _____, Carlotta considered dropping out of school.

4. It's time to let go of the _____.

5. As the parade _____ the reviewing stand, the band members tipped their hats.

6. The relay runner _____ the baton to the fastest runner on the team.

B. On a separate sheet, write two sentences using *passed* and two using *past*.

PRINCIPAL/PRINCIPLE

1. **Principal** means "main" or "most important." It is an adjective. It can also be a noun meaning "the head of a school" (the main or most important person in the school).

   The principal problem here is that you will not compromise.
   The principal closed the school because the water pipes froze.

2. **Principle** is a truth or a standard. It is a noun.

   You cannot play on our team because you do not understand the principles of fair play.

Memory tip: Principal includes the word *pal*, and a principal should be a student's pal.

25.16 ACTIVITY

A. Fill in the blanks in the following sentences with *principal* or *principle*.

1. Now that Leah Stanich is the _____ of Woodside Elementary School, she misses teaching.

2. I agree with the _____ of freedom of the press, but not when people's privacy is invaded.

3. The _____ matter before the school board is whether to change the high school curriculum.

4. I understand the _____ behind this algebra problem, but I do not know the procedure for solving it.

5. Right now, my _____ concern is for the well-being of my children.

6. Lucinda will not back down because she believes in the _____ she is fighting for.

B. On a separate sheet, write two sentences using *principal* and two using *principle*.

QUIET/QUIT/QUITE

1. **Quiet** means "without noise" or "calm." It is an adjective.

   Joyce cannot sleep unless the house is completely quiet.

2. **Quit** means "stop" or "give up." It is a verb.

   Peter finally quit smoking.

3. **Quite** means "exactly" or "very." It is an adverb.

   This is not quite the birthday Eleni hoped for.
   I am quite surprised by your actions.

25.17 ACTIVITY

A. Fill in the blanks in the following sentences with *quiet*, *quit*, or *quite*.

1. Mario studies in the library because it is _____.

2. I am not _____ sure how to help you.

3. Thomas _____ the basketball team because he tore a ligament in his knee.

4. Grandmother is _____ capable of taking care of herself.

5. The _____ in the country helps me relax.

6. Marla's New Year's resolution is to _____ biting her nails.

B. On a separate sheet, write two sentences using *quiet*, two using *quit*, and two using *quite*.

RISE/RAISE

1. **Rise** is an irregular verb meaning "get up" or "go up." It has these forms: *rise, rising, rose, risen.*

Present:	rise(s)	*Terry rises every day at dawn.*
Present participle:	rising	*The sun is rising in the east.*
Past:	rose	*I rose to greet Father Clooney.*
Past participle:	risen	*The choir has risen from its seats.*

2. **Raise** is a regular verb meaning "lift up" or "force up." It has these forms: *raise, raising, raised, raised.*

Present:	raise(s)	*She raises her hand and waves.*
Present participle:	raising	*Kyle is raising his feet so I can sweep under them.*
Past:	raised	*I raised the curtain to start the play.*
Past participle:	raised	*Dominic has raised the shelf an inch.*

25.18 ACTIVITY

A. Fill in the blanks in the following sentences with the correct forms of *rise* or *raise*.

1. He _____ the curtain to reveal the grand prize.

2. The sun _____ over the Atlantic Ocean.

3. The mayor had _____ to speak when the lights went out.

4. Every morning, Jeremy _____ the flag.

5. She has _____ the blinds to let the sun in.

6. Lee and Chris are _____ the heavy trunk onto the table.

7. Each day, he _____ at three o'clock to feed the baby.

8. When Helena entered the room, the guests _____ to greet her.

9. I always _____ my arm to hail a taxi.

10. Sam is _____ early to go fishing.

B. On a separate sheet, write two sentences using a form of *rise* and two using a form of *raise*.

SIT/SET

1. **Sit** is an irregular verb meaning "sit down" or "rest." It has these forms: *sit, sitting, sat, sat*.

Present:	*sit(s) The cat <u>sits</u> by the fire.*
Present participle:	*sitting I am <u>sitting</u> next to Brad.*
Past:	*sat We <u>sat</u> in the back of the church.*
Past participle:	*sat I have <u>sat</u> in one spot all day.*

2. **Set** is an irregular verb meaning "place" or "arrange." It has these forms: *set, setting, set, set*.

Present:	*set(s) The caterer <u>sets</u> a lovely table.*
Present participle:	*setting We were <u>setting</u> the chairs in a row.*
Past:	*set Margery <u>set</u> her books on the desk.*
Past participle:	*set I had <u>set</u> my briefcase on the roof of the car before driving off.*

25.19 ACTIVITY

A. Fill in the blanks in the following sentences with the correct forms of *sit* or *set*.

1. Joyce _____ the controls on the TIVO to record her favorite program, and then she left the house.

2. Every day at five o'clock, Kwame _____ the table for dinner.

3. We have _____ here long enough.

4. The students _____ their first drafts on the instructor's desk before leaving class.

5. The passengers are _____ on the plane, patiently listening to the preflight instructions.

6. I _____ in the library for an hour, waiting for you.

7. Because Hank and I are nearsighted, we usually _____ up front in theaters.

8. The mourners were filing by the coffin and _____ flowers on it.

9. We have _____ in these bleachers so long that our backs hurt.

10. Yesterday, Ira and Marco _____ up the tables for the garage sale.

B. On a separate sheet, write two sentences using a form of *sit* and two using a form of *set*.

SUPPOSE/SUPPOSED

1. **Suppose** means "assume." Its past tense form is *supposed*.

   I *suppose* Lesley will be joining us for dinner.
   Everyone *supposed* the snow storm would ruin the weekend.

2. When **supposed** comes between a helping verb (*am, is, are, was, were*) and *to*, it means "should."

   My sister *is supposed to* pick us up here.
   I *was supposed to* help Joy with the decorations.
   We *are supposed to* study together at noon.

→ **GRAMMAR ALERT**

Because the *d* at the end of *supposed* and the *t* at the beginning of *to* are pronounced as one sound, writers may mistakenly omit the *d* in *supposed*.

No: You were *suppose* to go with me.
Yes: You were *supposed* to go with me.

No: A student is *suppose* to study.
Yes: A student is *supposed* to study.

25.20 ACTIVITY

A. Fill in the blanks with *suppose* or *supposed*.

1. According to legend, Rome was _____ to be founded by twin brothers, Romulus and Remus in 753 B.C.E.

2. I don't _____ that anyone still believes that legend, however.

3. Archaeologists long _____ that, by the eighth century B.C.E., there was a settlement of huts on the top of Rome's hills.

4. Early Rome (753–509 B.C.E.) is _____ to have had seven kings.

5. The Etruscans, who influenced Rome for about a hundred years, are _____ to have turned it into a city.

6. We can _____, therefore, that the Etruscans were the most important early influence on Rome.

B. On a separate sheet, write two sentences using *suppose* and two using *supposed*.

THAN/THEN

1. **Than** is used to compare. It is a conjunction.

   Diana is taller than Sue.

2. **Then** refers to time. It is an adverb.

   I should be ready by then.

Memory tip: Think of the *a* in both *than* and *compare;* think of the *e* in both *then* and *time.*

25.21 ACTIVITY

A. Fill in the blanks in the following sentences with *than* or *then*.

1. Dr. Dodge explained the assignment and _____ dismissed the class.

2. Skinless chicken breast is healthier _____ beef.

3. First preheat the oven and _____ assemble the ingredients.

4. It is more difficult to be a teenager _____ many adults realize.

5. If you leave _____, you will miss dessert.

6. I would rather be intelligent _____ good-looking.

B. On a separate sheet, write two sentences using *than* and two using *then*.

THERE/THEIR/THEY'RE

1. **There** refers to direction or place. It can also be used as a sentence opener.

   Put your packages down <u>there</u>.
   <u>There</u> are no seats left.

2. **Their** shows ownership.

   The children played with <u>their</u> toys.

3. **They're** is a contraction meaning "they are."

   If Phil and Janet come, <u>they're</u> sure to complain all evening.

   Memory tip: Use *they're* only when you can substitute *they are.*

25.22 ACTIVITY

A. Fill in the blanks with *there, their,* or *they're.*

1. _____ are many interesting facts about left-handed people.

2. Apelike animals, such as lemurs and galagos, primarily use

   _____ left hands.

3. Look at a keyboard and see that the most popular letters (*a, e, r, s, t*) are

   _____ on the left side, so the left hand does most of the

   typing.

4. The Italian words for "left" and "left-handed" are *mancino* and *mancini;*

   _____ translated as "defective" and "deceitful."

5. Wearing a medal on the left side is a custom because the crusaders wore

   _____ emblems close to _____ hearts.

6. _____ once was a disease called "left-disease," which turned

   out to be paralysis.

B. On a separate sheet, write two sentences using *there,* two using *their,* and
   two using *they're.*

THREW/THROUGH

1. **Threw** is the past tense of *throw.* It is a verb.

   Hank <u>threw</u> the ball to second base.

2. **Through** means "in one side and out the other." It is a preposition. It can
   also be an adjective meaning "finished."

   The train passed <u>through</u> the tunnel.
   The play will be <u>through</u> at ten o'clock.

25.23 ACTIVITY

A. Fill in the blanks in the following sentences with *threw* or *through.*

1. I was the first one _____ with the history test.

2. Lanie was so angry she _____ her keys across the room.

3. Nigel wadded up the paper and _____ it into the wastebasket.

4. The chef put the beef _____ the meat grinder.

5. Dale _____ the ball up in a desperation shot.

6. We drove _____ Pennsylvania on our way to New York.

B. On a separate sheet, write two sentences using *threw* and two using *through*.

TO/TOO/TWO

1. **To** means "toward." It is a preposition. It is also used with a verb to form the infinitive, as in *to eat*.

   Let's go to class now   I hate to take pills.

2. **Too** means "also" or "excessively." It is an adverb.

   Christina needs a menu, too.   It is too cold in here.

3. **Two** is a number.

   Scott has two brothers.

25.24 ACTIVITY

A. Fill in the blanks in the following sentences with *to, too,* or *two.*

1. My roommate and I are going _____ the dining hall.

2. _____ get there on time, we must leave now.

3. _____ movies are playing in the student union tonight.

4. You, _____, can learn karate.

5. Stephen King books are _____ scary for Kim.

6. We will leave at _____ o'clock.

B. On a separate sheet, write two sentences for each of these words: *to, too,* and *two.*

USE/USED

1. **Use** is a verb meaning "make use of." Its past tense form is *used.*

   I hope you can use the sweater I bought you.
   Henri used the last towel and did not replace it.

2. When followed by *to,* **used** means "in the habit of."

When I was younger, I <u>used to</u> sleep late on Saturday.

I <u>used to</u> like spicy food, but now I do not.

GRAMMAR ALERT

Because the *d* at the end of *used* and the *t* at the beginning of *to* are pronounced as one sound, writers may mistakenly omit the *d* from *used.*

No: *Harriet <u>use</u> to live here.*

Yes: *Harriet <u>used</u> to live here.*

No: *I am <u>use</u> to a harder mattress.*

Yes: *I am <u>used</u> to a harder mattress.*

25.25 ACTIVITY

A. Fill in the blanks in the following sentences with *use* or *used.*

1. Carlotta is not _____ to so much free time, so she does not know what to do with herself.

2. If you _____ a plate, please wash it and put it away.

3. I gave Michael the book because he can _____ it more than you can.

4. Eventually, my brother became _____ to the extreme heat of the tropics.

5. I would like to leave for the gym and _____ the weights for an hour.

6. It often takes a full year for people to get _____ to college life.

B. On a separate sheet, write two sentences using *use* and two using *used.*

WERE/WE'RE/WHERE

1. **Were** is the past tense of *are.*

They <u>were</u> late because of heavy traffic.

2. **We're** means "we are."

<u>We're</u> happy to help you.

3. **Where** refers to location.

<u>Where</u> are you going?

Memory tip: Like *here, where* refers to location, and *where* contains the word *here:*

w $\boxed{here}$

Memory tip: Do not use *we're* unless you can substitute *we are.*

A. Fill in the blanks in the following sentences with *were, we're,* or *where.*

1. _____ not sure which road to take, so we should check the map.

2. _____ do you think I should go for vacation?

3. I don't know about you, but _____ happy to be here.

4. Joan and I thought the waiters in that restaurant _____ very rude.

5. This is the town _____ my father was raised.

6. The critics _____ charmed by the lead actor's performance.

B. On a separate sheet, write two sentences using *were,* two using *we're,* and two using *where.*

WHO'S/WHOSE

1. **Who's** is a contraction that means "who is" or "who has."

   Who's going with you?   Who's been sitting here?

2. **Whose** shows ownership.

   He is the boy whose dog is lost.

Memory tip: Use *who's* only when you can substitute *who is* or *who has.*

A. Fill in the blanks in the following sentences with *who's* or *whose.*

1. The person _____ car is parked outside has a flat tire to change.

2. _____ portrait is hanging on the wall?

3. _____ been using my comb?

4. _____ been telling you such silly stories?

5. _____ idea was this, anyway?

6. _____ going to help me carry groceries?

B. On a separate sheet, write two sentences using *who's* and two using *whose.*

WILL/WOULD

1. Use **will** to point to the future from the present.

   I believe I <u>will</u> win the lottery.

2. Use **would** to point to the future from the past.

   I believed I <u>would</u> win the lottery.

25.28 ACTIVITY

A. Fill in the blanks in the following sentences with *will* or *would*.

1. I understand that you _____ paint my house for $3,000.

2. Nicholas agreed that buying a new furnace _____ save on future heating costs.

3. The doctor explained that speech therapy _____ help Lee speak more clearly.

4. After an hour of discussions, the jury decided that the defendant

   _____ go free.

5. We know that you _____ do your best.

6. Mother and Father hope that Kenny _____ join us for supper.

B. On a separate sheet, write two sentences using *will* and two using *would*.

YOUR/YOU'RE

1. **Your** shows ownership.

   Bring <u>your</u> umbrella, because it may rain.

2. **You're** means "you are."

   <u>You're</u> just the person I wanted to see.

Memory tip: Do not use *you're* unless you can substitute *you are.*

25.29 ACTIVITY

A. Fill in the blanks with *your* or *you're*.

1. Writing lets you learn from _____ mistakes.

2. When _____ able to write often, you learn about yourself as a writer.

3. _____ a writer every time you write, no matter how unimportant the writing is.

4. The more attention you give to _____ writing, the more you will learn.

5. The more you write, the more confident you will feel about what _____ doing.

6. Study_____ readers' comments and _____ certain to learn much about writing.

B. On a separate sheet, write two sentences using *your* and two using *you're*.

Composing at the computer

Your computer's grammar and spell checkers will catch some, but not all, errors with frequently confused words, so be sure to edit carefully to find errors with these word pairs and trios.

 IF ENGLISH IS NOT YOUR FIRST LANGUAGE

For nonnative speakers of English, **homophones**—words that sound alike but have different spellings and meanings—can be troublesome. For example, distinguishing between *hear* and *here* or *hole* and *whole* can be tricky. There are many more homophones in English than appear in this chapter. Thus, you may want to keep a separate list of these words to study as you encounter them in your reading or as your instructor points them out in your writing.

25.30 COLLABORATIVE CHAPTER REVIEW ACTIVITY

Develop a fill-in the blank quiz by writing ten sentences using different frequently confused words from this chapter. Place a blank where each frequently confused word should go, and indicate correct and incorrect choices for the blank. Pair up with a classmate and take each other's quizzes.

25.31 CHAPTER REVIEW ACTIVITY

Fill in each of the following blanks with a frequently confused word that fits the definition given. Choose words from the list here and on the next page.

accept	here	principal	they're
except	its	principle	threw
advice	it's	quiet	through
advise	know	quit	to
affect	no	quite	too
effect	knew	raise	two
all ready	new	rise	we're
already	lay	set	were
beside	lie	sit	your
besides	lose	than	you're

buy	loose	then
by	passed	there
hear	past	their

1. Past tense of *throw:* _____

2. Understand: _____

3. Shows exclusion: _____

4. Influence: _____

5. Purchase: _____

6. It is: _____

7. Not old: _____

8. A truth or standard: _____

9. Offer a suggestion: _____

10. Used to compare: _____

11. Also: _____

12. Stop: _____

13. In one side and out the other: _____

14. Previously: _____

15. Most important: _____

16. Receive: _____

17. Near: _____

18. Very: _____

19. Previous time: _____

20. In addition to: _____

21. Not tight: _____

22. They are: _____

23. A sentence opener: _____

24. Negative: _____

25. Listen: _____

26. Alongside of: _____

27. Misplace: _____

28. Shows ownership by more than one person: _____

29. You are: _____

30. A nearby place: _____

31. Went by: _____

32. Result: _____

33. Past tense of *are:* _____

34. Shows ownership by something not human: _____

35. Without noise: _____

36. Toward: _____

37. All set: _____

38. Past tense of *know:* _____

39. Suggestion or opinion: _____

40. We are: _____

41. 2: _____

42. Get up: _____

43. Place: _____

44. Lift up: _____

45. Rest on a surface: _____

25.32 CHAPTER REVIEW ACTIVITY

The following passage contains twelve errors with frequently confused words. Cross out the incorrect words and write the correct ones above them.

EXAMPLE   Many students find a study group ~~quit~~ *quite* helpful.

[1]For many students, the best advise I can offer is to form a study group, because a study group can positively effect grades. [2]A study group is a small, informal group of students who work together to learn course material. [3]Beside working to learn course material, members of study groups meet to study for tests. [4]Its possible to form study groups for particular tests or to meet consistently throughout the term. [5]Typically, a study group is suppose to meet a week or two before a test and plan a strategy for studying. [6]Members share there understanding of what will be on the test, but their also supposed to develop a list of review questions together to guide their individual study. [7]A few days before the test, members of the study group meet to discuss answers to the review questions, go over the material, and share any new insights. [8]They may also quiz one another to identify any weaknesses or gaps in they're knowledge.

[9]Your likely to find that a study group helps you organize and structure material, so you can approach your study in a systematic way. [10]The study group will also help you share and except alot of different perspectives on material that you might of overlooked otherwise. [11]Finally, study groups motivate you to do your best work, because you're no longer working just for yourself.

GETTING IN GEAR: IDEAS FOR WRITING

The American justice system relies heavily on eyewitness testimony, but in times of confusion—like that depicted in the photograph—mistaken identity is so common as to make such testimony questionable at best. For a discussion of this issue, see www.nsf.gov/discoveries/disc_summ.jsp?cntn_id=1007115&org=NSF. Note that the site provides a video test of your own "eyewitness aptitude." How good an eyewitness would you make?

writing topic: In this chapter, you learned about words that are often confused, but there are many kinds of confusion in life—some kinds more serious than others. Write about a confusion you have experienced and explain either the effect of the confusion or how you resolved the confusion (or plan to resolve it).

suggestions for prewriting

- Try mapping. In the center of a page, write "kinds of confusion," and draw a circle around it. Branch off ideas from that circle by following the mapping instructions on page 9. (Think about your classes, your social life, your work, and your family life, both now and in the past.)
- Select one or more ideas from your map and freewrite about it for about ten minutes.

suggestions for drafting

- Your thesis or topic sentence (depending on whether you are writing an essay or a paragraph) can mention the reason for confusion; it can also mention the effect or method of resolution, something like these: "When I took an advanced calculus class against my advisor's advice, I became hopelessly confused" or "The only way to end the frequent mix-ups where I work is to put an end to office gossip."
- First explain the confusion and then explain its effect or resolution.

suggestion for revising: To move smoothly from your discussion of the confusion to a discussion of its effect or resolution, you can use transitional sentences like these: "The effect of the confusion was surprising," "The mix-up in directions put us in danger on the trip." "To deal with the confusion in math class, I went to the math lab." "To end the confusion about who caused the misunderstanding, I may have to write everyone a letter."

suggestion for editing: Edit one extra time, checking for frequently confused words.

RECHARGE: Lesson Summary

A number of words are frequently confused because they look or sound alike. Be careful to use these words correctly.

PART SEVEN REVIEW
Editing for multiple errors

The following passage has 10 errors with frequently confused words and 9 misspellings. Cross out and write above the line to correct the mistakes.

[1]People generaly love a good magic show. [2]These days, magicians perform spectacular tricks, making things like the Empire State Building and tigers disappear. [3]Even so, people still love the old standards. [4]For example, we no its not really happening, but its hard not to gasp when the magicain begins to saw through the box toward the trapped woman's abdomen. [5]This popular ilusion is designed so that a woman appears to be laying full length in a box that rests on a table. [6]Her hands and head protrude through holes in the ends of the box. [7]In some versions of the trick, her hands and ankels are tied with ropes, which come threw the sides. [8]The magician procedes to saw the box in half. [9]The two halves are than seperated, but you can't see inside because metal sheets have slid down over the cut ends of the box. [10]Finally, the two halves are pushed together again, the sheets of metal are removed, and miraculously the woman is whole and very much alive.

[11]How is this done? [12]The fact is, the ilusion involves to women. [13]When the props are brought onto the stage, one woman is all ready hidden in the table. [14]As the woman on stage climbs into the box, the one whose hidden climbs up into the box through a trap in the table and pokes her feet out the end. [15]She sets up, with her head bent forward between her knees. [16]The other

woman draws her knees up to her chin. [17]Only an empty space lies in the path of the descending saw.

READING AND WRITING IN RESPONSE TO TEXTBOOKS

The following excerpt, which is adapted from an introductory psychology text-book, explains how we determine what people are like.

[1]Consider for an moment the enourmous amount of information about other people to which we are exposed. [2]How are we able to decide what is important and what is not, and to make judgments about the characteristics of others? [3]Social psychologists interested in this question study principals of **social cognition**—the processes that underly our understanding of the social world. [4]They have learned that individuals have highly developed **schemas,** sets of cognitions about people and social experiences. [5]These schemas organize information stored in memory, represent in our minds the way the social world operates, and give us a framework to categorize, remember, and interpert information relating to social stimuli. . . .

[6]We typically hold schemas for particular types of people in our enviornments. [7]Our schema for "teacher," for instance, generally consists of a number of characteristics: knowledge of the subject matter he or she is teaching, a desire to impart that knowledge, and an awareness of the student's need to understand what is been said. [8]Or we may hold a schema for "mother" that includes the characteristics of warmth, nurturcnee, and caring. [9]Regardless of their accuracy . . . schemas are important because they organize the way in which we recall, recognize, and categorize information about others. [10]Moreover, they allow us to make predictions of what others are like on the basis of relatively little information, since we all ready tend to fit people into schemas we no even when their is not much concrete evidence to go on.

Source: Adapted from Robert S. Feldman, *Essentials of Understanding Psychology,* 4th ed. (McGraw-Hill, 2000), p. 520. Copyright © 2000 The McGraw-Hill Companies. Used by permission of The McGraw-Hill Companies.

1. Cross out the 11 misspelled and frequently confused words. Write the corrections above the line.

2. Which word in sentence 2 is an exception to spelling rule 3 (adding an ending to words with a final *e*)?

   _____

3. In the first paragraph, which incorrectly spelled word might have been correctly spelled if it were broken into parts?

   _____

4. Which two words have an incorrect spelling that suggests incorrect pronunciations?

_____

writing topic: The textbook excerpt says that "we tend to fit people into schemas . . . even when there is not much concrete evidence to go on." How often do you think we make mistakes when we fit people into schema? Give examples to support your claim.

Capitalizing and Punctuating Correctly

My attitude toward punctuation is that it ought to be as conventional as possible. The game of golf would lose a good deal if croquet mallets and billiard cues were allowed on the putting green.

—Ernest Hemingway, author of *The Sun Also Rises, The Old Man and the Sea,* and other novels

Reflection: What do you think would happen if there were no punctuation rules?

WHAT YOU WILL LEARN

When to capitalize

When to use periods, question marks, and exclamation points to end sentences

When to use commas

How to use apostrophes with contractions and possessives

How to punctuate quotations

WHY YOU WILL LEARN IT

so that you know when to use capital letters

so that you know how to end sentences correctly

so that you can separate sentence elements

so that you can use shortened forms and show ownership

so that you can reproduce the words of other people

CHAPTER 26

Using Capital Letters and End Marks

CHAPTER GOALS

By the end of this chapter, you will learn to

Apply twelve important capitalization rules

Use periods, question marks, and exclamation points

You learned early that sentences begin with a capital letter and end with a period. In this chapter, you will learn other capitalization rules and other marks for ending sentences.

RULE 1. CAPITALIZE NAMES OF PEOPLE AND ANIMALS

Capitalize

George Bush	Lucinda	Puffy
Hank	Malcolm X	Rover

Do Not Capitalize

man	girl	cat
boy	leader	dog

I asked Gloria if I should name my dog Rags.

Capital letters appear in *German shepherd* and *French poodle* because nationalities are capitalized.

RULE 2. CAPITALIZE TITLES BEFORE PEOPLE'S NAMES

Capitalize

Aunt Helen	President Bush	Rabbi Schwartz
Judge Tipton	Private Williams	Reverend Jones
Mayor Browning	Professor Smith	Senator Hernandez

Do Not Capitalize

my aunt	a president	a rabbi
a judge	a private	the reverend
the mayor	a professor	our senator

The guest of honor, Governor Ruiz, who used to be the mayor of our city, shook hands with my Uncle Roy and your aunt.

422

RULE 3. ALWAYS CAPITALIZE THE PERSONAL PRONOUN *I*

Lesley and I are leaving for a weekend vacation.

RULE 4. CAPITALIZE NAMES OF NATIONALITIES, LANGUAGES, AND RELIGIONS

In both noun and adjective form, the names of nationalities, languages, and religions should be capitalized.

Capitalize

African art	Canadian border	Chinese food	Irish
American	Catholic	German	Judaism

We went to the museum to see the exhibit of Indian jewelry and then went out for Thai food.

26.1 ACTIVITY

Fill in the blanks according to the directions given.

EXAMPLE Use a nationality:

I have never been fond of ___Mexican___ cooking.

1. Use a language:

   Mario regrets that he never studied _____.

2. Use the name and title of a senator:

   Several politicians attended the fundraiser, including _____.

3. Use the name of an animal:

   As a child, I had a parakeet named _____.

4. Use the name and title of a religious leader:

   The sermon was delivered by _____.

5. Use a nationality:

   Circle Cinema is showing a series of _____ films this weekend.

6. Refer to yourself with a pronoun:

   Marcus hopes that _____ will help him.

RULE 5. CAPITALIZE NAMES OF SPECIFIC GEOGRAPHIC LOCATIONS

Capitalize

Blue Ridge Mountains	Nashville, Tennessee	Route 66
Grand Canyon	Oregon	the South
Lake Michigan	Pacific Ocean	South America

Do Not Capitalize

the mountains	a city	the highway
canyon	state	south
a lake	the ocean	continent

We drove on Route 80 and then on a two-lane highway until we got to the foothills of the Allegheny Mountains.

RULE 6. CAPITALIZE NAMES OF SPECIFIC ORGANIZATIONS, COMPANIES, INSTITUTIONS, COLLEGES, AND BUILDINGS

Capitalize

American Red Cross	Friars Club	Republican Party
Chrysler Corporation	General Foods	St. Elizabeth Hospital
Disneyland	Ohio University	Sears Tower

Do Not Capitalize

organization	club	political party
car manufacturer	company	hospital
amusement park	university	building

Jerry applied for a job with General Foods, but he really wanted to work for an insurance company.

RULE 7. CAPITALIZE NAMES OF HISTORIC EVENTS, DOCUMENTS, AND PERIODS

Capitalize

Battle of Gettysburg	Magna Carta	Roaring Twenties
Declaration of Independence	Renaissance	Vietnam War

Do Not Capitalize

important battle	charter	wild era
document	historical period	war

The peace treaty following World War did not end all wars.

RULE 8. CAPITALIZE REFERENCES TO GOD AND SACRED BOOKS AND DOCUMENTS

Capitalize words that refer to God or a supreme being of any religion, as well as the pronouns that refer to these words. Also capitalize the names of sacred books and documents.

Capitalize

Allah	God	the Lord	the Torah
the Bible	the Koran	the Old Testament	the Trinity

Do Not Capitalize

a deity	the gods	a sacred scroll

Many people who do not believe in any religion still pray to the Almighty and ask Him for help.

26.2 ACTIVITY

Fill in the blanks in the following sentences according to the directions given.

EXAMPLE   Use a specific geographic location:

I wish I could travel to *Houston, Texas*   .

1. Use the name of a specific company or business:

After graduation, I would like to work for _____.

2. Use a specific historic event, period, or document:

I have always wanted to learn more about _____.

3. Use the name of a sacred book or document:

In religion class, the children are studying _____.

4. Use the name of a specific organization:

This year I will make a charitable donation to _____.

5. Use the names of specific geographic locations:

When I lived in _____, I enjoyed visiting _____.

6. Use specific historic events, periods, or documents:

I did well on the part of the test covering _____, but I had

trouble with the part on _____.

RULE 9. CAPITALIZE NAMES OF MONTHS, DAYS, AND HOLIDAYS

Capitalize
Independence Day   January   Tuesday

Do Not Capitalize
holiday   month   day   spring

My favorite holiday is Thanksgiving, which is always on the same day: Thursday.

RULE 10. CAPITALIZE SPECIFIC BRAND NAMES

Capitalize
Buick   Jello   Pepsi
Cheerios   Nike tennis shoes   Pillsbury brownie mix

Do Not Capitalize
car   gelatin   cola
cereal   tennis shoes   brownie mix

With my birthday money, I bought a London Fog raincoat, Reeboks, and a wool sweater.

RULE 11. CAPITALIZE THE FIRST AND LAST WORDS OF A TITLE AND EVERYTHING IN BETWEEN EXCEPT ARTICLES, CONJUNCTIONS, AND PREPOSITIONS

In titles, always capitalize the first and last words. In between, capitalize everything except articles (*a*, *an*, and *the*), conjunctions (joining words, such as *and*, *but*, *or*, and *since*), and prepositions (words such as *of*, *at*, *to*, *from*, *by*, and *in*).

> *In the Heat of the Night*   *The Sound of Music*
> *Sleepless in Seattle*   *The Once and Future King*

> *I hate it when schools ban books, particularly when they are as good as The Catcher in the Rye.*

CONNECT FOR SUCCESS: Capitalize Correctly in Your Classes

A number of words and phrases in each of your classes will be capitalized routinely, and you should learn what they are. For example, in business classes, names of companies, such as Mutual of Omaha, will be capitalized according to rule 6; in history classes, historic events, such as the Battle of the Bulge, will be capitalized according to rule 7; in literature classes, titles of literary works, such as *Death of a Salesman*, will be capitalized according to rule 11.

RULE 12. CAPITALIZE NAMES OF SPECIFIC COURSES

Capitalize

Algebra 112	Introduction to Psychology	Principles of Accounting
History 101	Physics Fundamentals	Spanish III

Do Not Capitalize

math	psychology	accounting
history	physics	language course

> *This semester I am enjoying Survey of Modern Drama, but I am struggling with Economics 101. I find economics boring.*

26.3 ACTIVITY

Fill in the blanks in the following sentences according to the directions given.

EXAMPLE   Use a brand name:

This week <u>Oreos</u> are on sale at the market.

1. Use the name of a movie with at least three words in the title:

   One of my favorite movies is _____.

2. Use a month:

   My birthday is in _____.

3. Use products with brand names (e.g., Wilson tennis racquet):

    I only want a(n) _____ and a(n) _____ for my birthday.

4. Use specific course titles:

    The professor teaching _____ is new this year, but the one

    teaching _____ is ready to retire.

5. Use the name of a specific holiday and a month:

    My favorite holiday is _____, partly because it is

    celebrated in _____.

6. Use the title of a book with at least three words:

    I already own a copy of _____.

26.4 COLLABORATIVE ACTIVITY

Pair up with a classmate and circle the first ten capital letters in a newspaper or magazine article. (Do not circle the capital letters that begin sentences.) Together, determine the reason for each capital.

ENDING SENTENCES

The period (.), the question mark (?), and the exclamation point (!) are **end marks.** They make the reader's job easier because they show where sentences end. They also convey meaning. To appreciate this fact, notice the different messages expressed in the following sentences, each with the same words.

> *The test is today.* [a statement of fact]
> *The test is today!* [shows strong emotion, perhaps surprise or fear]
> *The test is today?* [asks a question—is the test today?]

The period

Use a **period** (.) to end a sentence that makes a statement, makes a request, or gives an order.

Makes a statement:	*Today is Harry's birthday.*
Makes a request:	*Please open the window.*
Gives an order:	*Leave me alone.*

26.5 ACTIVITY

In the following blanks, write sentences according to the directions given. Use a period at the end.

EXAMPLE   Make a statement:

Joyce has moved here from Santa Fe.

1. Make a statement:

   _____

   _____

2. Make a request:

   _____

   _____

3. Give an order:

   _____

   _____

The question mark

Use the **question mark** (?) to end a sentence that asks a direct question. Here are some examples:

> _May I join you?_
> _Where is the nearest gas station?_
> _How is that possible?_

Some sentences pose a question, but that question is not in the speaker's or writer's exact words. These sentences are **indirect questions,** and they end with periods, not question marks.

Direct question:	_When does the play begin?_
Indirect question:	_I wonder when the play begins._
Direct question:	_Joel asked, "Will you help me?"_
Indirect question:	_Joel asked whether I would help him._

26.6 ACTIVITY

On a separate sheet, write three sentences that ask direct questions. Be sure to use question marks.

The exclamation point

Use an **exclamation point** (!) to express strong feeling. Here are three examples:

> _The house is on fire!_
> _I can't believe you said that!_
> _Get out of here before it's too late!_

Do not overuse the exclamation point. You should rely on your words to carry most of your strong feelings.

 PUNCTUATION ALERT

Do not use the exclamation point with a period or a question mark.

No:	_Why are you doing that!?_
Yes:	_Why are you doing that?_

PUNCTUATION ALERT

Use only one exclamation point at a time.

No: *Leave me alone!!*

Yes: *Leave me alone!*

26.7 ACTIVITY

On a separate sheet, write three sentences that show strong feeling. End each one with an exclamation point.

Composing at the computer

Because e-mail is supposed to be a fast method of communication, some people omit capital letters and end punctuation so they can write quicker. However, in e-mail you write for school or work, follow the rules you have learned in this chapter.

IF ENGLISH IS NOT YOUR FIRST LANGUAGE

1. If your native language is not based on the English alphabet (that is, if your language is Arabic, Chinese, Japanese, or another language that uses a different alphabet or alternative script), you may have some trouble seeing the importance of the difference in size between capital and lower-case letters. Try to pay particular attention to this feature of English when you read.

2. If your native language is a Romance language, you may not be accustomed to capitalizing the names of languages, religions, nationalities, and days of the week, so pay particular attention to the need to capitalize these words in English.

3. Remember that word order is different for direct and indirect questions.

   A. In a direct question, the helping verb *comes before* the subject.

      Is Alice going with us?

      Helping verb: *is*
      Subject: *Alice*
      Main verb: *going*

   B. In an indirect question, the helping verb *comes after* the subject in the part of the sentence that suggests the question.

      I asked whether Alice is going with us.

      Helping verb: *is*
      Subject: *Alice*
      Main verb: *going*

IF ENGLISH IS NOT YOUR FIRST LANGUAGE CONTINUED

C. In an indirect question, do not place all or part of the verb before the subject.

No: *The student asked why is the answer wrong.*
                                V   S

Yes: *The student asked why the answer is wrong.*
                                   S   V

26.7 CHAPTER REVIEW ACTIVITY

In the following passage, circle the letters that should be capitalized.

1938- President and Mrs. Roosevelt at Easter service.

[1]Together, franklin and eleanor roosevelt made a tremendous impact on the nation during its period of greatest economic need. [2]His new deal fought the great depression with intervention and a concern for social welfare. [3]Part of the reason for the success of the new deal was the dynamic personality of president franklin roosevelt, although it received much of its inspiration and power from congress and the american people as well. [4]Another source of aid to the people of the united states came from roosevelt's wife, eleanor, who recast the office of the

first lady with her fights for the underdog. [5]Her political activism is responsible for shaping the role of the first lady to one of white house activist.

[6]Some people criticized the new deal because it did not help sharecroppers and it preserved the inequities of corporate and industrial capitalism. [7]Nonetheless, new deal programs helped revive the democratic party, particularly in the traditionally democratic south and among big city labor organizations and ethnic groups. [8]Among new converts were african-americans and many women. [9]Two of the most important legacies of the new deal are economic stabilizers to ward off another depression and the establishment of a limited welfare state.

Source: Adapted from James West Davidson et al. *Nation of Nations,* 3rd ed. (New York: McGraw-Hill, 1998), pp. 930–31. Copyright © 1998 The McGraw-Hill Companies. Used by permission of The McGraw-Hill Companies.

26.8 CHAPTER REVIEW ACTIVITY

Write sentences according to the directions given. Be prepared to explain your choice of end punctuation.

1. Write a sentence that might be spoken in a restaurant. The sentence should make a statement.

   _____

   _____

2. Write a sentence that might be spoken in the classroom. The sentence should ask a direct question.

   _____

   _____

3. Write another sentence that might be spoken in the classroom. This sentence should ask an indirect question.

   _____

   _____

4. Write a sentence that expresses strong feeling.

   _____

   _____

5. Write a sentence that a parent might speak to a child. This sentence should make a request.

   _____

   _____

6. Write a sentence that a police officer might speak to a suspect. This sentence should give a command.

   _____

   _____

When the United States dropped two atomic bombs on Japan in 1945, one on Hiroshima (depicted in the photo) on August 6 and one on Nagasaki on August 9, World War II came to an end in the Pacific. The decision to end the war this way remains controversial. Many people maintain that the bombs saved lives; others claim that dropping the bombs was a mistake. You can read documents about the decision to drop the bombs at www.dannen.com/decision/ and decide for yourself.

writing topic: In this chapter, you learned about ending sentences with correct punctuation. Endings are important in many aspects of life. For example, using atomic bombs to end the war with Japan left a legacy we still feel today. Write about an important ending in your life, one that had a lasting effect, either positive or negative. For example, you might write about ending a friendship, quitting a job, graduating from high school, divorcing your spouse, or moving away from your childhood home. Describe the ending and its impact. Do you feel any different about the ending now that some time has passed?

suggestions for discovering ideas
- List as many endings as you can that you have experienced in the past ten years.
- Select one of the endings from your list and freewrite about it.

suggestions for drafting

- Your thesis or topic sentence (depending on whether you are writing an essay or a paragraph) can mention what came to an end and the effect of the ending, something like this: "When I quit smoking, I became very anxious."
- Try describing the ending first. Then go on to explain the effect of the ending.

suggestions for revising

- When you describe the ending, you will probably arrange details in chronological (time) order. For coherence, check to see if you need transitions that indicate time, such as *next, then, at the same time, later,* and *finally.*
- When you explain the impact of the ending, look for opportunities to use specific words. For example, instead of saying that, when you changed schools you "felt bad," say that you "felt insecure about making friends" and "self-conscious" about your accent.

RECHARGE: Lesson Summary

1. Capitalize the following.
   - names of people and animals (*Lorenzo, Spot*)
   - titles before people's names (*Professor Lorca, Uncle Henry*)
   - the personal pronoun *I*
   - nationalities, languages, and religions (*Spanish art, English*)
   - specific geographic locations (*Lake Michigan, Idaho*)
   - specific organizations, companies, institutions, colleges, and buildings (*American Legion, United Nations, Ford Motor Company*)
   - historic events, documents, and periods (*the Constitution, the Civil War*)
   - references to God and sacred books and documents (*the Bible, Jehovah*)
   - months, days, and holidays (*March, Monday, Christmas*)
   - specific brand names (*Coca-Cola, Reynolds Wrap*)
   - first and last words of a title and everything in between except articles, conjunctions, and prepositions (*From Here to Eternity*)
   - names of specific courses (*Introduction to Organic Chemistry*)

2. End sentences with a period for a statement of fact, a question mark for a question, or an exclamation point for strong emotion.

   I can come.
   Can I come?
   I can come!

CHAPTER 27

Using Commas

To appreciate the importance of commas, notice that the second sentence, with commas, is much easier to read than the first sentence, without them:

> *Without asking the boy the woman took his shovel pail and goggles and as far as I could tell she left.*

> *Without asking the boy, the woman took his shovel, pail, and goggles and, as far as I could tell, she left.*

USING COMMAS TO SEPARATE ITEMS IN A SERIES

A **series** is made up of three or more items. Use commas to separate the items in a series.

> *I bought <u>milk, bread, and cheese</u> at the store.*
> *The audience <u>clapped loudly, stood up, and cheered</u> on opening night.*
> *We searched for the kitten <u>under the porch, in the garage, behind the house, and in the basement.</u>*

 PUNCTUATION ALERT

Do not use a comma with a pair.

> *We ate <u>a sandwich and soup.</u>*

Do not use a comma if the items in a series are separated by *and* or *or*.

> *Peg enjoys <u>skiing and surfing and swimming.</u>*
> *We can <u>visit Grandma or go to a movie or stay at home.</u>*

27.1 ACTIVITY

Write a sentence using each of the following series or pairs. Be careful to use commas when they are needed.

EXAMPLE   calculus   trigonometry   or advanced geometry

> *I will take calculus, trigonometry, or advanced geometry in*
>
> *summer school.*

434

1. Kenny   Miguel   or Phil

_____

_____

2. the sweater   or the jacket

_____

_____

3. swims daily   lifts weights   and eats a low-fat diet

_____

_____

4. Memphis   and Nashville   and Knoxville

_____

_____

5. paint the living room   and repair the roof

_____

_____

6. roast beef   mashed potatoes   and gravy

_____

_____

7. ate supper   studied   watched television   and went to bed

_____

_____

8. listen carefully   take notes   and ask questions

_____

_____

9. hard work   and ambition

_____

_____

10. at home   at work   or at the gym

_____

_____

USING COMMAS AFTER INTRODUCTORY ELEMENTS

An **introductory element** is a word, phrase, or dependent clause that comes before the subject of a sentence. Here are some examples:

Troubleshooting

If you need to review dependent clauses or phrases, see pages 131 and 182.

Introductory word:	*Surprisingly,* ⟨*John*⟩ *agreed with us.* (subject)
Introductory phrase:	*Without a doubt,* ⟨*this snowfall*⟩ *will close the schools.* (subject)
Introductory dependent clause:	*If you are not busy,* ⟨*I*⟩ *would like you to come with me.* (subject)

Place a comma after an introductory word, phrase, or dependent clause.

Introductory word:	*Smiling, I walked away.*
Introductory phrase:	*In the cellar, we have a Ping-Pong table.*
Introductory dependent clause:	*Since you enjoy live theater, Joe bought you season tickets to the Community Playhouse.*

27.2 ACTIVITY

Place a comma after each introductory word, phrase, or dependent clause.

EXAMPLE According to one psychologist, people have poor self-images.

1. A generation ago psychologist Carl Rogers concluded that most people have low self-esteem.

2. In studies of low self-esteem even low-scoring people respond in the midrange of possible scores.

3. Actually most of us tend to view ourselves favorably, which is a phenomenon known as "self-serving bias."

4. After they are told they have succeeded people readily accept credit.

5. However people attribute their failures to such external factors as bad luck or the situation's inherent "impossibility."

6. For example athletes commonly credit themselves for their victories but attribute losses to bad breaks, bad referee calls, or the other team's superior effort or dirty play.

7. When people compare themselves with others self-serving bias is apparent.

8. According to surveys most businesspeople see themselves as more ethical than the average businessperson.

9. In the Netherlands most high school students rate themselves as more honest, persistent, original, friendly, and reliable than the average high school student.

10. Even if they have been hospitalized for accidents the majority of drivers claim to be safer and more skilled than the average driver.

27.3 COLLABORATIVE ACTIVITY

With two classmates, choose six of the following words, phrases, and dependent clauses, and use them to begin sentences that you compose. Be sure to follow each word, phrase, or clause with the subject of the sentence. Also, be sure to use commas after the introductory elements. Use a separate sheet.

EXAMPLE   at noon

At noon, I always break for lunch.

at midnight	laughing
before you leave	under the bed
concerned	when the game ended
confused	while you were gone
in the middle of the night	whistling softly

USING COMMAS WITH COORDINATION

In Chapter 7, you learned that an **independent clause** has a subject and a verb and can stand as a sentence. Now is a good time to review that material.

Independent clause: *the dog barked all night*
Sentence: *The dog barked all night.*

Independent clause: *we could not sleep*
Sentence: *We could not sleep.*

Troubleshooting

If you need to review coordinating conjunctions, see page 115.

Coordination is the joining of two independent clauses in one sentence, using one of the following **coordinating conjunctions.**

and	for	or	yet
but	nor	so	

The dog barked all night, so we could not sleep.

In Chapter 7, you learned that, when you join independent clauses with a coordinating conjunction, you should place a comma before the conjunction. Here are some examples:

The doctor stitched the wound ⟨, and⟩ she wrote a prescription for pain.
I asked you a question ⟨, but⟩ you did not answer.
You can leave with Lauren now ⟨, or⟩ you can leave with Alonzo later.
The street department closed the road ⟨, so⟩ workers could repair the water pipe.

 PUNCTUATION ALERT

Do not use a comma unless an independent clause appears on *both* sides of the coordinating conjunction.

No comma: *I parked the car and went into the house.* [There is no independent clause after *and*.]

27.4 ACTIVITY

Use a coordinating conjunction to combine each pair of independent clauses into one sentence. Remember to use commas correctly.

EXAMPLE   the Radio Act of 1927 is about eighty years old.
it still demonstrates the basic principles underlying broadcast regulation

The Radio Act of 1927 is about eighty years old, but it still demonstrates the basic principles underlying broadcast regulation.

1. the Radio Act of 1927 made the electromagnetic spectrum publicly owned
    it eliminated private ownership of radio frequencies

    _____

    _____

2. it required radio stations to operate in the public interest
    it prohibited government censorship of broadcast networks

    _____

    _____

3. an important provision was the creation of the Federal Radio Commission (FRC)
    the FRC established radio coverage areas

    _____

    _____

4. broadcasters could accept the decisions of the FRC
    they could call for a judicial review

    _____

    _____

5. Congress passed the Communications Act of 1934 to streamline government regulation of communications
    it created the Federal Communications Commission (FCC) with broader powers

    _____

    _____

    _____

6. the FCC's powers relate to all wireless and wire forms of communication (including the telephone)
    the FCC does not have power over communication used by the military or government

    _____

    _____

    _____

27.5 ACTIVITY

Place commas where they are needed in the following sentences. Two sentences are correct.

1. Our electricity was not restored for two days so all the food in the refrigerator spoiled.

2. The lecture series was well publicized but very few people attended.

3. We asked you to chair the committee for you are the most organized member.

4. I woke up to a heavy snowfall and went out to shovel the driveway.

5. Kevin jumped over the fence and then he ran across the backyard.

6. I will not vote for Pelligrini and I will not campaign for him.

7. The tutors in the Writing Center can react to your draft or they can answer specific questions about writing.

8. Gretchen arrived early enough to eat with us but too late to see Harold.

9. Luigi has been in this country for only a year yet he speaks our language well.

10. Frank is the best ball handler on the team so he usually sets up all the plays.

11. National Public Radio is interesting to listen to and it is entertaining.

12. I will tell you what happened but I am not sure you will believe me.

USING COMMAS WITH NONESSENTIAL ELEMENTS

A **nonessential element** is a word, phrase, or dependent clause that is not necessary (it is "nonessential") for identifying a person, a place, an object, an idea, or an emotion referred to. In the following examples, the underlined elements are nonessential.

The governor, who is running for reelection, will visit our town. ["Who is running for reelection" is nonessential because it is not necessary for identifying who will visit.]

Carl, anxious to make the team, is lifting weights daily. ["Anxious to make the team" is nonessential because it is not necessary for identifying who is lifting weights.]

Hilton Head, a beautiful coastal town, is our destination. ["A beautiful coastal town" is nonessential because it is not necessary for identifying the destination.]

Nonessential elements are set off with commas. Use two commas if the nonessential element is in the middle of the sentence and one comma if it is at the end of the sentence.

Nonessential element
in the middle: *My guitar teacher, Al Smith, plays in a rock band.*

Nonessential element
at the end: *I had an interview with the personnel director, an interesting person.*

Words, phrases, and dependent clauses necessary for identifying a person, a place, an object, an idea, or an emotion are **essential elements.** They are *not* set off with commas. Here is an example:

No commas: *The hotel that I visited had clean rooms.* ["That I visited" is necessary to identify which hotel is referred to.]

27.6 ACTIVITY

Underline the nonessential elements in the following sentences, and then set them off with commas. One sentence is correct.

EXAMPLE   The truckers' strike, <u>now in its second week</u>, shows no sign of ending.

1. Kevin Costner the star and director of many popular movies will visit our city.

2. Hans and Carrie bought a house a two-bedroom cottage.

3. Nashville known as "Music City, USA" is an exciting place to live.

4. I have always admired my grandmother who raised four children by herself during the Great Depression.

5. Rita Rudner who is a gifted comedian is currently appearing in Las Vegas.

6. You should take your broken watch to Claude Kingsley who is a reputable jeweler and watch repairperson.

7. The woman who works here is also a township trustee.

8. I just finished reading *Killer Angels* a Pulitzer prize–wining book about the Battle of Gettysburg.

9. Monopoly which has been a popular game for many years is still a best-seller.

10. Carly had to say good-bye to Mandy her best friend for ten years.

USING COMMAS WITH PARENTHETICAL ELEMENTS

A **parenthetical element** interrupts the flow of a sentence. It can be omitted without significant loss of meaning. Parenthetical elements are expressions such as these:

as a matter of fact	however	of course
believe it or not	in fact	on the other hand
by the way	in my opinion	therefore
for example	it seems to me	without a doubt

Notice in the following examples that the underlined parenthetical expressions can be removed with no significant loss of meaning:

With parenthetical expression: *This restaurant, <u>it seems to me</u>, has excellent service.*

Without parenthetical expression: *This restaurant has excellent service.*

Parenthetical elements are set off with commas. Use one comma for a parenthetical element that comes first or last. Use two commas for a parenthetical element in the middle.

Therefore, that answer is wrong.
More people, if you ask me, oppose violent programming.
Phillips is the best choice for mayor, in my opinion.

27.7 ACTIVITY

Write sentences in the following blanks according to the directions given. Be sure to use commas correctly.

EXAMPLE   Use "of course" in the middle:

You can, of course, make up your own mind

1. Use "as a matter of fact" at the beginning:

   _____

   _____

2. Use "in fact" at the beginning:

   _____

   _____

3. Use "in my opinion" in the middle:

   _____

   _____

4. Use "without a doubt" in the middle:

   _____

   _____

5. Use "however" at the end:

   _____

   _____

6. Use "it seems to me" at the end:

   _____

   _____

USING COMMAS WITH DATES AND ADDRESSES

Two rules govern the use of commas with dates and addresses.

1. Use commas to separate items in dates.

   The baby was born on Tuesday, November 2, 2005, in Northside Hospital.
   Saturday, October 30, is my wedding day.

If no day is given, then a comma is not used between the month and the year.

   The new manager began work in June 2004.

2. Use commas to separate items in addresses.

   Orlando, Florida, is the home of Disney World.
   My address is 5171 Sampson Drive, Youngstown, Ohio 44505.

As the example 2 shows, no comma is used before the zip code.

27.8 ACTIVITY

Complete the following sentences according to the directions given, being sure to use commas correctly.

EXAMPLE   Complete the sentence with the city and state where your school is located:

My school is located in *Ann Arbor, Michigan.*

1. Complete the sentence with the date of your birth:
   I was born _____

2. Complete the sentence with your address:
   Currently, I live at _____

3. Complete the sentence with the month and year you entered college:
   I began college in _____

4. Complete the sentence with a city and state you would like to visit:
   I wish I could go to _____

AVOIDING MISUSED COMMAS

If you keep the following in mind, you will not use commas incorrectly.

1. Do not use a comma with a pair.

   No: *We ate a sandwich, and soup.*
   Yes: *We ate a sandwich and soup.*

2. Do not use a comma if the items in a series are separated by *and* or *or*.

   No: *Peg enjoys skiing, and surfing, and swimming.*
   No: *We can visit Grandma, or go to a movie, or stay at home.*
   Yes: *Peg enjoys skiing and surfing and swimming.*
   Yes: *We can visit Grandma or go to a movie or stay at home.*

3. Do not use a comma after *and* in a series.

   No: *My birthday presents included a sweater, a CD, and, a bracelet.*
   Yes: *My birthday presents included a sweater, a CD, and a bracelet.*

4. Do not use a comma between a subject and verb.

   No: *The children on the playground, ran in circles.*
   Yes: *The children on the playground ran in circles.*

IF ENGLISH IS NOT YOUR FIRST LANGUAGE

1. If your native language does not use English script, punctuation may be new to you. Ask a writing center tutor or someone else you trust to help you edit for punctuation.

2. Do not use a comma whenever you would pause in speaking. This method, used in some languages, is unreliable in English.

27.9 CHAPTER REVIEW ACTIVITY

Add eleven commas where they are needed in the following paragraph. Be prepared to explain the reason for every comma you use.

[1]The gazelle a kind of antelope is a member of the cattle family. [2]Usually found in Africa or Asia the gazelle is a graceful animal with horns that sweep upward. [3]Depending on the animal's species the horns may be heavy streamlined or bent into a V or U shape. [4]These horns can be 14 inches long. [5]All the males have horns and in some species the females also have horns. [6]About 26 inches high at the shoulder the gazelle is very fast. [7]It can in fact outrun a greyhound. [8]The gazelle is one of the swiftest land animals and it is one of the most graceful.

27.10 CHAPTER REVIEW ACTIVITY

Add twenty-eight commas where they are needed in the following paragraphs. Be prepared to explain the reason for every comma you use.

[1]Kareem Abdul-Jabbar with his extraordinary height of 7 feet, 2 inches is a top record-holder in basketball. [2]When he retired in 1989 he became the first player to score more than 38,000 points. [3]Among his other records were seasons played games played field goals and shots blocked.

[4]Abdul-Jabbar the man who invented the skyhook was born Ferdinand Lewis Alcindor Jr. on April 16 1947 in New York City New York. [5]He adopted his Arabic name in 1971 six years after he joined the Black Muslim movement. [6]As a high school basketball player Lew Alcindor led his team to a 95–6 record and scored 2,067 points. [7]He received more than 100 offers of college scholarships and chose the University of California at Los Angeles. [8]He enrolled there and he led UCLA to three consecutive National Collegiate Athletic Association championships. [9]He was the only player chosen three times as the collegiate All-American.

[10]Upon graduation from UCLA Abdul-Jabbar was the leading draft choice for the professional teams and was soon claimed by the Milwaukee Bucks. [11]At center position he continued to play spectacularly. [12]In 1970 he was rookie of the year. [13]The next year he was awarded the Maurice Podoloff Trophy which is presented annually to the most valuable player in the National Basketball Association. [14]This award incidently is one Abdul-Jabbar went on to win six times. [15]In 1980 he was traded to the Los Angeles Lakers. [16]He helped the Lakers win the championship in 1980 1982 1985 1987 and 1988. [17]He became the second NBA player to score more than 30,000 career points and he became the NBA's all-time field-goal scoring leader. [18]When he finished his twentieth season in the NBA in 1989 this great athlete retired.

27.11 COLLABORATIVE CHAPTER REVIEW ACTIVITY

Pair up with a classmate; on a separate sheet, write sentences to illustrate every comma rule in this chapter. Be sure to label each sentence to indicate which rule it illustrates.

GETTING IN GEAR: IDEAS FOR WRITING

© 2006, Reprinted courtesy of Bunny Hoest and Parade Magazine.

The cartoon illustrates the fact that an improperly placed comma can affect meaning and cause misunderstanding. To learn more about using commas to prevent misunderstanding, visit www.ucalgary.ca/UofC/eduweb/grammar/course/punctuation/3_4j.htm.

writing topic: Misunderstanding can occur for many reasons and have a range of effects from humorous to tragic. Tell about a misunderstanding you experienced and explain its cause and/or effects.

suggestions for prewriting
- List five misunderstandings in which you have been involved.
- Select one of the misunderstandings and freewrite about it. If you need more ideas, do a second, more focused freewriting.

suggestion for drafting: Your topic sentence (for a paragraph composition) or thesis (for an essay) can mention the misunderstanding and its cause, its effect, and/or how serious it was, like one of these:
- "When my roommate forgot to give me a phone message from my boss, I almost lost my job."
- "I hurt my best friend when she misunderstood a comment I made."
- "My family and I are still laughing about the surprise fiftieth birthday party I gave for my father, who was really only forty-eight."

suggestions for revising
- Ask a reliable reader to note whether it is clear exactly what happened and why it was a misunderstanding. If something is not clear, ask your reader to suggest ways to solve the problem.
- Look for opportunities to vary your sentence openers, as explained in Chapter 23.

suggestion for editing: Edit an extra time to check for correct comma usage, paying particular attention to opening words, phrases, and dependent clauses.

RECHARGE: Lesson Summary

1. Use commas to separate items in a series.

   In Spain, we saw beautiful churches, historic mosques, and breathtaking mountains.

2. Use a comma after an introductory word, phrase, or dependent clause.

   Because of the fog, our flight was canceled.

3. Use a comma before a coordinating conjunction joining independent clauses.

   Oprah Winfrey is a television star, but she is also a philanthropist.

4. Use commas to set off nonessential words, phrases, and dependent clauses.

   The child, barely four years old, already knew how to read.

5. Use commas to set off parenthetical elements.

   The stock market, in my opinion, is too volatile right now.

6. Use commas to set off items in dates and addresses.

   The wedding has been rescheduled for Saturday, May 29, 2008, at five o'clock.

   The Metropolitan Museum in New York City, New York, is a national treasure.

CHAPTER **28**

Using Apostrophes

The apostrophe has two main purposes: to help form contractions and to signal ownership. In this chapter, you will learn about both of these purposes.

USING APOSTROPHES WITH CONTRACTIONS

A **contraction** is formed when two words are combined and one or more letters are omitted. An apostrophe (') stands for what is omitted. Some common contractions are shown in the following list.

Two Words	One-Word Contraction with Apostrophe for Omitted Letter(s)	Omitted Letter(s)
are not	aren't	o
cannot [exception]	can't	no
could not	couldn't	o
did not	didn't	o
do not	don't	o
does not	doesn't	o
he is	he's	i
he will	he'll	wi
I am	I'm	a
I had	I'd	ha
I have	I've	ha
I will	I'll	wi
is not	isn't	o
it is/it has	it's	i/ha
let us	let's	u
she did	she'd	di
she will	she'll	wi
should not	shouldn't	o
there is	there's	i
they are	they're	a
they would	they'd	woul
we are	we're	a
were not	weren't	o

Troubleshooting

To be sure you understand the difference between the contraction *it's* and the possessive *its*, see page 254.

Two Words	One-Word Contraction with Apostrophe for Omitted Letter(s)	Omitted Letter(s)
where is	where's	i
who has	who's	ha
who is	who's	i
you are	you're	a
you have	you've	ha

Note: The contraction form of *will not* is the unusual form *won't*.

 SPELLING ALERT

Be sure to place the apostrophe at the site of the omitted letter or letters.

No: *did'nt*

Yes: *didn't*

28.1 ACTIVITY

Fill in the following blanks with the correct contraction forms. Remember to use apostrophes for omitted letters.

EXAMPLE he will = _____*he'll*_____

1. I am = _____
2. we are = _____
3. cannot = _____
4. I will = _____
5. they would = _____

6. he is = _____
7. she did = _____
8. it is = _____
9. will not = _____
10. should not = _____

28.2 ACTIVITY

Underline each contraction in the following sentences. Then write what the contraction stands for in the blank.

EXAMPLE _____*Here is*_____ Here's the book I've wanted.

_____*I have*_____

1. _____ They'll be here in an hour.

2. _____ I can't go because it's late.

_____

3. _____ The receptionist said she'd be with me in a minute.

4. _____ It's been years since I've seen you.

_____

Part 8

5. _____ I'll help you if you're sure your instructor won't mind.
   _____

6. _____ I wouldn't worry just yet, because you've still got time to
   _____ solve your problem.

7. _____ Let's try to figure out who can't come to the party.
   _____

8. _____ Where's the picture frame you said you didn't want
   _____ anymore?

28.3 ACTIVITY

Write the contraction form above the underlined words. Remember to use apostrophes for omitted letters.

EXAMPLE   Sometimes the history books <u>do not</u> *don't* create an accurate impression of the soldiers who fought the Revolutionary War.

DISPIRITED SOLDIERS.

1. <u>It is</u> amazing that we won the Revolutionary War, because the colonies <u>did not</u> have a standing army, and the soldier volunteers <u>were not</u> well trained.

2. The volunteers were farmers who <u>could not</u> fight during harvest time, so <u>they would</u> return home when they had to harvest the crops.

3. The rich <u>would not</u> fight, so the burden fell to the poor and the young.

4. By 1777, Congress had realized we <u>were not</u> going to win the war without more capable soldiers, so there <u>was not</u> anything else they could do but institute the draft.

5. Each town had a quota to fill, but <u>there is</u> evidence that the rich paid the poor to fight for them.

6. Thus, the Continental Army <u>was not</u> much more than an army of young boys and the poor, most of whom <u>could not</u> vote because of lack of property and age.

28.4 ACTIVITY

From the list beginning on page 446, pick six contractions, including any that are new to you or that you have not used correctly in the past. On a separate sheet, write sentences using the contractions you have chosen.

CONNECT FOR SUCCESS: Check before Using Contractions in Your Classes

Contractions are not appropriate in the most formal writing, and some instructors prefer that you do not use them. To be on the safe side, check with your instructors to learn how they feel about contractions in student writing.

USING APOSTROPHES TO SHOW OWNERSHIP

Possessive forms show ownership by indicating that one person or thing belongs to another person or thing. As the following examples show, the apostrophe is used to signal possession.

Jake's flute [The flute belongs to Jake.]

Maria's idea [The idea belongs to Maria.]

the hotel's towels [The towels belong to the hotel.]

The following rules will help you use apostrophes to show possession.

1. If a *noun* does not end in *-s*, form the possessive by adding an apostrophe and an *s*. Use this rule for both singular and plural nouns.

Noun Not Ending in -S + 'S = Possessive
dog + 's = dog's   *The dog's collar is too tight.*
car + 's = car's   *The car's transmission must be replaced.*
children + 's = children's   *The children's toys are lost.*

2. If a *singular noun* ends in *-s*, form the possessive by adding an apostrophe and an *s*.

Singular Noun Ending in -S + 'S = Possessive
Doris + 's = Doris's   *Doris's ankle is sprained.*
Mr. Stills + 's = Mr. Stills's *Mr. Stills's garden is beautiful.*
dress + 's = dress's   *The dress's hem is torn.*

3. If a *plural noun* ends in -*s*, form the possessive by adding just an apostrophe.

    Plural Noun Ending in -*S* + ' = Possessive

    neighbors + ' = neighbors'   *My neighbors' houses were robbed.*
    boys + ' = boys'   *The boys' basketballs need air.*
    parents + ' = parents'   *Some parents' discipline techniques are questionable.*

→ **GRAMMAR ALERT**

Possessive pronouns do not take an apostrophe.

Yes	**No**
mine	mine's
yours	your's
his	his's
hers	her's
its	it's [*it's* means "it is" or "it has"]
ours	our's
their	their's

→ **GRAMMAR ALERT**

Do not use an apostrophe with plurals that do not show possession.

No: *The students' asked several questions.*
Yes: *The students asked several questions.*

28.5 ACTIVITY

In each of the following items, write the word that shows what is owned in the first column. Write the word that identifies the owner in the second column.

	What Is Owned	The Owner
EXAMPLE the cat's toy	*toy*	*cat*

	What Is Owned	The Owner
1. the plant's root system	_____	_____
2. the moon's glow	_____	_____
3. sociology's perspective	_____	_____
4. my mother's ring	_____	_____

5. a child's smile _____ _____

6. Freud's psychoanalytic _____ _____
   theory

28.6 ACTIVITY

Rewrite the following phrases so that ownership is shown with possessive forms. Remember to use apostrophes.

EXAMPLES   the coat belongs to Mohammed *Mohammed's coat* _____

the books belong to the boys *the boys' books* _____

1. the hat belongs to the girl _____

2. the hats belong to the girls _____

3. the house belongs to Boris _____

4. the equipment belongs to the worker _____

5. the equipment belongs to the workers _____

6. the question belongs to James _____

7. the boots belong to the soldier _____

8. the boots belong to the soldiers _____

9. the papers belong to the men _____

10. the poem belongs to John Keats _____

11. the vote belongs to the senator _____

12. the votes belong to the senators *edn* _____

13. the responsibility belongs to the boss _____

14. the stories belong to O'Henry _____

15. the victory belongs to the players _____

28.7 ACTIVITY

Combine each pair of sentences into one sentence by using a possessive form.

EXAMPLE   The return policy is liberal.
The return policy belongs to the store.

The store's return policy is liberal. _____

_____

PART 8 CAPITALIZING AND PUNCTUATING CORRECTLY

1. Dr. Carlito has new office hours.
   The office hours are posted on his door.

   _____

   _____

2. Although I was careful, I tore the blouse.
   The blouse belonged to Cassandra.

   _____

   _____

3. The carpenters were pounding.
   The pounding gave me a headache.

   _____

   _____

4. The writings influenced the development of democracy.
   The writings were by John Locke.

   _____

   _____

5. The meetings are held in the library.
   The meetings are for hospital volunteers.

   _____

   _____

6. The techniques are controversial.
   The techniques belong to the filmmaker.

   _____

   _____

7. The conclusion was weak.
   The conclusion belonged to the essay.

   _____

   _____

8. The sale attracted many new customers.
   The sale belonged to the business. [*Hint: Business* is singular.]

   _____

   _____

9. The profits were the highest in recent history.
   The profits belonged to the businesses. [*Hint: Businesses* is plural.]

   _____

   _____

10. The car is double-parked.
    The car belongs to Luis.

   _____

   _____

28.8 ACTIVITY

Write sentences on a separate sheet using the possessive forms of the following terms.

1. friend
2. friends
3. teacher
4. teachers
5. Ms. Sykes
6. children

Composing at the computer

Be careful not to rely too heavily on your computer's spell checking function. It will not distinguish between contractions with omitted apostrophes and sound-alikes. Thus, it will not tell you when *cant* should be *can't*, when *wont* should be *won't*, and when *Id* should be *I'd*. Also, it will not distinguish between *its* and *it's*.

IF ENGLISH IS NOT YOUR FIRST LANGUAGE

You may find the forms *its* and *it's* confusing. Remember the following.

1. **Its** is a pronoun that shows ownership; it does not have an apostrophe, just as other pronouns that show ownership do not have apostrophes (*his, hers, theirs*).

   The toy train came off its tracks.

2. Use **it's** (with an apostrophe) only to mean "it is" or "it has."

   It's not easy to work and attend school. [It is not easy.]

   It's been years since you began studying yoga. [It has been years.]

28.9 CHAPTER REVIEW ACTIVITY

Fill in the blanks in the following sentences according to the directions given.

EXAMPLE   Use the contraction form of *are not*:

Students who ___aren't___ registered by Tuesday must drop the class.

1. Use the contraction form of *it is*:

   I explained that _____ too late to add a class.

2. Use the possessive form of *voter*:

   A _____ party affiliation affects how he or she responds to political news.

3. Use the contraction form of *does not*:

   If it _____ rain soon, the crops will die.

4. Use the possessive form of *animals:*

   This zoo tries to reproduce the _____ natural habitats.

5. Use the contraction form of *who is:*

   _____ responsible for this mix-up?

6. Use the possessive form of *Chris:*

   _____ plan has several advantages.

7. Use the contraction form of *they are:*

   Elections have meaning only if _____ competitive.

8. Use the possessive form of *salespeople:*

   I like to shop here because I trust the _____ advice.

9. Use the contraction form of *I am:*

   _____ taking yoga to improve my flexibility.

10. Use the possessive form of *crowd:*

    The _____ cheering distracted the quarterback.

28.10 CHAPTER REVIEW ACTIVITY

Add ten apostrophes where they are needed for possessives and contractions.

EXAMPLE   One North Carolina jury's members came from a surprising place.

[1]Wal-Mart shoppers are accustomed to finding a range of products in the store, but it came as a surprise when Cleveland County Civil and Criminal Superior Court used the store to fill its need for jurors. [2]However, thats exactly what happened in Shelby, North Carolina, when Judge Don Bridges asked the sheriffs office to solve the courts problem. [3]Apparently, the court ran out of prospective jurors. [4]The court needed last-minute jurors because some people didnt show up for jury duty, and others were disqualified. [5]Judge Bridges's order gave the sheriffs deputies three hours to round up fifty-five people, so deputies went to Wal-Mart and started handing out the judges subpoenas. [6]Some shoppers timelines were very tight; they had only thirty minutes to report to court. [7]Some shoppers complained, but deputies said they had no choice. [8]They admitted that it wasnt the best solution to the problem, but they werent aware of anything else they could do. [9]Fortunately, the jurors sense of civic duty—to say nothing of their sense of humor—kept them good-natured about the proceedings.

GETTING IN GEAR: IDEAS FOR WRITING

People can get news from many sources, including television networks, twenty-four-hour cable news channels, radio, the Internet—and, of course, newspapers like the one shown here. Google News has put a new spin on getting news, which you can check out at http://news.google.com/ The site has stories from over 4,500 worldwide news sources in English, and it is updated every fifteen minutes. You can get a variety of perspectives on the same news story, you can customize your version of Google News to focus on specific stories, and you can trace the history of a story.

writing topic: Explain what you think the most serious problem or issue is facing the United States today. Be sure to note why you think the problem or issue is the most serious.

suggestion for prewriting: Skim all the articles on the front page of your local newspaper or browse the Google News site. Then freewrite for about fifteen minutes on one of the subjects you read about.

suggestions for drafting
- Write an informal outline or an outline map to guide your draft. If you find you do not have enough ideas, do some additional prewriting.
- If you give multiple reasons for the seriousness of the issue or problem, you can arrange them in a progressive order.

suggestion for revising: Be sure you have shown why the problem or issue is serious. To do so, do you need to add more reasons or add more explanation to the reasons you have already given?

suggestion for editing: Edit one extra time to check your use of apostrophes for contractions and for possessive forms.

RECHARGE: Lesson Summary

1. Use an apostrophe to form contractions.

   - A contraction is formed when two words are combined and one or more letters are left out. The apostrophe takes the place of the missing letter or letters.
   - Contractions include words such as *didn't (did not), you're (you are),* and *there's (there is).*

2. Use an apostrophe to show ownership.

   - Add an *'s* to form the possessive of nouns that do not end in -s *(car + 's = car's engine; men + 's = men's room).*
   - Add an *'s* to form the possessive of singular nouns ending in -s *(boss + 's = boss's report).*
   - Add an *'* to plural nouns ending in -s *(trees + ' = trees' leaves).*

CHAPTER 29

Punctuating Quotations

CHAPTER GOALS

By the end of this chapter, you will learn to

Distinguish between direct and indirect quotations

Punctuate direct quotations

Many times when you write, you want to include the spoken or written words of others. This chapter will show you how to do that.

UNDERSTANDING DIRECT QUOTATIONS

A **direct quotation** is the reproduction of someone's exact spoken or written words. The exact words quoted are enclosed in quotation marks (" "). Here are some examples:

> *Marla said, "The soup is cold."* [The exact words Marla spoke are between the quotation marks.]
>
> *"Call me Ishmael," wrote Herman Melville.* [The exact words Melville wrote are between the quotation marks.]
>
> *"If I were you," Rami remarked, "I would take the job."* [The exact words Rami spoke are between two sets of quotation marks.]

A direct quotation has two parts:

- the exact words quoted
- a statement that notes who spoke or wrote the words

Here is an example:

> *Leo said, "I did well on the English test."*

> Exact words quoted: *I did well on the English test.*
>
> Statement that notes who spoke: *Leo said.*

Three arrangements are possible when you write direct quotations.

1. The exact words quoted can come at the beginning of the sentence.

   > *"Interest rates will rise if the trade agreement is signed," the economist predicted.*

2. The exact words quoted can come at the end of the sentence.

   > *The economist predicted, "Interest rates will rise if the trade agreement is signed."*

3. The exact words quoted can be divided between the beginning and the end of the sentence.

   "Interest rates will rise," the economist predicted, "if the trade agreement is signed."

PUNCTUATION ALERT

Look again at the preceding example sentences to see that periods and commas go *inside* quotation marks.

29.1 ACTIVITY

Place quotation marks around the exact words quoted in the following sentences. Remember, exact words can come at the beginning, at the end, or both at the beginning and the end. Periods and commas go *inside* quotation marks.

EXAMPLES   "You may not enter here," the security guard said.
                      "This model," the clerk explained, "is the best buy for the money."

1. Rhonda took a sip from the glass and gasped, This milk is sour.

2. I'll be with you shortly, the barber said.

3. A computer, he remarked, is a wise investment for a college student.

4. The cheerleaders shouted, Get that ball and score!

5. We need to simplify our lives, I announced.

6. Tell me what is wrong, the teacher said, and I will try to help.

PUNCTUATING DIRECT QUOTATIONS

To write direct quotations correctly, pay attention to these factors:

- quotation marks
- commas
- end marks
- capitalization

How these four factors are handled will depend on the nature of the quotation and where the quotation is placed in the sentence.

When the quotation comes first

When the quotation comes first, follow these models to punctuate and capitalize:

"We can leave now," she said.
"Can we leave now?" she asked.

Quotation marks:	Enclose the exact words quoted.
Comma:	Place a comma before the second quotation mark if the quotation makes a statement.

End mark: Place a question mark before the last quotation mark if the quotation asks a question. Use a period at the end of the sentence.

Capitalization: Capitalize the first word of the quotation. Do not capitalize the first word indicating who spoke unless it is a name, such as "Jeff" or "Ms. Akers."

29.2 ACTIVITY

Troubleshooting

Don't worry if you can't remember everything about punctuating quotations right now. Just check the models, and eventually you will remember on your own.

The following sentences have a direct quotation first. Rewrite the sentences in the blanks, using the correct punctuation and capitalization.

EXAMPLE This smoke detector needs batteries the fire inspector told me

"This smoke detector needs batteries," the fire inspector

told me.

1. Over 80 percent of the program schedule on major pay-cable services consists of theatrical motion pictures my communications instructor explained

   _____

   _____

2. There is no reason to be upset Mother explained

   _____

   _____

3. Is the clock fast I asked

   _____

   _____

4. We try to help children become independent problem solvers the school principal mentioned

   _____

   _____

5. I'm sorry to have bothered you the elderly man whispered

   _____

   _____

6. This is ridiculous Sheila muttered to herself

   _____

   _____

When the quotation comes second

When the quotation comes second, follow these models to punctuate and capitalize:

The child whined, "I want a drink."
The child asked, "Can I have a drink?"

Quotation marks:	Enclose the exact words quoted.
Comma:	Place the comma after the statement of who spoke or wrote the words.
End mark:	Place the end punctuation inside the last quotation mark.
Capitalization:	Capitalize the first word of the quotation.

29.3 ACTIVITY

The following sentences have direct quotations second. Rewrite the sentences in the blanks, using the correct punctuation and capitalization.

EXAMPLE The teenager behind the counter asked do you want fries with your burger

The teenager behind the counter asked, "Do you want fries with your burger?"

1. The coach yelled watch out for the fast break

_____

_____

2. The librarian said if you cannot be quieter, you will have to leave

_____

_____

3. I asked myself where did I go wrong

_____

_____

4. My sociology teacher said socialization is the process whereby people learn the values, behavior, and attitudes appropriate for their culture

_____

_____

_____

5. The bus driver explained I can only accept exact change

_____

_____

6. The preschool teacher explained outdoor play provides children with many opportunities to solve intellectual problems

_____

_____

_____

When the quotation is split

When the quotation is divided into two parts, follow these models to punctuate and capitalize:

"Before class is over," said Professor Samuels, "let me know if you have any questions."

"We should leave now," said Dan. "The concert is over."

"Is it true," Katrina asked, "that you resigned?"

Quotation marks:	Enclose the exact words quoted.
Comma:	Place a comma before the second quotation mark. Place another comma after the statement of who spoke or wrote the words when the first part of the quotation does not form a sentence.
End mark:	Place a period or a question mark before the last quotation mark. Place a period after the statement of who spoke or wrote the words when the first part of the quotation forms a sentence.
Capitalization:	Capitalize the first word of the quotation. Capitalize the first word of the second part of the quotation only when the first part of the quotation is a sentence.

29.4 ACTIVITY

The following sentences have direct quotations divided in two parts. Rewrite the sentences with the correct punctuation and capitalization.

EXAMPLE   Before you leave said Donna I need to speak to you

"Before you leave," said Donna, "I need to speak to you."

1. Given the opportunity bragged the statistician I can prove anything with statistics

2. You can do it I told myself all you have to do is concentrate [*Hint:* The thought forms two sentences.]

3. The earliest example of executive power in the colonies noted the political science professor was the position of royal governor

4. Why is it Laura asked that everything goes wrong at once

5. If you believe in yourself I always say you can accomplish anything

_____

_____

6. Dinner is at six o'clock said Mimi please don't be late [*Hint:* The spoken words form two sentences.]

_____

_____

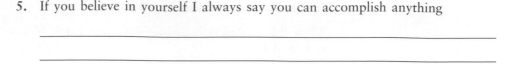

CONNECT FOR SUCCESS: Use Direct Quotations in Your Courses

Research papers you write in your other courses will generally include direct quotations. You may also need to use direct quotations in briefer papers you write. For example, in an essay about gun control for a political science class, you may decide to quote the Second Amendment to the Constitution, like this:

According to Amendment II, "A well regulated Militia, being necessary to the security of a free State, the right of the people to keep and bear Arms, shall not be infringed."

UNDERSTANDING INDIRECT QUOTATIONS

An **indirect quotation** *refers* to someone's words or thoughts but *does not reproduce* those words or thoughts exactly. Instead, it reports *about* what the person said or thought. Indirect quotations do not appear in quotation marks.

Direct Quotation— Exact Words or Thoughts Are Reproduced	Indirect Quotation— Exact Words or Thoughts Are Not Reproduced
The clerk said, "I'll be back."	*The clerk said he would be back.*
Lee advised, "Count to ten before speaking in anger."	*Lee advised me to count to ten before speaking in anger.*
The waiter asked, "Do you want separate checks?"	*The waiter asked whether we wanted separate checks.*
I wondered, "Where are we going?"	*I wondered where we were going.*

 PUNCTUATION ALERT

Thoughts may be handled either as direct quotations or as indirect quotations.

Direct quotation: *I said to myself, "I can do this."*
Indirect quotation: *I told myself that I can do this.*

29.5 ACTIVITY

Rewrite the indirect quotations in the following sentences to make them direct quotations.

EXAMPLE   I wondered whether I would get the job.

I wondered, "Will I get the job?"

1. The speaker explained that conformity can lead to disastrous effects.

_____

_____

2. The police officer explained that the crime may never be solved.

_____

_____

3. Joseph replied that he was certain a compromise could be reached.

_____

_____

4. The electrician said that rewiring the lamp costs $50.

_____

_____

5. The usher asked where we were sitting.

_____

_____

6. Helga thought to herself that she would win the race.

_____

_____

29.6 ACTIVITY

Rewrite the direct quotations in the following sentences to make them indirect quotations.

EXAMPLE   Roberto said, "We can have the meeting at my apartment."

Roberto said that we could have the meeting at his

apartment.

1. The hairdresser said, "Long hair is often considered unprofessional in the workplace."

_____

_____

2. My professor said, "Psychologists use the scientific method to understand behavior."

_____

_____

3. The teacher asked, "Does anyone need help with the assignment?"

    _____

    _____

4. The pediatrician explained, "By age four, children can work together."

    _____

    _____

5. Louisa muttered, "I never want to see Frankie again."

    _____

    _____

6. Juan thought, "I need a tutor to help me."

    _____

    _____

 IF ENGLISH IS NOT YOUR FIRST LANGUAGE

When you change from a direct to an indirect quotation, the following changes are sometimes made, depending on meaning:

1. Changes in the verb tense

    Direct quotation: *Max said, "Helga is at the store."*
    Indirect quotation: *Max said that Helga was at the store.*

2. Changes in the pronoun

    Direct quotation: *Phillipe mentioned, "I need a haircut."*
    Indirect quotation: *Phillipe mentioned that he needed a haircut.*

3. Changes in the adverb

    Direct quotation: *Dr. Juarez said, "I want your papers now."*
    Indirect quotation: *Dr. Juarez said he wanted our papers then.*

4. Changes in the demonstrative adjective

    Direct quotation: *Chris asked, "May I have this candy?"*
    Indirect quotation: *Chris asked if he could have that candy.*

29.7 CHAPTER REVIEW ACTIVITY

Write sentences according to the directions given.

EXAMPLE   Write a sentence you might hear spoken at a movie theater. Put the direct quotation before the statement of who spoke at the end.

"I want to sit close to the screen," Marco said.

1. Write a sentence you might hear spoken in a shopping mall or grocery store. Place the direct quotation before the statement of who spoke.

   _____

   _____

2. Write a sentence you heard recently in a classroom. Place the direct quotation after the statement of who spoke.

   _____

   _____

3. Write two sentences a dentist might speak to a patient. Place the first sentence at the beginning and the second sentence at the end. In between, indicate who spoke the words.

   _____

   _____

4. Write an indirect quotation to complete the following sentence:
   The children asked whether

   _____

   _____

5. Write something you might say to yourself before an examination. Place the direct quotation after the statement of who thought the words.

   _____

   _____

6. Write a sentence you spoke today. Place the direct quotation before the statement of who spoke.

   _____

   _____

29.8 CHAPTER REVIEW ACTIVITY

The following passage has direct quotations that lack correct punctuation and capitalization. Correct the passage by adding the missing punctuation and capitalization.

EXAMPLE   ThaoMee Xiong's classmate said, "To ~~to~~ me she is remarkable."

[1]It's a long way from the Southeast Asian country of Laos to Mt. Holyoke College, but for ThaoMee Xiong it's been a journey of success. [2]The high point so far was being named to *USA Today*'s All-USA College First Academic Team. [3]Xiong is all the more remarkable, given that she immigrated with her family from Laos to Thailand and then to Wisconsin. [4]In Wisconsin, she not only entered a totally different culture but also faced the challenge of learning to speak and write the language of that culture.

[5]I've always struggled with writing and have never been confident with it she says. [6]Once I get an idea for a paper, I try to do some research on the subject to see if there's enough information on the topic before I start writing about it Xiong explains and then I just start writing.

[7]Although writing is difficult for Xiong, speaking before groups of people is more comfortable. [8]She explains I find speaking a lot easier and feel far more confident than when I write. [9]She says that in high school she took up forensics and participated in mock trials. [10]I found this helped me a lot with language and speaking she notes it taught me not to be fearful of speaking in public.

[11]In high school, I was one of the few students of color Xiong says. [12]Because she was a minority, she felt a certain responsibility. [13]I always felt it was my responsibility to speak up and get my issues out there Xiong notes. [14]She goes on to explain that she had some concerns about her community, and she was dealing with the feeling of always being put on the spot. [15]Xiong states speaking up helped.

[16]I often wonder to myself if I were in her position, could I have done as well as Xiong

Source: Adapted from Robert Feldman, *Power Learning* (New York: McGraw-Hill, 2005), p. 196. Copyright © 2005 The McGraw-Hill Companies. Used by permission of The McGraw-Hill Companies, Inc.

GETTING IN GEAR: IDEAS FOR WRITING

As the photographs illustrate, families come in a variety of configurations. What do you think the American family looks like? How many families have a single parent? Gay parents? Mixed race components? To learn a little more about what American families look like today, you can visit the Women's Educational Media Web site at www.womedia.org/taf_statistics.htm.

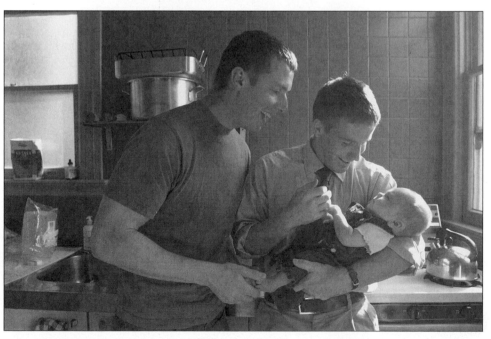

writing topic: Tell about a memorable moment you have spent with one or more family members. Be sure to make clear why the moment is so memorable.

suggestions for prewriting

- Write a map with "memorable family moments" in the center. You might begin branching off from there by noting names of family members.
- Study your map, identify a memorable moment to write about, and freewrite about that moment.

suggestions for drafting

- Your thesis or topic sentence (depending on whether you are writing an essay or a paragraph) can mention the family member and the moment, something like this: "I'll always remember the moment my father told me about his experience in the Vietnam war." Or your thesis or topic sentence can indicate why the moment was memorable, like this: "When my sister ran away from home, I learned the meaning of fear."
- Because you are telling a story, your details will be arranged in the order they occurred. (This is chronological, or time, order.)

suggestion for revising: Look for opportunities to use direct quotations. Reproducing the words people spoke will make your story more vivid.

suggestion for editing: Check your direct quotations against the models in this chapter to be sure you have capitalized and punctuated correctly.

RECHARGE: Lesson Summary

1. Direct quotations are punctuated according to where in the sentence the exact words appear.

   Quotation first: *"Your table is ready," the waiter said.*
   "Is our table ready?" we asked.

   Quotation second: *The waiter said, "Your table is ready."*
   The waiter asked, "Do you want the nonsmoking section?"

   Quotation divided: *"Your table is ready," the waiter said. "Do you want the nonsmoking section?"*
   "Your table is ready," the waiter said, "but it is in the smoking section."
   "Are you sure," the waiter asked, "that you want the chicken?"

2. Be sure to distinguish between direct and indirect quotations.

   Direct quotation: *I said, "I will not pay $50 for that ticket."*
   Indirect quotation: *I said that I would not pay $50 for that ticket.*

3. Thoughts are punctuated like direct quotations.
   "I hope I can do this," I thought.

PART EIGHT REVIEW
Editing for multiple errors

Edit each passage for capital letters, end punctuation, commas, apostrophes, and quotation marks.

A. Sometimes truth is stranger than fiction—even in sports. Consider the story of a baseball player named Bert Haas who once used his breath to stop a run from scoring.

Haas was playing third base for the montreal royals of the international league during a 1940 game. The jersey city giants had a runner at third base, when batter Woody Jensen tried to start a squeeze play. After Jensen dropped a bunt toward third base the ball rolled slowly along just inside the foul line.

The runner at third ran for home and Jensen sprinted for first base. Bert Haas realized that he wouldn t be able to throw out the runner at either base so he got down on his knees and began to blow the ball toward the foul line. It kept rolling fair so he blew again and again. Keep blowing screamed the montreal infielders. Just before the ball reached third base it rolled foul. The runner had to return to third base and the batter had to return to the plate.

Strangely jersey city did not protest. However Frank Shaughnessy who was president of the international league thought he should say something. With a twinkle in his eye Shaughnessy proclaimed after this, no player is permitted to blow a ball foul.

B. At the first stroke of midnight, the happy crowd on times square shouts, happy new year! You, too, are probably accustomed to celebrating each new year on january 1. However no festival has been observed on so many different dates as the welcoming of another year. The ancient greeks for example started the new year with the new moon after june 21. Before the time of julius caesar the roman new year started on March 1.

What about today In most predominantly christian countries the year begins on January 1 but other countries and religions observe New Years Day on different dates. The chinese celebrate twice—once on january 1 and once on the New Years Day reckoned according to the chinese lunar calendar. This second date can occur anytime between January 21 and February 19. People in Indonesia also celebrate twice—once on january 1 and once on the islamic new year. the russian orthodox church celebrates on a date determined by the julian calendar, which places the day on January 14. The jewish New Year, rosh hashanah, is usually celebrated at the end of September or the beginning of October. In vietnam each new year usually begins in February; Iran celebrates on March 21.

Each religious group in India has its own date for the beginning of the year. One hindu celebration comes in April or May. The people of Morocco observe the beginning of the year on the tenth day of muharram which is the first month of the islamic year.

By the way the custom of sending New Years cards is a very old one. The Chinese have been doing it for more than a thousand years. Their cards were used when people visited. They carried the visitors name but no greeting or message.

READING AND WRITING IN RESPONSE TO TEXTBOOKS

The following excerpt is adapted from an introductory business textbook. It explains a relatively new trend in the way people work together.

[1]The trend toward teams has led companies to alter their office arrangements completely, so that individuals can have separate offices and still meet in teams when needed. [2]At the aluminum company, Alcoa's senior executives work in open cubicles and gather around a communications center with televisions, fax machines, newspapers, and tables to encourage impromptu meetings. [3]Alcoa had downsized, reengineered, and changed its old hierarchical structure, but it still wasn't getting the results it wanted. [4]The physical environment simply wasn't designed for teamwork, so the company moved to a new facility.

[5]Small start-up companies in Silicon Valley and huge companies, such as IBM and Mobil, are all creating new office designs for the twenty-first century. [6]*Business Week* says, "Privacy is being replaced with productivity, hierarchy with teamwork, and status with mobility." [7]People can now work anywhere, anytime, in their offices, automobiles, or homes. [8]Teams are linked by computers so that team members can be anywhere and still operate as part of the team. [9]Computer networks have made it possible for managers and employees to stay at home and still be constantly in touch with other team members, all over the world. [10]Can you picture a time when huge office buildings are a thing of the past and employees will live and work where they please, while linked by computer? [11]That is rapidly becoming a reality for many firms.

Source: Adapted from William G. Nickels, James M. McHugh, and Susan M. McHugh, *Understanding Business,* 5th ed. (New York: McGraw-Hill, 1999), p. 216. Copyright © 1999 The McGraw-Hill Companies. Used by permission of The McGraw-Hill Companies.

1. Explain why commas are used in the following sentences:

     A. Sentence 2 _____

     B. Sentence 3 _____

     C. Sentence 4 _____

2. Why is a question mark used in sentence 10? How does the question help

   students learn the material? _____

   _____

3. Explain the use of the apostrophe in the following sentences:

   A. Sentence 2 _____

   B. Sentence 3 _____

4. Explain the use of capital letters in the following sentences:

   A. Sentence 2 _____

   B. Sentence 6 _____

   _____

5. Rewrite the direct quotation in sentence 6 as an indirect quotation. Which

   way is better? Why? _____

   _____

   _____

writing topic: The textbook excerpt asks you whether you can imagine a time
when "employees will live and work where they please, while linked by computer."
Explain what you think that will be like for workers.

Writing in Response to Reading

My alma mater was books, a good library. I could spend the rest of my life reading, just satisfying my curiosity.

—Malcolm X, African-American activist

Reflection: What was Malcolm X saying about the role of reading in his life?

WHAT YOU WILL LEARN

The connection between reading and writing

Strategies for reading critically

WHY YOU WILL LEARN IT

so that you understand how reading can improve writing

so that you can become a better reader

CHAPTER 30

Reading and Writing Responses to Reading

Perhaps you are wondering what a chapter about reading is doing in a book about writing. The fact is that reading and writing are connected in important ways. This chapter will explain those connections and how you can become a better reader. If you become a better reader, you will become a better writer.

THE CONNECTION BETWEEN READING AND WRITING

Writing and reading are connected because you will often be asked to write in response to class readings. That is, after reading assigned books, handouts, library materials, and other required texts, you will write essay examination answers, reports, book reviews, essays, journal entries, postings to class Web sites, summaries, and analyses.

Reading and writing are also connected because reading can improve writing. The more you read, the more you know, and the more you know, the more ideas you have to include in your writing. When you read newspapers and magazines, you learn about current events, and you can bring that information to your writing. Has your philosophy instructor directed you to write about an issue related to medical ethics? Perhaps you read a magazine article on stem cell research that can prompt a topic and supporting details.

Reading also provides models for writing. Pay attention to how other writers do such things as organize ideas, develop support, use description, give examples, and provide transitions, and try some of these techniques.

Reading also improves your vocabulary, and the more words you know, the better you can express yourself. If you read an article in *Time* that refers to a politician's *brazen* behavior, consider using that word the next time you want to describe someone's bold and shameless actions.

Perhaps most important, reading helps you understand your audience. As you read, you become accustomed to thinking like a reader. Then, as a writer, you are better able to make decisions about such aspects as how many examples to use, whether to write a humorous opening or a serious one, and what kind of detail will be most convincing. In other words, successful writers understand readers because they *are* readers, so they know what readers need and want.

THE STEPS FOR CRITICAL READING

As college students, you read a great deal, and you must read this material thoughtfully. Thoughtful reading is **critical reading**. Critical reading is not reading to find fault; it is reading done with energy, careful thought, and full attention. To read critically, you must understand what you read and form opinions about the material. The steps explained next can help you become a skillful critical reader.

Step 1: preview the reading

Get an idea of what is in store by doing the following:

- *Read the title.* Does the title offer any hints about the content of the reading? Some titles do, but some don't.
- *Check the author's name.* Do you already know that the author is a humorist, a liberal, a newspaper columnist, or a political figure? Have you read anything by this person before? If you have any previous knowledge of the author, you may get some clues about what to expect from the reading at hand.
- *Skim the first paragraph.* It might let you know the thesis of the piece or the broad topic the writer is discussing.

Preview "The Truth about Our Little White Lies" on page 476. Then compare your observations with the ones made by another reader, which follow. (Because there are no right or wrong previewing observations, the following might be different from yours.)

The title:	*The title suggests that the essay will be about harmless lies and that it will tell me facts about these lies.*
The author's name:	*I don't know anything about this author; she is new to me.*
The first paragraph:	*The first paragraph points out that white lies are common. If the whole essay focuses on that point, it will be saying what I already know.*

Step 2: mark up the reading

If you own the reading material, use a pencil or pen to mark it up in the ways explained. (If you prefer not to write directly on the material, or if you do not own it, use Post-it notes.)

- *Underline twice the central point of the reading (the thesis).* If the central point is implied (suggested) rather than stated, write it out yourself.
- *Underline once the main ideas that develop that central point.* Be careful not to underline too much—just identify the main ideas.
- *Circle words you do not know.* Make an educated guess about their meanings from clues in the text.
- *Write your reactions in the margin.* If you like a particular passage, draw a star or write an exclamation point next to it. If you strongly agree with something, write "yes!" or "I agree." If you disagree, write "no" or "I disagree." If you don't understand something, write a question mark next to it. In addition, write any other responses that you have, such as these: "Where's the proof?" "too emotional," "funny," "good example," "reminds me of Dr. Small's lecture on group behavior." Don't worry about being right or wrong, because there are no correct and incorrect reactions. Just respond.

The following is an example of what a reading can look like when a critical reader marks it. Because marking a text is as individual as the reader, your marked texts will look different.

THE TRUTH ABOUT OUR LITTLE WHITE LIES
KAREN S. PETERSON

Implied thesis – We all tell white lies for several reasons.

Wonder how the kids would feel about this.

leaving out

1   Gail Safeer, a graduate student in suburban Washington, D.C., doesn't let on to people that two of her three children were born during a previous marriage. "I don't correct people when they assume all three are my husband's," she says. "It's nobody's business. It's a little white lie of [omission,] like not telling somebody her husband is running around. . . . White lies are not daily currency in my life," adds Safeer. "But we all do it."

Wow! How does he know this? Seems high.

thinking about

2   Indeed we do. <u>Each of us fibs at least 50 times a day</u>, says psychologist Jerald Jellison of the University of Southern California in Los Angeles, who has spent a decade [musing] on the truth about our lies. He says <u>we lie most often about the Big Three—age, income and sex—areas where our egos and self-images are most vulnerable.</u> To protect them we even lie non-verbally with gestures, silences, inactions and body language. "You can even lie with your emotions," says Jellison. "The smile you don't mean, or the classic nervous laugh. A man asks a woman, 'Your place or mine?' and then chuckles. If she's offended, he can always elaborate on that laugh by saying, 'Can't you take a joke? I was only kidding.'"

Difference between little and big lie not clear. Some students say they studied less for a test than they really did. Why?

3   These types of lies are what Jellison calls "little white lies," the kind we throw around as casually as old sneakers but which he claims are our "social justifications." "<u>We lie because it pays</u>," he says. "We use [lies] <u>to escape punishment for our small errors.</u> . . . Also, our social justifications help us <u>avoid disapproval.</u> 'I gave at the office,' or 'I'm sorry.'"

That's OK

I always know when I lie–I disagree.

smoothly

4   <u>Our most common reason for lying is to spare someone else's feelings</u>, says Jellison. "We often tell ourselves that, <u>but usually we're trying to protect our own best interests.</u> I'll feel that if I tell you the truth, you'll get mad." Adds B. L. Kintz, a psychology professor at Western Washington University in Bellingham: "<u>We lie so often,</u> with such regularity and fluency, so automatically and [glibly] that <u>we're not even aware we're doing it.</u> The little self-serving deceptions, the compliments we don't mean, stretching the point in a social situation—they are part of reality. Lying is simply something that is."

I wonder how much people lie to me.
! well put

5   Jellison couldn't agree more. He believes that <u>white lies are the oil for the machinery of daily life.</u> "Society actually functions fairly well on many small

deceptions. They contribute the little, civilized rituals that comfort us. . . . The idea that we must always tell the truth is too simplistic," he says. "Is lying 'right' or 'wrong'? is an impossible question to answer."

Hard, but not impossible. Jellison seems to imply that little white lies are OK. This needs to be discussed more.

6   Be it right or wrong, <u>we have become so accustomed to lying and being lied to that we only see it as harmful in daily life when we don't realize that it's happening to us.</u> "We take for granted some degree of lying from politicians, government, business, advertising," says psychiatrist Dr. Irving Baran of the USC San Diego Medical School. "We don't get excited about an ad that hypes some product in a way we know isn't true. But the rub comes when we go to someone we need and trust and are deceived. A banker for a loan who says he's got the best interest rate going. A real estate agent who convinces us his is the best package available. An insurance agent pushing an unsound policy. An auto dealer who doesn't tell you the product's safety record. Then our backs go up, and what isn't true—hurts."

Conclusion needed.

Karen S. Peterson, "The Truth About Our Little White Lies," © 1983 USA TODAY. Reprinted with permission.

Step 3: reread

Sometimes one reading is enough. More often, college reading requires more. To identify all the important ideas, understand everything, and respond thoughtfully, you will have to read the material two or more times. The second time you read, check the dictionary definitions of circled words and see how close your educated guesses were. Also, each time you read, mark the text if you have new responses.

Step 4: write in your journal

Writing about what you read helps you remember ideas, consider points, evaluate issues, and develop ideas for writing in response to your reading. Journal entries can be anything you like. You might try the following:

- Freewriting about anything and everything that occurs to you about the reading. (See page 6 for more on freewriting.)
- Writing a paragraph that relates one or more of the ideas in the reading to something you have experienced, something you know, or something you are studying in another class.
- Writing about whether you liked the reading and why or why not.
- Explaining whether or not you agree with the author and why.

For more on journaling, see page 10.

   Here is a sample journal entry, which is a paragraph response to an idea in "The Truth about Our Little White Lies":

   People ask me all the time things like "How does this look?" or "Do you like my hair?" or "Is this outfit ok?" and I usually say something complimentary. That is often a white lie, I know, and I used to think I was just making people feel good. Now I'm starting to think that people would rather hear the truth and that it's better to say something like "Your hair isn't unattractive, but I think I like your old hairstyle better." The reason I think that is because I ask questions like that all the time, and I no longer trust the answers I get. If I'm telling white lies to others, they are probably telling them to me. When I ask how something looks or a similar question, I really want to know, even if the answer is disappointing. I am going to start telling the truth about these matters so that people will tell the truth to me in return. In this case, I don't think white lies are very helpful.

CONNECT FOR SUCCESS: Use Critical Reading Strategies for Textbooks

Use the critical reading strategies explained in this chapter to help you understand and remember information in your textbooks.

- When you preview the material, pay special attention to helpful features, such as introductory notes, headings, bold type, captions, charts, and end-of-chapter summaries.
- When you mark up textbooks, do not worry about finding a thesis. Instead, concentrate on underlining main ideas and important examples. (Many students prefer to highlight important ideas rather than underline.) Avoid marking too much. You will want to review your marked-up textbook when you study for exams, and if you have marked more than the main ideas and important examples, you may find yourself trying to memorize too much.
- When you reread, determine whether there is material you do not understand. If there is, write out specific questions to ask your instructor in class.
- When you write in your journal, write in ways that will help you understand and remember important material. For example, list or summarize main points, outline chapters, and write and answer study questions.

Using context clues for unfamiliar vocabulary

When you encounter an unfamiliar word during reading, you can often reason out the meaning using **context clues**, the information from the words and sentences that come before and after the unfamiliar word.

- Look for **synonyms** (words that have approximately the same meaning as the word you are unsure of) for clues. Synonyms are often signaled with commas or the word *or*, like this:

  Parochial schools, private Catholic schools, have become more popular in the past five years. [*Parochial schools* is a synonym for *Catholic schools.*]

  The template, or pattern, for public education goes back to colonial America. [*Template* is a synonym for *pattern.*]

Sometimes the synonym comes in another sentence.

  State lawmakers doubt that charter schools will be a panacea for our educational woes. Unfortunately, they do not know what the cure-all is. [*Cure-all* is a synonym for *panacea.*]

- Look for words and phrases that help you figure out meaning by suggesting contrast. These are words such as *unlike, in contrast, on the other hand, instead of, but,* and *although.*

Although we thought the task would be <u>Herculean</u>, it took very little effort. [Can you tell that *Herculean* means "requiring great effort or strength"?]

- Look for examples that suggest meaning. Examples may be introduced by words and phrases such as *for example, for instance, including,* and *such as.*

  I have had many <u>mentors</u> in my life, including my high school track coach, who taught me discipline; my third-grade Sunday School teacher, who helped me have faith in myself; and my mother, who taught me never to give up. [Can you tell that *mentors* are teachers or counselors?]

- Use your experience and knowledge to figure out meaning. Something you already understand can help you understand something you are unsure of.

  Fearing <u>reprisals</u> against its star witness, the FBI put him in the witness protection program. [If you know that the FBI is a law enforcement agency and that the witness protection program is for people who might be killed if they testify against someone, then you can figure out that *reprisals* means "revenge."]

READINGS

THEY SHUT MY GRANDMOTHER'S ROOM DOOR
ANDREW LAM

Award-winning essayist and short-story writer Andrew Lam is an associate editor with the Pacific News Service and a commentator on National Public Radio's "All Things Considered." Born in Saigon, Vietnam, he came to the United States when he was eleven years old. The war he refers to in the essay is the Vietnam War. Drawing on his experiences in both Vietnam and the United States, Lam contrasts the two cultures' views of death and offers an explanation for those differences. You will probably have no trouble determining which view the author finds superior.

1   When someone dies in the convalescent home where my grandmother lives, the nurses rush to close all the patients' doors. Though as a policy death is not to be seen at the home, she can always tell when it visits. The series of doors being slammed shut remind her of the firecrackers during Tet.

2   The nurses' efforts to shield death are more comical to my grandmother than reassuring. "Those old ladies die so often," she quips in Vietnamese, "every day's like new year."

3   Still, it is lonely to die in such a place. I imagine some wasted old body under a white sheet being carted silently through the empty corridor on its way to the morgue. While in America a person may be born surrounded by loved ones, in old age one is often left to take the last leg of life's journey alone.

4   Perhaps that is why my grandmother talks now mainly of her hometown, BacLieu; its river and green rich rice fields. Having lost everything during the war, she can now offer me only her distant memories: Life was not disjointed back home; one lived in a gentle rhythm with the land; people died in their homes surrounded by neighbors and relatives. And no one shut your door.

5   So it goes. The once gentle, connected world of the past is but the language of dreams. In this fast-paced society of disjointed lives, we are swept along and have little time left for spiritual comfort. Instead of relying on neighbors and relatives, on the river and land, we deal with the language of materialism: overtime, escrow, stress, down payment, credit cards, tax shelter. Instead of going to the temple to pray for good health we pay life and health insurance religiously.

6   My grandmother's children and grandchildren share a certain pang of guilt. After a stroke which paralyzed her, we could no longer keep her at home. And although we visit her regularly, we are not living up to the filial piety standard expected of us in the old country. My father silently grieves and my mother suffers from headaches. (Does she see herself in such a home in a decade or two?)

7   Once, a long time ago, living in Vietnam we used to stare death in the face. The war in many ways had heightened our sensibilities toward living and dying. I can still hear the wails of widows and grieving mothers. Though the fear of death and dying is a universal one, the Vietnamese did not hide from it. Instead we dwelt in its tragedy. Death pervaded our poems, novels, fairy tales and songs.

8   But if agony and pain are part of Vietnamese culture, pleasure is at the center of America's culture. While Vietnamese holidays are based on death anniversaries, birthdays are celebrated here. American popular culture translates death with something like nauseating humor. People laugh and scream at blood and guts movies. The wealthy freeze their dead relatives in liquid nitrogen. Cemeteries are places of big business, complete with colorful brochures. I hear there are even drive-by funerals where you don't have to get out of your own car to pay your respects to the deceased.

9   That America relies upon the pleasure principle and happy endings in its entertainments does not, however, assist us in evading suffering. The reality of the suffering of old age is apparent in the convalescent home. There is an old man, once an accomplished concert pianist, now rendered helpless by arthritis. Every morning he sits staring at the piano. One feeble woman who outlived her children keeps repeating, "My son will take me home." Then there are those mindless, bedridden bodies kept alive through a series of tubes and pulsating machines.

¹⁰ But despair is not newsworthy. Death itself must be embellished or satirized or deep-frozen in order to catch the public's attention.

¹¹ Last week on her 82nd birthday I went to see my grandmother. She smiled her sweet sad smile.

¹² "Where will you end up in your old age?" she asked me, her mind as sharp as ever.

¹³ The memories of monsoon rain and tropical sun and relatives and friends came to mind. Not here, not here, I wanted to tell her. But the soft moaning of a patient next door and the smell of alcohol wafting from the sterile corridor brought me back to reality.

¹⁴ "Anywhere is fine," I told her instead, trying to keep up with her courageous spirit. "All I am asking for is that they don't shut my door."

Andrew Lam, "They Shut My Grandmother's Room Door, 1989. Used by permission.

UNDERSTANDING CONTENT

On Writing

Explain the use of the apostrophe in *patients'* (paragraph 1), *grandmother's* (paragraph 6), *America's* (paragraph 8), and *don't* (paragraph 14). Why do the apostrophes appear where they do?

1. What is the main difference between the way Americans and Vietnamese view death?

2. How is the attitude of Americans toward death reflected in American culture?

3. How does Lam explain the Vietnamese attitude toward death?

4. In addition to their different attitudes toward death, what other contrasts between Vietnamese and Americans does Lam point out?

EXPLORING IDEAS

1. Which attitude toward death does Lam prefer? How can you tell?

2. What is the significance of the closed door?

3. In paragraph 4, Lam says that for his grandmother, "Life was not disjointed back home." In paragraph 5, he says, "The once gentle, connected world of the past is but the language of dreams." What point do you think Lam is making when he contrasts the disjointed life and the connected world?

4. If you were a nursing home administrator, what procedure would you implement for dealing with the death of a resident?

REFLECTING ON YOUR READING PROCESS

What did you think the title meant when you previewed the essay? What did you understand it to mean after your first or second reading?

GETTING IN GEAR: IDEAS FOR WRITING

The elderly are the fastest-growing age group in the United States. As the photographs depict, some older Americans will be blessed with good health and other circumstances, so they will be able to maintain an active, independent lifestyle, but others will need more care. To learn about issues important to both active seniors and those needing more care, visit the American Association of Retired Persons Web site at www.aarp.org and www.aging-parents-and-elder-care.com/index.html.

writing topic: What do you think of the way we treat the elderly in this country? You can consider such issues as whether we respect the elderly appropriately, help them maintain a satisfactory quality of life, and provide adequate healthcare, housing, and assisted living facilities and nursing homes. Are there any changes that should be made? If so, what are they?

suggestions for discovering ideas

- If you have any elderly friends, relatives, or neighbors, think about how these people are treated and about the quality of their lives.
- Freewrite about how we treat the elderly and about how they should be treated.

suggestions for drafting
- Include examples to show how the elderly are treated, or cite reasons you think they are or are not treated well.
- If you recommend a change, explain why that change is a good idea, or explain how the change can be made.

suggestion for revising: Use the checklist for revising a paragraph on pages 33–34 or the checklist for revising an essay on page 65.

suggestion for editing: Edit twice. The first time, look for the kinds of errors you have made in the past; the second time, look for all other errors.

YOU BECOME WHAT YOU WEAR
KATHLEEN CARLIN

After working as a surgical nurse, Kathleen Carlin returned to school and earned two degrees, one in English and one in sociology and anthropology. As part of the Family Support Network, she has helped families with problems associated with child abuse, and as a volunteer for Yellowstone County Sheriff's Department, she has helped crime victims.

"You Become What You Wear," which records some of the details of a sociology experiment Carlin engaged in as a college student, illustrates how quickly people make judgments about others based on their dress. It was first published in 1996 in Commonweal, *a biweekly review of public affairs, religion, literature, and the arts edited by Catholic laypeople.*

1   A standard criticism of sociological research projects is that they go to great lengths to prove what most people with common sense already know. Without exactly taking sides for or against that criticism, I want to describe a sociological exercise that might seem to validate it—except that, for me and a classmate (and maybe for some who read this account), the experience made a truism come alive.

2   What we did: During spring break from a local college, my friend and I went downtown to shop. First, however, we made ourselves virtually unrecognizable to our friends and even to our families. We wore clothing slightly inappropriate for the weather, clean but wrinkled, clearly out of sync with the styles worn by most visitors to the area. We carried plastic bags of nameless possessions. Both of us were slightly unkempt. My friend wore a faded flannel shirt and T-shirt, a wrinkled skirt over sweat pants. I wore a wool hat that concealed my hair, an unfashionable coat and scarf, and glasses with clip-on sun shades.

3   The aim was to look like street people and to observe what difference that made in the way other people responded to us—whether the appearance of poverty

would place a stigma on us. We were also prepared to act out some mildly unusual behaviors that might speak of some emotional disabilities, without appearing seriously disturbed or dangerous. As it turned out, there was no need for histrionics; people turned us off or tuned us out on the basis of appearance alone.

4   Our first stop (after parking our cars near the railroad tracks) was in the bargain store of a local charity, where we politely asked access to a bathroom and were refused. Next we entered the lobby of a large hotel, where we asked for a coffee shop and a bathroom. The bellhop said, "You must go to the twentieth floor." We weren't up to trying our gig at an exclusive restaurant, so we wandered around the first floor and left. From there we went to a pawnshop, where we more or less blended with the patrons, and then on to the upper-scale stores and coffee shops during the lunch hour.

5   It was stigma time. Some of the children we encountered stared, pointed, and laughed; adults gave us long, incredulous looks. Clerks in stores followed us around to watch our every move. In a lunchroom a second assistant hurried to the side of the cashier, where they took my $2 check without asking for an ID; it seemed worth that price to have us out the door. At one doorway a clerk physically blocked the entrance apparently to discourage our entry.

6   We had money to cover small purchases, and, apart from wearing down-scale clothing, we did nothing in any of these settings to draw attention to ourselves; we merely shopped quietly in our accustomed manner. At one establishment we did blow our cover when we ordered croissants with a latté and an espresso; that may have been too far out of character for "bag ladies." Elsewhere we encountered derision, mockery, distrust, and rude stares.

7   So what did we learn? Mostly what we expected, what everybody knows: people judge by appearances. Just looking poor brings with it a stigma, accompanied by the withdrawal of much of the social civility most of us take for granted. Lacking the culturally acceptable symbols of belonging in this milieu, we became, to a degree, objects, with less inherent dignity as persons.

8   There was, however, one surprise—more accurately, a shock. It became clear most strongly at the shop I mentioned earlier, the one where a clerk conspicuously positioned herself in the entryway on seeing us. I had just noticed the place and had turned to my companion, saying, "I've never seen this store. Let's go in." She looked at me with dismay: "You're not really going in there, are you?"

9   I knew what she meant and shared her feeling. The place felt out of bounds for us. In a very few hours, we found ourselves accepting and internalizing the superficial and biased judgments of ourselves that prevailed among the people we

On Writing

Explain the reason for the semicolon in paragraph 3 and for the two semicolons in paragraph 5.

met; we stigmatized ourselves. It's a good lesson to learn, maybe especially for sociologists.

Kathleen Carlin, "You Become What You Wear" (1996). © 1996 Commonweal Foundation. Reprinted with permission. For subscriptions: www.commonwealmagazine.org.

UNDERSTANDING CONTENT

1. Is Carlin's thesis in the first paragraph, the last paragraph, or both? Explain.

2. Why did the author and her friend dress "out of sync with the styles worn by most visitors to the area" when they went downtown?

3. How were the author and her friend treated when they dressed down-scale? Why were they treated that way?

4. What did Carlin learn that she expected to learn? What did she learn that came as a surprise?

EXPLORING IDEAS

1. Explain the meaning of the title. How does the title relate to the last paragraph?

2. If Carlin and her friend had gone into an impoverished area dressed in upscale clothes, how do you think people would have responded? Why?

3. In paragraph 9, Carlin says, "We stigmatized ourselves." What does she mean? Do you agree that people stigmatize themselves? Explain.

4. In paragraph 1, Carlin says that her experiment seems to prove what "most people with common sense already know." Why, then, does she write the essay? Does the essay serve an important purpose? Explain.

REFLECTING ON YOUR READING PROCESS

Select one of the reactions you wrote in the margin. In two or three sentences, explain why you had that reaction. As an alternative, if your reaction has changed on further reflection, explain how it has changed.

GETTING IN GEAR: IDEAS FOR WRITING

Used by permission of Talbot's.

The screen shot, from Talbot's Web site at www.talbots.com, is one example of how clothing is marketed to women. Explore this site, as well as some magazine and television advertisements. Do any of the marketing efforts help explain why so many women buy Talbots clothes?

writing topic: Teenagers are often obsessed with clothes. Why do you think that is? Explain one or more reasons for the obsession, such as parents, advertisers, or teenagers themselves.

suggestion for prewriting

- Think about your high school days and freewrite about how you and your friends felt about clothes—and why.

suggestions for drafting

- Be sure your thesis or topic sentence includes a claim.
- If you want to save your most convincing point for last, arrange your details in a progressive order.

suggestion for revising: Ask a reliable reader to evaluate whether your reasons are convincing.

suggestion for editing: Read your work aloud one time to listen for errors you may have overlooked in print.

HAVE A NICE DAY
THOMAS H. MIDDLETON

"Have a nice day!" we are regularly told. But is the speaker sincere? Maybe not, says Thomas Middleton, but the sentence is harmless enough—and sometimes it even does some good. Interestingly, this essay originally appeared in 1979 in the Saturday Review, *yet it remains relevant today, as "Have a nice day" continues to be used routinely.*

1   Shortly after the quasi-annual Los Angeles fire disaster last year, we met Gordon Jenkins, the composer-conductor, and his wife, Beverly. The Jenkinses had lived in one of the oldest and most charming houses on Broad Beach Road in Malibu. Broad Beach was one of the areas most severely affected by the fire.

2   Mr. Jenkins told me that when the fire leaped down the hills and started blazing across the street from their home, and the smoke billowed in, they were forced to leave. They drove to a motel and checked in for the night. Early the next morning, they went back home. As you drive along Broad Beach, what you see from your car is a row of garages. As a rule, the garages hide the houses, which are built along the beach. The Jenkinses' garage, being made of cement, was intact. When they went around the garage to where their house had stood the day before, they found only ashes. They had lived in the house for over 31 years.

3   They went back to the motel for what I suspect was a crushingly dismal breakfast.

4   On their return to Broad beach, they found that the police were blocking off the street. The policeman who stopped them told them no one but residents could enter the area. Mr. Jenkins told him that he was a resident, or that at any rate he had been a resident, his house having burned to the ground the day before. The cop checked his driver's license and waved them through, calling, "Have a nice day!"

5   The Jenkinses got about 200 feet down the road before the "Have a nice day" sank all the way in and their gales of laughter burst out. Surely, no other phrase could have made Gordon and Beverly Jenkins laugh all the way to the ashes of their home. That mindless pleasantry brightened a dark day.

6   "Have a nice day" is ubiquitous these days, at least in this part of the country. It is said constantly by supermarket checkers, filling-station attendants, receptionists, and just about everyone else who deals regularly with the public.

7   I have friends and relations, not necessarily curmudgeonly, who loathe the expression on the grounds that it is almost always said automatically and that, like most automatic utterances, it is almost always insincere.

8   My own feeling is that it is a pleasant enough pleasantry. I grant that "Have a nice day" probably helps no more than my wife's admonition, "Don't fall down." That's what Jeannie says whenever I'm standing on a narrow ledge or a stepladder. I'd do my best not to fall down even if she didn't tell me not to. Still, it's good to know that she cares.

9   There is a difference between "Have a nice day" and "Don't fall down" in that the person who tells me to have a nice day may not be sincerely concerned over what kind of day I'll have, whereas if I should fall off the ladder, Jeannie's day could be seriously flawed.

10   Years before I heard "Have a nice day," I was in the habit of telling people to have a good time, and I always meant it sincerely, for whatever good it might do. I remember long ago when I used to drive young Tom to school on those infrequent days when he'd miss the bus or the weather would be particularly foul. As I dropped him off, I always said, "Have a good time," and he always said, "Thanks," until one day, after my customary "Have a good time," he turned rather peevishly and said *"Geez,* I'm going to *school!"*

11   I said, "I know. Have a good time while you're learning something, or learn something while you're having a good time. They're not mutually exclusive." He brightened and said, "Hey, ri-i-ght! Thanks!"

12   I think "Have a nice day" provides one of those little indications that we do care, even if only slightly, about one another's welfare. It has taken its place for a time in the storehouse of phrases we use for civility's sake, and on at least one occasion it brought unexpected laughter in a time of heavy tragedy.

13   Have a nice day.

Thomas H. Middleton, "Have a Nice Day"© 1979 Thomas H. Middleton. Used by permission of the author.

UNDERSTANDING CONTENT

1. In your own words, state the thesis of the essay.

2. According to the essay, why do some people think that those who say, "Have a nice day" are almost always "insincere"?

3. Gordon and Beverly Jenkins laughed when the police officer told them to have a nice day. Why?

4. Middleton makes note of the fact that the Jenkinses lived in their house for thirty-one years. Why is that information significant?

EXPLORING IDEAS

1. Why does Middleton use humor rather than treat his topic in a serious way?

2. Do you routinely say, "Have a nice day"? Why or why not?

3. Why do you think the policeman told the couple to "Have a nice day"? Was his remark appropriate?

4. What does the Jenkinses' laughter indicate about them and suggest about how they might have coped with the tragedy?

REFLECTING ON YOUR WRITING PROCESS

When you skimmed the first paragraph during your preview of the reading, what expectations did you form for the essay? Were those expectations born out when you did your first reading? Explain.

GETTING IN GEAR: IDEAS FOR WRITING

On Writing

Anecdotes are brief stories that can illustrate a point. For example, paragraphs 1 through 5 form an anecdote to illustrate that "Have a nice day," even when used mindlessly, can brighten a day. In addition to illustrating, anecdotes often add interest and liveliness to writing. What would this piece have been like without the anecdote?

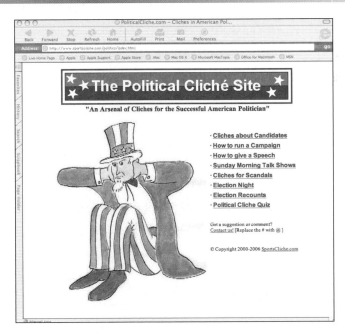

Like "Have a nice day," many expressions are commonly heard. For example, in every political campaign and election, commonly heard expressions include "This campaign will focus on the issues," "The race is too close to call," and the candidate "has a clear vision for our future." You can see more of these political clichés at http://www.sportscliche.com/politics/index.html.

writing topic: Select a commonly heard expression and do what Middleton does: First illustrate the expression with a brief story (an anecdote) and then explain whether or not the expression can be part of a positive form of interaction.

suggestion for prewriting: If you need help settling on an expression, you can visit clichésite.com, or you can use a current slang expression or ethnic term (such as *chutzpah* or *gringo*).

suggestion for drafting: Write an outline before drafting, arranging the details for your anecdote in chronological order.

suggestion for revising: Ask a reader with good judgment about writing to tell you whether your anecdote does a good job of illustrating the expression.

suggestion for editing: Point to every word and punctuation mark, lingering over each one for a second or two to study it for correctness.

FISH CHEEKS
AMY TAN

Amy Tan was born in California in 1952 to parents who came to the United States to escape the Chinese Civil War. In 1987, Tan traveled to China with her mother. That trip inspired her to write The Joy Luck Club *(1989), the bestselling book that was made into a movie. Tan's other novels include* The Kitchen God's Wife *(1991),* The Bonesetter's Daughter *(2001), and* Saving Fish from Drowning *(2005). She has also written children's books and magazine articles, including "Fish Cheeks," which first appeared in* Seventeen, *a magazine for adolescent girls.*

1   I fell in love with the minister's son the winter I turned fourteen. He was not Chinese, but as white as Mary in the manger. For Christmas I prayed for this blond-haired boy, Robert, and a slim new American nose.

2   When I found out that my parents had invited the minister's family over for Christmas Eve dinner, I cried. What would Robert think of our shabby Chinese Christmas? What would he think of our noisy Chinese relatives who lacked proper American manners? What terrible disappointment would he feel upon seeing not a roasted turkey and sweet potatoes but Chinese food?

3   On Christmas Eve I saw that my mother had outdone herself in creating a strange menu. She was pulling black veins out of the backs of fleshy prawns. The kitchen was littered with appalling mounds of raw food: A slimy rock cod with bulging eyes that pleaded not to be thrown into a pan of hot oil. Tofu which looked like stacked wedges of rubbery white sponges. A bowl soaking dried fungus back to life. A plate of squid, their backs crisscrossed with knife markings so they resembled bicycle tires.

⁴   And then they arrived—the minister's family and all my relatives in a clamor of doorbells and rumpled Christmas packages. Robert grunted hello, and I pretended he was not worthy of existence.

⁵   Dinner threw me deeper into despair. My relatives licked the ends of their chopsticks and reached across the table, dipping them into the dozen or so plates of food. Robert and his family waited patiently for platters to be passed to them. My relatives murmured with pleasure when my mother brought out the whole steamed fish. Robert grimaced. Then my father poked his chopsticks just below the fish eye and plucked out the soft meat. "Amy, your favorite," he said, offering me the tender fish cheek. I wanted to disappear.

⁶   At the end of the meal my father leaned back and belched loudly, thanking my mother for her fine cooking. "It's a polite Chinese custom to show you are satisfied," explained my father to our astonished guests. Robert was looking down at his plate with a reddened face. The minister managed to muster up a quiet burp. I was stunned into silence for the rest of the night.

⁷   After everyone had gone, my mother said to me, "You want to be the same as American girls on the outside." She handed me an early gift. It was a miniskirt in beige tweed. "But inside you must always be Chinese. You must be proud you are different. Your only shame is to have shame."

⁸   And even though I didn't agree with her then, I knew that she understood how much I had suffered during the evening's dinner. It wasn't until many years later—long after I had gotten over my crush on Robert—that I was able to fully appreciate her lesson and the true purpose behind our particular menu. For Christmas Eve that year, she had chosen all my favorite foods.

Copyright © 1987 by Amy Tan. First appeared in *Seventeen* Magazine. Reprinted by permission of the author and the Sandra Dijkstra Literary Agency.

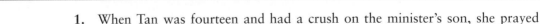
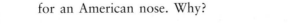

UNDERSTANDING CONTENT

On Writing

Tan uses very specific words—words such as *fleshy* and *bulging* in paragraph 3. Cite four other specific words in the essay. What does the specific word choice add?

1. When Tan was fourteen and had a crush on the minister's son, she prayed for an American nose. Why?

2. Why did Tan cry when she learned that the minister's son was coming for Christmas Eve dinner?

3. Why did Tan's mother cook "a strange menu" (paragraph 3)?

4. When Tan was fourteen, how did she feel about her Chinese heritage?

EXPLORING IDEAS

1. "Fish Cheeks" originally appeared in *Seventeen,* which is read mostly by adolescent girls. Why would an audience of teenage girls be interested in this essay?

2. What lesson can be learned from "Fish Cheeks"? Is this lesson one that readers of *Seventeen* need to hear? Explain.

3. Should Tan's mother have prepared a more Western menu for her Christmas eve dinner? Why or why not?

4. Many years after the incident, Tan realized that her mother had prepared Tan's favorite foods on that Christmas Eve. Explain the significance of the menu.

REFLECTING ON YOUR WRITING PROCESS

What was your first impression of the title when you previewed the reading? What did the title mean to you when you completed your first reading?

GETTING IN GEAR: IDEAS FOR WRITING

Every culture has its own traditions for important life-cycle events, such as weddings and funerals. The photograph depicts a bride and groom in traditional Chinese ceremonial dress. You can learn about the traditions of many cultures by clicking on the country that interests you at http://dir.yahoo.com/Regional/Countries.

writing topic: As an adolescent, Amy Tan experienced a conflict between her Chinese heritage and the American culture she wanted to be part of. Tell about a cultural, generational, gender, or other conflict you experienced. Did the conflict teach you anything?

suggestion for prewriting: Freewrite about one or more of the following:
- conflicts between your cultural heritage and American culture
- conflicts between your generation and your parents' generation or your children's generation
- conflict between you and people of the opposite gender

suggestion for drafting: Write an outline before drafting. If you include a story that illustrates the conflict (the way Tan does), arrange those details in chronological order.

suggestion for revising: Look for opportunities to enliven your writing with specific, vivid words, the way Tan does.

suggestion for editing: Point to every word and punctuation mark, lingering over each one for a second or two to study it for correctness.

BABY NAMES, BIG BATTLES
TUNKU VARADARAJAN

A British citizen who was born in India, Tunku Varadarajan was the bureau chief for the London Times *in New York and the editorial features editor of* The Wall Street Journal. *He is currently a columnist for OpinionJournal.com, a* Wall Street Journal *website. In the following piece, which originally appeared in* The New York Times *in 1999, Varadarajan notes that choosing a baby's name is an important process with lifelong impact. It is also a process that can be difficult for parents in the United States who are from a different culture.*

1 My wife has just given birth to a son. Tomorrow, the twelfth day after he was born, our family will perform an ancient but simple Hindu ritual. We will sign a prayer and make a small offering to the gods, after which I will put my lips to his little ear and say to him three times: "Your name is 'Satya.'" Thirty-seven years ago, in Delhi, my father observed the same rite, intoning my name thrice into my right ear.

2 Satya [SUT-ya] is the Sanskrit word for "truth." For me, and for my wife, it has two clear virtues as a name: its meaning is a handsome one, and its brevity sits snugly with my protracted surname.

3   We arrived at Satya after a process that was as arduous, and almost as lengthy, as the boy's gestation. Parents will always quarrel over their child's name—with each other, with friends, with relatives. There is no privacy in the process, and a number of names, which I cherished fleetingly, fell by the wayside as soon as someone said, "You can't call him *that!*" These battles over a baby's name are magnified when a parent is, like I am, not from a Judeo-Christian background.

4   Although my American wife has her roots in North Carolina, she was rather keen that her son should have an Indian name. My initial protestations that he should, perhaps, be called "something American" were given the shortest shrift. Walter was simply out of the question, as was Lancelot.

5   My wife was right, of course. Saying, "Your name is Walter" would have sounded absurd at the end of a Hindu naamakaran, or naming ceremony.

6   Naming a child is not easy for parents in America who come from non-European backgrounds, from cultures where Ashutosh, Chae-Hyun, and Naeem are common names. We have to ask ourselves a number of important questions. How will the child's foreign name sound to American ears? (That test ruled out Shiva, my family deity; a Jewish friend put her foot down.)

7   Will it provoke bullies to beat him up on the school playground? (That was the end of Karan, the name of a warrior from the Mahabharata, the Hindu epic. A boy called "Karen" wouldn't stand a chance.)

8   Will it be as euphonic in New York as it is in New Delhi? (That was how Sameer failed to get off the ground. "Like a bagel with a schmear!" said one ruthless well-wisher.)

9   There were other questions: Does it make a jarring sound, especially when mispronounced—as it surely will be—by other people? Does it mean something rude in English? Will he have to spend the rest of his life spelling it out over the telephone, letter by wretched letter?

10   My wife and I could have resorted to an option that many Indian parents in the United States employ: going for a perfectly orthodox Indian name that "sounds American." Over the last few months, as our ear for names grew more acute, we've encountered children called Neel (Neil), Dev (Dave), Jai (Jay) and even Dilin (Dylan).

11   We've also noted names that sound American when shortened to nicknames, like Samar (Sam), Ishaan (Sean) and Sidhartha (Sid). Our problem with these Indian names—I call them "Ameronyms"—is that they limited us to a meager short list. Besides, they are growing to be rather common among Indians in this country.

On Writing

Cite two examples of parenthetical words or phrases set off with commas or dashes. (See page 440 for a discussion of commas and parenthetical words and phrases.) What effect do these constructions have on Varadarajan's prose?

12 But one evening, about a month ago, my wife called excitedly from the next room. She'd found a name for our son at last. Leafing through a book of Indian baby names—published in Bombay and purchased by us in Jackson Heights, Queens—she had come across Satya. Here was an Indian name that didn't sound American. It couldn't even be snipped or tweaked to sound American. But we loved it so much that we forgot America. We were naming him for ourselves, after all, and not for America. We can hardly wait, now, to whisper the words: "Your name is Satya."

Tunku Varadarajan, "Baby Names, Big Battles," © 1999 Tunku Varadarajan. Used by permission of the author.

UNDERSTANDING CONTENT

1. Why does the author think that Satya is a good name for his son?

2. What made choosing a name so difficult for the author and his wife?

3. A Jewish friend objected to the name Shiva. Why? If you do not know, ask someone who is Jewish or check a dictionary.

4. What requirements did the author have for a suitable name for his son?

EXPLORING IDEAS

1. Did the author put undue emphasis on the choice of a name for his son? Explain.

2. Should the author and his wife have chosen an American name, such as John or Bill, for their son? Why or why not?

3. Why do you think that many Indians are choosing Indian names that sound American for their children?

4. How does the author feel about his Indian heritage?

REFLECTING ON YOUR READING PROCESS

Most likely, some words were unfamiliar to you. How many such words did you circle and look up? Which of those words do you think you might be able to use in your other classes?

GETTING IN GEAR: IDEAS FOR WRITING

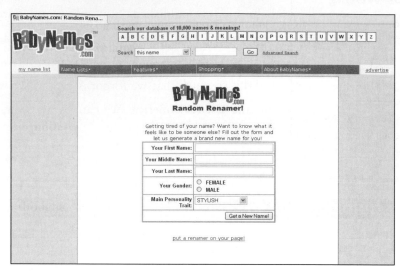

© babynames.com. Used by permission of babynames.com

Do you wonder what it would feel like to have a different name? If you visit www.babynames.com, you can rename yourself using the name generator shown in the screen shot. You can also see the top 100 baby names.

writing topic: Do you like your first name? Explain why or why not and explain how your first name has affected you.

suggestions for prewriting
- Freewrite about the importance of a person's first name and how you feel about your own first name.
- Think about a time someone noticed your name, either positively or negatively. How did the notice make you feel?

suggestions for drafting: Your topic sentence or thesis (depending on whether you are writing a paragraph or an essay) can mention your name and how you feel about your name, something like this: "I am happy that my name is Rosetta because it is distinctive."

suggestion for revising: Ask yourself these questions:
- Will my reader understand how I feel about my name and why I feel that way?
- Is there any place where my reader might lose interest?
- Is there any place where my reader might not understand what I mean?

suggestions for editing
- Take a break before you edit to increase your chances of seeing errors.
- Trust your instincts. If you feel that something is incorrect, it probably is—even if you are not sure of the nature of the problem. Visit your campus writing center for help naming and correcting an error.

THANK YOU, M'AM
LANGSTON HUGHES

Best known as a poet, Langston Hughes (1902–1967) is also respected as a playwright, critic, and fiction writer. He was an important figure in the 1920s' blossoming of literature and music known as the Harlem Renaissance. "Thank You, M'am" is his short story about a confrontation between a young boy and a savvy woman, an encounter that did not go at all as the boy had expected. As you read, consider what you would have done in the woman's place.

1   She was a large woman with a large purse that had everything in it but a hammer and nails. It had a long strap and she carried it slung across her shoulder. It was about eleven o'clock at night, and she was walking alone, when a boy ran up behind her and tried to snatch her purse. The strap broke with the single tug the boy gave it from behind. But the boy's weight, and the weight of the purse combined caused him to lose his balance so, instead of taking off full blast as he had hoped, the boy fell on his back on the sidewalk, and his legs flew up. The large woman simply turned around and kicked him right square in his blue jeaned sitter. Then she reached down, picked the boy up by his shirt front, and shook him until his teeth rattled.

2   After that the woman said, "Pick up my pocketbook, boy, and give it here."

3   She still held him. But she bent down enough to permit him to stoop and pick up her purse. Then she said, "Now ain't you ashamed of yourself?"

4   Firmly gripped by his shirt front, the boy said, "Yes'm."

5   The woman said, "What did you want to do it for?"

6   The boy said, "I didn't aim to."

7   She said, "You a lie!"

8   By that time two or three people passed, stopped, turned to look, and some stood watching.

9   "If I turn you loose, will you run?" asked the woman.

10   "Yes'm," said the boy.

11   "Then I won't turn you loose," said the woman. She did not release him.

12   "I'm very sorry, lady, I'm sorry," whispered the boy.

13   "Um hum! And your face is dirty. I got a great mind to wash your face for you. Ain't you got nobody home to tell you to wash your face?"

14   "No'm," said the boy.

15   "Then it will get washed this evening," said the large woman starting up the street, dragging the frightened boy behind her.

16   He looked as if he were fourteen or fifteen, frail and willow-wild, in tennis shoes and blue jeans.

17   The woman said, "You ought to be my son. I would teach you right from wrong. Least I can do right now is to wash your face. Are you hungry?"

18   "No'm," said the being-dragged boy. "I just want you to turn me loose."

19   "Was I bothering *you* when I turned that corner?" asked the woman.

20   "No'm."

21   "But you put yourself in contact with *me,*" said the woman. "If you think that that contact is not going to last awhile, you got another thought coming. When I get through with you, sir, you are going to remember Mrs. Luella Bates Washington Jones."

22   Sweat popped out on the boy's face and he began to struggle. Mrs. Jones stopped, jerked him around in front of her, put a half-nelson about his neck, and continued to drag him up the street. When she got to her door, she dragged the boy inside, down a hall, and into a large kitchenette-furnished room at the rear of the house. She switched on the light and left the door open. The boy could hear other roomers laughing and talking in the large house. Some of their doors were open, too, so he knew he and the woman were not alone. The woman still had him by the neck in the middle of her room.

23   She said, "What is your name?"

24   "Roger," answered the boy.

25   "Then, Roger, you go to that sink and wash your face," said the woman, whereupon she turned him loose—at last. Roger looked at the door—looked at the woman—looked at the door—*and went to the sink.*

26   "Let the water run until it gets warm," she said. "Here's a clean towel."

27   "You gonna take me to jail?" asked the boy, bending over the sink.

28   "Not with that face, I would not take you nowhere," said the woman. "Here I am trying to get home to cook me a bite to eat and you snatch my pocketbook! Maybe you ain't been to your supper either, late as it be. Have you?"

29   "There's nobody home at my house," said the boy.

30   "Then we'll eat," said the woman. "I believe you're hungry—or been hungry—to try to snatch my pocketbook."

31   "I wanted a pair of blue suede shoes," said the boy.

32   "Well, you didn't have to snatch *my* pocketbook to get some suede shoes," said Mrs. Luella Bates Washington Jones. "You could of asked me."

33   "M'am?"

34 The water dripping from his face, the boy looked at her. There was a long pause. A very long pause. After he had dried his face and not knowing what else to do dried it again, the boy turned around, wondering what next. The door was open. He could make a dash for it down the hall. He could run, run, run, run, *run!*

35 The woman was sitting on the day-bed. After awhile she said, "I were young once and I wanted things I could not get."

36 There was another long pause. The boy's mouth opened. Then he frowned, but not knowing he frowned.

37 The woman said, "Um-hum! You thought I was going to say *but,* didn't you? You thought I was going to say, *but I didn't snatch people's pocketbooks.* Well, I wasn't going to say that." Pause. Silence. "I have done things, too, which I would not tell you, son—neither tell God, if he didn't already know. So you set down while I fix us something to eat. You might run that comb through your hair so you will look presentable."

38 In another corner of the room behind a screen was a gas plate and an icebox. Mrs. Jones got up and went behind the screen. The woman did not watch the boy to see if he was going to run now, nor did she watch her purse which she left behind her on the day-bed. But the boy took care to sit on the far side of the room where he thought she could easily see him out of the corner of her eye, if she wanted to. He did not trust the woman *not* to trust him. And he did not want to be mistrusted now.

39 "Do you need somebody to go to the store," asked the boy, "maybe to get some milk or something?"

40 "Don't believe I do," said the woman, "unless you just want sweet milk yourself. I was going to make cocoa out of this canned milk I got here."

41 "That will be fine," said the boy.

42 She heated some lima beans and ham she had in the icebox, made the cocoa, and set the table. The woman did not ask the boy anything about where he lived, or his folks, or anything else that would embarrass him. Instead, as they ate, she told him about her job in a hotel beauty-shop that stayed open late, what the work was like, and how all kinds of women came in and out, blondes, red-heads, and Spanish. Then she cut him a half of her ten-cent cake.

43 "Eat some more, son," she said.

44 When they were finished eating she got up and said, "Now, here, take this ten dollars and buy yourself some blue suede shoes. And next time, do not make the mistake of latching onto *my* pocketbook *nor nobody else's*—because shoes come

by devilish like that will burn your feet. I got to get my rest now. But I wish you would behave yourself, son, from here on in."

⁴⁵ She led him down the hall to the front door and opened it. "Goodnight! Behave yourself, boy!" she said, looking out into the street.

⁴⁶ The boy wanted to say something else other than, "Thank you, m'am," to Mrs. Luella Bates Washington Jones, but he couldn't do so as he turned at the barren stoop and looked back at the large woman in the door. He barely managed to say, "Thank you," before she shut the door. And he never saw her again.

"Thank You, M'am" from Short Stories *by Langston Hughes. Copyright © 1996 by Ramona Bass and Arnold Rampersad. Reprinted by permission of Hill and Wang, a division of Farrar, Straus and Giroux, LLC.*

UNDERSTANDING CONTENT

On Writing

In Chapter 29, you learned about punctuating direct quotations. When you use conversation to reproduce someone's exact words, you are using direct quotations. Hughes uses a great deal of conversation in his story. What does it contribute? How would the story be different without the conversation?

1. Why did Roger try to steal the purse?

2. Was snatching Mrs. Jones's purse something that Roger planned? How can you be sure Roger is telling the truth about whether he planned to steal the purse?

3. Do you think the title of the story is a good one? Explain.

4. Why does Mrs. Jones take Roger to her house, even though he tried to mug her?

EXPLORING IDEAS

1. Using the evidence in the essay for clues, list words and phrases that describe Roger. Then list ones that describe Mrs. Jones.

2. What do you think of the way Mrs. Jones handled the situation with Roger? Explain your view.

3. Why is it significant to Mrs. Jones that Roger's face is dirty, and why is it important that she take him home to wash it?

4. Why does Roger ask Mrs. Jones if she needs him to go to the store?

REFLECTING ON YOUR READING PROCESS

Did you read "Thank You, M'am" a second time? If so, what did you discover that you did not notice with your first reading? If you did not do a second reading, do so now and note something new that you discovered with that second reading.

GETTING IN GEAR: IDEAS FOR WRITING

Many people need help from time to time. For example, Mrs. Jones extended a helping hand to Roger, and the photograph shows one person helping another. One way *you* can lend a helping hand is to become a volunteer in your community. To discover volunteer opportunities near your school or home, visit www. volunteermatch.org/.

writing topic: Tell about a time you tried to help someone or wanted to help someone. Or tell about a time someone tried to help you. Explain what happened. Perhaps you tried to help someone and it didn't work out, or perhaps you wanted to help but didn't know how to do it or were afraid to. Or perhaps someone helped you and made a big difference in your life—or tried to help you and failed.

suggestion for prewriting

To come up with ideas, answer the following questions:

- What happened?
- Who was involved?
- Where did it happen?
- When did it happen?
- Why did it happen?
- What, if anything, was learned?

suggestions for drafting

- Since you are telling a story about a time you helped someone or a time someone helped you, your details will be arranged in chronological order.
- If you get stuck while drafting, skip the problem and push on. Return later to the part you had trouble with.

suggestion for revising: Read your draft out loud. If it sounds choppy, add transitions (page 45) and vary sentence openers (Chapter 23) to smooth out your sentences. Also, try revising to include coordination (Chapter 7) and subordination (Chapter 8).

suggestion for editing: Edit once for each kind of error you tend to make. Then edit again to check for any other errors.

FOR ONE TEACHER, A LESSON ABOUT E-MAIL AND PRIVACY
ELIZABETH STONE

In this 1999 New York Times *piece, college English professor Elizabeth Stone explains that she once imagined chatting with students in the cafeteria over coffee. Little did she know that she would be chatting with them online—whether she found it convenient or not.*

1   It's 3 in the morning, and not a creature is stirring, except for the mouse. My mouse. I can't sleep, which is why I'm in my nightie, online at the computer, my study dark except for the light cast by my monitor.

2   Suddenly, there is the telltale tinkle of Instant Message, America Online's system for real-time communication among its members, followed by a note from a student—let's call her Rachel, or Elmo1972—across my screen. "HI PROFESSOR!! IT'S ME, RACHEL!!!" That presumes that I don't already know who Elmo1972 is.

3   Which I do.

4   Here we are again, I think, just the two of us, alone in the dark in the middle of the night.

5   Undaunted by my failure to respond as instantly as the Instant Message genre suggests I should, Rachel types me another message.

6   "What are u doing up so late???!"

7   When I became a college professor, I imagined having conversations after class with students over coffee in the cafeteria. I did not imagine that I would be a presence on their Buddy Lists, someone to be dragooned into insomniac pajama parties in cyberspace.

8   Nor did I imagine that they might learn more about me than I care to have them know—like my nocturnal online habits. And I didn't envision that, like Rachel, they would be able to leap out of the cyberbushes at me, any time day or night.

9   "I'm marking your paper," I finally type back "That's what I'm doing." I remind myself I have to block Rachel's screen name so she won't know when I'm online, a way of drawing a curtain between my personal life and hers. I've said this to myself before and didn't do it, but this time I will, less because I don't want to be on call 24 hours a day (though I don't) than because I don't like being imagined in my nightgown.

10   "Marking my paper? Oh phat!!" she types back.

11   "Well, see you in class," I reply, hoping she'll take the hint.

12   She doesn't.

13   "How do u like it so far?"

14   "Can't go into it now or I'll never get them all done."

15   Eventually, I manage to end the conversation.

16   "Sleep tight," she types by way of adieu.

17   The day I first gave students my e-mail address, I knew it would add a new dimension to our professional relationship. And in the beginning, I thought it would be a simple one.

18   They could send me papers via e-mail.

19   I could use e-mail to send them back.

20   They could send me questions via e-mail.

21   I could use e-mail to send back answers.

22   Since I teach journalism, I could send them to websites to read the *Denver Post* the day after the Littleton killings or tell them to check out the new study on coffee posted at the National Institutes of Health or give them an assignment to find out as much information as they could about a classmate, armed with only that person's phone number.

23   I tried to mold this new aspect of our relationship around the traditional pedagogical core. I changed my screen name from ElizaS to the more restrained Eliz-Stone. I was their teacher, after all.

24   Some of the initial rough spots were familiar ones, only in a new key. I found, to my chagrin, that I could misplace just as many e-mail papers as I did the hard-copy kind. For their part, excuses for missing work remained essentially unchanged. "I know I left it in your mailbox" altered not at all, while "my dog ate it," merely changed to "my computer ate it."

25   What I didn't anticipate were the options available to those students of mine who, like Rachel, were AOL subscribers—and that was nearly half of them, as it turned out. For users like us, the first part of an e-mail address is the screen name. Once my students knew my screen name, they could slap it onto their Buddy Lists.

26   Then whenever I went on line, my name would appear in a small window on their monitors.

27   I began to think of the Buddy List window as a sort of online *Rear Window*, from which they could secretly watch my comings and goings.

28   I knew more about them, too, than I once had, often from their screen names alone.

29   Sports zealots—like a Mets fan, Piazza1979—were obvious. When Flipper70 hobbled in on crutches one day saying her tendon had snapped, I figured out, correctly, that she was a gymnast.

30   Sometimes, though, what was right before my eyes proved mysterious. Gigglez122 is one of the most somber students I've ever had. Does she have a merry side? Does she yearn to? Sabachik is Irish. I don't know what to make of Blu-Lady, Punkissa and Snowinlove. Last year, there was EatsDirt. I didn't dare inquire.

31   Recently, a screen name I didn't recognize emblazoned itself across my screen in an Instant Message note. "WAIT!" BBoop181 said, "DON'T SHUT ME OUT! IT'S ME, RACHEL!"

32   "What happened to Elmo?" I typed back.

33   "u blocked Elmo," she said, her font dripping with accusation. "I know because Ken and I were both online one day while we were talking on the phone. Ken could see u come online from his Buddy List, but I couldn't see u on mine. That's when I knew."

34   I had been caught. After years of teaching, I knew how to handle lots of ticklish problems—kids who were unhappy with their grades or depressed or falling asleep in class or on the verge of dropping out—but this ticklish Elmo issue was a new one.

35   But Rachel seemed oddly unfazed.

On Writing

In casual e-mail correspondence, people often use shorthand spellings because they can be quick and easy. Note, for example, the use of *u* for *you* in paragraphs 33 and 36. However, in more formal usage, whether for e-mail or not, use conventional spelling

³⁶ "So anyway, now that I reached u, could u do me a favor? That paper I e-mailed u yesterday? My printer is broken. Do u think u could print me out a hard copy?"

Elizabeth Stone, "For One Teacher, a Lesson about E-Mail and Privacy," *New York Times*, September 2, 1999. Copyright © 1999 by The New York Times Co. Reprinted with permission.

UNDERSTANDING CONTENT

1. How did Professor Stone anticipate using e-mail and online resources when she first gave students her e-mail address?

2. Now that students have her e-mail address, Stone is uncomfortable with the results. Why?

3. Stone finds her students' screen names interesting. Why?

4. Explain the reference contained in the first sentence: "Not a creature is stirring, except for the mouse."

EXPLORING IDEAS

1. Using her e-mail communication with Professor Stone for clues, how would you describe Rachel's personality?

2. Using the clues in the essay to help you decide, how would you describe Professor Stone?

3. If you were Professor Stone, would you feel as she does about AOL's Buddy List? Why or why not?

4. If you were Professor Stone, how would you have handled the correspondence with Rachel and the invasion of privacy?

REFLECTING ON YOUR READING PROCESS

Did you read the essay a second time? Why or why not? List the characteristics of an essay likely to require a second reading.

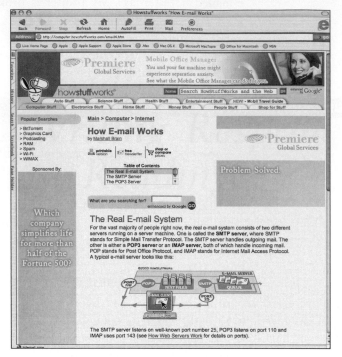

© 2006 HowStuffWorks, Inc. Used with permission.

Have you ever wondered how e-mail works? If so, you can find out by visiting the How Stuff Works Web site at http://computer.howstuffworks.com/email4.htm.

writing topic: Explain the role of computers in your life. Do computers make things easier for you? Are they a frustration? Cite examples to support your claim.

suggestion for prewriting
- List the ways computers make your life easier. Then list the ways they create problems.
- Study your lists and decide which point or points you want to write about. If necessary, write another list that focuses on that point or points.

suggestion for drafting: Develop an informal outline by numbering the ideas in your list in the order you will write them up. If you make several points about computers in your life, you can use a progressive order.

suggestions for revising
- Ask a reader with good judgment about writing whether you have done a good job of explaining why computers are a help or a problem for you. If you have not, add examples or an anecdote (brief story) to show, not just tell.
- For smooth transitions, you can introduce your examples with the transitions *for example* and *for instance*.

suggestion for editing
- Take a break before you edit to increase your chances of seeing errors.
- Trust your instincts. If you have a feeling that something is incorrect, it probably is—even if you are not sure what the problem is. Visit your campus writing center if you need help naming and correcting an error.

THE AFGHAN-AMERICAN: TORN BETWEEN LOVE FOR TWO NATIONS
MARCO R. della CAVA

Journalist Marco R. della Cava has written many articles for USA Today *about a wide variety of topics, including the Internet publication* Salon *and the satirical newspaper* The Onion, *psychic Uri Geller, the crash of EgyptAir 990, and computer use by Native Americans. The article reprinted here first appeared in* USA Today *in 2001. It was one of several pieces della Cava wrote to chronicle how people have been affected by the terrorist attacks on the World Trade Center and the Pentagon. As you read this piece, you will notice the young woman's conflict over her cultural identity, a conflict that looms large as a result of the attack.*

1   Nooria Kakar's young life has been mostly all-American. Growing up in Schenectady, N.Y., she hung out with friends, flirted with boys and helped organize high school dances. After majoring in business at San Jose State University (where she now works in human resources), she set her sights on being a lawyer.

2   But like many immigrants, Kakar lives a double life. At age 17, she married a man chosen by her parents and relatives. At 20, she had a child. At home, she changes from Western to traditional Afghan garb.

3   Prior to Sept. 11, "I never even gave thought to visiting Afghanistan," she says. Now, Kakar is thinking of moving there along with her husband, Abdul Mateen, 28, and son, Jamal, 2.

4   While many Americans now are grappling with tangible issues such as unemployment, Kakar's struggles are philosophical. On a recent lunch break at a neighborhood Burger King (where she declined food or drink in deference to her Ramadan fast), she poured out her conflicted thoughts. Here is her story, in her words.

5   I'm from Kandahar, and I'm ethnically Pashtun. I was born on Jan. 1, 1979. I lived there for four or five years. I remember my grandfather's house that I lived in after my father was killed by the Soviets.

6   My father was a teacher. I guess they didn't want him to spread his anti-communist beliefs. My mom tells me that people came to the door and took him away. The next day, they found my father in our fields, shot dead. My life hasn't been the same since.

7   When we left Afghanistan, I lived in Pakistan for about four years, in Quetta and then Karachi. Then my oldest uncle got into the United States and applied for the rest of the family to come. It was a battle to get us in, but eventually we did, all 13 of us.

8   We almost moved to California, where my uncle was, but it was too expensive. So instead we went to Upstate New York, where I stayed until 1995, when I came here to San Jose.

9   It was a small-town life in Schenectady, only one high school. We lived in public housing, about 50 families in our complex. We all stuck together: parties, weddings, playing. That helped me stay in touch with my traditions.

10   My mom always covers her head, but my sister and I don't. It's a generational thing. I have always been very aware of my traditions and my country, but in my values, I feel very American.

11   In Afghan culture, they don't encourage girls to go to college and get a degree. It's more like, get married and have a kid. But I always wanted to make sure I could be me.

12   When I was 17, I got married to an Afghan guy from California. My husband is my uncle's wife's brother. Our marriage was set up. My only request was to go to school and have my freedom.

13   When I went to San Jose State, we were struggling to live on our own and support ourselves. I left at 6 a.m. and came home at 11 p.m., which is again not what an Afghan girl does.

14   Prior to Sept. 11, I had a very set future. I was going to go to school, I was going to graduate, and we were going to work hard. My husband, who works as a cashier now, was going to get his own business, we were going to buy a house, going to save for our son's college education. I was very ambitious and optimistic. I don't know about that now.

15   I'm a pessimist now, which I've never been. For some reason, I feel very guilty. I've talked to other younger Afghan people, and many feel the same way, because we can imagine being in those camps being bombed.

16   As an Afghan, I think the U.S. (military) action is totally wrong. They're killing innocent people. But from my American perspective, I really want my government to capture whoever perpetrated Sept. 11. I'm conflicted.

17   I've always been a very patient person, but now if someone said something (against) Afghanistan, I don't think I'd have the patience to sit there and explain how I feel. So I tell people almost immediately, "Hey, that's where I was born," just so they know before they say anything.

18   There are times when I feel that I have to prove myself as being one or the other, Afghan or American. But I'm not, I'm both. Before Sept. 11, I used to sit there and ask my mom, "Are your people ever going to accept me as an Afghan?" Probably not, because I grew up here and I have a different, a very American, personality.

19 But now I feel the same thing about America. I feel I'll never be totally accepted as American, no matter how I dress, act or talk. I am who I am. I don't want to be seen as 100% of either one. I want to be able to stay right where I am, but I'd like to be supported by both sides.

20 I was going to go and get a law degree, but I think that's off for now. I'm researching agencies that are sending people to Afghanistan. I have an application from the Red Cross. I want to go and help out, that's my future.

21 The way I think about Afghanistan is the way I think about my son. What do I want for him? I want hospitals for him, clothes, food, an education, and that's what I want for the children there. They're in the same situation I was in 20 years ago.

22 In a perfect world, I'd go help the Afghan people *and* become a lawyer. But my goals for myself don't really matter in this moment in time. If I just help to save one child over there, my law degree is worth giving up.

23 It's funny. I have a wall at home that I've been using to put up my college degree, and any other honors I might have won.

24 I am very proud of it, and I envisioned that wall getting more and more full. But next to it is a wall with just a tiny map of Afghanistan, which my husband put up. Now, that tiny map has a lot more meaning than my wall.

Marco R. della Cava, "The Afghan-American: Torn between Love for Two Nations," *USA Today,* December 17, 2001. © 2001 USA Today. Reprinted with permission.

On Writing

"The Afghan-American: Torn between Love for Two Nations" first appeared in *USA Today*. The article's paragraphs are much shorter than usual for an essay, but not for a newspaper article. Why are newspaper paragraphs so short?

UNDERSTANDING CONTENT

1. Why does della Cava say Nooria Kakar lives a double life?

2. In what ways does Kakar depart from Afghan traditions? In what ways does she adhere to Afghan traditions?

3. How did the September 11 attacks change Kakar?

4. Why does Kakar want to return to Afghanistan?

EXPLORING IDEAS

1. The author describes Kakar's post–September 11 issues as "philosophical" (paragraph 4). In what way are they philosophical?

2. Kakar says that not covering her head is a "generational thing" (paragraph 10). Explain what she means.

3. Kakar wants to "be supported by both sides" (paragraph 19). How possible do you think that is?

4. Does Kakar seem like a person you would like to get to know better? Explain.

REFLECTING ON YOUR READING PROCESS

Select one of the impressions you formed when you read. In a few sentences, explain why you formed that impression.

GETTING IN GEAR: IDEAS FOR WRITING

A "watershed moment" is a public or private event that marks a turning point, a time when things change permanently, or at least for a long time. The attack on the World Trade Center and Pentagon on September 11, 2001, was a watershed moment. You can read accounts and analyses of the events from around the world at the Library of Congress Web archive: http://1cweb4.loc.gov/911/index.html.

writing topic: Tell about a watershed moment in your life. Explain what happened and how you were affected, being sure to note in what ways you were permanently altered.

suggestion for prewriting: To identify the watershed moments in your life, list all the important events you can think of. The events need not be as dramatic and far reaching as terrorist attacks, and they might be public or private. You can include such events as a move to a new city, a parent's job loss, or the gain or loss of a friend.

suggestions for drafting
- Think of your writing as having two parts, one that tells what happened and one that gives the effects of what happened.
- The part that tells what happened will likely have a chronological order, and the part that gives the effects may have a progressive order.

suggestion for revising: Use the checklist for revising a paragraph on pages 33–34 or the checklist for revising an essay on page 65.

suggestion for editing: You may have occasion to use the words *affect* and *effect* in this writing. To be sure you understand the difference, study the explanation beginning on page 394.

THE FIGHT
MAYA ANGELOU

Writer, singer, dancer, and African-American activist Maya Angelou is perhaps best known for her autobiographical I Know Why the Caged Bird Sings *(1969).* Her later books include All God's Children Need Traveling Shoes *(1986),* My Painted House, My Friendly Chicken and Me *(1994), and* Oh Pray My Wings Are Gonna Fit Me Well *(1997). In the following excerpt from* I Know Why the Caged Bird Sings, *the store referred to located in Stamps, Arkansas. The fight referred to occurred when African-American heavyweight champion Joe Louis fought the Italian heavyweight champion, Primo Carnera, in 1935. For the black people who cheered Louis on, the fight was not just another sporting event.*

1   The last inch of space was filled, yet people continued to wedge themselves along the walls of the Store. Uncle Willie had turned the radio up to its last notch so that youngsters on the porch wouldn't miss a word. Women sat on kitchen chairs, dining room chairs, stools and upturned wooden boxes. Small children and babies perched on every lap available and men leaned on the shelves or on each other.

2   The apprehensive mood was shot through with shafts of gaiety, as a black sky is streaked with lightning.

3   "I ain't worried 'bout this fight. Joe's gonna whip that cracker like it's open season."

4   "He gone whip him till that white boy call him Momma."

5   At last the talking was finished and the string-along songs about razor blades* were over and the fight began.

6   "A quick jab to the head." In the Store the crowd grunted. "A left to the head and a right and another left." One of the listeners cackled like a hen and was quieted.

7   "They're in a clench, Louis is trying to fight his way out."

8   Some bitter comedian on the porch said, "That white man don't mind hugging that niggah now, I betcha."

9   "The referee is moving in to break them up, but Louis finally pushed the contender away and it's an uppercut to the chin. The contender is hanging on, now he's backing away. Louis catches him with a short left to the jaw."

10   A tide of murmuring assent poured out the doors and into the yard.

11   "Another left and another left. Louis is saving that mighty right . . ." The mutter in the Store had grown into a baby roar and it was pierced by the clang of a bell and the announcer's "That's the bell for round three, ladies and gentlemen."

12   As I pushed my way into the Store I wondered if the announcer gave any thought to the fact that he was addressing as "ladies and gentlemen" all the Negroes around the world who sat sweating and praying, glued to their "master's voice."†

13   There were only a few calls for R. C. Colas, Dr. Peppers, and Hire's root beer. The real festivities would begin after the fight. Then even the old Christian ladies who taught their children and tried themselves to practice turning the other cheek would buy soft drinks, and if the Brown Bomber's victory was a particularly bloody one they would order peanut patties and Baby Ruths also.

14   Bailey and I lay the coins on top of the cash register. Uncle Willie didn't allow us to ring up sales during a fight. It was too noisy and might shake up the atmosphere. When the gong rang for the next round we pushed through the near sacred quiet to the herd of children outside.

15   "He's got Louis against the ropes and now it's a left to the body and a right to the ribs. Another right to the body, it looks like it was low . . . Yes, ladies and

---

*Singing commercials for Gillette razor blades.
†A famous advertising slogan for RCA, "His master's voice" was accompanied by a picture of a dog listening to a phonograph.

gentlemen, the referee is signaling but the contender keeps raining the blows on Louis. It's another to the body, and it looks like Louis is going down."

16   My race groaned. It was our people falling. It was another lynching, yet another Black man hanging on a tree. One more woman ambushed and raped. A Black boy whipped and maimed. It was hounds on the trail of a man running through slimy swamps. It was a white woman slapping her maid for being forgetful.

17   The men in the Store stood away from the walls and at attention. Women greedily clutched the babes on their laps while on the porch the shufflings and smiles, flirtings and pinching of a few minutes before were gone. This might be the end of the world. If Joe lost we were back in slavery and beyond help. It would all be true, the accusations that we were lower types of human beings. Only a little higher than the apes. True that we were stupid and ugly and lazy and dirty and, unlucky and worst of all, that God Himself hated us and ordained us to be hewers of wood and drawers of water, forever and ever, world without end.

18   We didn't breathe. We didn't hope. We waited.

19   "He's off the ropes, ladies and gentlemen. He's moving towards the center of the ring." There was no time to be relieved. The worst might still happen.

20   "And now it looks like Joe is mad. He's caught Carnera with a left hook to the head and a right to the head. It's a left jab to the body and another left to the head. There's a left cross and a right to the head. The contender's right eye is bleeding and he can't seem to keep his block up. Louis is penetrating every block. The referee is moving in, but Louis sends a left to the body and it's the uppercut to the chin and the contender is dropping. He's on the canvas, ladies and gentlemen."

21   Babies slid to the floor as women stood up and men leaned toward the radio.

22   "Here's the referee. He's counting. One, two, three, four, five, six, seven . . . Is the contender trying to get up again?"

23   All the men in the store shouted, "NO."

24   "—eight, nine, ten." There were a few sounds from the audience, but they seemed to be holding themselves in against tremendous pressure.

25   "The fight is all over, ladies and gentlemen. Let's get the microphone over to the referee . . . Here he is. He's got the Brown Bomber's hand, he's holding it up . . . Here he is . . ."

26   Then the voice, husky and familiar, came to wash over us—"The winnah, and still heavyweight champeen of the world . . . Joe Louis."

27   Champion of the world. A Black boy. Some Black mother's son. He was the strongest man in the world. People drank Coca-Colas like ambrosia and ate candy

bars like Christmas. Some of the men went behind the Store and poured white lightning in their soft-drink bottles, and a few of the bigger boys followed them. Those who were not chased away came back blowing their breath in front of themselves like proud smokers.

28   It would take an hour or more before the people would leave the Store and head for home. Those who lived too far had made arrangements to stay in town. It wouldn't do for a Black man and his family to be caught on a lonely country road on a night when Joe Louis had proved that we were the strongest people in the world.

From *I Know Why the Caged Bird Sings* by Maya Angelou. Copyright © 1969 and renewed 1997 by Maya Angelou. Used by permission of Random House, Inc.

UNDERSTANDING CONTENT

On Writing

Explain the reason for each of the following capital letters: *Momma* (paragraph 4), *Christian* (paragraph 13), *Baby Ruths* (paragraph 13), *Himself*, (paragraph 17), *Brown Bomber's* (paragraph 25), *Christmas* (paragraph 27).

1. Which paragraphs tell something about what life was like for African Americans during slavery and afterward in the South? What do those paragraphs say life was like?

2. What image of white people is presented in the selection?

3. One of the elements of the story that helps set it in the 1930s is the description of the store. Cite two other references that help identify the time.

4. What connection exists between the outcome of the fight and the pride of the African-American community?

EXPLORING IDEAS

1. Why do you think that "the old Christian ladies who taught their children and tried themselves to practice turning the other cheek" (paragraph 13) support the fight?

2. Why do you think Angelou makes this statement: "It wouldn't do for a Black man and his family to be caught on a lonely country road on a night when Joe Louis had proved that we were the strongest people in the world" (paragraph 28)?

3. For what purpose do you think Angelou tells the story of the fight?

4. What is the significance of the fight and the story?

REFLECTING ON YOUR READING PROCESS

Did you follow the four steps for critical reading explained in this chapter? Why or why not?

GETTING IN GEAR: IDEAS FOR WRITING

The photograph is of Joe Louis, known as "The Brown Bomber." To learn more about Louis and to see additional photos, visit this *Detroit News* Web site: http://info.detnews.com/history/story/index.cfm?id=52&category=sports.

writing topic: Joe Louis was a hero—a symbol of pride, hope, victory, and strength. As heavyweight champion, he was an important figure in a racially divided country. Explain what today's sports heroes symbolize. As an alternative, select a sports figure and tell what that person symbolizes—good or bad.

suggestion for prewriting: Write a map with "what sports heroes symbolize" (or use a specific person) in the center. (For more on mapping, see page 9.)

suggestion for drafting: Back up your points with examples of sports heroes who symbolize the qualities you mention.

suggestion for revising: Look for opportunities to add details that show, not just tell. For example, instead of saying that "Lance Armstrong symbolizes strength in the face of adversity," be more specific: "Lance Armstrong symbolizes strength in the face of adversity. Even after cancer surgery and chemotherapy, he continued competing in the Tour de France."

suggestion for editing: Edit last, after revising. That way, your full attention is on looking for errors. Also, you will not be editing material that you strike out during revision.

ONLY dAUGHTER
SANDRA CISNEROS

A writer of both poetry and prose, Sandra Cisneros draws on her Mexican-American heritage, focuses on the cultural and social conflicts related to her upbringing, and presents the perspective of Chicana (Mexican-American women). She is one of the first Hispanic-American writers to achieve commercial success. Among her books are The House on Mango Street *(1983),* Woman Hollering Creek and Other Stories *(1991),* My Wicked Ways *(1992), and* Loose Women: Poems *(1994). "Only daughter," which first appeared in* Glamour *magazine in 1990, tells about current and past influences on Cisnero's writing.*

1 Once, several years ago, when I was just starting out my writing career, I was asked to write my own contributor's note for an anthology. I wrote: "I am the only daughter in a family of six sons. *That* explains everything."

2 Well, I've thought that ever since, and yes, it explains a lot to me, but for the reader's sake I should have written: "I am the only daughter in a *Mexican* family of six sons." Or even: "I am the only daughter of a Mexican father and a Mexican-American mother." Or: "I am the only daughter of a working-class family of nine." All of these had everything to do with who I am today.

3 I was/am the only daughter and *only* a daughter. Being an only daughter in a family of six sons forced me by circumstance to spend a lot of time by myself because my brothers felt it beneath them to play with a *girl* in public. But that aloneness, that loneliness, was good for a would-be writer—it allowed me time to think and think, to imagine, to read and prepare myself.

4 Being only a daughter for my father meant my destiny would lead me to become someone's wife. That's what he believed. But when I was in the fifth grade and shared my plans for college with him, I was sure he understood. I remember my father saying, *"Que bueno, mi'ja,* that's good." That meant a lot to me, especially since my brothers thought the idea hilarious. What I didn't realize was that my father thought college was good for girls—good for finding a husband. After four years in college and two more in graduate school, and still no husband, my father shakes his head even now and says I wasted all that education.

5   In retrospect, I'm lucky my father believed daughters were meant for husbands. It meant it didn't matter if I majored in something silly like English. After all, I'd find a nice professional eventually, right? This allowed me the liberty to putter about embroidering my little poems and stories without my father interrupting with so much as a "What's that you're writing?"

6   But the truth is, I wanted him to interrupt. I wanted my father to understand what it was I was scribbling, to introduce me as "My only daughter, the writer." Not as "This is my only daughter. She teaches." *Es maestra*—teacher. Not even *profesora.*

7   In a sense, everything I have ever written has been for him, to win his approval even though I know my father can't read English words, even though my father's only reading includes the brown-ink *Esto* sports magazines from Mexico City and the bloody *¡Alarma!* magazines that feature yet another sighting of *La Virgen de Guadalupe* on a tortilla or a wife's revenge on her philandering husband by bashing his skull in with a *molcajete* (a kitchen mortar made of volcanic rock). Or the *fotonovelas,* the little picture paperbacks with tragedy and trauma erupting from the characters' mouths in bubbles.

8   A father represents, then, the public majority. A public who is disinterested in reading, and yet one whom I am writing about and for, and privately trying to woo.

9   When we were growing up in Chicago, we moved a lot because of my father. He suffered bouts of nostalgia. Then we'd have to let go of our flat, store the furniture with mother's relatives, load the station wagon with baggage and bologna sandwiches and head south. To Mexico City.

10   We came back, of course. To yet another Chicago flat, another Chicago neighborhood, another Catholic school. Each time, my father would seek out the parish priest in order to get a tuition break, and complain or boast: "I have seven sons."

11   He meant *siete hijos,* seven children, but he translated it as "sons." "I have seven sons." To anyone who would listen. The Sears Roebuck employee who sold us the washing machine. The short-order cook where my father ate his ham-and-eggs breakfasts. "I have seven sons." As if he deserved a medal from the state.

12   My papa. He didn't mean anything by that mistranslation, I'm sure. But somehow I could feel myself being erased. I'd tug my father's sleeve and whisper: "Not seven sons. Six! and *one daughter.*"

13   When my oldest brother graduated from medical school, he fulfilled my father's dream that we study hard and use this—our heads, instead of this—our

hands. Even now my father's hands are thick and yellow, stubbed by a history of hammer and nails and twine and coils and springs. "Use this," my father said, tapping his head, "and not this," showing us those hands. He always looked tired when he said it.

14   Wasn't college an investment? And hadn't I spent all those years in college? And if I didn't marry, what was it all for? Why would anyone go to college and then choose to be poor? Especially someone who had always been poor.

15   Last year, after ten years of writing professionally, the financial rewards started to trickle in. My second National Endowment for the Arts Fellowship. A guest professorship at the University of California, Berkeley. My book, which sold to a major New York publishing house.

16   At Christmas, I flew home to Chicago. The house was throbbing, same as always; hot *tamales* and sweet *tamales* hissing in my mother's pressure cooker, and everybody—my mother, six brothers, wives, babies, aunts, cousins—talking too loud and at the same time, like in a Fellini* film, because that's just how we are.

17   I went upstairs to my father's room. One of my stories had just been translated into Spanish and published in an anthology of Chicano writing, and I wanted to show it to him. Ever since he recovered from a stroke two years ago, my father likes to spend his leisure hours horizontally. And that's how I found him, watching a Pedro Infante movie on Galavision and eating rice pudding.

18   There was a glass filmed with milk on the bedside table. There were several vials of pills and balled Kleenex. And on the floor, one black sock and a plastic urinal that I didn't want to look at but looked at anyway. Pedro Infante was about to burst into song, and my father was laughing.

19   I'm not sure if it was because my story was translated into Spanish, or because it was published in Mexico, or perhaps because the story dealt with Tepeyac, the *colonia* my father was raised in and the house he grew up in, but at any rate, my father punched the mute button on his remote control and read my story.

20   I sat on the bed next to my father and waited. He read it very slowly. As if he were reading each line over and over. He laughed at all the right places and read lines he liked out loud. He pointed and asked questions: "Is this So-and-so?" "Yes," I said. He kept reading.

On Writing

A **rhetorical question** is asked to create an effect; no answer is expected. Sometimes it emphasizes a point or gets the reader to think about something. Rhetorical questions appear in paragraphs 5 and 14. What purpose do they serve?

---

* *Federico Fellini (1920–1993) was an Italian film director, whose movies were known for their personal expression and artistic fantasy.*

21 When he was finally finished, after what seemed like hours, my father looked up and asked: "Where can we get more copies of this for the relatives?"

22 Of all the wonderful things that happened to me last year, that was the most wonderful.

UNDERSTANDING CONTENT

1. How did Cisneros's family circumstances affect her as an aspiring writer?

2. Cisneros says that everything she has written has been for a particular person. Who is that person? Why does she write for that person?

3. Explain the difference between the attitude of Cisneros's father toward his sons and his attitude toward his daughter.

4. The fact that Cisneros's father showed pleasure reading her story was "the most wonderful" thing that happened to her that year. Why?

EXPLORING IDEAS

1. Cisneros says the fact that she is the only daughter in a family with six sons explains everything. What specifically does it explain?

2. In her original title, Cisneros chose not to capitalize the *d* in *daughter*. What is the significance of the lowercase letter?

3. Explain the double meaning of *only* in the essay's title. Is the title a good one? Why or why not?

4. What does Cisneros convey about her profession when she describes writing as "embroidering my little poems and stories" (paragraph 5)? Why do you think she uses this phrase?

REFLECTING ON YOUR READING PROCESS

What did you think the title meant when you previewed the essay? How did your understanding change after your first or second reading?

GETTING IN GEAR: IDEAS FOR WRITING

Title IX of the 1972 Education Amendments Act prohibits gender discrimination "under any education program or activity receiving federal funds." This protection against sex discrimination applies from preschool through graduate school. Although Title IX has not ended sex discrimination in education, it has certainly eliminated a great deal of it. The photographs reveal some of the differences that existed between men's and women's athletics before Title IX. To read about the specific protections provided by Title IX, visit www.dol.gov/oasam/regs/statutes/ titleix.htm.

writing topic: Discuss whether or not there are different expectations for males and females in the United States. If you like, you may limit your discussion to expectations in one area, such as athletics, politics, parenting, education, the workplace, or the media.

suggestions for prewriting

- Write a map with "expectations for males and females" in the center. You can branch off from the center with different aspects of society, such as education, sports, marriage, careers, and appearance. (For more on mapping, see page 9.)
- Select one aspect of society from your map (such as education) and freewrite about expectations for males and females as they relate to that aspect.

suggestions for drafting

- Your topic sentence or thesis (depending on whether you are writing a paragraph or an essay) can mention the aspect of society and whether the expectations for males and females are different, something like this: "In the workplace, expectations for males and females are not as similar as we like to believe."
- It might be effective to arrange your detail in a progressive order.

suggestion for revising: Since you are comparing or contrasting genders, you may need to use transitions such as *similarly, in like fashion, in the same manner, in contrast, on the other hand,* and *however* to move smoothly from one point to another.

suggestion for editing Remember to use commas to set off transitions.

PROUD TO BE ADD
COURTNEY HOUSAM

Courtney Housam was a first-year student at Southern Methodist University when she wrote this article for ADDitude magazine (2001), a publication for and about people with attention deficit disorder (ADD). ADD causes people to be easily distracted and impulsive. When it occurs with hyperactivity, it is called attention deficit/hyperactivity disorder (ADHD). The essay is an adaptation of one she presented at her high school senior assembly.

1   I am sitting in ninth period statistics class as we discuss probability. My classmate reads from the textbook about the probability of two randomly selected M&M 's being red. I'm thinking, "Why would you want a red M&M , because yellow is definitely better. But then again, I wouldn't want M&M's—I'm kind of in the mood for some Sour Patch Kids, but not too many, because your tongue starts to hurt if you eat a lot of those. Maybe I should just get a bagel after school. With cream cheese. Yeah . . . veggie cream cheese."

2   As I get called on: "Courtney, what was your calculation?" and I answer "Uh . . . I don't know. Can you repeat the question?" I am met with an angry glare. I'm Courtney Housam. I am ADD.

3   I've spent a lot of time in detention because of looking out the window in history class, losing assignments, and forgetting books at home. In the beginning, I never learned—not because I was a rebel, but because it was so hard to stay focused, organized, together. In middle school, a psychologist told me it was common for ADD kids to "fake it" their entire academic lives, paying attention 20 percent of the time and somehow pulling the rabbit out of the hat come exam week. Maybe you are familiar with this concept.

4   ADD means I'm easily distracted. Any change in the environment catches my eye and disrupts any earlier train of thought. I have difficulty following multi-step directions and sticking with what I'm thinking. I assure you that if you tell me to "take a right, go three blocks, turn left, watch signs for Cottman Avenue and follow straight to the stop sing—but don't forget to go to the gas station first," I will be out of gas, lost on a side street in Northeast Philadelphia.

5   Impulsivity impairs my self-control. I tend to make quick decisions and to jump to conclusions before thinking things through. Many times I'll say what's on my mind or make rash decisions without considering the consequences. People with ADD often find themselves fidgeting or talking nonstop as a way of releasing excess energy. I have a constant urge to be on the go.

6   "Take a chill pill!" If I had a dollar for every time I've heard that phrase, I'd be worth more than Bill Gates. Ritalin* does help me calm down and focus my thoughts. Miraculously, I can remember to turn in my history paper on time and clean out my book bag. When I started on Ritalin, my C average jumped to A-plus.

7   On the other hand, what's wrong with being loud, speaking with enthusiasm and entertaining radical thoughts? Maybe we should worry less about medicating people into tranquility and take time to appreciate their eccentricity.

8   Although many ADD qualities may seem destructive or dangerous, there are also many positive aspects of this condition. ADD people are some of the most intuitive, creative, intelligent people around. Thomas Edison and Benjamin Franklin are both believed to have had it.

9   I hate being asked if I took my medicine today. I believe that ADD is a difference, not a disorder. For me, Ritalin is a helpful tool. But if the aberration were considered part of the norm, there would be no need to fix it. I am proud to say that I have ADD and I would have it no other way.

Courtney Housam, "Proud to Be ADD," December 2001. Reprinted with permission from *ADDitude Magazine*. For more articles like this one, to subscribe, or to sign up for the monthly e-newslwetter, visit *ADDitude* online, www.additudemag.com.

On Writing

In Chapter 21, you learned about the importance of parallelism. Cite an example of parallelism in paragraph 7 and paragraph 8.

UNDERSTANDING CONTENT

1. List four words and phrases to describe the style of people with attention deficit disorder.

2. What are the positive aspects of ADD?

3. What are the negative aspects of ADD?

4. How does the author feel about having ADD?

Ritalin is a drug often used to help control the symptoms of ADD and ADHD.

EXPLORING IDEAS

1. How do you think teachers react to students with attention deficit disorder?

2. Do you agree or disagree with Housam's statement that "maybe we should worry less about medicating people into tranquility and take time to appreciate their eccentricity"? Explain.

3. In paragraph 9, Housam says that, if ADD were "part of the norm, there would be no need to fix it." Why don't we consider ADD part of the norm?

4. In paragraph 3, Housam says a psychologist told her that children with ADD are often "pulling the rabbit out of the hat come exam week." What does the psychologist mean?

REFLECTING ON YOUR READING PROCESS

The headnote gives you some background information on the author of the essay. Did that information affect your reaction to the essay and its ideas? Explain.

GETTING IN GEAR: IDEAS FOR WRITING

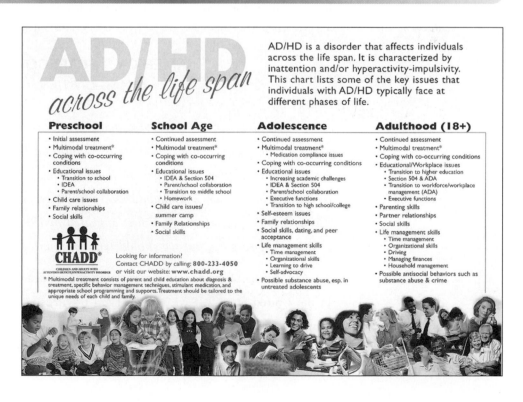

The poster explains that attention deficit disorder is a lifetime condition that manifests itself in particular ways at different times of life. To learn more about ADD (and to purchase the poster), you can visit the Web site for Children and Adults with Attention Deficit/Hyperactivity Disorder (CHADD) at www.chadd.org.

writing topic: According to some psychologists, as much as 5 percent of the population has attention deficit disorder, and many prominent people have ADD. As Housman notes, both Thomas Edison and Benjamin Franklin may have had it. Perhaps, then, ADD should not be considered "abnormal." Explain one or more ways we decide what is "normal."

suggestions for prewriting
- List the factors that influence what we consider normal. Consider the media, school, our parents, religion, and so on.
- Freewrite about one or two factors on your list.

suggestions for drafting
- Develop an outline before you draft. You may want to arrange your details in a progressive order.
- Use examples to illustrate how our sense of "normal" is affected.

suggestion for revising: Think about your reader and read your draft the way that person will. Then ask yourself these questions:
- Is there are any place the reader might lose interest?
- Is there any place the reader might not understand what I mean?
- Is there any place the reader might not be convinced of what I am saying?

suggestion for editing: Try placing a ruler under the first line of your writing. Examine just that line—slowly—for errors. Then move the ruler down to the next line and look for errors. Continue in this fashion to the end of your writing.

AMERICA'S SCAPEGOATS
CHANG-LIN TIEN

A naturalized citizen who emigrated from China, Chang-Lin Tien (1935–2002) was the chancellor of the University of California, Berkeley, from 1990 to 1997. An internationally known expert in thermal science and engineering, he was recognized as a scholar, a humanitarian, and an informal ambassador to Asia. In "America's Scapegoats," which first appeared in 1994 in Newsweek's *"My Turn" column, Tien argues that we should take pride in our immigrant heritage.*

1   My life has been far more satisfying than I dreamed possible when I arrived in the United States, 38 years ago. I am privileged to head a world class institution, the University of California, Berkeley. My former Ph.D. students are professors at major universities. My engineering research has contributed to America's space technology, nuclear-reactor safety, and energy technology.

2   Yet no matter the scope of my accomplishments, when many Americans see my face and hear my Chinese accent, they think of me as an immigrant, first and foremost. In the eyes of many, that has come to mean a drain on public services, a competitor for jobs and a threat to a cohesive society.

3   I have watched the campaign to discourage immigration with growing concern. Whether we preside over universities or work the fields, immigrants are becoming the scapegoats for America's ills. I don't object to controlling the volume of immigration. Today, with unprecedented shifts in the global population, no nation can afford to throw its borders wide open. But we are in danger of forgetting that America was built by immigrants, and that our immigrant heritage is the wellspring of our nation's strength and vitality.

4   Even as a university chancellor, I am no stranger to the sharp sting of anti-immigrant hostility. Perhaps the most dramatic incident took place when I represented Berkeley a few years ago at a football rally after the Citrus Bowl. As I walked to the stage, a few people in the audience chanted, "Buy American, Buy American." This was profoundly disturbing. I am American and proud of it.

5   Just looking like an immigrant can make you the target of heckling. Any of us of Asian, Latin American and Middle Eastern heritage knows this. Several friends and family members have been subjected to taunts of "Go back to your own country." It's difficult for them to respond; like Bruce Springsteen, they were born in the U.S.A. This anti immigrant mood is not new. Throughout our history, whenever the economy suffered, immigrants became easy targets. But today, it is not only the immigrants who suffer. Ultimately, all Americans stand to lose, native and foreign born alike.

6   Now our nation faces the formidable challenge of forging a unified society from highly diverse constituencies. The population is undergoing a rapid transformation, and by the middle of the 21st century, the majority of Americans will trace their roots to Latin America, Africa, Asia, the Middle East and the Pacific Islands.

7   Evolving into a cohesive society based on respect and understanding is far from automatic. Throughout human history, racial and ethnic tensions have divided and destroyed peoples and countries. The ethnic strife that ripped apart Brooklyn's Crown Heights and South Central Los Angeles is a sobering reminder of the challenge posed by rapid diversification.

8   Yet if there is a nation that promises to be a model for how to make diversity work, it is the United States. This is the nation with the strongest and deepest democratic roots. This is a nation with a living Constitution that guarantees

rights to all its citizens. This is a nation that has taken pride not in its homogeneity, but in its immigrant heritage.

9 It was America's promise that drew me here in 1956. Even as a penniless graduate student from China, I believed I could make a contribution in this land of opportunity. Indeed, I am deeply grateful to America for offering opportunities difficult to find anywhere else in the world.

10 Today, however, in the headlong rush to restrict immigration, we are jeopardizing this promise. Hundreds of state and federal measures have been introduced to curb legal and illegal immigration. The backers of these proposals often rely on inflammatory anti immigrant rhetoric to rivet the attention of Americans, ignite their rage and move them to action.

11 In the hoopla, the debate is now moving away from the legitimate question of how much immigration America can sustain. Instead, we're blaming immigrants for many of our most urgent problems and trying to convince ourselves that we'll solve them by simply restricting immigration.

12 Effective immigration policy must be grounded in reason, not emotion. Racial and cultural, hostilities fanned by the present anti immigration frenzy must cool down. Then, I am confident, we can make immigration work for America, just as it has from the time of our nation's infancy.

13 After all, in my 38 years here, I have seen this nation make amazing progress. When I came here to study in the South, I encountered Jim Crow segregation. Whites rode in the front of buses and blacks in the back. This racial system did not apply to Asian-Americans and left us in an ugly limbo. It troubled me and left a life-long impression. The rest of the country was not free from racial discrimination. When I joined the Berkeley faculty, in 1959, my wife and I could not live in certain Bay Area neighborhoods.

14 In less than four decades I have seen the enactment of civil-rights legislation that has created opportunities for all Americans. I have seen universities open doors to students who reflect our diverse society. I have seen women and men of all backgrounds become leaders in government, business, science, arts and education. Now I look forward to seeing the promise of America fulfilled. We can turn our national motto of *e pluribus unum,* or "one out of many," into more than an expression in a dead language. What it will take is the same kind of unwavering commitment that forged one nation from highly diverse colonies more than two centuries ago.

15 Immigrants are not the cause of America's major problems. It's time America stopped putting all the blame on immigrants and started facing up to the difficult

reality of a world in transition. Let's seize the opportunity to transform America into a model of diversity for the future.

Chang-Lin Tien, "America's Scapegoats," *Newsweek,* October 31, 1994. Copyright © 1994 Newsweek, Inc. All rights reserved. Reprinted by permission.

UNDERSTANDING CONTENT

On Writing

In sentence 2 of paragraph 5, notice that the singular verb *knows* is used with the indefinite pronoun *any*. As explained on page 186, *any* can be either singular or plural, depending on meaning. In this case, it has the singular sense of "any *one* of us."

1. The author was a highly educated, unusually productive U.S. citizen, yet often he was not perceived as such because he looked like an immigrant. How was he often perceived?

2. Explain the meaning of the U.S. motto *e pluribus unum,* which means "one out of many."

3. When people try to pass laws to severely limit immigration, what important fact are they forgetting?

4. According to Tien, why is the United States the country that stands the best chance of becoming a model for successful diversity?

EXPLORING IDEAS

1. In paragraph 12, the author says that "we can make immigration work for America, just as it has from the time of our nation's infancy." What do you think this statement means?

2. In your own words, explain Tien's position on immigration and why he feels as he does. Do you agree with him? Why or why not?

3. Why do you think some people blame immigrants for America's problems?

4. The author closes by calling for us to "transform America into a model of diversity for the future" (paragraph 15). Suggest two or three ways we can heed his call.

REFLECTING ON YOUR READING PROCESS

This is the last reading in the book. Has your reading process changed this term? If so, explain how. If not, explain why not.

GETTING IN GEAR: IDEAS FOR WRITING

A symbol of freedom, the Statue of Liberty has welcomed over 12 million immigrants to the United States through New York Harbor and Ellis Island. Inscribed on the base of the statue is Emma Lazarus's poem "The New Colossus," which reads in part:

> Give me your tired, your poor,
> Your huddled masses yearning to breathe free,
> The wretched refuse of your teeming shore.
> Send these, the homeless, tempest-tost to me,
> I lift my lamp beside the golden door!

To read all of "The New Colossus" and to learn about the history of the Statue of Liberty, as well as to see some interesting statistics, visit the National Park Service Web site at www.nps.gov/stli/prod02.htm#Statue%20of.

writing topic: In paragraph 5, Tien says that "just looking like an immigrant can make you the target of heckling." Are people who look like immigrants the only ones who are heckled because of their looks? Why does the way a person looks sometimes make that person a "target of heckling"?

suggestion for prewriting: Write two lists. First list people who are heckled because of their looks. Then list the reasons these people are heckled.

suggestions for drafting
- Develop an outline before you draft. You might want to put your reasons in a progressive order.
- If you have trouble coming up with details for your draft, freewrite about one or more ideas in your list.

suggestion for revising: Give your draft to a reader with good judgment about writing and ask that person to suggest any details you should add.

suggestion for editing: In this writing, you may need to refer to people in general by writing sentences such as this: "When a person immigrates to the United States, he or she may be ridiculed." To be sure you use pronouns correctly, review the information on page 274.

Appendices

PART TEN

Editing for a Mix of Errors

Like most writers, you probably make more than one kind of mistake when you write, so you should practice editing to find and correct a mix of errors. You already had some of this practice when you completed the "Power Up" activities at the end of Parts 2–8. For additional practice, this appendix offers you eight pieces of writing to edit for a wide range of errors.

When you work through the passages in this appendix—and when you correct errors in your own writing—you can improve your editing skills if you use the strategies explained on pages 54–55. In addition, make note of the errors your instructor points out in your writing, learn the rules that apply to those errors, and visit your campus writing center for extra practice and reinforcement.

ACTIVITY 1

Edit the passage to eliminate the following:

> Three comma splices (Chapter 9)
> Three subject-verb agreement errors (Chapter 10)
> One pronoun-antecedent errors (Chapter 16)
> Two parallelism errors (Chapter 21)
> One error punctuating a quotation (Chapter 29)

[1]**Schizophrenia** refers to a class of disorders in which severe distortion of reality occurs. [2]Perception, emotion, and the way a person thinks may deteriorate. [3]There may be withdrawal from social interaction, there may be displays of bizarre behavior. [4]Although several types of schizophrenia have been observed, the distinctions among them are not always clear-cut, moreover, the symptoms displayed may vary considerably over time. [5]Nevertheless, a variety of characteristics reliably distinguish schizophrenia from other disorders.

[6]An individual with schizophrenia do experience a decline from a previous level of functioning. [7]Thus, the individual can no longer carry out their activities. [8]A person with schizophrenia use logic in a peculiar way and does not follow conventional linguistic rules. [9]For example, one schizophrenic said I don't have a diploma, but I'm

a doctor, and I'm glad to be a mental patient, because it taught me how to be humble; I use Cover Girl creamy natural makeup.

[10]People with schizophrenia can have either delusions, perceptual disorders, or they can have emotional disturbances. [11]One of the most common delusions experienced by people with schizophrenia are feeling controlled by someone else. [12]A common perceptual disorder is hallucinations. [13]Finally, people with schizophrenia tend to withdraw, they have no interest in others. [14]In extreme cases, they live in their own, isolated world.

Source: Adapted from Robert S. Feldman, *Essentials of Understanding Psychology,* 4th ed. (New York: McGraw-Hill, 2000), pp. 463–64. Copyright © 2000 The McGraw-Hill Companies. Used by permission of The McGraw-Hill Companies.

ACTIVITY 2

Edit the passage to eliminate the following:

> One run-on sentence (Chapter 9)
> One comma splice (Chapter 9)
> Two tense shifts (Chapter 14)
> Three spelling errors (Chapter 24)
> Two errors with a frequently confused word (Chapter 25)
> Two apostrophe errors (Chapter 28)

[1]On a sunny day in San Mateo, California, Lars Ulrich, drummer for the top-selling heavy metal band Metallica, wasnt signing autographs, nor was he getting ready for a concert. [2]Ulrich and a band of lawyers were delivering the names of more than 300,000 Web users who had ilegally downloaded song files on Napster. [3]Ulrich, who had been on a public crusade against Internet file-swapping, wants Naptster to bar these users from downloading more Metallica songs.

[4]At its high point, Napster had approximately 58 million registered users. [5]Some shared music more than others, understandably the big record lables and the Recording Industry Association of America (RIAA) were very worried. [6]Much of the debate about the Napster incident centered around the question of whether consumers have a right to copy trade music under the "fair use" doctrine. [7]This principal has been at the heart of controversy between content producers and users longer then people have been copying CDs to cassettes' to play in their cars.

[8]In 2001, the court rules that Napster encouraged the wholsale infringement of copyright. [9]Hilary Rosen, president of the RIAA, said that Napster should stop violating the copyright laws. [10]Napster users felt differently they apparently still do, because while the service has ceased operating, new services have sprung up. [11]One source estimates that as many people swap music and video files today as they did when Napster was operating.

Source: Adapted from Joseph R. Dominick, Fritz Messere, and Barry L. Sherman, *Broadcasting, Cable, the Internet, and Beyond,* 5th ed. (New York: McGraw-Hill, 2004), p. 97. Copyright © 2004 The McGraw-Hill Companies. Used by permission of The McGraw-Hill Companies.

ACTIVITY 3

Edit the passage to eliminate the following:

> Two sentence fragments (Chapter 6)
> One verb form error (Chapter 11)
> Two pronoun-antecedent agreement errors (Chapter 16)
> One error with adjective or adverb forms (Chapter 18)
> One dangling modifier (Chapter 19)
> Two apostrophe errors (Chapter 28)

[1]While walking his dog in 1948, a brainstorm stuck George de Mestral. [2]Noticing that cockleburs clinged to his pants and to his dog, the Swiss engineer had a thought. [3]He took some of the burs home with him and studied it under a microscope. [4]He saw an intricate pattern of tiny hooks that could grab onto anything with loops—and thats when de Mestral realized he had a replacement for the zipper. [5]He created a nylon model. [6]Which he named Velcro, a combination of the French words *velour* and *crochet*. [7]Because it is modeled on a natural occurring design, the invention is unusual. [8]Although de Mestral, who died in 1990, received other patents. [9]Velcro is his legacy.

[10]Velcro did not replace zippers or make it obsolete, but it now holds together everything from the space shuttle to artificial heart valves. [11]A piece of Velcro only 2 inches square can have 3,000 hooks and loops and support a 175-pound person hanging on a wall. [12]Lets see a zipper do that! [13]In fact, in one of his most famous gags, David Letterman leapt onto a wall of Velcro and lodged there, like an insect caught in a web.

ACTIVITY 4

Edit the passage to eliminate errors in the following areas. This time, you are not being told how many errors there are.

> sentence fragments (Chapter 6)
> person shift (Chapter 17)
> dangling modifiers (Chapter 19)
> parallelism errors (Chapter 21)
> possessive forms (Chapter 28)

[1]HIPAA (**Health Insurance Portability and Accountability Act of 1996**) is a federal law governing many aspects of health care. [2]Such as electronic transmission standards and the security of health care records. [3]As part of this act's Administrative Simplification provisions, the HIPAA Privacy Rule protects individually identifiable health information. [4]Health information is information about a patients' past, present, or information about future physical and mental health and payment for health care. [5]If a patient's information is created or received by a health care

provider electronically and if it can be used to identify the person, it is *protected health information* (PHI). ⁶Except for treatment, payment, and health care operations, the Privacy Rule limits the release of protected health information without your consent.

⁷To conform to the HIPAA Privacy Rule, a written Notice of Privacy Practices. must be given by medical practices. ⁸This document describes the medical offices practices regarding the use and disclosure of PHI. ⁹It also establishes complaint procedures, explains disclosure procedures, and it discusses how consent for other types of information release is obtained.

¹⁰Medical practices are required to display the Notice of Privacy Practices in a prominent place in the office. ¹¹They must also give patients a form called the **Acknowledgment of Receipt of Notice of Primacy Practices** ¹²And make a good faith effort to obtain a patients' written acknowledgment of having received and read the Notice of Privacy Practices.

Source: Adapted from Susan M. Sanderson, *Computers in the Medical Office,* 4th ed. (New York: McGraw-Hill, 2005), p. 6. Copyright © 2005 The McGraw-Hill Companies. Used by permission of The McGraw-Hill Companies.

ACTIVITY 5

Edit the passage to eliminate errors in the following areas. This time, you are not being told how many errors there are.

subject-verb agreement (Chapter 10)
verb forms (Chapters 11 and 12)
spelling (Chapter 24)
end marks (Chapter 26)

¹The average life span of paper bills are about a year, and for a dollar bill it's even less. ²Old money must be took out of circulation because torn and wrinkled bills is a nuisance. ³Perhaps you have wondered what is done with old money?

⁴Every day, the Treasury Department of the U.S. government recieves worn and dirty bills from banks and other sources. ⁵Would you believe it gets as much as 5 tons of money a day? ⁶The old money is cancel—that is, it is took out of circulation. ⁷Then the bills are destroyed in a machine called a macerator. ⁸A million dollars a minute is did away with by the macerator. ⁹If you has damaged paper money, it isn't necesarily worthless. ¹⁰If three-fifths of the note are preserved, you can send it to the Treasury and redeem it at full value.

¹¹The paper on which the notes are printed use to be of various sizes. ¹²From 1861 to 1928, it was 7 and 7/16 inches by 3 and 1/8 inches. ¹³However, in 1928 it was made smaller, and the new size be what we have today—6 and 5/16 inches by

2 and 11/16 inches. [14]The money is print by the Bureau of Engraving and Printing in Washington.

ACTIVITY 6

Edit the passage to eliminate the errors. This time, you are not being told either the kind or the number of errors.

[1]One of the tasks of the early years are for the brain cells to make connections with each other and create pathways. [2]They do this by growing branches called **dendrites.** [3]Babies are born with many more cells then they need, so the first years involve what some call "pruning." [4]The cells that aren't never used disappear. [5]"Use it or lose it" is a common expression stated by those who teach about the implications of brain research. [6]The message here is that infants and toddlers need the kinds of experiences that help them make the optimum number and right kinds of connections and pathways that result in healthy, wholesome development.

[7]What make a difference to brain development are commonsense things. [8]Infants and toddlers who have warm relationships that result in their feeling close connected to someone are more likelier to have optimal brain development than those who are shuffled around and feel constantly insecure. [9]Even when there is attachment and especially when there is not. [10]Shielding babies from stress is important. [11]When violence is part of family life; babies can be stunted in their brain development. [12]From a secure infancy and a safe toddlerhood come children who are curiouser, more interested, and more competent learners. [13]Teachers and parents need to understand that babies and toddlers who don't get no nurturing or who witness or experience violence will not develop to their potential.

ACTIVITY 7

Edit the passage to eliminate the errors. This time, you are not being told either the kind or the number of errors.

[1]Have you ever wondered why people get goose bumps when it be cold? [2]Goose bumps are a holdover from the time human beings were covered with hair. [3]When the temprature is hot, little muscles at each hair relax. [4]Which causes the hair to relax as a result. [5]Then, sweat glands pump out body heat in the form of sweat. [6]Blood vessles enlarged to take more heat to the skin to get rid of it.

[7]Conversely, when its cold, the duct to the sweat glands get more smaller to conserve heat. [8]Blood vessles get smaller, also to save heat, then little muscles pull up the hair on the body.

[9]When our bodies were covered in hair and the hair stood up. [10]It provided excellent insulation against the cold. [11]Hair standing up doesn't provide good insulation no more because we no longer have enough fur for that. [12]However millions of years ago a human being probably did. [13]That hair standing up kept them warmer. [14]Interestingly, today those little muscles we still have on the end of each hair continues to make goose bumps.

[15]Cold is not the only stimulus that can cause a persons hair to stand on end. [16]Fear and anger can cause the same reaction. [17]The same being true for other mammals, including cats and dogs. [18]There fur gets more big when they are angry or afraid and now you knows why. [19]The science that explain the workings of the human body in terms of how it has develop in response to the environment is called evolutionary biology. [20]What a fascinating field it is.

ACTIVITY 8

Edit the passage to eliminate the errors. This time, you are not being told either the kind or the number of errors.

[1]Long before the advent of modern medicine, even before the discovery of vitamins and minerals, people relied on herbs to cure their ills. [2]Many cultures still believe that a simple herb could cure or prevent health problems. [3]Today there is an explosion of interest in "natural" products, which has dramatically increased the use of herbal remedies. [4]This "back-to-nature" phenomenon has develop because of warnings about food preservatives and additives or products that are said to be cancer-causing. [5]The emphasis on *natural* and *nature* has generate a multimillion-dollar enterprise. [6]There have been a great increase in the number of health food stores selling natural organic vegetables, vitamins, and cosmetics. [7]It no longer appeals only to certain cultural or ethnic groups, but also to the general population.

[8]Several familiar and much needed medications come from plant sources. [9]Digitalis (*Lanoxin*), use in the treatment of heart disease, come from the foxglove plant. [10]Vincristine (*Oncovin*) and vinlastine (*Velban*), made from the periwinkle plant, are common antineoplastic agents employed frequent in the treatment of Hodgkin's disease, leukemia, and breast and testicular cancer. [11]Reserpine (*Sepasil*), which made from rauwolfia derivatives, comes from a shrub growed in India and the tropics and is use to treat high blood pressure.

[12]As a health care team member in a doctor's office, clinic, or hospital, you are in a position to question patients about the use of herbal remedies and inform him or her about those that are harmful. [13]However, all too often, health care professionals not asking such questions, and patients are not volunteering this information. [14]Obtaining a complete list of the herbs that a patient is using is essential in identifying potential herb interactions with prescription medications.

Source: Adapted from Donna F. Gauwitz, *Administering Medications: Pharmacology for Health Careers,* 5th ed. (New York: McGraw-Hill, 2005), pp. 114–15. Copyright © 2005 The McGraw-Hill Companies. Used by permission of The McGraw-Hill Companies.

Reviewing the Parts of Speech

In grammar study, words are identified according to how they function in a sentence. In English, words can function eight ways, and each of those functions is a **part of speech.** The eight parts of speech are

nouns	adverbs
pronouns	prepositions
verbs	conjunctions
adjectives	interjections

Understanding the parts of speech will help you learn grammar, so that you can edit your writing more successfully. In fact, the parts of speech are mentioned so often in this book that you will probably refer to this appendix often.

NOUNS

1. A **noun** names a person, a place, an object, an emotion, or an idea.

   Persons: *teacher, plumber, Joyce, Karl, Dr. Mann, sisters, doctors*

   Places: *yard, Chicago, Argentina, city, bedrooms, township*

   Objects: *boats, shoe, Kmart, stores, window, Buick, paint, house*

   Ideas: *thought, wisdom, cowardice, beliefs, democracy*

   Emotions: *jealousy, love, anxiety, hatred, happiness*

   <u>Lonnie</u> brought his <u>notes</u> on <u>economics</u> to <u>class.</u>

2. Nouns can be either *singular* or *plural.* **Singular nouns** name only one person, place, object, emotion, or idea; **plural nouns** name more than one.

   Singular nouns: *daughter, Mr. Flynn, ocean, Peru, Empire State Building, movie, feeling thought,*

   Plural nouns: *daughters, countries, pictures, feelings, thoughts*

   <u>Italian Bistro</u> featured its most popular <u>dishes</u> on the <u>menu</u> and offered a <u>discount</u> to <u>children.</u>

ACTIVITY 1

Underline each noun and above it write s if it is singular and p if it is plural.

A-9

EXAMPLE   Many geographic $\overset{P}{\underline{\text{regions}}}$ are named after an $\overset{S}{\underline{\text{explorer}}}$.

¹In the sixteenth century, a mapmaker in Germany named Martin Waldseemuller gave America its name. ²Waldseemuller drew a map of the New World and called the region America. ³The mapmaker could have used many different names for the regions now called North America and South America but chose a name derived from the explorer Amerigo Vespucci. ⁴Vespucci made many expeditions and was the first explorer to have an important realization—that the continents of North America and South America are not Asia.

PRONOUNS

A **pronoun** substitutes for a noun or refers to a noun. Here are some of the most commonly used pronouns:

I, me, my, mine
you, your, yours
he, him, his
she, her, hers
it, its
we, us, our, ours
they, them, their, theirs

Mario brought his daughter to work. but his boss said she could not stay.

The students told their teacher that the book was unclear. so they did not understand it.

For a more complete discussion of pronouns, see Chapters 15, 16, and 17.

ACTIVITY 2

In the following paragraph, underline each pronoun and draw an arrow to the word it substitutes for or refers to.

EXAMPLE   The Chinese first printed their books on paper.

¹In China, people used wood blocks to print their books. ²The method was slow, but it was faster than printing by hand. ³In Europe, books were printed by hand, usually by monks. ⁴The books were so valuable that the monks copying them were chained to their desks, so they wouldn't steal them. ⁵In the 1400s, Johannes Gutenberg invented a printing machine. ⁶It used separate metal pieces for each letter. ⁷They were arranged in order to create a page of words. ⁸His machine revolutionized printing. ⁹It made the printing of large numbers of books possible.

VERBS

1. **Action verbs** express physical or mental activities, including actions, processes, and thoughts. They are words such as these:

consider	eat	go	love	think
do	enjoy	hit	talk	try

    The artist <u>sells</u> his paintings cheaply.

    The dogs <u>barked</u> all night.

    I <u>believe</u> in you.

2. **Linking verbs** do not express physical or mental activities. They connect the subject of a sentence to a word or words that rename or describe that subject. Most linking verbs are forms of *be*. These are the linking verbs:

am	was	appear/appeared	taste/tasted
be	were	feel/felt	smell/smelled
is	been	seem/seemed	look/looked
are	being	sound/sounded	become/became

    That salesperson <u>is</u> grouchy. [*Is* links the subject *salesperson* to grouchy, which describes salesperson.]

    The roast <u>smells</u> delicious. [*Smells* links the subject *roast* to *delicious*, which describes *roast*.]

    My brother <u>was</u> class president. [*Was* links the subject *brother* to class president, which renames *brother*.]

3. A verb can be more than one word; it can be made up of an action verb or a linking verb and one or more of the following **helping verbs**:

am	were	must	do	had
be	been	might	did	shall
is	being	could	does	will
are	may	would	have	
was	can	should	has	

    The plane <u>will be</u> on time.
    We <u>should have left</u> an hour ago.

4. One of the most important characteristics of verbs is that they express present, past, and future tense (time).

    Present: *Today I <u>begin</u> a new diet.*
    Past: *Yesterday I <u>began</u> a new diet.*
    Future: *Tomorrow I <u>will begin</u> a new diet.*

    For a more detailed explanation of verbs, see the discussion beginning on page 82.

ACTIVITY 3

Underline each verb and label it AV if it is an action verb, LV if it is a linking verb, and HV if it is a helping verb.

EXAMPLE Many people <u>have</u> <u>learned</u> little about the Pledge of Allegiance, because this history <u>is</u> rarely <u>taught</u> in schools.

¹The Pledge of Allegiance was written in 1892 by Francis Bellamy in honor of Columbus Day. ²Originally, the words were "I pledge allegiance to my Flag and the Republic for which it stands—one nation indivisible—with liberty and justice for all." ³The pledge was popular in schools and was recited daily. ⁴In 1923, the U.S. Flag Association made some changes. ⁵It replaced "my Flag" with "the flag of the United States of America." ⁶In 1954, Congress made another change when it added "under God."

ADJECTIVES

Adjectives describe nouns and pronouns.

> *This milk is <u>sour</u>.*
> *The <u>new red</u> car is parked on a <u>steep</u> hill.*
> *She is <u>understanding</u>.*

A, an, and *the* are special adjectives called **articles**.

> <u>The</u> accident left Carla with <u>a</u> broken leg and <u>an</u> ankle injury.

For a more detailed discussion of adjectives, see Chapter 18.

ACTIVITY 4

Underline each adjective and article and draw an arrow to the noun or pronoun described.

EXAMPLE   <u>A</u> <u>new</u> car has <u>a</u> <u>distinctive</u> smell.

1. Marcus is anxious because he lost the car keys.

2. The new employees were told to report to the third floor for an orientation meeting.

3. I felt bad about forgetting to bring the birthday present.

4. An expiration date on milk cartons is a reliable indication of freshness.

5. The peer pressure experienced by teenagers can lead to dangerous behavior.

ADVERBS

Adverbs are also describing words. They describe verbs, adjectives, and other adverbs.

> *The sun is shining <u>brightly</u>.* [*Brightly* describes the verb *is shining*.]
> *Helga's humor is <u>very</u> sarcastic.* [*Very* describes the adjective *sarcastic*.]
> *You are speaking <u>too</u> loudly.* [*Too* describes the adverb *loudly*.]

For a more detailed discussion of adverbs, see Chapter 18.

ACTIVITY 5

Underline each adverb and draw an arrow to the word described.

EXAMPLE   Kara and Atwan travel <u>frequently</u>.

1. The chief executive's speech on the company's finances caused too many investors to sell their stock.

2. An accident forced us to take a detour, which delayed us significantly.

3. The slightly confused students asked their instructor to explain the answer more slowly.

4. I was extremely tired after taking the two-hour examination in the unusually hot classroom.

5. The police officer ran quickly yet cautiously when he heard screams.

PREPOSITIONS

A **preposition** shows how a noun or pronoun relates to an other word in the sentence. A preposition often shows how things are positioned in time or space. Prepositions are words such as these:

at	by	of	to
before	in	on	under
between	near	through	with

The dog ran between the trees and into the doghouse.
I though you would be gone by now.

Some prepositions, such as those in this list, are made up of two or more words:

according to	in front of
ahead of	in spite of
because of	instead of
in addition to	out of

For a more detailed discussion of prepositions, see Chapter 20.

ACTIVITY 6

Underline the prepositions in the following paragraph.

EXAMPLE Some people in the United States did not want English for the official language.

[1]During the Revolutionary War, many Americans desired complete separation from England. [2]These people wanted no ties with England and even advocated discontinuing the use of English. [3]In fact, for some people, this desire persisted after the war. [4]For example, the first speaker of the House of Representatives, Frederick Muhlenberg, discussed making German instead of English the language of the United States—probably because Muhlenberg's family came from Germany. [5]Some lobbied for French as the official language, and others leaned toward Spanish, Greek, or Hebrew. [6]Despite their efforts, English has remained the official language of the United States throughout our history.

CONJUNCTIONS

Conjunctions are joining words. There are three kinds of conjunctions: *coordinating conjunctions, subordinating conjunctions,* and *conjunctive adverbs.*

1. **Coordinating conjunctions** join words, phrases, and clauses of equal importance in a sentence. The coordinating conjunctions are

and	for	or	yet
but	nor	so	

   Bill <u>and</u> Theresa are brother <u>and</u> sister. [The coordinating conjunctions join words of equal importance.]

   You will find the keys on the table <u>or</u> in the car. [The coordinating conjunction joins phrases of equal importance.]

   I heard what you said, <u>but</u> I don't believe it. [The coordinating conjunction joins clauses of equal importance.]

2. **Subordinating conjunctions,** which begin dependent clauses (page 131), join the dependent clauses to independent clauses (page 131). Some common subordinating conjunctions are

after	because	unless
although	before	until
as	if	when
as if	in order that	where
as long as	since	while

   <u>While</u> you were out, your boss called.
   We bought the house cheaply <u>because</u> the owner was anxious to sell.

   For a detailed discussion of subordinating conjunctions, dependent clauses, and independent clauses, see Chapters 7 and 8.

3. **Conjunctive adverbs** are used with semicolons to join independent clauses. Some common conjunctive adverbs are

consequently	instead	therefore
furthermore	meanwhile	thus
however	nevertheless	

   The violent storm knocked out the town's electricity; <u>furthermore,</u> it left thousands of people injured.

   For more on using conjunctive adverbs to join independent clauses, see page 118.

ACTIVITY 7

Underline the conjunctions and label each one CC if it is a coordinating conjunction, SC if it is a subordinating conjunction, or CA if it is a conjunctive adverb.

>   *SC*
>
> **EXAMPLE**   <u>Although</u> the president lives in the White House, the vice-president
>
>   lives elsewhere.

[1]The president of the United States lives in the White House; however, the vice-president lives in a home with the official title "The Admiral's House." [2]The house is named "The Admiral's House" because it is on the grounds of the U.S. Naval

Observatory, where it once served as the home of the chief of the observatory.[3] After Walter Mondale became the first full-time resident in 1974, every vice-president has lived in this Victorian house, on the corner of 34th Street and Massachusetts Avenue, NW, in the District of Columbia. [4] Before Congress decreed "The Admiral's House" the official residence, vice-presidents lived in hotels, or they bought or rented temporary quarters. [5] The vice-presidential residence is not as grand or well-known as the White House. [6] Nevertheless, it does have 9,150 square feet of floor space, so it is certainly not cramped.

INTERJECTIONS

Interjections express strong emotions or make an exclamation. They are words such as these:

help	oops	wow
hooray	ouch	yes
oh	whew	yikes

Interjections can be punctuated with a comma or an exclamation point.

Oh, I remember you.

Wow! I got the highest grade on the test.

ACTIVITY 8

On a separate sheet, write five sentences with interjections.

WORDS AS MORE THAN ONE PART OF SPEECH

Because a word's part of speech is determined by how it is used in a sentence, a word can be one part of speech in one sentence and a different part of speech in another sentence. In fact, many English words can be more than one part of speech. Here are examples, using the words *love*, *peace*, and *since*:

Love as a verb:	*I love New York city in the spring.*
Love as a noun:	*Damien's love of football is well known.*
Peace as a noun:	*After months of negotiations, the two countries declared peace.*
Peace as an adjective:	*The peace talks ended with the signing of a new treaty.*
Since as a conjunction:	*I have been depressed since my dog died.*
Since as preposition:	*I have been depressed since June.*

REVIEW ACTIVITY 9

Above each underlined word, indicate its part of speech. The first sentence is done as an example.

[1] The Grand Canyon *is* (vb) *located* (vb) in Arizona. [2] Many theories explain how the canyon was made, but the most popular theory says it was cut by the Colorado

River over a period of 15 million years . [3]Although it is the largest land gorge in the world, it is not the deepest canyon in the United States. [4]The deepest canyon is King's Canyon, which runs through the Sierra and Sequoia National Forests in California. [5]King's Canyon plunges steeply to 8,200 feet at its deepest point.

Acknowledgments

Peterson, Karen S.: "The Truth About Our Little White Lies," © 1983 USA TODAY. Reprinted with permission.

Lam, Andrew: "They Shut My Grandmother's Room Door," 1989. Used by permission.

Carlin,Kathleen: "You Become What You Wear" (1996). © 1996 Commonweal Foundation. Reprinted with permission. For subscriptions: www.commonwealmagazine.org.

Middleton, Thomas H.: "Have a Nice Day"© 1979 Thomas H. Middleton. Used by permission of the author.

Tan, Amy: "Fish Cheeks" Copyright © 1987 by Amy Tan. First appeared in *Seventeen* Magazine. Reprinted by permission of the author and the Sandra Dijkstra Literary Agency.

Varadarajan, Tunku: "Baby Names, Big Battles," © 1999 Tunku Varadarajan. Used by permission of the author.

Hughes, Langston: "Thank You, M'am" from *Short Stories* by Langston Hughes. Copyright © 1996 by Ramona Bass and Arnold Rampersad. Reprinted by permission of Hill and Wang, a division of Farrar, Straus and Giroux, LLC.

Stone, Elizabeth: "For One Teacher, a Lesson about E-Mail and Privacy," *New York Times,* September 2, 1999. Copyright © 1999 by The New York Times Co. Reprinted with permission.

della Cava, Marco R.: "The Afghan-American: Torn between Love for Two Nations," *USA Today,* December 17, 2001. © 2001 USA Today. Reprinted with permission.

Angelou, Maya: "The Fight" From *I Know Why the Caged Bird Sings* by Maya Angelou. Copyright © 1969 and renewed 1997 by Maya Angelou. Used by permission of Random House, Inc.

Cisneros, Sandra: "Only Daughter" Copyright © 1990 by Sandra Cisneros. First published in *Glamour*, November 1990. Reprinted by permission of Susan Bergholz Literary Services, New York. All rights reserved.

Housam, Courtney: "Proud to Be ADD," December 2001. Reprinted with permission from *ADDitude Magazine* For more articles like this one, to subscribe, or to sign up for the monthly e-newslwetter, visit *ADDitude* online, www.additudemag.com.

Tien, Chang-Lin: "America's Scapegoats," *Newsweek*, October 31, 1994. Copyright © 1994 Newsweek, Inc. All rights reserved. Reprinted by permission.

Photo Credits

Index